TOTAL WAR

Volume II: *The War in Asia*

Peter Calvocoressi
& Guy Wint

BALLANTINE BOOKS • NEW YORK

We are grateful to Martin Gilbert of Merton College, Oxford, and to the Macmillan Company for their kind permission to use the maps on pages 198, 349, 369, which have been adapted from the following:

Russian History Atlas edited by Martin Gilbert. Cartography by Arthur Banks. Copyright © 1972 by Martin Gilbert.
Recent History Atlas edited by Martin Gilbert. Cartography by John Flower. Copyright © 1966 by Martin Gilbert.
Jewish History Atlas edited by Martin Gilbert. Cartography by Peter Kingsland. Copyright © 1969 by Martin Gilbert.
American History Atlas edited by Martin Gilbert. Cartography by Peter Kingsland. Copyright © 1969 by Martin Gilbert.

Library of Congress Catalog Card Number: 72-3402

SBN 345-23476-6-195

This book was originally published by Pantheon Books, Inc. as one volume. Published by arrangement with Pantheon Books, Inc.

First Printing: September, 1973

Printed in the United States of America

Cover art by George Jones

BALLANTINE BOOKS, INC.
201 East 50th Street, New York, N.Y. 10022

CONTENTS

THE WAR IN ASIA

Part I

ASIAN CONFLICT

Part II

OCEAN CLASH

Contents

Part III
THE HIGH TIDE OF WAR

Part IV
THE DEFEAT OF JAPAN

LIST OF MAPS

Foreword

THE idea for this book was Guy Wint's. He died before it was finished and the loss has been inestimable. He was a man who knew much, thought carefully, was insatiably curious and revelled in the unexpected. Rarely did I spend an hour in his company without being presented with a comparison or parallel which I would never have thought of for myself. History gave him immense satisfaction. He loved its grand sweeps and the business of disentangling these from the dense detritus of the past. History also provided him with entertainment, of a tolerant rather than a cynical kind, for with a strong belief in the effectiveness of the individual in public affairs—which he typically saw as drama—he combined an indulgent affection for the occasional human absurdities which the record bleakly reveals. In his writings therefore, and even more so in conversation which he specially enjoyed until his first stroke made it painful for him, he was a scholar with a difference which his friends recognized though might find hard to define.

One day he told me that he had come across a young person who was not only baffled by the role of Finland in the Second World War but could not make out which side Italy had been on. This conversation showed him that the war had become part of the past for our younger contemporaries and that it might be a good idea to write a book showing why it happened and how it went. We knew from the start that we did not want to write a military or campaign history and were not qualified to do so, but apart from that negative consideration we were at first uncertain about what the book ought to contain. We wished to give a substantial amount of space to the sources of war but it was more difficult to decide which aspects of the war in progress to treat at length. We felt that it was essential to tell enough about the actual fighting to enable the reader to know who was winning at any particular point, but we were not so much concerned to give a round-by-round account of the fighting as to show why particular campaigns were fought, when and where they were fought, and also what happened behind what used to be called 'the lines'.

The arrangement of the book was also a problem, about which a word here is in place. We began by planning a chronological treatment in which a section about one part of the world would be followed by a section covering much the same period in another part of the world, after which the story narrated in the first part would be taken up where it had been broken off, and so on several times over until we got to 1945. We agreed that I should be primarily responsible for the European, Atlantic, African and Middle-Eastern theatres, while he should take as his prime task the whole of the rest of Asia and the Pacific. But we soon abandoned the plan to march in alternating tandem from the beginning to the end of our story—for two main reasons. First, we concluded that it would be horribly confusing for our readers to have to do so much switching from one half of the world to the other; and second, we came to believe that the wars in the two hemispheres were much less closely interdependent than we had at first supposed. They were of course contemporaneous or nearly so, and they raised questions of priorities—specially on the Anglo-American side and specially in relation to the wars at sea—which were sometimes crucial. But in their origins and to a large extent even in their courses Hitler's wars on the one hand and the Sino–Japanese and American–Japanese wars on the other constitute distinctly intelligible stories which can, we thought, more conveniently be told in sequence (with the necessary cross-commenting) than in parallel.

When Guy Wint died he had covered his alloted sphere. (The whole of his work on this book was done between his first and second strokes.) But the latter sections of what he wrote were still on his death in a rudimentary stage. We have done our best to follow up all the traces of the material he has used, but if something has not been acknowledged we should like to hear. It was his habit to write and re-write many times over; his first drafts were always many times the length intended for their final form, which was achieved only after a series of refining revisions. Consequently there remained much work to be done, and this work was undertaken by Freda Wint. Besides her natural interest and talents Mrs Wint had the advantage of having discussed much of the book with her husband before his death. Nevertheless she has had to assume a significant responsibility as well as setting aside very many hours of labour in order to bring Guy Wint's last drafts into publishable shape. I myself and the readers of this book are greatly beholden to her. She was greatly helped by Dr Ian Nish who most kindly read all that Guy Wint had written and was generous with expert comment and advice.

For myself I have a special debt to record. I had always supposed that I could not work with a research assistant but only by myself. Yet my other commitments forced me to try the experiment. It has been from my point of view a triumphant success and I very happily acknowledge the great debt which I owe to Rosemary Righter for the work she did for me and the way she did it. I now believe that being a research assistant is more difficult than having one. Without Mrs Righter's stimulating help I should not only have taken twice as long over my task but would also have missed a number of telling points.

My wife read every word of various drafts of every chapter that I wrote and has very greatly helped me to clarify my mind and my text. In illustrating this text with excellent maps Arthur Banks has wrought with an enthusiasm and a skill which are as gratifying to me as they must be helpful to the reader.

Finally, I wish—and I know too that Guy Wint shared this wish—to thank Dieter Pevsner and André Schiffrin, publishers and friends, for the interest they have shown in our work as it went along and notably for the extensive oral and written criticisms which they have made at various times. I happen to know that publishers have busy lives and so I appreciate all the more warmly the amount of time and thought that these two set aside for our benefit.

PETER CALVOCORESSI

The War in Asia

I

ASIAN CONFLICT

1

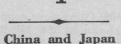

China and Japan

THERE are two principal countries of the Far East with an ancient civilization, China and Japan; and the war in the Far East had its origin in the quarrel between them. This developed gradually out of events which began about a century earlier and set afoot historical processes which were seemingly uncheckable. With apparent fatalism inflammable materials were stacked.

Ultimately, the fire started and flames enfolded the two countries in a most bitter war of survival. This in turn caused a wider blaze in the Pacific; and the fire in the East coincided with Hitler's fire in Europe. The conflagrations merged, and the wars become one. Almost all the peoples of the Far East and South Asia were engaged.

The start of this great drama came with the different ways that China and Japan responded to the unfamiliar intrusion of the West into Asian affairs.

In East Asia China, even in its decadence, has always been a most absorbing topic. It has lain across the map of Asia, establishing standards and precedents, rather as the Roman Empire dominated the ancient western world. Traditionally, East Asia had no system of international relations in which independent countries coexist with one another, such as was known from the earliest times in Europe, but was a system in which all the lesser countries revolved like satellites around the great central structure, which was regarded by all men as central, necessary and almost unchanging. In the middle of the nineteenth century, this was still true, even though China was standing on the verge of one of the most calamitous periods of its history that was to cause its very name to be a reproach. It still dominated the political imagination, both of its inhabitants, and of visitors to the Far East. So much history had gone into its making, and so revered was Chinese civilization in Asia, that traces of mortal disease did not at first cause extreme alarm. Nevertheless China belonged to the ancient world, which, in 1850, was passing rapidly away.

What was threatening China was the impact of the western world. China was known as the Middle Kingdom for it seemed the centre round which all things revolved and it had flourished through so many ages because it was unique. Now, for the first time in its history, it was coming into contact with powers which had totally different traditions and which were totally ruthless. They came from the other side of the world, but, from the alarm they caused, and from the absence of normal human rapport, they might have come from Mars. These powers, well organized politically, were not inclined to concede to China a moral superiority.

The history of China and the West is chequered. The record of the foreign powers is not so black as it is painted, whether by Chinese communists or by liberal western historians, who are overwhelmed, often quite unreasonably, by guilt. In some ways China's suffering was inevitable. It was the necessary result of the unavoidable process of a withdrawn state being thrust upon the world. Many of its experiences can be seen today to have been renascent; they conferred new and valuable matter upon an ancient civilization. The version put about by the communists is exaggerated, perverted and untrue. But something like their view is held by most of the Chinese people. The myth has been agreed upon. It must be attended to in any account of what really happened.

China, according to this view, was, for nearly a hundred years, harried by several foreign powers which had projected themselves into the Far East by their navies and their fleets of merchantmen; and for most of the time it fought a losing battle against them.

The agony of China began in the middle of the last century. It was compelled by foreign governments to open itself for trade, which meant consenting to having its tariffs fixed by these agents; to accord to foreigners extra-territorial rights, which rendered them immune from Chinese law; and to permit them to set up in some of the choicest parts of the Empire small foreign communities which were thereafter protected from Chinese jurisdiction by warships and small bodies of troops. These were the famous Treaty Ports, now of dolorous memory. In addition, the same rights were exacted for Christian missionaries, who were let loose to subvert the ancient Confucian system. The Chinese government was powerless to resist. It had neither the technical means (in arms and warships), nor the political stamina, nor the control of its own people, nor the ability to organize them.

Externally nothing had changed except for the establishment of neat, well-ordered townships side by side with the sprawling cities of China. They were clean; they appeared innocent. In this innocuous guise, imperialism came to China and soon began its work without anybody recognizing that it was initiating a new age. The first trade treaty, the Treaty of Nanking of 1842, which opened the five ports to British trade and residence, contained crippling restraints on China's sovereignty, but at the time was regarded as relatively innocuous. The Treaty provided that foreigners should administer their own justice to aliens and so appeared to be relieving the Chinese of a vexatious duty and to be keeping the foreigner at arm's length, which was very much the Chinese desire.

Moreover, by specifying areas where foreigners could live, it appeared to have spared the Chinese demands for the sale of land elsewhere. The foreigner was generally prohibited from acquiring real estate in China—a kind of apartheid set-up. But the foreigner had been given the means to enforce his will, and used it ruthlessly. He partly got round the rule that he should not own land by inducing the Christian missionaries, specifically exempt from the prohibition which applied to foreign businessmen, to hold the land in their name.

At first the Chinese did not understand what was being done to them, or how serious was the damage done to them in the Treaty Ports. But the misdeeds of the imperialists slowly became clear to everyone, and gradually produced a mood of terrible baffled rage.

China had not only to fear imperialism when it was sea-borne. Before the coming of the foreign ships, it had been conscious of the land threat from its neighbour, Russia. This threat endured without interruption and in varying degrees of intensity. By land or sea China was surrounded by adversaries. It was still the Middle Kingdom, but no longer the axis round which the world turned; rather it could boast the name because it was the centre against which the spoliative instincts of the world were directed.

China was, it is true, saved from conquest and annexation. This was because the foreign powers arrived not alone, but in multiplicity, because each was jealous of the other, because each realized that its trading rights depended on none achieving full political control of China. The Chinese Empire was thus permitted to continue.

It is important not to overstate the case. There were many personalities among the foreigners in China who bore nothing but goodwill to the country. There were institutions which were actively philanthropic. Foreign influence often brought about great changes, almost by accident. The Treaty Ports were often impressive for their neatness of construction and they disseminated new standards of public administration over a limited area. But the Chinese argued that this kind of imperialism did the maximum harm to China while ensuring that the imperialist powers conferred no countervailing benefits.

Thus, groups of foreigners—nearly all businessmen—lived in China, organized entirely according to the customs and conventions of their homeland and subject to their own laws, in juxtaposition to the Chinese who were still subject to their ancient form of government. Most of the foreigners had only one interest; to make money through trade. Inevitably, even if the foreign communities had had no intention to influence Chinese society, the free action of the foreign groups deeply modified the Chinese society all around them, especially because the Chinese government was unable to place limits on their activities. The operations of buying and selling, the freedom to conduct almost all forms of enterprise which private initiative could suggest, the freedom of money and its free use—all tended to erode the old Chinese civilization, which the Chinese, bound by treaty, were unable to safeguard.

The Chinese were in the position of a man bound hand and foot, watching the activities of an assailant who was openly plotting his ruin. As a result of the unwelcome guests, Chinese society was changing; but China could do nothing about it. Chinese anger mounted against the foreign communities, but China was impotent.

The Chinese feeling raged more strongly against the Chinese who collaborated with foreigners than against the foreigners themselves. The Chinese who showed himself unduly obliging to the foreigner, who set himself to make money by taking advantage of the conditions of foreign business, who was willing to act as the agent of the foreign business community and performed the indispensable role of interpreter and middleman, roused angry resentment. This class was called the compradors, from the Portuguese word meaning 'to provide': they were China's universal agents, at the disposal of the foreigner. Without the compradors, the pattern of the new type of imperialism would never have come into being.

The comprador class became extremely rich and prosperous. Eventually many of the Chinese nationalists came from this class. So did many people who contributed in various ways to the new China: in arts, in science, in medicine. For many decades the Chinese creative energies seemed to be located in this class. The fact that it was hated was never sufficiently appreciated by foreigners, whose needs had called it into being.

*

The principal state in the hostile group ringing China was Great Britain, but there was one foreign country which behaved in a way unlike the others, the United States of America, which had a different history and different traditions from those of the European nation-states like Great Britain.

The United States, which came into being as the result of rebellion against Britain, did not form a new national state of its own, but was, rather, a repository of the elements of the western world which showed, by emigrating to America, that they desired to have a new political civilization. The United States did not altogether escape the nineteenth-century trend of western countries to be aggressive and self-assertive, but was distinctly less predatory, less remorseless, than the others.

Thus in its relations with China the United States pursued a milder course than its western peers. True, it was drawn into the harrying. When the other states took the extra-territorial privileges, for the protection of their nationals, the United States joined in; and it took its share among the other powers in setting up the International Settlement at Shanghai. But its pursuit of China was not relentless, and it did not demand exclusive concessions of its own, which were the aim of other governments and which came to be dotted all over China like so many colonies. The United States' interest was in international trade—in contrast to Britain whose special concern was with the investment of capital in China—and in promoting it the United States was no more scrupulous than other states in forcing its activities upon China, which, officially, did not welcome them. But in this international trade the American concern was more with the attitude of other western powers than with that of China. The United States had always the fear that these would end in a policy of splitting up China into various spheres of interest, from which American interests would be excluded or discriminated against.

Hence the United States' aim of preserving the open door into China. On this principle American official policy turned. It sought to establish a system by which all the powers voluntarily restricted the use of political influence to secure for themselves an economic privilege such as was not enjoyed equally by other powers. The American activity on these lines culminated in securing in 1900 the assent of powers interested in the China trade to this 'Open Door doctrine' and in guaranteeing American support for China's territorial integrity. The United States regarded this as a pro-Chinese policy, anti-imperialist, and in fact it was more so than suited the habits and interests of the other powers. But it is understandable that later generations of Chinese should have pointed to the solid gains which it was the United States' intention to gain from it. They were not impressed by the advantages that this non-cooperation of the United States with the other powers undoubtedly brought to China, and regarded these as incidental and not philanthropic.

Nevertheless, the U S was philanthropic. From the 1870s a section of the American public became aware of China as a great Asiatic people which might with justice call upon the United States for aid. This was the United States' first public response to the needs of a section of the world community; a response which has since become progressively wider, and embraced successively Japan, the states in Europe assisted by the Marshall Plan, and states of Latin America. They had no legal or other claim on the U S; the U S had no obligation to them. It responded in their cases to the simple fact that they had needs which the United States could fill, and the U S did not pass them by on the other side. Often, of course, there was, mixed with the practical philanthropy, a great deal of hypocrisy, of unscrupulous dealing, of serving a concealed interest, of power hunger only a little better than Europe's. because it was veiled; but, though these existed, it was a remarkable fact that there was a genuinely philanthropic policy in which these found a place.

The initiators of the wave of goodwill were the American missionaries. Thousands of these were active in China and, through them, links were forged between innumerable small towns in the United States and similar units in China. To a remarkable extent the American people actually took the Chinese people by the hand, and led them over the first stages of their modernization. Politically the organs of government in the United States impressed the Chinese people, many of whom recognized the remarkable behaviour of the U S, even though their vast pride suffered from the American patronage. It was natural for the descendants of two thousand years of mandarins to feel disgust at becoming pupils of such a commercial people, lacking a long history, as the Americans. Relations were therefore not easy. But Chinese, in a more judicious mood, had to admit that this relationship was the most satisfactory that China had experienced in modern history.

This adventure in philanthropy was a part of the history of the American people, not the American government. It was not officially inspired. The thousands of American missionaries, the vast expenditure, the use of skill and manpower, were all of them privately directed. So also American businessmen for the most part took their own risks and reaped their return, and largely did not employ American organized public force. The interplay of the missionary and the businessman, the clash between disinterest and the long-term interest which American activity promoted, was of course one of the principal themes for the historian of the time to savour. And in the United States the widespread goodwill to China set up currents which, in a society as democratic as that of the U S, were bound to influence the state and produce subtle changes in its policy towards China. So intertwined were most of the impulses of the United States.

*

Confronted with such acute danger, China made sporadic efforts to modernize itself and to generate a counteractive power; this should have been possible by reason of its size, its population and the reasonableness of its people. But for a long while its governing class was so set in conservative ways —as an essential part of their Confucian civilization—that the efforts failed. To reform and reorganize, China had to go through a shattering revolution, leave its ancient political civilization and venture out on ways new and untested. It had to experience a slow rebirth.

For a time the Chinese mandarins, the higher civil servants of the Confucian bureaucracy, had supposed that the secret of the terribly formidable strength of the West lay in some technical devices which had been added to the instruments of government. If they could discover what these were, the government of the ancient empire would be rejuvenated, and able to stand up for itself. Steam power, explosives, modern weapons were all of them the candidates for the shattering secret of western power. But the empire's attempt to purchase these devices from the West left it no better off. It was clear that the Chinese government lacked the talent to reorganize its society so that it might adapt itself to make proper use of these. It could not mobilize China. It remained inert, and a powerless victim to those who chose to victimize it.

Under constant strain, the old system of government was ceasing to act. The old régime had been based on the principle that a harmony had to be imposed on the disharmonious elements of which society consists. The policy was largely based on government by exhortation, and by displaying the example (at least in theory) of universal benevolence; and this proved workable because of the Confucian ideas which prevailed in all areas under Chinese rule. Confucianism, as much as the secular institutions of the old China, held the state together. But the old Confucian philosophy was being undermined as Chinese society, for the first time in two thousand years, began to change fundamentally. In the rough world which had developed, China had to discover new principles on which to base its government.

Some Chinese looked abroad at the new system of parliamentary democracy which was becoming so fashionable. Could this be the secret which made the West so strong, and could its institutions not be taken over by China? For a time there was enthusiasm and hope about these ideas. But it should have been clear that they were not likely to be a helpful model to China, which had its own powerful political traditions, built by more than two thousand years of history, and not readily set aside. Nor could a system of government be easily imported and acclimatized, which had been built up so painfully in Europe, which was the product of so many attitudes of action and habit, themselves born of wars, revolution, and the slow work of many centuries. China was too unlike Europe, and China was made a dangerous gift by its friends who intemperately supported this nostrum.

The course which China took was therefore quite unpredictable; it was empirical and, even today, with hindsight, it is hard to trace out what experiments it made, and how much China suffered.

One of the reforms which it made apparently without realizing the profound consequences which it had, was to abolish the civil service. This it did in 1905; the examinations by which it was recruited were suspended. Earlier, the existence of this college of administrators, chosen to serve the empire by competitive public examinations, had been regarded, with some justification, as one of the strong points of Chinese civilization. But in the first decade of this century, the Chinese civil service was held to be old-fashioned and conservative. It was selected from among the classes which

were steeped in Confucianism, and this made it the enemy of
reform. The classes in favour of modernization all combined their resentment against it as constricting the development of the country. It was supposed that by striking it
away, China would release forces which would transform
it. That the mandarinate preserved standards of government
and maintained the unity of the country was totally ignored.
A great blow was struck at public order by its abolition,
but the country thought that it was a blow in the cause of
progress and liberation.

The Manchu Empire survived the sacrifice of the mandarins by only six years. The empire and its outworn apparatus were discarded in 1911: it had stood in the way of
reform; probably a revolution was the necessary prelude to
recovery. But the first results of the fall were catastrophic.
The power of the empire was divided between war-lords, who
commanded their own provinces. This was the worst and
most helpless period of Chinese history. Chinese politics
seemed to be without rhyme or reason. Power drifted from
one war-lord to another with no meaningful result. The rise
or fall of one provincial satrap or another brought no lighten-
ing of the gloom. There was no change, no regeneration, no
significance.

The dawn for which men hoped first became visible with
the rule at Canton, a city in the south of China, of the group
called the Kuomintang, which had emerged from a revolutionary party of the last days of the Manchus. This group
proclaimed itself the nationalist party of China and held its
first National Congress in 1924. It was at first primitive, over-
laid with the colour of circumambient war-lord governments,
incompetent, corrupt, and very weak. But it was in certain
aspects new, and had, at least in form, a modern party
organization which was in part borrowed from western countries, though the methods of its operations were mainly
drawn from China itself. It functioned in an authoritarian
way, owing its power to its army and police, but it claimed
that this method of government was a transitory one. After
a period during which it held the nation in tutelage, it would
transfer the basis of government, and would become liberal
and democratic. In after years, the length of this period of
tutelage, the holding of the Kuomintang to its promise of

democratization, became one of the principal questions of Chinese politics.

The Kuomintang slowly widened its authority; and came to be looked on as the party of national regeneration. It was a focus which attracted the support of all Chinese everywhere, who longed for a sign that China was at last reasserting its national strength.

It was the turning of the tide. Nationalism, with all the social and political reorganization which that connoted, began to do its work upon the Chinese people. The leader of the Kuomintang, Dr Sun Yat-sen (1866–1925), had described the great weakness of China, in its enforced competition with the western powers, as the absence of any cohesive power which could hold the people together. China, he said, was like a tray of sand: shake it and it fell apart. But, in China as in other parts of the world, the power of nationalism was to introduce a new faculty of maintaining social unity. How and why is one of the *arcana imperii* of the time. But it was abundantly clear that, as the movement proceeded and gathered strength, China was behaving quite differently from the recent past. The tray of sand was shaken; and the grains now tended to cohere in patterns which promised well for the future.

A fact which should have recommended the Kuomintang in the 1920s to serious attention by the outside observer was that in its organization and spirit it was not a copy of the western parliamentary parties. It was something devised for China, produced by Chinese thought to meet specific Chinese needs. It owed something to Soviet practice—many of the features in the organization of the party being borrowed from Russia at a time when Sun Yat-sen was enthusiastic, but had little understanding of communism—and, with a rosy eye-wash, it professed to look forward to a time of universal democratic rights. But the Kuomintang—as it was to function in the 1930s—was a party of nationalist authoritarianism.

*

Cutting across the political vicissitudes of the times was a social crisis. In a sense China was doomed to experience disorders in any case. China has a long history, and has endured a time of acute crisis once in every three or four hundred years which is marked by troubles, the fall of a dynasty, civil commotion of a prolonged and hopeless kind. Various causes have been suggested for this clearly marked cyclical course of Chinese history, but the most probable is that it is caused by pressure of population.

In the time of prosperity—when a dynasty is at the peak of its fortunes—the population is within manageable limits. The prosperity continues; the population grows; it becomes too large; there is intense pressure on the land; there are rising rents, and a diminishing food surplus for the towns; there are social distress, outbreaks of civil war and banditry, reverses in the struggle to maintain the frontier; there are corruption and extraordinary administrative decadence. After a time there comes the near or total collapse of government. China enters on a nadir of its history, from which there comes eventual recovery as the population regulates itself. Malthusian checks come into play, the extreme pressures are relaxed, the natural Chinese civilization reasserts itself.

There can be no doubt that China had entered on one of those adverse phases in the latter part of the eighteenth century. The Manchu dynasty ended its golden age in the unnaturally long reign of the Emperor Chien Lung (who reigned from 1736–96), and the population increased ominously. In the nineteenth century it would have been due for its time of troubles, regardless of the troubles brought on it by its new problems of foreign relations. The middle years of the century saw the Taiping rebellion and the revolt of the Chinese Muslims against the government, both classic cases of a population explosion, both resulting in a very great slaughter. The two political maladies came together— the troubles from the cyclical character of Chinese history and the troubles from the totally new and exceptional strain of encountering its rivals in the world. Each set of troubles complicated the other; each intensified the other; recovery became ever more difficult.

The Kuomintang, and Chinese nationalism, promised to bring relief to the political problems of China in the 1930s. At the same time there were signs that the social causes which had brought political collapse were about to be ameliorated by process of time, and it seemed likely that the efforts of the Kuomintang at social and economic improvement would not continue to be dogged with adversity. These signs, however, were hard to read correctly, and may have been misconstrued.

For the relative slowness of China's regeneration there are a number of reasons. The rebirth of a nation—it was nothing less—takes time, which cannot be cut short beyond a certain measure. It is a natural process, not entirely controllable by political or human means. But China's peculiar and horrifying experience of the last century remains to some extent a mystery. China's progress in our day has been so rapid, so revolutionary, that it is hard to understand why in the fairly recent past it took so long to get off the ground. In the last resort one is left with the bare statement—that a crisis of population coincided with a crisis of foreign relations, that the results of both became merged, and that it took more than a century to work out the consequences.

*

The other country, Japan, had an altogether different experience and its past must also be studied if Japan's place in the world cataclysm is to be understood. Japan was a lesser country than China. Generally its population was only about one sixth of China's. But it was inhabited by a people, which, by vigour, by a genius for imitation, and by artistic and warlike qualities, had made itself unique in the history of Asia. Japan had built up a civilization in many respects peculiar and outstanding. It responded to the stimulus of the coming of the westerners in a way which transformed the history of the region.

Since the beginning of the seventeenth century Japan had been exercised by the problem of relations with the West. It read the writing on the wall in the shadow cast by the Portuguese and Spanish galleons which at this time used to visit Japanese ports. Should Japan encourage them or should it deter them? After a brief period of cultivating their friendship it withdrew itself into seclusion. It persecuted mercilessly, as possibly enemies of Japanese security, the missionaries about whom at first it had been enthusiastic. It cut all ties with the external world, diplomatic, cultural and, as far as this was possible, economic. It was the classic case of a hermit kingdom. This policy of exclusiveness preserved Japan intact until the United States, in the year 1853 and again in 1854, dispatched a naval squadron under the command of Commodore Perry and compelled it to resume normal intercourse and foreign trade.

Thereupon Japan was in danger of being reduced to a colony by the imperialist powers. For its escape it had to thank the diplomatic adroitness, the skilful reasonableness of a few leading Japanese statesmen during the first years of the 1870s while Japan was renewing its contacts with the world. Once they had lost their first instinctive anti-foreignness they exposed themselves with zeal to all western influences. Japan's survival beyond this critical interval it owed to the remarkable changes which were brought about in Japanese society as a result of contact with western countries. From a militarily weak country, with a contemptible technology, Japan in a few years became like a hedgehog, which the imperialist powers, even at the height of their aggressiveness, thought twice about mauling.

Japan's history, which made this national strength possible, has been one of social change—a marked contrast to the sluggish conservatism of China's official social history. Japan was able to accept change because the Japanese were born relatively free of an overpowering tradition. Its governing circles were able, in contrast to the Chinese, to produce men who were imaginative, forceful, and free of the deadening desire that life should be preserved exactly as it had been known in previous centuries. They were daring and iconoclastic. They were not bound by a thwarting public opinion, as was the mandarinate in China.

In China, the society, the civilization, took precedence over the government. It was a civilization not disposed for change. But in Japan the government was not held in invisible fetters by public opinion and by the past.

Furthermore a Japanese government which desired to make changes was more likely to be able to implement them. Society was more responsive to governmental direction: it was more at its mercy. For this the main reason was geography. Japan consisted of a chain of islands, all of them comparatively small, all of them accessible by sea. Thus a fairly good system of communication could be established.

This alone made it very different from China: in China there were, by the standards of that day, majestic roads, but, even so, the population in the outer provinces was at three months distance from the seat of central government. In consequence the ability of the centre to regulate the affairs of a large part of China was much reduced. But in Japan, no such inhibition palsied the national administration. Its efforts did not peter out in vast distances which separated it from its subjects.

The progress of Japan was rapid and, to the western powers spreading their influence through the world, unprecedented. In 1868 occurred the so-called Meiji Restoration. This was a revolution, not a restoration, although this great political change in Japan was dressed up as a revival of things past. An old, vestigial system of an Emperor, long confined to a kind of museum existence, and preserved partly for religious reasons, was called into employment; the existing system of government, a highly traditional one presided over by hereditary prime ministers or Shoguns, was suppressed. The new system was organized by the Samurai, the ex-feudatories of Japan's feudal past which it was abandoning. Exercising their remarkable talent for mimesis, they copied from what their intelligence judged to be the essentials of the formidable western system. The Japanese surprised themselves by the ease with which they were able to reproduce in Japan most of what went into the making of western civilization. From Britain they copied the organization of the navy; from Germany the army, the educational system and some political institutions; from France an outline of the legal system. The degree of modernization was greater in appearance than in reality, for often the old, and essentially Japanese institutions and modes continued behind a façade of reform. Nevertheless, reform there was, and Japan began to operate with a revolutionary change in efficiency.

Soon the Japanese sensed that their basic aim—which was to attain a military power which would enable them to resist on level terms with the western powers—was slowly being realized. They felt strength beginning to pulse through the political system. From this time on, Japanese thought about the political miracle of their awakening was increasingly obsessed by considerations of power.

For the European onlooker, the spectacle of Japan at this time was of remarkable interest. For him it was a new experience to kick an ancient civilization, and to find that it did not crumble. It was bracing and fascinating. Enough of the old, graceful, picturesque, fragile civilization of old Japan still survived to make the process of the metamorphosis of Japan of almost incredible interest; and, in addition, of poignant pathos. American, British and French men of letters grasped the occasion of describing what was happening before their eyes, and the result was a series of books describing the topography, anthropology, ethics and aesthetics of Japan in transition. Among them Redesdale's *Tales of Ancient Japan* is especially valuable in the picture which it gives of the national ethos, and of the reaction to it of a civilized and imaginative westerner.

This was the elegiac tribute of the West to a country which showed spirit in resistance. It was quite different from the contemptuous tone and temper of the writings about India and China at the time. And for the foreigners who were blind to the more subtle qualities of a nation's progress, the rapid expansion of trade and of the whole economy were impressive and sobering.

*

By 1890 it was plain that the once real threat that Japan would fall a victim to western imperialism had spent itself. Instead, Japan shocked the western powers by joining with them in harrying and nibbling at China, whose disorders invited pressure.

In 1894 Japan became engaged in war with China, and won a spectacular victory. It was the first of the succession of Sino-Japanese wars. By the peace settlement Japan secured the off-shore Chinese island of Formosa. It also proposed to annex South Manchuria in full sovereignty. But this antagonized the West, which still regarded China as their destined prey, and they were unwilling that Japan should go hunting with them. Under intense pressure from Russia, France and Germany, Japan gave up this Manchurian conquest.

In this incident nearly all the ingredients of international politics in East Asia up to 1945 are already plain. Japan perceived that events were presenting it with an extraordinary opportunity: Japanese were to speak, until their final defeat in 1945, of 'Japan's hour of destiny', the fleeting opportunity of which they must take advantage. In East Asia, in the Japanese view, there must be a hegemony of either Japan or China: the concept of coexistence seemed to have no place.

In general, in the comparison between the two, Japan was the weaker power. The immense size of China, the antiquity and impressiveness of its civilization, its economic superiority when this could be mobilized, must in the end prove decisive. All the warlike qualities of the Japanese people and the advantages of geographic position could not prevail against this opposition. But over the short period, in a time of instability and of unnatural weakness of China, Japan would have the advantage of stealing a march on China, of becoming, despite the historical position of the two, the stronger partner; and then, if Japan was willing to rely on its will and on the use of force, it could count on maintaining for an indefinite period the advantage which it had. Japan would stake all upon its ability to repress by force the natural event of a revival of Chinese power.

*

From that determination came the events which led Japan to its fateful participation in the Second World War. Japan's resolution to stake all its future upon the employment of force came to determine most things in the life and domestic achievements of its gifted people.

It was an audacious resolution, and a rather horrifying one. It meant choosing to act against the progressive forces of the age, and allying with the darker tendencies, which were never far below the surface. It involved Japan in courses of action which gradually led to its having a reputation for cruelty and insensitivity and it coarsened the emotional life. Inevitably Japan turned away from the more delicate things in its civilization. Japan had chosen to follow *Bushido*, the way of the warrior, and to concentrate its interests on making itself feared as the ogre of the Far East. Japan was dazzled by its feudal past, and did not sufficiently take note of the fact that military effort in the new conditions of industrialism was quite unlike that of

Japanese tradition. Bushido in the twentieth century was to be unlike that of the days of the Samurai and Daimyos. With fevered resolution Japan found itself impelled on the road of national brutality, and this was hard because in a part of their minds, the Japanese, like the Germans, desire to be loved, and find it difficult to understand that their actions make them monstrously unlovable.

*

The contrast between this alarming and determined imperialism, and the natural diffidence of a great many Japanese, perhaps the majority, has often been commented on. The Japanese have a tendency to be abnormally apologetic for themselves and unassertive. As a people, they reprobate individualism. It strikes the Japanese as selfish. This trait is one of the most pronounced in the Japanese character, and is at the root of much that is peculiar in politics, in ethics, in Japanese tradition. It explains why they have rarely produced great assertive figures to take charge of the affairs of the nation individually.

But the very modesty of individual Japanese explains much of what was horrible in recent Japanese history. When the fashion for national aggressiveness set in, few people had the decisiveness, the resolution and the courage to oppose it. What was the individual Japanese doing in taking it on himself to resist the rush of the whole people, even if their direction was to the Gadarene lake? This artistic people, when its emotions were touched, was capable of a national behaviour which was arrogant, demanding, fierce and sinister in the extreme. A naturally diffident people became ready to sweep aside all the restraints which stood in its way. But the fact that there was another side to Japan, another aspect to the machine of conquest, needs to be kept constantly in mind if Japanese action is not to be a continuous puzzle.

It was some time before this hardening of the Japanese attitude towards China became plain. This is often forgotten: it is wrongly assumed that the Japanese hostility became rigid much earlier than in fact it did. For a long while Chinese and Japanese had viewed each other with natural affection. Japan remained, in a peculiar way, tied to China by linguis-

tic, cultural and religious connections. The two languages
were distinct from one another, but the Japanese had borrowed the Chinese characters, and could write Japanese in
these. This proved a powerful bond of attachment. In the
modern period many of the leaders of Chinese nationalism
had been inspired by modern ideas by residence as students
in Japan. They looked back on that period with nostalgia.
Japan, where the conditions of life were not so very different
from China's, was for these young men the convenient forcing house and museum of western attitudes, the place where
western institutions were on show but had not become too
uncomfortable, and where life was not a leap in the dark.
Morever in Japan there still survived, by habit if not as the
result of conviction, the consoling sense that China was a
land with a magnificent past.

A belief that Japan could be the natural protector of
Chinese nationalism, and that together the Chinese and Japanese peoples might discomfort the western world; the fascination of the Chinese at discerning the Japanese methods
of surviving in the dangerous world and getting level terms
with its horrific visitors: these facts tended to postpone an
inexorable break between China and Japan. The Chinese
and Japanese still preserved a special feeling for each other,
even when the Japanese were behaving most brutally and
insensitively. For a long while the Chinese had the instinct
that they should be patient, and that the day might come
when the temporary clouds between the two countries would
disappear and that Japan would become useful to them. They
cherished Japan's successes, as, for example, its victory in
1905 in the Russo-Japanese war, as a matter for the common
pride of Asians.

In the end, the relations between China and Japan took a
turn for the worse, and became cooler. Events on both
sides contributed to this. Chinese nationalism became more
unrestrained and irresponsible: it revealed more clearly its
ultimate goal. Japan set itself with more determination to
thwart reviving Chinese ambition; and the internal events in
Japan had rendered inactive the groups which fostered understanding and indulgence. Relations became colder; but
only disastrously so during the 1930s. When this happened,
much of the warm regard of each country for the other,
especially among the more traditional classes, still continued

in latent form. It was suppressed, but it was always there just below the surface, an imponderable factor in the situation of the Far East.

*

While this national resolution was slowly forming as the response to the circumstances of the time, it should be remembered that the circumstances were different from those of today. Japan made a disastrous choice, which was to lead to untold retribution and havoc, but at the time of its first moves toward empire building its decisions did not appear so eccentric. In the later part of the nineteenth century, force was still the final tool in the conduct of international relations; all countries accepted this, and Japan was not peculiar. Britain's conquest of India still stood out as the brazen example of what imperialism might succeed in doing. The only deterrent was in the calculation of consequences, and these were at that time clear of such devastating things as the atom bombs, or even, for the most part, of the horrors of wars of attrition.

For all its apparent modernization, many features of the Japanese state continued to be very different from those of the West. In contrast with the western powers, Japan, though it wore the trappings of a modern state, continued to be at least mentally attached to the Middle Ages. This accounted for its often bewildering reaction to the situation in which it found itself. It explains the frequently surprising recourse to the methods of the past. They did not represent an abrupt move to reaction by the Japanese, as they were apt to be interpreted by the West. Rather they were the intrusion into modern ways of the instinct of an earlier day, which had never died completely in Japan. Japan, though suitably made up for the part of a contemporary power, never was quite at home in the modern world; it was wearing a kind of fancy dress, and the West dimly recognized the fact. The West was never entirely at home with Japan, for it sensed a certain eerie mystery, as of a survivor from a past civilization.

The psychological drama behind Japan's attempt to prevail by force, and especially behind the attempt to prevail over China, is exceedingly interesting.

Throughout their history the Japanese have always exhibited symptoms of schizophrenia, exemplified in their attitude towards China. Japan admired China, and simultaneously it despised it; it was tied to China and yet yearned to be free. Its attitude combined the pious reverence of a child towards a grandparent with the disrespect which eventually led to war with its cultural ancestor. For the civilization of Japan, though ultimately it was due to the Japanese spirit playing upon the various influences which went into its making, was, in its remote origin, derived from China. From China came the initial impulse, and the Japanese could never put this out of their minds. On one hand they accepted, in an excess of self-abasement, the traditional Chinese view of the Japanese as being a race of 'deformed dwarfs'; on the other, they felt themselves superior, and proclaimed themselves with neurotic insistence to be the children of the Sun Goddess—'the race of Yamato'—and destined to rule the entire world, even a world as powerful, rich and wide as their extended knowledge of the nineteenth and twentieth centuries proved it to be. This ambivalence and the unreality behind so much of Japanese action—together with the extremes of violence alternating with extremes of self-control—are the key to understanding a great deal of Far-Eastern history.

The relations with China always preoccupied the Japanese. Even when Japan was led, via China, into war (which few people in Japan really desired) with the United States, Britain and finally Russia, it was essentially a by-product of this great absorbing interest. When Japan went to war with the U S and Britain, it was because the West intervened between Japan and its victim China. In a sense, Japan was perfectly sincere in claiming that it wished to protect China: it was protecting it from the western aggressors so that it could be preserved intact for Japan.

However, it must not be supposed from this description that Japan acted monolithically. For a country as regimented as was Japan, there were always surprising divergencies from the norm. From time to time there rose movements which altered the policy of the government, and even at times seemed to offer the prospect of a reversal of policy. But, seen in perspective, Japan's drive on China continued with little interruption throughout the period.

2

The Anglo-Japanese Alliance

JAPAN followed this resolute policy of maintaining its ascendancy over China for half a century down to 1945. It was hampered in its execution by the jealousy of the western powers, which believed that they had a monopoly in exploiting China. In asserting itself in China and the Pacific Ocean, Japan ran the risk of increasing opposition from these powers. It had discovered early that they would not willingly leave it in peace to bully China: not because they were sympathetic with China, but because they objected to Japan's rise.

In pursuit of its purpose, Japan had to resort to one of the oldest devices of diplomacy. Ringed by a group of unsympathetic powers, Japan set itself to split their united front, to woo one of them as its ally and advertise its useful role in return for patronage. If it could enlist the friendship of one of the larger powers, for which it was prepared to pay a price, it reckoned on being able to hold in check the others, and to avoid being compelled by them to forgo advantages at China's expense (as had happened in 1895).

Where could it find the friendly patronage? Which great powers could it woo away from the conventional attitude of suspicion of Japan as an upstart? Above all, how could Japan supply a great power with an inducement to take certain risks to gain its friendship? These problems exercised Japanese statesmen at the turn of the century.

Opinion was divided. It was generally agreed that the extreme enemy of Japan, the frustrator of all its schemes of advance, was its immediate neighbour, Russia. Nevertheless

24

one school favoured an apparently direct appeasement of Russia, and, when it had the upper hand, began negotiations which might have found a way for Japan and Russia to coexist. Another school wanted an alliance with Germany. Already Japan felt the attraction of Germany; in its programme of modernization it had borrowed from Germany the outline of its constitution, and also it had copied much in the organization of its army. In the formative years of Japan's foreign policy Japan had soundings with Germany which looked towards a much closer link.

But eventually another school prevailed. It was the group which was inclined to rely on the Japanese navy. Japan was a group of islands; it was a maritime power; it felt that it was obeying its predestined fate in accepting a maritime solution of its problems. It did so by throwing in its lot with Britain. Japan, perched off-shore of the land mass of Asia, was aware that its conditions of life were very much the same as those of Britain, which was similarly an island off-shore of the land mass of Europe. The geopolitical attractions of an alliance with Britain were reinforced by a strong emotional reaction in Japan. The political attitudes of the western powers since the enforced opening up of Japan to foreign trade in the middle of the nineteenth century had been marked by galling restraints on its mainland explorations, for instance, in the restriction of its spoliation in China in the war of 1894–5, and in some quarters by a cultural insensitivity, of which the term 'yellow peril' was an example. The British readiness to come to an understanding not only promised a political alliance of real value but also wiped out a sense of previous humiliations and produced a response of warm friendship in Japan. Thus in 1902, there was concluded the Anglo-Japanese Alliance, which gave Japan the partner which it sought.

The alliance was an event of fundamental importance in Japanese history. The complicated diplomacy which preceded and followed it are a clue to all that happened in the Far East. History had taken hold of Japan, and placed it eventually in the position from which it drove on, blindly, but with a certain exhilaration, to its fated part in the Second World War, and to its doom. Too much attention cannot be given to these events by anybody wishing to find out what really happened. With one eye turned towards Pearl

Harbor, and, what lay beyond, to Hiroshima, the complexities of the years which followed on the alliance must be unravelled.

The alliance was in effect a neutralizing arrangement so far as Japan was concerned. It provided that if either of the two partners became engaged in war with a Great Power, the other should give notice that it would come in on the side of its ally if it were attacked by another of the Great Powers. The effect of this upon Japan was that probably it would be relieved of the prospect of a war with more than one adversary. Thereby the neutrality of the other powers was likely to be assured. For example, under the protection of the treaty, Japan could safely make war on Russia, being reasonably assured that it would not be assailed by any power which otherwise might be inclined to come to the aid of Russia. The British power, promising war against any ally of Russia, or any combatant of Japan, was enough to secure the neutrality of all other powers. So, by a minimum use of actual force, the danger of war involving several countries was very much reduced.

The alliance worked as it was intended. It produced the results which were foreseen. In 1904 Japan did fight Russia as a result of the unappeasable rivalry between the two countries: rivalry for the control of north China as Japan uncovered its ambitions. The watching world was surprised at Japan's temerity at challenging such a mighty antagonist, and was astonished at Japan's survival. Its victory was less complete than popular legend might suggest. Japan was exhausted and grasped at peace after eighteen months of successful but gruelling hostilities. It was in no position to demand to annex Manchuria, though it might seem to have gained the right to do so. But by the treaty which restored peace, Japan was given the right to safeguard the South Manchurian Railway which was built with Japanese capital. This was fateful. From this military base, the power of Japan was to spread over and to menace all of China.

This first of Japan's great wars also set a precedent of undiplomatic conduct. Japan began it by a surprise attack on the Russian navy: it dispensed with a declaration of war. But in this war, at least, Japan's treatment of its prisoners and its observance of international conventions on clemency were exemplary.

In the same way that the alliance served Japan, it also served Britain. In effect, it provided that the British interest in the Far East would be protected in case Britain became involved in war in Europe. If that happened, Britain would rely on Japan to keep its empire and interests intact in the Pacific. And so it happened when Britain had to fight the first European war. The treaty was not quite perfectly observed, at least in spirit. Some Japanese, influential ones, could not help speculating on what Japan must do if Britain should lose the war, a possibility which they did not seem to see with regret; and the positive aid Japan gave was less than might have been expected of an honourable ally. It felt that it had done everything which could be asked of it when it had liquidated the German colonies in China. But concerning the effect of the treaty as a whole, Britain was content.

Throughout the two decades which it lasted the alliance was the corner-stone of Japanese policy. Under its umbrella Japan safely took the first steps to the establishment of its empire. The irony was that the extension of this empire was to lead Japan into the most disastrous war of the 1940s, and war with its former ally. It pressed ahead with its imperial enterprises when jangled events had deprived it of the British alliance, and had transformed Britain into an enemy, or a wished-for victim. It is no wonder that the Anglo-Japanese Alliance was, by old-fashioned and conservative Japanese, looked back on with melancholy regret. It represented the time of safety. It was the instrument which had brought Japan respect, growing power, and no doubts or perplexities. It was a tower of strength to Japan psychologically. It had been the dependable way, felt the solider elements in Japanese society, amid other kalaeidoscopic attractions, and Japan had been wise not to forsake it.

*

The alliance was allowed to die at the Washington Conference in 1921. The issues in the Far East had grown more complex and divided. In 1915, when the balance of forces in the East was disturbed by the western powers being engaged in war in Europe—which for the eastern countries was a kind of European civil war—Japan seized its opportunity and presented the government at Peking with a virtual ultimatum which has been called the Twenty-One Demands. Acceptance of these would have ended even the circumscribed independence of Northern China: it would have transformed it into a Japanese protectorate. The pattern of probable events had been made clear in Korea, which Japan had taken over as a protectorate and later annexed. China was saved by the diplomatic intervention of the United States.

Instead of obtaining the surrender of China, Japan in 1917 became entangled in negotiations with the United States which seemed to give a recognition of its claims on mainland China, though in vague form; and then, on peace being restored, it had the mortifying experience of coming to the Washington Conference, convened by the United States in 1921, and of being compelled to join with the remaining powers interested in the Pacific in pledging itself to respect China's integrity and independence.

The Washington Conference contemplated a period in which Treaty Ports and extraterritoriality in China would be no more. The powers were willing that China should eventually be admitted to the comity of states as an equal, and welcomed the signs of modernization. The instrument embodying these agreements, called the Nine Power Treaty, was to be for twenty years a memorial of the limitations put upon Japan from having a free hand to decide the shape of the Far East. In Japan itself the change of mood in the powers who were party to the treaty was received with consternation, which would have been greater if most Japanese had not regarded it as hypocrisy. In Japan the fires of imperialism had still to become at their most incandescent.

That such a high-minded document could be produced, and seriously debated, was a sign that great changes were coming over the whole world. The instincts of imperialism had begun to subside in all the countries involved, Japan excepted; the climate of opinion was changing, and there was a reconsideration in many countries of their long-term objectives. In all lands, the doubts of the liberal intelligentsia were undermining the former certainties. It was even asked whether it was certain that imperialism in certain countries really paid; whether the profit from the economic rampage over China was equal to the costs and dangers of keeping China down. There was an unfamiliar readiness to receive politely the advances of Chinese nationalism. Above all, the instinctive resort to force showed signs of waning; there was more readiness to treat China as other countries were treated.

In these new circumstances the British decided to terminate their Japanese alliance; and thereby struck a heavy blow at Japan's sentiment and security. On balance Britain considered that the treaty had come to have disadvantages which outweighed its attractions. The immediate motive for not renewing it was pressure from the Canadian government, which in turn reflected opinion in the United States, which had begun to feel the naval rivalry with Japan. The first phase of American tension with Japan happened as the result of American armament and exertion during the first European war; the American navy felt its strength, and the United States was less inclined than formerly to share the seas with other powers. The chief reason for Britain's acquiescence in the American pressure to break the Anglo-Japanese Alliance was the belief that, if Britain was faced with a choice between American goodwill and that of Japan, the decision must go in favour of Anglo-Saxon solidarity. Yet perhaps few such fateful decisions have been made so casually, with so little national debate, and with such small realization of what had been done, and what it meant for the future.

The ending of the treaty confirmed that the world was to divide upon racial lines. By rebuffing Japan, this event compelled Japan to recognize itself as being on the Asian side. It confirmed the tendency of some Japanese—and some westerners—to see the tensions of this part of the world as consisting in the white versus the yellow race. Japan, cast out again from the inner ring of powers which had the last word in world affairs, would in the end seek to overthrow this same inner ring. It would do so in the name of the equality of races. In its manoeuvres it could no longer be assured of the neutralization of most of the western powers; and undoubtedly it would make a commotion in seeking to forward its interest in a world grown more hostile to it.

As a compensation for the old Anglo-Japanese Alliance, Japan had to content itself with an agreement for limitation of naval power, in which Japan's status as one of the greatest naval powers in the world was recognized. Japan was accorded a ration of three compared with that of five which was taken by the United States and Britain. But this was a poor substitute. It did nothing to give Japan a friend in the harsh world of competitive politics. On the contrary, it underlined the opposition of interests between it and greater powers. Whereas it had been able to count on the British navy as a possible ally while the United States pursued its policy guided only by American interests, after the naval agreement both the United States and Britain were lumped together as potentially unfriendly powers.

A further step in embittering relations took place in 1924, when the American Congress, alarmed by a sudden influx of Japanese, passed an Exclusion Act which barred Asiatics, including Japanese, from any hope of being accepted as immigrants. About the same time Australia became notorious for a White Australia Policy. These steps, more than any other, convinced the Japanese that, whether they wished it or not, the great world of contemporary history insisted that they were to be Asian; and Japan would take them at their word, and would seize the Asian leadership.

Japan, having been disowned by its partner among the great powers, was thereafter forever in a restless search for an ally which would offer it the same security as Britain had done. For a long while it did not find it, and as it cast around, its neuroses of alarm and resentment were deepened and became always more dangerous.

The Japanese efforts to thwart by force the recovery of China had been checked by diplomacy and by the intervention of other powers. Japan was induced to retreat. It was still lacking in self-confidence. It had not yet developed the willingness to outrage the rest of the world. But the stage was being set for the more determined confrontation from which Japan would not back down so easily; the Chinese would be goaded to stubborn effort to defend their revolution and the recovery of their vital power; Japan would be lured by the attractions of a dangerous new ally in the West which it would calculate would give it the security it had sought; and all the powers concerned would in the end drift into a war in the complications arising out of this fatal competition.

3

The Japan which struck

AT the start of hostilities between two countries it is customary to take stock of their rival strength. Japan, both in its own eyes and in the eyes of the rest of the world, began the conflict, of which the first phase opened in 1931, with overwhelming advantages. Most eye-witnesses to the initial clash would have been astonished if they had had a glimpse of what it would eventually grow into. It was expected that Japan would settle the quarrel in a small-scale colonial war, such as the world had been accustomed to in the recent past.

Japan had reason for its confidence. It was a modern state, recognizably like the states of the western world. It had a formal constitution like a western country. It was indeed a copy of these, and it included such institutions as a constitutional monarchy, a cabinet, a civil service, and two houses of parliament with rather more than consultative powers. It had, moreover, a modern industrial structure. Its achievements in making a success of a western-style economic system is one of the wonders of Far-Eastern history, the more remarkable because the traditions of Japan had appeared to tell against commercial success. The ethos of Japan remained unbusinesslike. There was, fairly widespread, a deep contempt for money. But this had not prevented the Japanese from setting money to do its work.

The state machinery was strong. Its administration, even if there was much corruption, was reasonably well organized. Though Japanese institutions were apt to strike the westerner as being odd and haphazard in the way they were run, they produced the result intended: they had the secret of effectiveness.

The national unity, which had been so conspicuous in the war with Russia nearly three decades earlier, had not been undermined as Japan entered on a more sophisticated life in the 1930s. Its people, in spite of an increase in wealth, continued to be easily regimented. The success of the government in doing this was due to the extraordinary competence and ubiquitousness of the police, which was one of the traditional features of administration in Japan. For centuries the police had been harrying the Japanese people. One of the victims of modern extremism was the curious, nonconformist cults of Japanese Buddhism. The police seemed to be infuriated by their existence, and persecuted them severely.

Though there were the beginnings of social unrest and of a communist party, this was as yet scarcely reflected in Japan's political life. Dangerous ways of thought were appearing among students—in themselves a surprisingly large class—nightmares to the police, and to the army which played a special part in keeping the morale of the nation untainted, they could console themselves that they were dealing with an eccentricity rather than a serious threat.

Though Japanese is an exceptionally difficult language to learn, the population was almost entirely literate. Knowledge, especially technical knowledge, was advanced. The newly literate populace, which was so different from other populaces in Asia, did not band against the government. Indeed, the Japanese people, though hardy and enterprising, remained extraordinarily docile to govern. They had an ancient tradition of turbulence, upheaval, and a readiness to make civil war: but these had become only a distant memory. Their martial quality had been mobilized, exclusively and entirely, in the national interest, and was embodied in the Japanese army.

*

For the result of the war, much would naturally depend on the capability of the army. The Japanese army had had a various history, and had passed through changes since the days of the Meiji Restoration, at which it was organized. In the 1930s it was a national army, the product of universal military service. But though this was its origin, it stood apart from the nation in a rather sinister way.

The young men of the army, when called to the colours, were trained in a manner which was calculated to ensure their obedience, to brutalize them, to make them unlikely to act like the rest of the Japanese people. They became docile instruments of the officer corps. Extraordinary stories leaked out of the barbarity of the system of military training. The Japanese army was not the nation in arms—since it rejected much in Japanese life which might have made it more capable of self-control in the aftermath of battle—but it was the Japanese peasantry in arms. Such a force was dangerous because it was liable to be swayed by terrible spasms of inane and savage barbarism. The rigid discipline under which it was kept in Japan was suddenly set aside when it found itself under foreign skies and in different surroundings. The woes of the Asian continent wherever the Japanese soldier was to tread were to be proof of this.

The corps of professional officers, the centre of this military system, was drawn from the entire nation and, at least in theory, was not limited to certain parts of the country or certain social classes. Boys who chose the army as their career were withdrawn at the age of sixteen from ordinary education, and were trained in the numerous military academies. Later, with factionalism playing its peculiar part in Japanese affairs, their careers depended on the faction in the army to which they attached themselves. They followed a certain conventional pattern in their lives, with different aims, interests, ethics from those of the majority of the Japanese people. They were less liable to be swayed by ordinarily changing ideas because their education had been distorted.

Japan, as its army had grown larger and more free of political control, became like one of the great military empires with which the West had long been familiar in Europe. The army was largely autonomous: its isolation and self-regard led it to think that it had a divine right to be the custodian of the national soul. In a great crisis the country was more likely to follow the hectic counsels of the army rather than the sober ones of civilian government.

This was particularly obnoxious because of the peculiar quality of Japanese militarism. This derived from the fact that, in traditional Japan, the use of arms had been a monopoly of a military caste called the Samurai. Officially the Samurai had been brought to an end soon after the Meiji Restoration. Nevertheless, the tradition which animated these professional soldiers continued to prevail in the modern army, and became dominant in the period of national assertiveness which prevailed in the thirties. By and large, the Japanese army officers of the professional, thorough-going kind, guided themselves by the code called Bushido, the way of the warrior. Bushido prescribed the life of the soldier at all points. It proclaimed that his ultimate fate was to be killed: to kill others first, but in the end to be slain. Bushido laid down everything that was possible in the relation of one Samurai with another, but was silent about, because it was contemptuous of, the rest of humanity. Harshness, endurance, the carrying out ruthlessly of impossible orders, the savage treatment of the underdog, the duty in circumstances of disgrace to commit *hara-kiri*—self-slaughter in a peculiarly painful manner—were its subject. Leadership was to be enforced by fear, by iron discipline, and was not to be exercised by any reserves of human magnetism.

It was a deeply pessimistic cult. Its parallels are perhaps only to be found in old German sagas; its horror and its hopelessness. It is significant that the revival of the typical Bushido outlook was associated with a type of politics such as that which prevailed amid the Nazis. The gloom and grimness of this tradition of Japanese militarism was symbolized in the deliberate drabness of the Japanese uniform. The army was without glitter. Alone among military powers, Japan exhibited no military panache. Bushido painted the heroic life as one which excluded compassion and which was directed only to success.

Perhaps because Japanese militarism was so outwardly unattractive, it was curiously anonymous. It did not carry any 'cult of personality', as did most European brands of militarism. A consequence was that Japanese generals, interesting personalities though they might be, were seldom popular. The national heart did not warm in contemplating them. It might feel pride or respect, but never affection.

The tragedy of Japan happened in such dangerous ideas

becoming so influential when, in the twentieth century, Japan possessed the power to make itself so formidable internationally. Japan's modern army machine was administered by men who took as serious guides of conduct a tradition quite out of date and barbaric. Of course, not all the officer corps lived by this repulsive code. Some were as civilized as the most progressive civilians, and by most of the country the ideas of the Samurai were regarded as absurd, medieval, deeply irrational, frightening and frightful. It was common to regard the cult as a plague centre in Japanese civilization which must be eradicated. But the fact that it was really an eccentricity in Japan made Japanese militarism the more difficult to keep under control, and it attached itself easily to wild and irresponsible aims. It escaped the censorship of commonsense of the whole of society. Little by little, this insane part of Japan succeeded in becoming dominant. Military, archaic Japan took captive twentieth century, ingenious, civilian Japan, and swept it along towards the challenge to the civilization of the world, which was the principal history of Japan in this time.

*

Japan was strengthened for war by a peculiar psychology of its people: so strange and well-marked that the study of its evolution has become one of the standard exercises of Far-East history. This psychology proceeded from certain moral conflicts which the Japanese, almost to a man, accepted as axiomatic. A Japanese longs, before all other things, for a world organized on the principles of harmony. Harmony is only to be achieved when everyone fills his predestined place, and asks for himself neither too much honour, dignities and awards, nor too little. It is an outlook curiously like that of the Middle Ages, at least in its theory. It is worship of 'degree, priority and place'. Above all it is an outlook which detests anarchy. The simple fact which the Anglo-American democracies found it hard to understand was the horror which the Japanese felt at an individual or group which had a clear conception of its own interests, as distinct and separate from those of the community, and which set out to realize them.

The Japanese also had a sense of being under an im-

mense obligation, which any amount of altruistic behaviour
could never requite, to their family predecessors, to the
Japanese Emperor as embodying the Japanese state, and to
the government of the day for making life tolerable. It was
possible for a Japanese government to make extreme drafts
upon this sense of obligation, and a diffused sense of responsibility in general among its people, and do so almost
without limit. In war the Japanese government could only
lose the support of the populace when it was evidently and
completely beaten in the field: it would not be beaten because
it had forfeited this support beforehand.

In organization for war, the Japanese system was the
stronger because of the Emperor-system with which the
whole was covered. Though in actual fact the Emperor had,
or at least exercised, little political power, as a figure-head
he was of the utmost possible importance. The Emperor, as
an institution, has now undergone change, probably permanent. It is true that the Emperor survived the war; but he
was to lose, by contact with the realities of the modern
world, so much of the mystique which at this period continued to surround the office that today some careful inquiry
is necessary to recapture it. He was no longer regarded as a
divine person. But in the 1930s it was widely accepted as
axiomatic that he was of different stuff from ordinary humanity.

Immensely awe-inspiring, extremely sacred, the incarna-
tion of all that was meant by the Japanese national spirit,
remote, mysterious, never criticized in press or parliament
—the Japanese Emperor obviously possessed the qualities
which made him the ideal mascot for war. What did it matter
if all the actual deeds of government were the acts of common or garden Ministers? In fact the role of the Japanese
Emperor, at least in its remoter origin, was as much sacer-
dotal and magical as it was governmental. It is significant
that the Japanese word meaning to observe a religious rite
is radically connected with the word meaning government.
Simply to dwell in the same country as the Emperor conferred felicity, and laid on his subjects a readiness to endure
sacrifice which recognized no limit.

The court of the Japanese Emperor was not notably
military in its atmosphere. He existed as a man, as well as

an idea, and it was hard for him to live up to the position required of him by the theorists of the Japanese state. It was strange to find that the Emperor Hirohito was a mild-mannered, courteous prince, and that he lived in a court which was a museum of venerated or picturesque objects. It was rather like the entourage of a British monarch. It was decorous and somewhat dull: but it was colourful—and was much more strongly marked by fragile aestheticism than is ordinary life in Japan. This was not really surprising, because, in the long history of the Japanese monarchy, it had seldom been associated with military leadership. Though in theory the Japanese monarch was the supreme commander, in military matters as in civilian, only the Emperor Meiji had taken this at all seriously. His successors, including Hirohito, reverted easily to the more ancient attitude. The Emperor Hirohito was head of the state, he received reports from ministers, and advised but played a strictly constitutional part. He did not sully the office with politics. The court class clearly did not want war.

*

A basic cause of all the misfortunes in Far-Eastern politics was the fundamentally precarious state of the Japanese economy. Japan had built up, especially during this century, an impressive industry, but was at bottom a poor country. It lacked raw materials. Its chief asset was its manpower, and it owed its economic advance to the organization of this. Its people were strenuous, punctual, persevering, disciplined, adaptable: out of these talents, combined with a leadership capable of putting these to use, there was constructed one of the most thriving economies of the world. Japan threw itself with zest into imitating the western countries.

Starting in the early days of the Meiji Restoration, Japan built up its industry, and the rest of its economy, systematically. Its constant impediment was that it had to build bricks without straw. But it succeeded. The result was that the Japanese economy followed a particular pattern. It imported almost all the raw materials for industrial use: iron, the rare metals, coal, oil, and, in the early days, machinery; it exported many of the products of industry.

The raw materials were sent to Japan, and the Japanese people, organized in a great productive machine, processed these and marketed the product. It lived thus upon the proceeds of being the workshop of the East, but one to which the raw materials were delivered from abroad, and one which was kept going by orders from abroad. This was the basic pattern which shone through, although of course much in the economy was exceptional to the system.

The broad lines of the Japanese economy were thus very similar to those of the British economy in Europe. There were differences; Japan never allowed its agriculture to become so small a part of the economy as did Britain when Britain concentrated on being the workshop of the world. Japan, unlike Britain, never took the decisive steps towards *laissez-faire*, and never abandoned the direction of its economic destinies to blind economic laws. It never, to the same extent, was confident, as Britain was at the time, that the economic machine, if left to itself, would automatically right itself, whatever the predicaments to which it was exposed by adverse political circumstance. The Japanese government had constantly in mind that Japan's prosperity was at the mercy of other countries allowing it unimpeded access to raw materials, and unimpeded access to markets for the sale of its products; and it sought, by countless means, to remedy this. Japan, like Britain at the present time, had a continual anxiety from its balance of payments. It lived dangerously. It knew that it must export or die.

Its great industrial machine, and along with this, the remarkable nexus of mercantile institutions which it built up, all depended on the inward flow of raw materials, and on being able to find a foreign market for the finished products. If ever this process was interrupted, or seriously dislocated, Japan would be halted, its national talents would be wasted, its prosperity disappear, its nakedness be exposed.

Such a restless, dynamic society, explosive and always ready to seek new opportunities, uneasily aware of the narrow conditions for its survival, was not easy to fit into the world around it. It was constantly producing new situations: its nature, and its indispensable quality, was to be at home in constant vicissitudes. Though, as a military empire, Japan stood for a certain stability, it was really, though it would have denied this, the force making for constant instability in the Far East.

*

As the twentieth century proceeded, it became a fixed idea in Japan that the country was in great peril, as the Japanese felt their economy to be ever more insecure. They had had experience of entrusting themselves to be carried forwards by the great expansion of world trade, and had been taught by successive trade cycles, to fear disaster. The grave effect of the world depression on Japan in 1930 strengthened the case of the army for finding a military solution to the economic dangers. World trade barriers which arose as a result of the depression caused desperate poverty in Japan. The army, with its intimate connection with the Japanese peasantry, was greatly concerned about the sensational collapse, in 1930, of silk purchases by the United States. This deprived the agricultural class of its second main source of income and caused widespread distress in the countryside. The younger army officers were frequently drawn from the class of small landowners, and viewed affairs with a countryman's eyes. It was significant that ideas of expansion through foreign conquest came, not from the generals in the first place, but primarily from the young officers.

If Japan were able to conquer the adjacent territory from which raw materials could be produced—such as Manchuria —and if it should obtain military control of some of the markets for buying Japanese exports, it could breathe at peace. It could have the assurance of maintaining its industrial greatness, of safeguarding the livelihood of the countryside and of solving problems of over-population. The peace, prosperity and progress of all Asia, as well as Japan itself, depended on this consummation. The Japanese military were able to argue that they supported not only a narrow national cause, but that they were crusaders for the whole of Asia. The well-being of the entire continent depended on the safeguarding of the Japanese economy. Only the western countries could think it an advantage that the Japanese talent should be thwarted.

This was the frame of mind behind the Japanese attempt

to gain absolute control of China, and, later, of South-East Asia. The Japanese believed themselves to be economically propelled. This does not mean that the war was an economic necessity, or that the Japanese soldiers who made it were economic puppets. But they made Japan's economic problems the justification of their military action, and, not insincerely, supposed themselves driven on by economic forces which compelled them to act as they did.

The developing views on economics of the army became a matter of concern to the large mercantile institutions which dominated the economy of the country. These institutions, with plenty of money to spare, found that, in the condition of Japanese politics of the day, it was prudent to buy support wherever it was possible—not only from politicians in the Diet, but from soldiers and from the cliques involved in canvassing the plans of the army. Undoubtedly the degree of this corruption can easily be exaggerated: there were many honest army officers, just as there were many incorruptible Diet members. But the links between the army, with its economic fixation, and the opportunist commercial interests, were well established, widely ramified, and liable to influence Japan's politics in an irregular manner.

The gathering popular discontent, which is inevitable in a difficult economic situation, expressed itself in growing criticism of the established organs of government, and of the regular methods of doing public business. There were a few dramatic assassinations, which should have been seen as ominous. Brash, resolute, prepared for violence, the new men who were in power in Japan inclined to radical measures when faced by a Chinese challenge. The new western attitude of appeasement, of spinning out for as long as possible their period of privilege but of eventually coming to terms with the changed world, seemed to them hardly comprehensible. The harsh facts of the economic depression supplied them with arguments for expansionism. They were set on reducing China, or at least north China, to a satellite of Japan.

*

In the late twenties, a document called the Tanaka Memorial was in fairly wide circulation in Tokyo. This document, which has always been described by the Japanese government as a forgery, was a memorandum to the throne by the Japanese War Minister, and outlined a plan to take military possession of all north China. Always it was the northern part of the country which interested Japan. Though the nationalist ferment was happening in the south, and from south China came the impulses which were making China a revived power in world politics and a danger to such countries as Japan, even the forward bloc of Japan imperialists was at first content that this should be left alone if Japan could obtain control of the vast resources of manpower and potential economic wealth in the north. All the while, Japanese diplomacy, and semi-secret organizations, were busy spreading Japanese influence in China, softening up the Governors of the Chinese provinces which had been marked down as potential victims, and making propaganda to counter the effects of the nationalist ideas spreading from south China.

Many political groups in Japan, even those which declared themselves activated by generally liberal principles, found themselves in sympathy with the policy of containing Chinese nationalism. At least, few strongly resisted it; many, however, were inclined to regard a decisive counter-move by Japan as being more of a dream than practical politics. But, as the country moved towards what was to be its great expansionist adventure in Asia, there began to appear sharp differences between the different sections of opinion. These were over the extent to which Japan should press China; over tactics, methods and timetable; over whether Japan should aim at direct conquest of Chinese territory, or some form of indirect control. As the critical period came nearer, the danger of collision with other powers grew increasingly plain, and there was disagreement about how they should be confronted. In particular the army and the navy came into conflict. The navy had favoured the old plan of advance behind the umbrella of good relations with the Anglo-Saxon naval powers, and for long was lukewarm towards Asiatic adventures. But the navy fiercely resented what seemed to be the pusillanimity of the civilian cabinets in tamely agreeing with the U S and Britain to Japanese naval limitation. It supported conspiratorial sorties which restored to assassinations as a protest; and in this set the army a fatal example to follow. The right wing in politics was also divided. There were differences between cautious conservatives and wild visionaries: between those who were carried away by a mythical view of Japanese history and those who interpreted the realities of the day with cool realism.

These differences became increasingly expressed in struggles between organized factions. In these, there took place the real conflict over the path which Japanese affairs were to take. In Japanese politics during these years the great decisions were not fought out in the formal seat of national debate, in the Japanese parliament, but were made as the result of fierce factional dispute. There were factions within the army, factions within the different sections of business, factions of the navy.

Political life of this kind—a tussle between factions fought in a jungle fashion—proved very congenial to Japan. It was more comfortably Japanese than was the contest between political parties carried on according to rules in the Japanese Diet. It was natural for a Japanese to look to a faction and its fortunes for forwarding his interests. The faction was organized in such a way as to give free play to Japanese paternalism. In Japan there is a disposition to see all problems in terms of personal relationships rather than as great political principles. This was more compatible with the breakdown of society into competing factions than it was with the struggle of political parties.

*

In 1931, Japan's conviction of its manifest destiny, its need for economic recovery, the restlessness and ambition of its new political leaders, especially of the army, converged. The year seemed to be the predestined time for action. The place for action was Manchuria.

Manchuria consisted of three provinces which were an integral part of China, but were not part of old China. It lay to the north of the Great Wall which had been built to shelter China from barbarian raids. It was the home of the Manchus, which had been the barbarian tribe which in 1664 had penetrated the defences, overthrown the Ming dynasty, and substituted for it the Manchu dynasty which had continued until 1911. Towards the end of its life, this dynasty nearly lost its original homeland to tzarist Russia. It had the mortification of proving powerless to protect it, and of seeing Japan wage the Russo-Japanese war to put an end to Russia's penetration of Manchuria instead of protecting it itself. As the result of that war, Japan did not annex Manchuria, but China did not recover its full and unconditional control of it, and Japan enjoyed special privileges.

The South Manchurian Railway Company, a corporation owned by the Japanese, had much authority and excessive control in the region. The railway company was operated by the Japanese in an expansive mood, and was used by them to build Japanese political power. It grew from being simply a railroad undertaking, operating the line which ran from north to south as the spine which held Manchuria together, into a general trading organization with vast interests in the development of the country: and it took on political functions which in turn led to Japan having to maintain a force for the defence of its employees.

In the civil war in China which followed the fall of the Manchu Empire in 1911, Manchuria suffered rather less than the rest of the country. A bandit named Chang Tso-lin was able to build up power with which he took over the territories. He recognized that in these provinces he could survive only if he had the protection of the Japanese, or, at least, that he could not flourish against Japanese wishes. He chafed at Japanese interference, but he submitted, and governed Manchuria, in all that was essential, as a Japanese puppet. In his old age, and perhaps in response to stirrings in China, he became restive.

He also had held a part of China south of the Great Wall. From there, in 1927, he was driven out by the expansion of the Kuomintang. The Chinese nationalist challenge had come in that part of China where Japan had become supreme. In Manchuria, Japanese capital was making very substantial profits, and it had become the lodestar for Japanese economic expansion. Japan was faced with the decision whether it would acquiesce in China's re-establishment of its control—in which case the Chinese pronouncements and record had left no reasonable doubt that they would terminate Japan's privileged position, at once or after a few years—or would stand and fight.

Chang Tso-lin himself did not try to resist. He could not do so. He bowed before the Kuomintang military success.

In the course of his evacuation of his southern territory in 1928, the train in which he was travelling was blown up, and Chang Tso-lin perished. It was said that the Japanese had found him unsatisfactory as the Japanese agent for resisting the Kuomintang, and had murdered him. There was some evidence to support this. If he died in this way, it marked the passage of the Japanese army into conspiracies in which they acted without the knowledge of civilians in the Japanese government, or with the knowledge only of those civilians of whose willingness to conspire with them they felt secure: conspiracies which were designed to force the hand of the government and to present it with a *fait accompli*.

Chang Tso-lin was succeeded by his son, Chang Hsueh-liang. He was much closer in touch with the mood of China south of the Wall. To what extent was not realized: the surprise was general when he formally accepted the sovreignty of the Kuomintang over Manchuria. It was a recognition of the power of the national idea. Chang Hsueh-liang admitted that the day of the war-lord was over. Chinese nationalism had coerced him into accepting its claims to dispose of Manchuria as Chinese soil, and of himself as a Chinese subject. But this claim, even though Chang himself submitted to it, could not be recognized by the Japanese. It was a challenge to Japan, which was obliged to resist it.

In September 1931, while the West was dealing with a British financial crisis, which drove Britain from gold and forced the devaluation of the pound—and which led among other things to the British naval mutiny at Invergordon—Japan struck. There was an incident on the South Manchuria railway at Mukden in which the line was tampered with. The Japanese army stood forward as the undisguised makers of its policy towards China and sent units throughout southern and central Manchuria. The Japanese government, with obvious misgivings by some of its members, was dragged along in its wake.

The war was begun light-heartedly. The Japanese, conscious of the strength of modern armaments, and for a long time inclined by the experience of their early victories to underrate China's power of resistance, put their complete confidence in the use of force. Their levity recalls the comment in *Coriolanus* of the Volsces greeting war:

Let me have war, say I. It exceeds peace as far as day does night: it is sprightly, waiting, audible, and full of event: peace is a very apoplexy, a lethargy, deaf, mulled, sleepy, insensible.

They would have been wiser to reflect on the comments of Thucydides at the beginning of the Peloponnesian war in ancient Greece. He makes a wise envoy argue that war is so full of accident and so difficult to control that one should always embark on it with deep anxiety, even if the results seem assured. Thucydides writes: 'Consider the vast influence of accident in war before you are engaged in it. As it continues it generally becomes an affair of chances, chances from which neither of us is exempt, and whose event we must risk in the dark.' But Thucydides was a Greek, not much read in Tokyo.

4

The China which was struck at

THE notable advantage of Japan in the 1930s was that it was a relatively well-organized and modern state attacking, in China, a society which was still in the early stages of adopting modern institutions. At the time, Japan's resolve to subdue China did not seem absurd or incredible. It faced, it is true, a huge adversary. That China was immense, and had unlimited manpower, might well have daunted it. Japan had only one-fifth of China's population. But there were many factors which told against China's deployment of its potential strength, and which made Japan's ambition seem less absurd.

There was the economic position. China had a totally inadequate industry for making war. Except for coal, with which China was bursting, it was generally short of accessible raw materials. Initially it had a pitifully small steel industry. Its equipment for generating power was completely insufficient. Its railway system had great gaps. Its roads, for modern needs, were, for the most part, terrible. It had no system for enlisting its scientists, who were produced in some quantity in the gifted Chinese race, in its war effort. Its population contained far too many illiterate peasants, far too small a middle class, for its economy to be properly organized. Such was the technical side of China's capacity for war-making. The facts encouraged aggressors against it.

In China the state did not have the same reality as it had come to have in Japan. China, in spite of chaos, held together as a society, but this was because of the natural cohesiveness of families and clans. The principles of its unity

46

were of very ancient origin. The family, and not the state, was the center of loyalty. In a day when the Japanese were becoming, in form at least, more and more like the typical nation-states of the West, the Chinese continued to be rather archaic, to breathe the air of the ancient world, to be sceptical of the overriding claims of the state upon the individual. It is true that, from these very qualities, China drew on a massive strength—something primeval—with which it could confront Japan. But, equally, it was at a deep disadvantage.

In an effort to redress this weakness China put its faith in nationalism. In doing this, it followed the pattern of all the peoples of Asia. Nationalism was their support. Peoples responded to it, and it gave them an impetus which propelled them past crises which would otherwise have overthrown them.

Nationalism was an astonishingly simple force. For all its surprising lack of intellectual content, it produced in country after country, the same result. Nationalism brought in new considerations, and a man was given by it new motives by which to govern his conduct. It burst the narrow confines in which men had been content to see the affairs of the world. It made a man feel that he belonged to and had objectives in common with the whole community, and not simply his own family. The majority of the Chinese people espoused nationalism with passion. Few were untouched by it. Its wings beat strongly in all recent history. It was the central, compelling force of the times. It was the root of the war, just as religion was the base of events in the Thirty Years War in Europe.

Of course it happened that nationalism, great as was the stir which it made, loudly as it raised its voice, had often to compromise. Too often it came off second best in China at this time in a struggle with the quiet voice of family obligation. It was seldom that the claims of nation would totally prevail over the more ancient social ties. Throughout the period, this was true of China, as it was also of most other agrarian societies. All men, or nearly all men, acted in ways which proved that the family was still the centre of their interest. Society was simply a federation of families. To keep this in mind is to understand many things about the modern history of Asia. Yet, by and large, nationalism prevailed in China in the 1930s. It was the force which animated politicians, and gave them the power to make China perform tasks which would otherwise have seemed impossible.

*

At the start of the war with Japan, China was governed by the quintessential national party, the Kuomintang. The Kuomintang had its origin in a number of societies, more or less secret, which had worked to overthrow the Manchus. As a single party it dates from 1912. When the old régime fell, the Kuomintang was not yet strong enough to claim the succession. It came, however, to power in Canton, and raised an army. With this, and with the support of the relics of the old system of government, it had made good its authority, subduing the war-lords who had· divided up the inheritance from the Manchus. It gradually became the dominant power throughout the country. But in doing so, it compromised, abandoned large parts of its revolutionary programme, and took care to make itself acceptable to the social classes which had great traditional authority in Chinese society. It took in tens of thousands of members who would have been shocked at the modernizing radical programme of the original founders. By the time Japan struck, it would have been hard to say exactly what the Kuomintang stood for. It was a purely national party. It was dedicated to advancing China's interests, and to protecting these against the foreigner, Japan included, and in this it was ferocious. But beyond that, it was hard to see any principles which it followed, except feathering the nests of its many members. Its government had to rule over a hotch-potch of interests, and for this a succession of compromises was necessary.

The party brought together the rural gentry and urban bankers and merchants, bosses of secret societies and trade unionists, brokers, soldiers and bandit leaders. Its attitude to the particular questions it faced was determined by expediency. Some classes, for example landlords and bankers, were more powerful socially than others, and the party mirrored, instead of trying to modify, the existing social system. The Kuomintang was a comprehensive party, never a party of genuine revolutionaries. In general the party had become more conservative the older and larger it grew, because each group that it included strove, before all else, for its own survival.

The Kuomintang liked to represent itself as a progressive, avant-garde party. The westernized and sophisticated classes, which made one of its influential parts, advertised it as being democratic. Certainly it was, in the intention of this wing, to be aligned with the progressive forces of mankind. But the enlightened part of the party leadership was all too aware that it sat with colleagues who were anything but liberal and democratic. They had also to reconcile their claim with the blatant fact that the Kuomintang operated a single-party system of government, that (with one temporary exception to be described later) it did not tolerate the existence of rival parties, and that it carried on government—if only as a temporary measure—as a Kuomintang dictatorship. It announced that it would become democratic in future but it fixed no date for this transition. The dictatorship aspect of the Kuomintang was to give many of its leaders a sense of unity with the Axis countries of Europe. It embarrassed greatly the pro-American and pro-British circles, which were very powerful among the Shanghai businessmen who formed the support of the Kuomintang with which westerners came most readily in touch. But they did not count in the party for as much as was supposed.

*

The Kuomintang, from its earliest days, owed its strength to the army. In fact the Kuomintang was the army. Its being, ethos, performance, all depended on the military. This was the outstanding fact about it, and the paradox is that this fact was never grasped by western observers. The westerners in China, in dealing with the rise of nationalism, commonly met and negotiated with the middle-class and civilian members of the party. Chinese militarism had a bad name, and the middle class, who struggled against it, were ready to assure the foreigner that their party—the Kuomintang—stood for the complete supremacy of the civilian element, which was what the West desired to hear. The westerner, in this and other matters in which the Kuomintang was interested in misleading him, too easily accepted the Chinese version of reality. After all, the civilians were often highly articulate and convincing. By contrast, the generals were for the most part ill-educated, and even the best of them trained in very poor military academies. The westerner seldom understood how the decisions as to power were taken in the Kuomintang; he did not understand how the mind of the generals moved. And yet for a true appreciation of Chinese history of the time, the politics of the generals were the essential study.

By Japan the peculiarly military nature of the Kuomintang was perceived, and Japan had a lively appreciation that, in dealing with the Kuomintang, its problem was to overthrow its army. The Japanese observer saw correctly that the struggle was one between the Japanese army, which claimed to control the development of Japanese society, and its rival, the Chinese military machine, which claimed the loyalty of the Chinese nation.

How, then, was the Kuomintang army made up?

*

The Kuomintang army was a painful thing to contemplate, especially in the early days of the Chinese revolution. Later, in the 1930s, it hired German military advisers, who made a part of it quite presentable. But the few smart, well-drilled regiments which they brought into being scarcely concealed that their work had essentially been window-dressing. Organization of the whole army continued to be dreadfully poor. The Kuomintang army appeared as much a rabble as did the army of the revolution in France in the years which followed 1793. But for a time these incarnated the spirit of the Revolution. In the same way, in an oriental and haphazard fashion, these soldiers were the life spirit of the Chinese revolution.

The Chinese army was an army of mercenaries. The leaders of the Kuomintang were content, unlike the Japanese, with raising an army by payment, as China always had done. This was peculiar for an army which was the instrument of revolution: a political force is more usually raised by making service compulsory. But China could raise a force of millions, at incredibly little expense, so overcrowded was the land. There were far more men than there was equipment. There was a rudimentary general staff. The financial administration of the army opened the door to corruption: the pay for whole regiments was made to colonels, who were left to fix the pay scales and conditions of service with their men. They were divided in their allegiance between the central and the provincial authorities, and between the centre and local generals, who were little more than respectable bandits. A Japanese, taking note of their indiscipline, had little cause to be anxious about them.

The weakness of the Chinese army reflected the essential backwardness of the social system. It was an army which was raised from the peasantry. This peasantry had so many just causes of grievance against the holders of power in China that it could not be relied upon to fight with any tenacity. Here is the key to the life of the country, here the explanation of all the events which have since followed.

The Kuomintang could not trust the rank and file of the army, and this lay at the core of the frustration of Chinese nationalism. The party, which claimed essentially to be the party of the nation, evolved a policy for which it could not expect the support of a sufficient part of the Chinese nation.

*

This was the most important fact about China in 1931. It leads to an examination of the realities of Chinese society.

The trouble of China at this period was that it was virtually without an effective administration. From this proceeded many of the peculiarities of Chinese society.

The government issued enlightened decrees—hence the good reputation internally of the Kuomintang. But there was no civil service to give effect to them; no government with an effective will; almost anarchy. The apparatus of the Chinese administration was adequate when it was worked by educated and dedicated men; but the spirit of the times had forced these into retreat. A rapid and appalling worsening took place. The machinery of government fell into decay. There was an abundance of officials, but these were not bound together in any articulated system. They stood out, but each acted on his own, without giving the impression of orderly administration. Most offices became objects for purchase. The magistrates and assistant magistrates, having bought their posts, set themselves to exploit their office to recoup themselves. They taxed remorselessly, and they sold justice. They were venal and incompetent in the performance of their principal functions which should have been to protect the people against those who always appeared to prey on them in the times of decay of government. In the atmosphere of general decline, the elements of society which felt themselves naturally strong organized themselves and usurped the functions of government. Usually this meant groups of landlords: in many areas they raised an unofficial militia, which terrorized the countryside and ran the locality: it seized grain from the peasants at low prices, intervened to back up the money-lender in exploiting the farmer, carried out a forced loan on the people to meet the government's demand for troops, put down forcibly the resistance of the bolder spirits, supported all kinds of obnoxious practices, such as protecting the opium trade, and gave more or less open protection to bandits. Sometimes the local bosses found themselves on different sides in support of different claimants on governmental power; and the pressures on the rank and file of society were thus doubled.

In spite of all this, it is important to remember that the Chinese peasant, if the whole circumstances of his life are considered, still probably enjoyed, at least at the start of this period, the best life of any peasant in any country in the world. China was in decay politically; it was in mortal danger from the powers around it; but for a long while the degree to which this affected the peasant, and the number of peasants whose lives felt the consequences, can be exaggerated. China had begun to fall to pieces, but this process had not yet reached a stage where, for the mass of the people, it discounted the other advantages of Chinese civilization. If the miseries over so large a part of the rest of the world are borne in mind, if the misfortunes and the quality of life caused by creeping industrialization are weighed up by the observer, the balance is tilted and the virtues of Chinese life appear very shining. The worst man-made calamities which the Chinese had to fear were famine and the insecurity of life due to there being no adequate rule of law. On the other side, he enjoyed the protection of the family, of public opinion, and the many things which are summed up in the term 'Chinese civilization'. At any rate, the peasant was not dissatisfied with his lot.

He would have been surprised to learn that he was pitied. The decay of China he regarded as a passing phenomenon: he must wait, be patient, and all would come well again. Misery was to break over him, but civil war, its root cause, did not become endemic until the middle of the second decade of this century. The checks and balances which limited arbitrary powers, the pressure of public opinion, still operated, and did not cease to do so until the break-up of society had proceeded a long way.

*

At the centre of life in China, there was, like a canker, the question of the ownership of the land. China had always been rent by a great schism. It was divided between the peasants who owned some land and the peasants who were landless. The schism was the fundamental one in Chinese life: from this division of the population, and all the facts incidental to it, there have followed, almost from the beginnings of Chinese history, many of the characteristic trends of its society and politics.

In 1931 five out of every six Chinese lived by agriculture: and the proportion had remained more or less constant throughout history. From his relation to the land depended most of what was significant to the status, to the life itself, of the typical inhabitant of the country. Land ownership gave a man the entitlement to a share in the good things of civilization. Without land he was virtually an outlaw. Education, which was the key to social advance and to status, was firmly in the hands of the landed. They controlled the village school. Without going to the school, there was no way of progressing upward on the educational ladder, and of taking advantage of the opening of careers to talent, which should otherwise have been a unique benefit of the Chinese social order.

A peculiarity of the Chinese agrarian system was that in spite of the social importance of land ownership, there was no rich landed class. There was nothing comparable to the Junkers, or to the landlords of eighteenth-century England or Ireland. There were a few excessively rich landlords, usually the product of families which had recently done extremely well in state service: but these were the exception, and were like fish out of water in the rural society. The landowners in China were very numerous, but each possessed land on a scale grotesquely small, and did nothing to make these privileges less painful to the landless labourers, and to the masses in the country districts who were totally unprivileged.

The division between the rural gentry and rural proletariat was exceedingly sharp and brutal. The landless were powerless: they were at the mercy of the landowners, who were also local officials, money-lenders, or merchants. (The only alleviation of their position was that if, by a miracle, they chanced to prosper economically, society put no obstacles in the way, legal or otherwise, of their acceptance.) The situation is now the constant theme of Chinese communist propaganda. Its contention is that in Chinese society one part has lived off and mercilessly exploited the other part. The classic film 'The White-headed Girl', represents very well the plight of the exploited class. Possibly their state of wretchedness is exaggerated, but not very much. In all China's long dynastic history, behind all the civilization and elegance of life, the reality was that it was the arena of a permanent class war. China has been permanently divided between two classes, one of whom has had nothing to lose but its chains, and has, through the centuries, sat down constantly with appalling insecurity. The Chinese landowners bled white the masses of the people. As it had been since the beginnings of time, so it was still in 1931.

This tension was reflected in the politics of the period. The Kuomintang, as it developed, came to be completely monopolized by the landowning class. Though it had originally had place for eccentrics, for deracinated Chinese, for émigrés who were the product of a different social system, it underwent a change as it spread widely throughout China, and was adapted for purposes of the class struggle. The landless were denied membership, or at least denied any office of power. The Kuomintang régime was essentially a landlord régime. The Kuomintang official or politician was bound together in a kind of freemasonry with most of the army officers. They all belonged to the exploiting class; they banded together against the landless. Any threat to the landed interest and the landlords closed their ranks, however much they might struggle and be divided over other matters; and as a result the landless mass had no escape, except to contract out of society, and take to a bandit life. Brigandage was thus endemic over every province of China; in China, alone among civilized countries, banditry was talked of as an everyday condition of life, to which the poor might resort from time to time as a matter of course. The provinces never had a police force which could cope with this stream of malcontents.

The nature of the Kuomintang had grave consequences in the organization of the army. Most of its rank and file were drawn from the landless class: on the other hand, all of the officers were from the landed. The officers were well enough contented with the policy of the party. The rank and file could not be. Thus there was always a sense of grievance in the army, and a sense of incipient revolt. The army might for a time be made loyal by occasional bounties by the popularity of some local commander. But over the long run the army remained sullen and of uncertain temper. It saw no reason to fight wars, or to incur danger, and found the lure of military life to lie in the plunder which was traditionally the reward of its exertions.

Here the contradiction at the centre of the Kuomintang— to use a Marxist phrase—became obvious. It was a party which, born out of revolutionary civil war, should have been carried forward by the army. But its leadership, after the early years, took fright, and did not countenance the army playing with revolutionary ideas such as the expropriation of the landlords. The army ceased to be revolutionary. Discipline was called in against radical sentiment. By this action, the Kuomintang ceased to be a genuine revolutionary force in Asia.

The social disruptiveness, which was the inevitable result of such a social system, was increased by a tendency which has always existed in Chinese society and which from time to time in Chinese history bursts out and determines the affairs of the country. This is a very deep sentiment among the Chinese people towards anarchy. This is found among all classes, landed and landless, and goes with Taoism and Buddhism, two religions which have always been popular in China. There is a deep distrust of government as such: the typical Chinese has an insuperable scepticism about its benefits, and a temperamental optimism about the chances of regulating life without the recourse to official paraphernalia. For the three decades after the fall of the Manchus, this instinctive trend in the country was powerful, especially among the landless. The rise of the Kuomintang happened essentially as a reaction to this, and was marked by a revival of Confucian ideas and the notions of the more realist figures of Chinese civilization. But at this time, the natural and amiable inclination of the Chinese towards anarchy was not yet passed. It weakened considerably the reformist aims of the Kuomintang.

*

The inclination of the Kuomintang rank and file to mutiny, and the dissent of much of the country from a social order dominated by the rural gentry, were expressed in the rise of a rival nationalist party and government, that of the Chinese communists. From the early 1920s, China had seen both the nationalist Kuomintang, and, though it was at first very weak, a Communist Party which also appealed to nationalism, though it claimed to be internationalist. The Chinese Communist Party was founded in 1922 by members of the intelligentsia. In its first months it had been a study center for fostering the readings of Marxist writings. These had had a great boom in interest due to the revolution in Russia; before that, Marxism had been practically unknown. The achievements of communist government in Russia gave Communism a great prestige in China: and Communism in China also began to receive direct aid from Russia: Moscow began to direct its disciples. The doctrine spread widely, and the Communist Party began to be of some consequence. At this time the Kuomintang still retained some of the radicalism of its early days, and a section of the party was not averse from some of the communist ideas. It looked with envy upon the support which Communism was gaining, and was prepared to collaborate with the communists in return for the accession of strength which this might bring to a coalition. In the mid-twenties, the two parties collaborated in advancing their common cause against the warlords. Together they established the Kuomintang power, sketchily it is true, throughout China.

But the communists, with their Marxist beliefs, were not a

safe ally for such a party as the Kuomintang. The communists were real revolutionaries, determined that one branch of political thought alone should prevail. The Kuomintang was a comprehensive party. Though it was itself a dictatorship, it was in reality much more a federation of parties, and it attempted nothing like the rigid thought control of Communism. Gradually it became clear to the Kuomintang that, by the understanding with the communists, its was nursing a viper in its bosom. It drove them out of the alliance.

The breach occurred in 1927, at the moment when the great port of Shanghai fell to the Kuomintang. This brought the vast accession of the economic backing of bankers and great commercial interests. The Kuomintang judged that its strength from this was worth much more than the strength which an alliance with Communism could bring it. It was willing to sacrifice the former association, which brought it a certain mass backing, to the new partnership, which brought it the immediate, tangible economic strength. It seized, shot and arrested as many of the communist leaders as it could lay hands upon. In Shanghai it used the secret societies, which were its habitual allies, for rounding up the known organizers of the communist party. It included in this purge a number of radical Kuomintang members of whose sympathies it felt unsure. Radicalism withdrew from the Kuomintang. From the time of the coup in Shanghai, the Kuomintang was definitely a conservative and right-wing party.

In retrospect it is obvious that these events in Shanghai were of great importance for Chinese history. But at the time they were not appreciated fully. The western observers, in particular, saw them as a blood-letting which strengthened the Kuomintang. The Kuomintang was, at this period, in the ascendant, and there was no comparison between it, and its sudden great prestige—its recognition as the legitimate government of China, and the millions of dollars with which it was watered by Shanghai business—and the communists, who led a hunted life, and who only appeared in the news as the comrades of China's notorious bandits.

The communist party took years to recover from this blow. In the interval the Kuomintang appeared supreme. But the communists survived, and reorganized. Their earliest actions, on recovering the zest for a campaign, had been frittered away in trying to organize secret anti-Kuomintang centres in the towns. They were under the influence of the Russians, and the Russians, from the experience of the October revolution, considered that the only way of making revolution was by inducing the industrial proletariat to take action. But such a tactic was entirely impossible in China: the towns did not dominate political life, industry was too small, the powerful armies could move in to suppress them. From the futility of these tactics, they were saved by the genius of the rising young figure, Mao Tse-tung. He was the discoverer of the way to make Communism an effective power in China. From 1928 he had shifted the effort to the rural areas. He discovered the power of the peasantry. He used the slogans of land reform to raise revolutionary armies. Through Mao Tse-tung the communists became again a power in China, however modest was their strength at first in comparison with that of the Kuomintang.

The communists, by making alliance with local bandit chiefs, managed to organize a small opposition government in the heart of the Chinese countryside. This was the famous Kiangsi Soviet, the first communist government in China. It owed its being and its survival to the general disorder sweeping China. But their ability to create a government was to have vast consequences in the direction of Chinese affairs. It meant that the radicalism which was endemic in China was being provided with a practical programme. It is true that in the past there had often been a ferment of desperation in the country, but it had remained always without an effective organization and effective ideas to attach itself to. The masses were ripe for revolution, but their emotions were never attached to some cause worthy of them. For example, the Taiping rebellion, in the middle of the last century, was a far more significant revolt than is today in general understood, and came near to overthrowing the Manchu government: but the Taiping acted under an ideology which was unworthy of their rebellion. It was a half-crazy messianic movement, which borrowed most of its ideas from the corrupted teaching of Christian missions. The movement failed because the Taiping did not offer a régime which, in the country's judgement, was comparable to that of the imperial régime.

It was now different. In Kiangsi, the communists had set

up an actual government. It had teachings, organization, slogans, all of which attracted the classes which were deeply hostile to the Kuomintang. It provided the standard round which they could rally. They had been able to set up on Chinese soil a Soviet government which had become the centre of revolutionary action.

At first the Kiangsi Soviet had simply the sympathy of the dispossessed and alienated masses elsewhere in rural China. It was conscious of waves of sympathy which washed round it, but it was unable to bear any effective support to its well-wishers. Over vast areas of the country, the Kuomintang was still unchallenged. Nevertheless, by founding the Kiangsi Soviet, and keeping it alive, the communists had kept open the possibility that one day they would eclipse the Kuomintang, and that, one day, the support of the country, still given to the Kuomintang, would be transferred in bulk to them.

At first, the significance of these events was overlooked by the outside world. Very little was known about them; the communists were underrated as a danger to the Kuomintang. The Japanese had a livelier appreciation than the westerners, but it was supposed that they were so much interested in blackening the face of the Kuomintang, as a disorderly, untrustworthy government, that their concern could be regarded as routine propaganda. Chiang Kai-shek, the military leader of the Kuomintang, judged however—rightly as events were to make clear—that the danger was acute and deadly. He threw a cordon round the communist district, and kept up a constant pressure upon it. He proclaimed that, if the communists were not extirpated, they might grow into a force which would eventually overwhelm the Kuomintang. They might transform all the existing politics in the Far East.

All this was eventually to prove a correct forecast. Chiang Kai-shek, who had received a very limited education, who was the product of rural China and who was obviously outshone in intellect by the *haute bourgeoisie* of the Kuomintang to which he had been linked, was found to have perceived the realities of China more correctly than did his more sophisticated colleagues, trained in the universities and banking houses.

Chiang not only judged events. He set himself to try to influence how these would move. It was his will which determined that at first the threat from Japan should be given less weight than the threat from the Chinese communists. As a result, the head-on clash between Japan and China was delayed for some years. He had a civil war on his hands, whose issue would be of greater consequence than that of any war between China and Japan. Therefore the civil war loomed far larger in his mind than a national war. The civil war came first.

Chiang Kai-shek was therefore in the unpopular position of demanding that Chinese should concentrate on fighting Chinese. He neglected to take account of the fact that Chinese national feeling demanded that Chinese should fight Japanese. Even though there were plenty of wealthy and propertied Chinese, who saw that Communism was a real threat to their interests, they were held back and checked by nationalism from whole-heartedly acting upon calculation. The majority were ashamed to do what calculation directed.

5

Manchuria 1931

IN September 1931, the Japanese army began a full-scale attack on the Chinese troops in Manchuria, taking as their pretext the bomb explosion on the railway line at Mukden. This section of the Japanese armed forces, known as the Kwantung army, had been stationed in Manchuria by the Sino-Japanese agreement of 1905 to protect the South Manchurian Railway. Its movements after the bomb incident (which the Chinese accused them of contriving) were so systematic, orderly and comprehensive that they had obviously been considered long in advance. The army was openly flouting normal civilian controls, and the Japanese government was uneasily following its lead and waiting for events to unfold.

The Japanese quickly overran Manchuria. Chang Hsuehliang evacuated it. In the fighting, only one Chinese general resisted seriously. He showed, by his field tactics, that he had studied the teaching of the old Chinese military texts on how to feign and double-cross. He won momentarily a great deal of popularity in the national press of China by the successful action which he fought on the Nonni River. But he received no support, either from the other generals or from the central government, which did not use its forces to support him. Early in 1932 the conquest of Manchuria was complete.

The Chinese government, in distant Nanking, played the card which it hoped would relieve it of danger without its being driven to resolute action. It appealed to the League of Nations. The League's prestige as a peace-keeping ma-

61

chine had been growing in Europe; in minor European disputes in the previous dozen years, the Council of the League
had at times intervened when peace was threatened; and
China was led to think that it might do so over Manchuria.
The League had never yet been engaged upon restraining a
Great Power, and this was the task it was now set. Undoubtedly the Kuomintang leaders, though realist enough
in home affairs, showed themselves surprisingly ingenuous in
supposing that text-book methods of collective security could
be followed, with effective results, in checking Japan.

Possibly the Kuomintang politicians were misled by a number of western enthusiasts who abounded in Nanking and
Shanghai, and who were later to be joined by refugees from
the rising storm in Europe. It had become a matter of
prestige to the Chinese to become the patrons of expatriate
dilettantes. A great banker like T. V. Soong derived face
from their permanent employment on his staff. This was
reminiscent of a classical period of Chinese history; in the
days before the establishment of the stable military empire,
when China consisted of a group of warring feudal kingdoms, roving scholars offered themselves to the Chinese kings,
who gladly employed them. Now as then, the scholars, though
cosmopolitan, had more influence on policy-making than most
of the regular politicians. They were dangerous advisers. Disillusioned by the western record, many of them made a cult
of the Kuomintang because it was an apparently revolutionary power which was willing to experiment with new
methods. They urged China to attach its fortunes to League
procedures.

The League was embarrassed by the confidence shown in
it. The skies were darkening over the world: the economic
crisis had set in, and the Great Powers looked with alarm at
being called upon to do anything which could further un-
settle the world's economy. They were faced with awkward
problems from the rise of Germany, and many of them
were more concerned with what they could do to take the
danger out of these problems than they were ready to risk
much on a hazardous experiment in a course so doubtful as
that of protecting China. The foreign ministers who com-
posed the League Council felt that the situation was far too
dangerous for them to gamble over the means of concerting
action against one of the Great Powers. They used the cus-

tomary expedient. They appointed an international commission of inquiry, which was presided over by an Englishman, Lord Lytton, who had been governor of Bengal, and was the grandson of the Victorian historical novelist, Bulwer Lytton.

While the Commission was preparing its report, the crisis took a new turn. The shock to China had been deeper, spread quicker and produced more results than Japan had expected. Events passed out of control. A commotion amongst the Chinese people, not any action by the Chinese government, was the unexpected factor. A boycott of Japanese goods took place, which was partly spontaneous and partly organized by Chinese secret societies. Violence broke out at Shanghai as a result of the boycott, and this provoked Japan to land troops there on 28 January 1932. They met with something like the resistance of a Popular Front, and soon they had to deploy four divisions. The defence, improvised on the spur of the moment, was impressive. This was one of the first demonstrations in modern times of which the world took effective notice, that the Chinese, or some of them, were a martial people. Hitherto the Chinese had fought their wars by incompetent professional armies, operating from books of rules which, though they might give occasional apt counsel as they had done on the Nonni river, were hopelessly out-of-date. The people, who were sceptics by tradition, expressed their contempt for all things military. But in this, as in everything else, China was changing, and the powers in contact with it had to take notice of the fact.

The resistance was at first hampered by the ambivalent, cautious, lukewarm attitude of the Chinese government. But by accident, there happened to be garrisoned, on the outskirts of Shanghai, the unit of the Chinese army known as the Nineteenth Route Army. This force was commanded by Tsai Ting-kan, an ingenuous, simple-minded man who had breathed in the simple slogans of the nationalists (and also, it appeared, of the communists). This officer, whose military training had been elementary, and who had received no indoctrination politically, and his troops, simple peasants with the most ordinary equipment, stiffened the resistance of the rest of the Chinese. The fighting lasted until 3 March when the Japanese at last broke through to the open country beyond the city. The confidence of the Japanese military re-

ceived a set-back from the unexpected resistance, and from
the international stir which Japan's action was making. Finally, mediation from the United States, Britain, France and
Italy managed to effect an armistice.

For a time the Nationalist Government of China, and
even a realistic and cynical politician like Chiang Kai-shek,
continued to put their faith in the League of Nations. The
Lytton Commission paid a visit to Manchuria in the summer of 1932, and it reported at the end of the year. It
made a fair-minded, rational assessment, which was written
with the dispassionate voice of history. It stated, with a good
deal of sympathy, the Japanese case, emphasizing how large
was the investment which Japan had made in Manchuria,
the Japanese right to have this protected, the natural Japanese resentment at the Chinese xenophobia, and Japan's
suspicion, which it thought not unreasonable, of an alliance
between communist Russia and Nationalist China. It agreed
that Japan could in fairness regard itself as having a special
position in Manchuria, and argued that lasting peace required
that this should be recognized in an international treaty,
which should contain safeguards for Japan which were genuine.

The Lytton Commission, however, did not scruple to say
that Japan had been an aggressor, though in polite and
reasoned language, and though it held that China had itself
been provocative, and was therefore in part guilty. The report was accepted by the League Council, and it was too
much for Japan to swallow. Japan objected to China, the par-
venu, being treated as equal with Japan, which thought of
itself as one of the established imperialist powers of the
world. Its reply was to resign from the League of Nations
in March 1933.

No attempt was made by the League Council to organize
sanctions against Japan, although Japan's action did not
technically relieve it of the threat: but it is obvious that
the powers snatched at the excuse eagerly. Also, by with-
drawing from the comity of nations, Japan relieved the
League of the effort to regulate internationally the privileged
position of Japan in Manchuria, which the Lytton Commission had agreed that it should have.

The final scene at Geneva was described as follows in
The Times:

Mr Matsuoka announced immediately after the vote that his government found themselves compelled to conclude that Japan and the other members of the League entertained different views of the manner to achieve peace in the Far East, and were obliged to feel that they had now reached the limit of their endeavours to cooperate with the League with regard to Sino-Japanese differences. The Japanese then walked out in a body. They maintained the self-possession of their race to the last, but many of them are known to have been cleft in their emotions.

Their departure was seen with ruffled feelings by some of the officials of the League of Nations, who, while they recognized that Japan was aggressive, felt themselves obliged to state that, on the various international committees and agencies which the League promoted, Japan had been a most valuable member. The hearts of some of them were heavy at what they felt had been the driving out of Japan from associating with enlightened governments, and at the increased opportunity which this gave to all the darker forces at work in Japan. Some of them recognized that it was a water-shed, and were melancholy that a greater effort had not been made to control the future direction of the tides.

There followed a very brief and humiliating campaign in which Japan conquered the province of Jehol, which was part of Inner Mongolia, and incorporated it into China. This was a mopping-up operation and, once again, the central government made no serious attempt to frustrate it. Jehol was historically of interest as it had been a vast hunting-preserve of the Manchu princes when these ruled in Mukden. After this came a long truce. It was to continue, uneasily, until July 1937.

6

Lull

IN spite of its apparently easy defeats, and in spite of its disappointments at Geneva, China did not lose face. In this Japan was disappointed. It had counted on its action being regarded in the public opinion of the world as an old-fashioned colonial operation, which, in the atmosphere of 1931, was still condonable. China, a manifestly unequal power, was to be put in its place. But the world, to Japan's surprise, was not inclined to revise its previous impression that China was genuinely in revival, and to write it off as now discredited.

As soon as the fighting in China was checked by a truce, China resumed its continuous, painful steps towards recovery as a power in world affairs. The Japanese became conscious, though at first they could scarcely credit it, that this Chinese ambition was now fostered by the former imperialists who had once treated it with so much contempt. In fact, Japan's determination to rise had now become so evident, and was seen with so much misgiving by other powers, that it was natural for its rivals to switch their interest benevolently to Japan's enemy. This slow, but lasting change was more evident in governments than in the sentiments of western businessmen, who, by the old habit of consorting with the Japanese, had for a long while found the change in their governments nearly as puzzling as did the Japanese.

In the next six years, from 1931–7, this progress continued. Domestically, for China, they were dominated by one man, Chiang Kai-shek. He drew ahead of his civilian colleagues in the government and came to hold in the public mind of China a position very much like that of the emperors of old. By foreigners he was equated with Chinese nationalism, its embodiment and its principal agent. Chiang was the dominant figure in China until the end of the Second World War. In this war, remarkable personalities were few in Asia. In Japan, for example, the whole melancholy conflict threw up no single figure who catches the imagination. Many people forwarded the drama but their personalities remain shrouded. In China, however, it is possible to tell what sort of man was Chiang Kai-shek. An attempt to analyse and assess his personality is necessary, for, in understanding what qualities he had and why they established his supremacy in Chinese government, many of the obscure facts about China's régime may be made plain.

Chiang was the successful general of the Kuomintang. He had mounted on the shoulders of the party and come to dominate it. His special characteristic was will-power. He knew just what he wanted, and was never idle in his pursuit of it. This gave him an advantage over most of his rivals and competitors in Nanking. He was gifted with a great self-confidence, which probably meant that he despised most of the other leaders of the party.

Devious, subtle, resourceful—these he had to be if he was to hold his position among the shifting sands of Nanking. His outstanding quality was an exceptional tenacity: he got his way through single-minded persistence. His mind being made up, he would never change. In this, but not in other ways, he was like Shakespeare's Julius Caesar:

> But I am constant as the northern star
> Of whose true-fixed and resting quality
> There is no fellow in the firmament.
> The skies are painted with unnumbered sparks,
> They are all fire, and every one doth shine,
> But there's but one in all doth hold his place.
> So in the world: 'tis furnished well with men
> And men are flesh and blood, and apprehensive,
> Yet in the number I do know but one,
> That unassailable holds on his rank
> Unshaked of motion: and that I am he.

He had a rather chilling attitude to the issues of life and death. If an object could be obtained with comparatively little sacrifice, so much the better. But if its purchase should cost 100,000 lives, he was willing, with scarcely any hesitation, to pay the price. He would have regarded this attitude as realist.

He was not especially clever, inspiring, good, proficient at public speaking or public appearance. He was the product of a provincial military college in China, and of a rather inferior Japanese education. With this background he was neither so well educated as to have ecccentric views, nor so badly as to appear scandalously ignorant. Accordingly the middle ranks, the mediocre, served him well as the medium out of which he rose to fame. He had a poor imagination, but as against this, an exceptionally good memory. He dissimulated, and always held back his real thoughts. His suspiciousness was boundless. But if he did not check this, he could point to it having served him well. He was habitually surrounded by so much deceit that only a carefully nurtured suspicion kept him aware of the plots of remarkable complexity which were the stuff of Chinese politics.

He had a flair for political manoeuvre, and was excellent at manipulating his colleagues. He knew, and was at home in, the labyrinth of Chinese affairs—in the secret societies, in knowing how to use money to build a personal empire, in knowing how to operate a front in politics, and what to say in public through that front. He had the political talent, which comes near political mysticism, for nearly always foreseeing how things would fall out, and for knowing what needed to be done in particular circumstances. This flair, which included judging a situation correctly—and not with the distraction of moral considerations—was perhaps the key to his success in politics.

He preferred to rule through the ubiquitous secret societies which were always one of the chief characteristics of China. Some of these societies were of ancient origin, had existed originally for respectable purposes, but had degenerated. Chiang took steps to bind the societies to himself. They secured discipline among their members by strong-arm methods, always secret. Chiang, being fundamentally uninterested in ideas, jumped at the opportunity of gaining China by means of authority in this twilight world, twitching a string here, a string there. The extent to which China, before the communist revolution, was a rabbit warren of secret societies, ramifying with weird ceremonies and tied up at distant removes to Confucianism, cannot be exaggerated. They caught in their net all who mattered in the government—bureaucrats, soldiers, businessmen. Because of these societies, Chinese public life was always shrouded in a certain mystery. Nothing happened in a quite straightforward way. In any transaction the trail at some stage went underground. Things could not be done without recourse to the secret society. And, more probably than not, Chiang would be involved.

If he never pursued lofty or exceptional aims, that meant he would be set on nothing he could not achieve. He kept his nose to the ground, and pursued ends which were strictly practical. He was cautious and did not expose himself recklessly to danger: but when danger found him, he could call forth the stoic courage of the better type of army officer to sustain him in it. Science and all the arts did not interest him. He became a Christian, and he used to read, and read again, familiar books: but he had no taste for new books. He was not speculative. He had no particular ideas about the way the world was changing, and probably was never in a position to understand this. When he did not understand a point, he was unwilling to speak, and became inscrutable.

He had the natural xenophobia of the uneducated man; but he had the wit to conceal this in his necessary dealings with foreigners. These found him puzzling, and they never established complete rapport with him. But some of them were very much impressed by the man, and agreed that he was dignified, not garrulous, and reserved. He had a cynical view of human nature. But by natural instinct he tended to consort with the type of man who was foreign to exceptional virtue. His cynical views thus proved correct, as far as those with whom he came into contact weere concerned. His rancour and vindictiveness against his enemies were constantly spoken of. But probably this rancour proceeded from considerations of prudence, which taught him that a man who was once his enemy was likely to remain so, and that generosity had few conquests, rather than from bitterness of mind.

In private life he was rather dull, faithful by routine to his intimates, determinedly egotistical. In the wider circles of life, he had no friends. Those who knew him well agreed that he was neither particularly wicked nor noticeably squeamish. A study of the countless crises he survived, and his way of dealing with them, might be added as an appendix to Machiavelli's book.

He was not magnetic and not lovable, though he was sometimes loyal to his colleagues and was admired for this. To outer show, he appeared ascetic, and if, as his enemies alleged, this was a pose, it did not appear so to the mass of the people. He felt the pull of the past and he played round with Confucian ideas, and the somewhat austere and chilly teaching of Chinese conservatives which ceased to be revolutionary and swung to the Right, was his guiding thought.

Yet that Chiang was in many respects a remarkable man cannot be denied; otherwise he could not have battled on, receiving countless checks, seldom achieving total success. Only his will and obstinacy were indomitable.

*

The interest of the nation was in reconstruction. The prime concern of Chiang Kai-shek was in fighting the communists.

Chiang was obsessed with the civil war. At first the communists occupied, and maintained a Soviet government in, part of the Kiangsi province and neighbouring territory. They hurled back five successive so-called bandit-suppression expeditions, each of them more elaborate than the last. In 1934 they decided that they could not withstand another, and that the time had come for a move in a way which has become classic in Chinese communist strategy: one step back in order to prepare for two steps forward. They broke through Chiang's encircling armies and made an astonishing march, in which they again and again repelled the forces sent to block their way, to the Tibetan borderlands in the far west of China, and up to the remote and mountainous province of Shensi. Ninety thousand men began this long march and the number which reached relative safety in the north-west was 20,000.

By this fantastic march the communists associated themselves with all that was remarkable in Chinese military history. They captured the imagination of the country in a way that was quite disproportionate to their size and their real importance. Arrived in Shensi, they set themselves to build a new Soviet government, as they had had before in Kiangsi, one which was milder than the Kiangsi model and which did not automatically frighten off all the propertied class of peasants. It made more appeal than had the Kiangsi model to rational feeling, less to class warfare. Moreover, it was hallowed by the record of the patriotic deeds of communists in the transit force from Kiangsi to the new home. When they took up the cry for war with Japan, they were heard with increased respect in China.

Chiang Kai-shek, however, did not consider that he had suffered a setback. He was still growing in strength, and was building up an élite section of the Chinese army, which was under his personal control and on which his authority ultimately rested. This was the section which was trained by German military advisers in the 1930s by an agreement which Chiang had negotiated with the German government. These officers, who succeeded in adapting themselves to the manners of the more military Chinese, spoke significantly about their warlike qualities when they were properly led. In startling contrast with the hordes of ragged Chinese troops, in their tattered uniforms which were all too familiar in China, the occasional khaki-clad regiment was now to be seen, very smart, alert, marching with precision: the élite of the Kuomintang.

In everything, things began to go well for China. Its great weakness had been disunity, and the lack of a modern political structure. Now, very slowly, and largely by means of the tortuous, devious policies of Chiang Kai-shek, which he pursued with resolution, China's political unification made progress. The Kuomintang prevailed in new provinces: the war-lords who survived had their powers reduced: the central government of Nanking found new ways of undermining them, and of making new contact with the people by new institutions. Chiang Kai-shek, alert, like the Japanese of the earlier generation, to take advantage of borrowing what seemed to him relevant from abroad, took over various devices from the contmporary example of Hitler for reinforcing his personal ascendancy. The country began to be studded by a secret organization called the Blue Shirts, whose members were pledged to advance his interest: this included thugs, but also highly respected professors from Peking university, who felt that the desperate needs of the country required that Chiang should be supreme. During this period there was only one retrograde moment when a nationwide unrest among Chiang's opponents led to an outbreak of civil war on the old pattern: but this was soon prevented by diplomacy.

In 1935 the Kuomintang, advised and assisted by experts lent to it by the Bank of England, greatly enhanced its prestige when it introduced a new currency throughout the whole country: and held it stable. The new system replaced the silver standard which had been made unworkable by the financial policy of the U S. The American government, under pressure from senators advancing the interests of silver producers, had raised the price of silver, and drove China to seek another basis for its currency. The success of the Kuomintang in bringing a fiat currency into areas which it had previously occupied by military means alone was the best sign of the consolidation of its authority. It gave both the Kuomintang and China a fillip: and braced it to face the approaching war. Britain, by giving aid in this reform, had shown that it considered the new China worth taking risks for, and that it was willing to develop its Far East policy on the hypothesis that China was becoming stable.

*

In these years an additional person of the drama was beginning to play an interesting and much publicized part. This was Madame Chiang, whom Chiang had married, as his second wife, in 1927. She was one of three ambitious and remarkable sisters, one of whom was the widow of Sun Yat Sen, the leading spirit among the founders of the Kuomintang, who had died in 1924 and was revered as a national hero. Her brother was T. V. Soong, the banker and Kuomintang politician. Madame Chiang supplied the female influence, which recalled to Chinese, who are extremely historically minded, many parallels in the dynastic histories of the past. In a way this increased their tendency to see Chiang as being like one of the founders of past dynasties. But, though her influence on Chiang was considerable, it must be seen for what it was, and not misinterpreted. She was not responsible for developing any new qualities in him: the stubborn will, which had made his place initially in the Kuo-

mintang, was all his own. Madame Chiang, who was Ameri-
can-educated, and in temperament had become more American than Chinese, was his window on the United States.
Through her, the relations of China and the U S became
closer than they would have been without her. Madame
Chiang gave her husband a glamour, an interest, which he
could not have hoped for himself in American's eyes. She
was a forceful personality, wilful and dogmatic, and, though
she lacked great political wisdom, she had an intelligence
which made her a useful intermediary with foreigners. Chiang's use of his wife was skilful.

In 1934, Chiang Kai-shek, assisted by his wife, launched
what was called a 'new life movement'. This was not very
popular: it was the subject of mirth among foreigners and
the sophisticated classes of urban China. It was an attempt
to revive the ancient Confucian virtues as the spiritual basis
of the new state. Confucianism had been repudiated soon
after the revolution which overthrew the Manchus; but a
void had been left, and the Kuomintang lacked a spiritual
basis on which to build the new order. Confucianism was not
really a religion; it was a code of ethics which from earliest
times had been accepted as the ideal of the Chinese people:
it served throughout history as the powerful pillar of the
state, and the fact that in China this role was performed
by ethics, which in other states was performed by the great
organized religions, has throughout been one of the characteristics and fateful elements of Chinese civilization. Confucianism performed the unlikely part of presenting in a
fossilized form the ethical outlook and views of the feudal
society which was the state of China two thousand years
ago. Attitudes which would have been appropriate in a good
Chinese feudatory continued to be advocated, though the
society which gave rise to them had long since changed. Confucianism urges submissiveness, demands reverence to the
old, deplores a headstrong attitude in individuals, prizes the
rites of courtesy, assumes that the business of women is to
obey in all things. The task which the Chinese set themselves
was to reinstate Confucianism, without allowing a too evident
Confucian control of all the institutions of public life.

The new life was to be puritanical. A gloom settled over
Chinese society. Nevertheless, by dint of propaganda, by the
use of all the government machinery for indoctrination, by

the use of various army bureaux for its propagation, and by manipulation of all the government powers of patronage, a not unimpressive Confucian revival began to make headway in China. The change in the intellectual climate of China, with the substitution of a rather narrow Confucian dogma for bland scepticism, was one of the notable features of the time.

*

In the middle thirties the sense that China was recovering, which increased Chinese self-confidence at home as well as affecting the policies of all the powers concerned in the region, caused the Chinese to feel an increasing resentment at Japan's constant pressure upon them. In 1934 Japan, its ambitions enlarging after the conquest of Manchuria, was demanding that an area, carved out of China's northern provinces, should be declared autonomous, and that the writ of the government of Nanking should cease to run there. Obviously the calculation was that in a short time it would pass under the control of Japan. The activities of Japanese agents caused a wave of indignation, and this was particularly strong among the students of Peking. Peking was always the seat of three or four universities, and their pupils, partly because of the regard which China traditionally paid to scholarship and to the learned life, enjoyed peculiar prestige. They were buoyed up by memory of the great demonstration which they had made fifteen years earlier against a particularly corrupt government because of its craven acceptance of foreign demands; this had never been forgotten by the government or by the students themselves; they had come to think of themselves as the custodian of the nation's conscience; they felt themselves morally obliged to be the nation's barometer. The Japanese overstepped the limit. Pressed too hard, the students erupted in December 1935, in a great demonstration against the Chinese officials who were subservient towards the Japanese.

Those who had the good fortune to be present on this occasion felt, even if obscurely, that they were taking part in a historic action. The beauty of Peking in the freezing midwinter, the sense of great issues happening which could only be dimly seen, the foreboding and the excitement, the sense of returning power and rising might in the Chinese people—of a people long oppressed feeling strength to quell the brute and boisterous force of the oppressor—all this made a memorable event in the history of China's ancient imperial city. Even though Peking at this time was demoted, and had temporarily ceased to be the capital city, the students must have sensed the drama of its being the setting for this great demonstration that marked China's national resurgence.

The growing nationalist temper was directed in part against Japan: in part against Chiang Kai-shek, because, though he was the military leader of China, he declined to act as its champion. Instead of calling China to arms he continued to sit in central China, and called for the national attention to be riveted there, to wars for the eradication of communism. In doing this, Chiang began to be regarded as almost a traitor to the Chinese nation. China, or at least its intelligentsia, was ready to go to war, but it felt that one hand was tied behind its back by the Generalissimo of its own armies, or at least was engaged in keeping down the peasantry—an action which the younger, generous section of the nation did not desire at all, and was only necessitated because the landed interests of the Kuomintang required it. How long would these interests continue to control Chiang? When would he become responsible to the will of the younger and more virile section of the nation?

The tension came to a head in December 1936. Chiang went to inspect the Manchurian troops who had been driven out of their homeland by the Japanese five years previously: their quality and their record as fighting men were both rather poor, and their employment had been a problem. They had declared themselves loyal to the Kuomintang: and had been used for blockading the communist forces, who were now in Shensi. Blockading is a tedious duty: the soldiers and officers felt themselves in a strange land: they desired only to be led back to their homes. So disgruntled were they that they fell easy victims to propaganda by the communists, whom they were supposed to be cutting off from all communications with the outside world. Rumour of this had reached Chiang, but he did not realize how deeply the rot went. It is very strange that he ventured himself among such disaffected troops with no proper bodyguard. Not for the first or last time in his career, the secret police, and

Intelligence services, who were a major factor in his government, failed him. He visited Chang Hsueh-liang twice, at his headquarters in Sian, and on his second visit, on the first night, he was surprised, while in a bungalow, by a rising of the Manchurian officers. He managed to escape in the darkness, and crawl up the garden, but he had hurt his back in getting away, and after a few hours he was discovered.

Chang Hsueh-liang sent telegrams to Nanking. A period of suspense followed. The mutineers tried to barter Chiang's release against an undertaking that he would declare war on Japan. So powerful was the national spirit that it impelled the officers to make this unrealistic demand, for it was plain that the war would be premature. Chiang refused absolutely to enter into negotiations with them, and tried, though power was all on their side and he was alone and defenceless, to over-awe them and compel them, buy superior strength of will, to set him free. He succeeded with Chiang Hsueh-liang, who had been at the head of the conspiracy, but who wilted under Chiang's rebukes, and who, in consequence, became his protector against some of the more extreme officers, who would have shot him on the spot. Whatever may have been felt later about Chiang, his bearing among his captors compels admiration.

In the outer world, the government in Nanking was extremely bewildered. There were signs of a break-up, and some of the key personalities began to prepare for a struggle for the post which Chiang seemed to be about to vacate. In Tokyo too, the government had no plans for such an unexpected contingency. Britain and America likewise waited.

The people with resolution were on the one side Chiang's dynamic and opinionated wife and his brother-in-law, T. V. Soong: and on the other side the leaders of the communists, who were only a few miles away. After Chiang's captors had drawn blank in their efforts at compelling him to negotiate, they sent for Chou En-lai and the political officers of the communists. It has never been cleared up whether the communists had known beforehand of the plot. One view is that, immediately after the kidnapping, Moscow had taken a hand in the direction of events. There was radio communication between them and Yenan, the capital of the communists in Shensi province; and the policy of Moscow, which was itself under menace from Japan, had been to preserve, at whatever sacrifice this might be to ideological sense, Chiang Kai-shek alive as the most useful and strongest ally against Japan. The kidnapping threatened this policy, and the interests of the USSR. Simultaneously, Madame Chiang and her brother flew to Sian. By acting whilst others talked, they had intervened to prevent the Nanking government from using its planes to bomb the mutineers. Such an action might have seemed justified: but it would probably have resulted in Chiang's immediate execution. His death might have suited the ambitions of some of the higher officers of the Nanking régime.

There were confused and secret deliberations at Sian. In the end the communists returned home, apparently convinced that Chiang would call off another large-scale offensive against their position in Shensi, which had been planned for the immediate future: and they seem to have been given some assurance that he would in future carry on a more lively defence against the Japanese. The communists were to be autonomous in the areas, not very extensive, which they actively held, and an attempt was to be made at associating a few communist dignitaries in the central government of the Kuomintang. Chiang flew back to Nanking, a free man, and accompanying him was Chang Hsueh-liang, who said that he repented of his mutiny and desired to make retribution. Certainly Chang had neglected to obtain reliable guarantees of his treatment, for on arrival at Nanking he was promptly tried and imprisoned for an indefinite term.

The incident had been dramatic: and was also fateful. It might as easily have ended in an opposite way. Chiang Kai-shek might have been executed by the communists or his captors: the history of Sino-Japanese relations would in that case certainly have developed in a different way. It throws light on the intelligent and subtle mind of the communists, whose roughness of manner had hidden their talent for diplomacy. They must have calculated that Chiang alone could lead China into war: and they were content to use him, and the huge and growing armies of the Kuomintang, for this purpose. Ostensibly Chiang agreed to this; he accepted that it was allegedly the national decision to respond to Japanese aggression by making war.

In reality he fought still to temporize, to procrastinate, to trip up the persons who were relentlessly pressing him forward, to complicate the issues, to drag new considerations to the front. In any case time was needed to make dispositions for war. He was the Reluctant Dragon—dragon because all Chinese emperors (and Chiang was virtually an emperor) are thought of as dragons—reluctant because he was warned by his sure political instinct that his position—and much else besides—would not survive the war.

But in July 1937 the Japanese attacked, and Chiang had to accept their challenge. The assessment which he made, and which forced his hand, was probably as follows.

The students, and the university professors, so vastly influential in the China of that day, so exaggeratedly more important than their numbers or physical power made credible, were, with few exceptions, for resisting. They compelled the country as a whole to take a stiff line, beyond what it would otherwise have thought possible. Also, for an end to patience—though it was hard to speak of a solid voice of such a disparate class, and one not used to having its views considered—were the army officers as a whole, underneath the top commanders. They were variously derived: many were corrupt; but the national spirit was apparent, in varying degrees, in most of them. The same was less true, as Chiang knew well, of some of the senior commanders, who were exposed to the blandishments of the Japanese, whose attitude changed from time to time according to the inducements offered to them, and who did not constitute an inspiring leadership. However, in 1937, most were willing to fight. The landed gentry, while not exactly enthusiasts for resistance, reflected the mood of China: their patience was strained beyond endurance.

Of the true middle class—the native bankers and moneylenders, the petty manufacturers, the craftsmen, the minor civil servants—the disposition was fairly solidly nationalist, and ready to oppose Japan. Some sections were less forward than others; there was always the contradiction between defence of their commercial or other advantage, and the gratification of feeling: none of them could have felt that war would bring them benefits. But they also felt, obscurely perhaps, that they were instruments in a conflict, and it was not in their power to stand aside. They may have deplored their fate, but most of them, while privately desiring to be left in peace, were ready to follow the national path. The merchant guilds, which played a considerable part in the organization of the economic life, had been very prominent in the organization of the resistance in Shanghai in 1931. It was indicative of the part which national sentiment was to play in the organization of the people in the Chinese war effort.

More individualist and more cynical was the attitude of the great bankers and financial magnates of the Treaty Ports. Some of them, indeed were with the war party: many had greater political regard for the security of their possessions.

The masses of people—the poor peasantry, the unskilled workers of the towns—the people who were to bear the main burden of the war in hardship and toll of life—were not consulted, and their opinions would have been taken as being of little weight. But among these, so far as they were informed, the temper was apt to be nationalist, and strongly nationalist. In the Asia of the past generation, it was always remarkable how news circulated, and how accurate the reports tended to be which circulated in the back streets and urban slums. The temper of the vast anonymous mass could not be overlooked.

*

These years, 1931–6, had been, for Japan also, a period of relentless pressure towards a formal war with China, which had come to be regarded as inevitable.

The first experience of Japan's adventure in the conquest of mainland China had not been impressive. Much of the outside world was disappointed and surprised. What the Japanese would do in Manchuria had been awaited with some curiosity. Some countries had been ready to be tolerant. The record of China's rule had been dreary, and it would not have needed any exceptional skill in administration for the Japanese to do better.

Japan decided to govern indirectly through friendly Chinese rather than to establish direct administration. Thus far the choice was wise. Already, as early as 1931, direct imperialism had acquired a bad name, and Japan could not hope to overcome this unless it succeeded in wrapping up reality in some more acceptable political form. Therefore, in 1932, they created a state which was designed to give comfort to the Chinese of the old days of the Empire. It was called Manchukuo, the state of the Manchus. To administer it, there were invited a number of families of the old régime, especially those who had been noticed as friendly to Japan. At their head was Aisin-Gioro Pu-yi, who had been the boy who was deposed in 1911 as the Manchu Emperor of China, and who made his services available to the Japanese for Manchukuo.

Pu-yi, who was to survive many vicissitudes, died only in 1968, and wrote a book *From Emperor to Citizen*, in which he describes at first hand what it was like to be a puppet emperor in the hands of Japan. He explains, for example, how the government of Manchukuo was appointed and changed. He describes how, on one occasion, the commander of the Kwantung army—the Japanese general who supervised the state—came to see him and informed him that his Prime Minister wanted to retire:

> He advised me to grant his request, and replace him with a new Prime Minister. I had already learned that Japan was dissatisfied with the existing incumbent, and I immediately agreed and proposed who should be appointed as his successor. I thought that the general, who had heard my views on Japan–Manchukuo friendship twice in recent days, would be bound to comply with my request. But to my surprise I ran straight into a brick wall. 'No,' he replied shaking his head. 'The Kwantung army has already considered the question and chosen a suitable man. Your Majesty need not worry about a thing.'*

The role of Pu-yi was purely token: he was to attract the attention, and ultimately perhaps the allegiance, of the Manchus, Mongols, and other border people who might play a part if there was war between Japan and Russia. But the Japanese did not propose to proceed very far with this indirect method of government. They soon dropped the pretence that they recognized Manchukuo as independent, and that it was only tied to Japan by a voluntary military alliance.

The Japanese military and the Japanese civil service were

*Pu-Yi: *From Emperor to Citizen: the Autobiography of Aisin-Gioro Pu-yi,* Foreign Language Press, Peking, 1965.

supreme in the country. The Japanese, though they had little racial feeling, were very arrogant: peoples who were subject to them saw their follies, feared their excesses, but secretly tended to despise them. The Japanese showed their worst qualities in their empire. In Japan itself there were people of intellectual and moral distinction: but the empire had proved a catalyst, sorting out the men of coarser fibre from the finer spirits. The dross was drafted as the agents of Japan's foreign venture. Soon they began to make a reputation which was to be a lasting impediment to the further spread of their rule. There were complaints of arbitrary actions, arrests, executions. The machinery of government was used diplomatically to promote the interests of the South Manchuria Railway Company and to foster the multitude of subordinate economic enterprises. The camp-followers became worse exploiters.

Yet, little by little, the army's Manchurian adventure proved disappointing, and, as the Japanese because of their excesses had to abandon the hope of any sincere or large-scale cooperation from the Chinese, the Japanese army, far from meditating ending it and cutting their losses, became increasingly interested in the provinces in China itself south of the Wall, at least in the provinces of the northern half of the country. The grass seemed greener in that valley than it had turned out to be north of the Wall. It became the fashion in Japan for ambitious young officers to seek service in the Kwantung army, and from that vantage point to smell out the situation in Peking, and in the northern provinces of China. Their hopes grew, and they were not deterred by the ill end which some of their colleagues came to because the Chinese had naturally become anxious about the Japanese Secret Service.

*

Japan's economic measures in Manchukuo, and its discouragement of the presence of western businessmen, began to be unfavourably commented on internationally. In north China its pre-invasion action was more spectacular and more sinister. It used its political prestige to further all kinds of economic activity, some very detrimental to China. In particular it fostered the opium trade.

Opium had first become an issue in China at the beginning of the previous century. The British, in forcing the trade upon China, had sought to counter the fact that China bought too little from the West, and thereby caused an adverse balance of trade, by creating a new Chinese want, opium. It was grown in great quantities in India, and could easily be shipped to Canton. The Chinese government protested, and pointed to its duty to protect the Chinese people from the effects of the drug. Two wars had to be fought to overcome its moral protest.

The subsequent history of opium contains a number of unexplained matters. Why did the country as a whole take to opium smoking? What were the effects of the drug upon people's efficiency? Why was the habit, which had been so widespread a few years earlier, checked so completely and with such ease when China eventually had its communist revolution? In the 1930s this ultimate solution of the problem was still far off. Opium had long ceased to be an article of western import: it had become instead a major Chinese product, and though it was not legalized, it was consumed everywhere. The Kuomintang régime drew from its trade a revenue which was outside the ordinary state budget, which was unpublished, but which was the most important item in the financing of its army. Opium, as it is usually taken in China, is a comparatively mild drug, and the Chinese addiction to it probably did them no great harm. A quite different effect, however, was produced by the derivatives of opium: heroin and morphine.

The Japanese set themselves to flood the provinces of north China with heroin and morphine. Partly they did so because of the very high profits obtainable; partly they had in mind the destructive effects of these two drugs. Their use would corrupt the population, and cause them to become apathetic, and weaken their will to resist. They protected rings of Korean drug peddlers. For a time the press was full of stories of these traders, of the protection illegally given them by the Japanese army and navy, and of the unfortunate inhabitants reduced to fawning submission to the bowls in which the morphine was wrapped.

Scenes such as these were confined to only a minute percentage of the map of China, and only a small proportion of the population was affected. But it was symbolic of the new imperialism and the lengths to which it might go. Japan made no effort at hiding it away; it showed its face unashamedly to the world, and the world, startled by Japanese cynicism, reacted more deeply against it than Japan perhaps foresaw. The West, which had the opium wars on its conscience, was more scandalized by the Japanese re-enacting the events of the buried past, than prepared to hail them as brothers in crime.

*

Japan's descent into Avernus, during these six brief years, and the corruption of its political system were rapid. Most of what happened prepared Japan for the later part it was to play. In this time Japan took, with great speed, a series of plunges, which ensured that, when the Pacific war came, it fought this in a spirit that surprised the world by its barbarity.

A rapid deterioration set in among most of the national institutions. Many of these had the obvious effect of easing the path to war: and they harmed the spirit of the country profoundly. When there was a lull in the development of external events, the crisis deepened internally.

The process can be traced from point to point. In Manchuria, in 1931, the decision to act had been made by the Japanese army. It dragged the civilian government in the wake of its *fait accompli*. The precedent was alarming, and was regularly acted on by the army in the years which followed, and accepted by the nation. No revolution took place, and no change of institutions was necessary: the civil service continued to operate, and remained comparatively unpurged. But in the government of the day, with a constitution not too precise, it was enough that one of the controlling forces should shift the balance of power in the administration: and the whole nature of government changed. The civil authority ceased to intervene in matters which were properly its concern, and left these to the army. It was a species of anarchy.

The development was aided by a peculiar feature of the constitution. It was laid down by law that the Ministers of the navy and army must be serving officers holding a certain rank. The implications became apparent. Through this provision the army and navy gained a veto over all the dealings of the cabinet whenever they chose to express it. It was only necessary that they should withdraw their nominees from the cabinet, and forbid other serving officers to join it, and a situation would come about in which the civilian Ministers, even of high prestige, were forced to supplicate the army for terms which would make it possible for the cabinet to continue its work.

A curious development, which struck all historians of Japan as reviving historical precedents, was that, in the army, the readiness to exploit these full powers was found among the younger officers. Situations were constantly developing in which the more senior officers hesitated and prevaricated: sometimes they did not know what to do, or were frankly appalled at finding themselves called on to take the responsibility in unfamiliar civilian affairs. The junior officers could exercise this without nervousness or scruple. This explains why so much army initiative originated at quite a low level.

Under army protection a large number of so-called patriotic parties began to operate. These, made up chiefly of thugs, led in part by retired army officers and held together by histrionics and cash, drove out of public life the moderate or old-fashioned men who wanted to preserve the more dignified ways of the past. These irrational, violent forces were a feature of the politics of the period. A civilian Minister, or a sober, responsible service officer, had to be ready at all times to be struck at by these gangs: and knew that they were often employed by their apparently respectable rivals. Their method represented the violent way of doing politics which had come in, and no moral slur attached to the use of gangs for assassination, nor could public opinion be rallied against them.

The patriotic societies were active in everything. Within months of the Mukden incident a serious wave of unrest, violence and assassination began. The most important incidents were the murder of the Finance Minister, Inouye Junnosuke, and the Prime Minister, Inukai Tsuyoshi. The societies sensed that the atmosphere had become suddenly propitious for their activities, and offered themselves to one faction or another. They interested themselves in all branches of government. But foreign affairs were their most dangerous concern. The Black Dragon Society—which took its name from the Japanese word for the Amur river which was the border between Manchuria and the U S S R—was particularly obnoxious. It organized the assassination of Prime Ministers: it tried to dictate to the Foreign Office: it sought to win members among the bureaucracy: by terror it dictated much of the ideological guidance which the Japanese government was accustomed to give to the people. The murderers of Premier Inukai declared at their trial that their motive had been to protest against the Japanese ratification of the London naval agreement which the Japanese government had incurred much displeasure by accepting. It was to be the last constructive agreement for peace that a Japanese government was to be allowed by public opinion to make.

The investigation of these plots showed that there was a deep malaise among the services. These wanted a radical change in the form of government, though in precisely what form it was hard to specify. The talk was of national renewal, and a general new birth of institutions. The young officers were divided. Some were primarily interested in bringing about a domestic revolution: others wanted it because it seemed the best way of promoting a more ruthless foreign policy. But in the end the two trends were united: a sterner foreign policy went with the renewal of institutions at home.

In February 1936 the turbulence of the new army reached its peak. There took place then an incident which embodied all the trends to violence of the time, and all the flouting of established political conduct. A plot was made by the younger officers in some of the most respected regiments. Plots, it will be gathered, were nothing new: it was the scope and audacity of this particular one which were original. The conspiracy was to murder the leaders of the cabinet and the most respected elder statesmen who advised the throne: and then, as an act of unheard-of impiety, to give an ultimatum to the Emperor for the appointment of a particular kind of Ministry. They failed because their plot was prepared inadequately, and because some of the leading figures escaped their would-be assassins. But for some days the politics of Tokyo, which at the time was snow-covered, was divided between a barracks which housed the rebellious officers who were waiting for high personages to throw in their lot with them, and the rest of the town, stunned by the enormity of what had been done, and with police and the loyal section of the army gradually mustering the resolution to step in with repressive action. Finally they moved in, there were trials, and after a considerable delay, some exemplary executions.

Japan had been saved from the dictation of a ruthless and flamboyant figure only because no such figure had the ability to seize the government. The tradition of Japan was against individual action. Even in times of great crisis it required that revolutionaries should act in committees. But the spectacle of the administration of a great empire ceasing altogether for a few days, and great offices of state being hawked round by captains and majors, caused all lookers-on to marvel and to shudder.

This abortive revolution, by its radicalism, led to a realization that the Japanese army, or a part of it, was ceasing to be right-wing. One of its causes was said to be the unfamiliar outbreak of political discussion among junior officers. This was partly the result of their becoming affected by Japan's economic problems. They were seeking solutions; they did not mind if they were radical. Hitherto the army, to the comfort of the better-off classes of the Japanese, had seemed to connote safety, conservatism, stability. But they had to recast their thoughts rather rapidly when they saw at least a section of the officers playing with what in Japan had been regarded as dangerous thoughts. Some reflective onlookers noticed that, if the army should turn towards Communism in its new adventurousness it would have a good chance of putting the whole country on a communist footing. Japan, with its heavy industry, with its huge industrial population which was accustomed to strict discipline, and its underlying taste for violence, would be admirable material for a communist dictatorship to work on.

This uneasiness, vague but pervasive, increased the danger of war. Many Japanese, fearful that the army, which already they felt was beyond control, might now move towards the acceptance of all kinds of radicalism in Japanese internal affairs, felt that its giddy mind would best be occupied by foreign quarrels.

The national temper began to be touched with hysteria. Thought control, imposed by the government, meant the virtual interruption of all forms of rational thinking. An official version of Japanese history, made up of fairy stories and full of absurdity, was made to prevail: it became dangerous to publish more serious matter. A much respected Japanese professor, Minobe Tatsukichi, was hounded from his job because it was found that he had stated in a book on political science that the Japanese Emperor was an organ of the constitution. He was too sacred to be defined. The deification of the Emperor, which formerly had been inherited from the Japanese past, grew now to absurd proportions and was especially ironical because it was known to be distasteful to the Emperor himself.

In these years, there also took place a distinct shift in the religious life of the country. Attention was less on the compassionate, often intellectually subtle religion of Buddhism; more emphasis was given to the religion which had coexisted with Buddhism for many centuries—Shinto, a rather simple form of animism and worship of the symbols of state. It had no intellectual corpus attached to it.

It became dangerous for a Japanese to diverge by however little from the norm in behaviour, sentiment, or thought. Japan had never been kind to the pronounced individual: and Japanese society had eyed any departure from conformity with uneasiness. (Only those cases where experimentalism had been backed up by a reputation of extreme religiosity were exempted.) The increasing tension in political life made the Japanese dislike eccentricity even more severely. In the years preceding the end of the Japanese military venture, there was an increasing sterility in Japanese literature and in all departments of creative life. Of true individualism, of the man with the social courage to stand up and denounce what society was doing, or the innovator who worked under the pressure of his *daimon* and ignored the praise or censure of the world, there was strikingly little.

7

The War resumed

THE second phase of the war began in an obscure skirmish between the Japanese and Chinese troops at a place not far from Peking called the Marco Polo Bridge. This encounter happened on the night of 7 July 1937. In the next few weeks, at first sporadic, later general fighting spread through all north China, and reached Shanghai. As far as can be discovered, none of the main Japanese generals, and certainly not Chiang Kai-shek, wanted war at this particular moment: and peace efforts were made constantly. But the situation was out of hand. The Chinese communists, who were now formally reconciled with the Kuomintang, used every opportunity to drive their allies on to war. The decision was forced by relatively junior officers in command in the field. Compulsively the fighting spread. The top commanders on both sides saw this and made unavailing efforts to check it, and excused themselves from responsibility.

The two years which followed were the chief phase of slaughter in the war between China and Japan: then came a renewed period of lull. The conflict was still separate from the Armageddon which was being prepared in the West, and at first remained a separate war, when the explosion occurred in Europe. Natually both sides followed with care the events in Europe, and at times they adjusted their policies accordingly. But the two wars were not to merge until December 1941. There were four years to go before that.

The history of these first years of fighting is fairly simple. As was expected, Japan quickly overcame the organized resistance in the north, and occupied the railway lines and the cities. It sent a powerful force to Shanghai, and the history of the landing there after the Mukden incident was repeated. The Chinese resisted for seven weeks, and there was jubilation in China. Improvising a guerrilla warfare, the Chinese discovered in some theatres the military prowess which has since been taken for granted. But at Shanghai, on breaking through in the end to open country, the Japanese this time crossed rapidly the 200 miles to Nanking, and occupied it without difficulty.

Chiang Kai-shek and his government had withdrawn to Hankow. In December 1937 they had lost Nanking, their capital; the slaughter and atrocities were far worse than in 1931. It was the history of an earlier time, of the Mongol ravages of Asia, of Timur and the cold terror he spread— a horror which his name can even now evoke in Central Asia. There are lurid tales of Timur sacking a city. If an army dared to oppose him Timur built up a pyramid of skulls of those he slaughtered. He camped in a tent of scarlet canvas outside the towns he besieged, thus symbolizing the massacres he intended to make. The ferocity of the Japanese at Nanking amazed the world. The massacre was done for the most part by Japanese conscripts, unfamiliar with war, perhaps neurotically working out of their system the extreme repressions in which they had passed so much of their lives. Some Japanese officers in other centres wept with shame and indignation when they heard the details of the ravage.

The effect was profound in other countries of the world. At first the news of the outrage was censored, but ultimately it got into the world press. Anxious though they were to avert their gaze from Asia, because of the preoccupations in Europe, the countries of the West turned their attention to Nanking, and were appalled by seeing a foretaste of what might soon be everywhere. From then on, the Japanese army was held to be uncivilized, savage and terrible.

In 1938 there was much fighting in north and central China. In the spring, in an effort to halt the Japanese advance, Chiang ordered the breaching of the Yellow River dykes. This failed to halt them; but it was estimated that over a million peasants were drowned in the flood which resulted. It began to be clear what torment had been let loose on the world. In October, the Japanese, in the south, took Canton and its hinterland. Canton was the original base of the Kuomintang. Its capture was significant, as it seemed to symbolize striking at the root of the Kuomintang. In the same month the Japanese, advancing up the Yangtse, had taken Hankow. This was not an easy victory, as many successes had been. There was heavy fighting: the Chinese engaged in positional warfare, and did not use guerrilla tactics. Some divisions showed the result of their having received German training from Chiang Kai-shek's German advisers. In the battle of Hsuchow the Chinese won triumphantly.

In spite of this, in October 1938, Hankow fell. Chiang Kai-shek's government withdrew to Chungking, the principal town (though not the capital) of the remote province of Szechuan, which bordered on Tibet, and which since 1935 had been prepared by Chiang as the national capital in an emergency. Chiang was now following what proved to be his masterplan for the war: to trade space for time; to care little for loss of territory provided the centre of resistance remained intact, to put faith in the huge distances in China, and to hang on in spite of defeats.

Gradually the truth about the Chinese armies became known in the outer world, which had at first been inclined to credit that China had become better organized than it was in fact. The organization went to pieces. Soldiers went into battle as part of a modern military formation, but this usually broke under strain, and they became pockets of fighting men. Hence came much of the nightmare quality which made this one of the most awful periods of China's recent black record. Administration was primitive; corruption was extreme. Army medical services and hospitals scarcely existed, and soldiers who were only slightly wounded usually perished. Volunteer medical aid began to appear from the sympathetic countries of the West, but all its doctors could do was to add to the swelling chorus of lamentation.

Chungking was well beyond the gorges in the Yangtse, which are one of the beauty spots of China. To attack Chungking was to involve the Japanese in such problems of logistics that Chiang was safe there. The Japanese did not follow him farther. A very long pause set in. There was no more large-scale fighting for six years. It might have been supposed that the war had petered out.

*

Japan took stock of what it had gained. Superficially it had conquered territory which contained 170 million people. China had lost its principal sea ports. It depended henceforward for foreign supplies on two routes, one an earth road from Russia through Turkestan, the other a road from Chungking to the south which ended in Burma: both were very long, poorly constructed, and liable to traffic blocks. For a time it had been able to use Hanoi, in Indo-China, but the bridges which carried the railway line which linked this port with Yunnan (in south-west China) were destroyed.

Such heavy fighting was not to happen again, even when this war was eventually swallowed up in the Second World War, and when China's weapons were much strengthened by aid from its allies.

Japan estimated the number of Chinese who had been killed during this period as at least 800,000: its own dead numbered only 50,000. Probably this is an over-estimate of the one, and an under-estimate of the other. Yet there was a great gap between the losses on both sides. Japan suffered its first reverses in the occupied districts in the north. Its control of the railways and towns did not give it control of the rural areas. It began to feel severely the effects of communist guerrilla action. At first it had supposed that it had the measures for repressing the communists, and, for a time, little was heard about the communist armies. This was to the dismay of the friends of China who had built up extravagant hopes on the reconciliation between Chiang and the communists. Eventually, though, the stubborn resistance of the communists began to take a toll. To have overcome it, to have attempted a stricter control which would have eliminated this, would have cost many millions of troops, which the Japanese could not afford. China had begun to draw the advantages from one of its assets, size. Because the Japanese could not pacify the vast areas of Hopei, Shantung, and Shensi provinces, which they had overrun, they constituted themselves as a target for guerrilla action.

Chiang Kai-shek sat in his fortress at Chungking and

waited. The city, though not beautiful as is Chengtu, the capital of Szechuan, was fitted for its purpose. Rainfall was heavy, and the clouds which overhung it for weeks on end, together with surrounding mountains which made it difficult to approach, prevented it from being an easy target of attacks from the air. It was bombed heavily for a time, but later was left in peace. The city was large, and had once been affluent. Chiang's task was to keep his government in existence, to survive the plots against him, to plot against others—to continue to be regarded as the symbol of nationalism. Alas, though wartime propaganda made the reputation of Chungking as a heroic centre of resistance, a long, slow demoralization set in among the Kuomintang establishment, the inevitable result among an army and bureaucracy condemned to too much idleness, and this proved in the long run too much for Chiang Kai-shek to combat. The Chinese of the Kuomintang and the army staff were a different people from the particularist Szechuanese, who resented their impact on their ancient provincial culture. Relations between them and the local people deteriorated steadily. 'Down-river gangsters' was the term used for Kuomintang officials by the Szechuanese people. Internal rot was the price the Kuomintang paid for the tactics of masterly inactivity.

Chiang Kai-shek was resting his hopes, not in the Kuomintang army, but chiefly in foreign aid, principally in American aid, which his diplomats in the United States tirelessly sought. Certainly there was abundant American goodwill to China, based chiefly on the vast American missionary enterprise in China. It seemed that China, before the war, had been willing to reconstruct its society according to American ideas, and this seemed to impose on the United States the obligation of protecting it internationally.

As far as China was concerned, Japan now turned its back on battles and daring campaigns, and engaged in political warfare and in political intrigue. The only military action was a single attempt in June 1940 to force the Yangtse gorges, which ended at Ichang. Japan decided that to carry on the war was to bring complication after complication, and, from now on, explored ways to end it. From this time, 1939–40, the Japanese army sought peace in China as constantly and assiduously (though maladroitly) as it had previously sought war. It was out of the question to arrange to annex the vast territory it had overrun, and to rule it directly as the British used to rule India. The need for civil servants would be immense, beyond anything which Japan could supply. It turned in consequence to indirect rule, to organizing north China as a puppet state (similar in general shape to Manchukuo), which would be under the rule of a single man or body of men upon whose loyalty they could rely, because it would be clear that, with Japanese aid removed, they would collapse.

Their first thought was to use Chiang Kai-shek himself. If they could have detached him from his nationalism, and made it worth his while, Chiang would have proved an excellent puppet. He would have had a full and apparently contented life hunting down communists. Realizing how greatly an alliance with Chiang would serve them, understanding that this was indeed the crisis of the war, the Japanese used the utmost finesse to bring it about. But neither the secret emissaries whom they sent tirelessly to visit him, nor the German Ambassador who proposed mediation, brought the Japanese any hopeful news. Chiang had little room to manoeuvre in. He had made his way to the top of the Kuomintang, but he had become a prisoner of the national movement, which would have broken him if he had sought to betray it. Chiang, who knew the dark corners of China's political life, and availed himself of the services of its inhabitants, knew well what agents it would employ.

Reluctantly the Japanese decided on an alternative plan. They set themselves to persuade respected nationalists, who were opposed to Chiang Kai-shek, to form a government which had all the outward shape of the Kuomintang, and which the Japanese could substitute for the official Kuomintang. They had resort to one of the most distinguished members of the Kuomintang, who had been almost a founding father of the party.

This man, Wang Ching-wei, one-time Vice-President of the Kuomintang republic, had previously built a career on the leadership of the left wing. He had never exhausted the fame which he had gained by being involved in a plot in the days of the Empire to murder a Manchu grandee. In private, his views were anything but radical and he had married a very wealthy wife, who came from a family of

Singapore millionaires. But his political talents had been acceptable to the revolutionary branch of the Kuomintang. After the fall of Canton and Hankow he seems to have accepted the Japanese argument that further resistance was useless, and to have argued that China, by recasting its foreign policy, could still come to terms with Japan which would be mutually advantageous. At Chungking, he conferred at length with Chiang Kai-shek. Though no record exists of their conversation, it is known that the two men debated in full the Japanese peace offer.

In December 1939 he recognized his failure, and left the capital. The Japanese were willing to see in him the best substitute head of a cooperative Chinese government. He had the aura of a major politician. He had the record of being a persistent rival of Chiang Kai-shek. Mostly Chiang had succeeded in keeping him out of office, and, when Wang Ching-wei had manoeuvred so that he compelled Chiang to share power with him, Chiang was suspected of a hand in the mysterious shooting which had removed him from office. The Japanese acted with resolution. Wang's name, the prestige of Nanking city, the attraction of the Kuomintang—renamed by Wang the Reformed Kuomintang—all these were used to give the new government such prestige as it could have in a Nanking which remembered vividly what it had been made to suffer.

The government came into being in 1940. A fairly long list of landholders, industrialists, former officials, diplomats out of employment, politicians who had ruined their prospects with the official Kuomintang, came to see if the vistas opened up under the new administration appeared brighter for them. Many were recruited for the régime. Many of the more or less respectable Chinese nationalists had begun to find the régime of the Reformed Kuomintang very beguiling, especially since it reconciled nationalism with the prospect of opting out of the war. Wang Ching-wei's government was a copy of the genuine Kuomintang. Its constitution was much the same; it contained the complications and intricacies which had puzzled all those who tried to follow Chinese politics. Its methods of administration were much the same.

In administration the régime was slightly less corrupt than

had been expected. It did little that was outwardly disgraceful. As the head of a puppet government, camouflaged for the general public in the colours of nationalism, Wang Ching-wei did neither more nor less than was expected of him: he fought for China's interests while being ready in the last resort to yield to Japan's superior strength. In China he played the same part as Marshal Pétain in France. But Wang's government never succeeded in living down the sense of national shame in which it was born; never managed to take independent life; it remained a creature of the Japanese; it never became a serious body internationally.

*

Meanwhile the pretence that the war was a joint one, of the Kuomintang and the communists against Japan, was wearing thin. The Chinese communists, in the regions which they had overrun in the north, maintained a lively propaganda against the Japanese. Guerrilla warfare was their special art. There was also activity by guerrilla bands who fought in the name of the Kuomintang. But the pretence, which had been built up immediately after the Sian incident, that the armies of the communists were to be fused with the armies of the Kuomintang under some kind of common command, never became a reality. The communists had no intention of surrendering the sole command of their army. That was their most effective instrument in Chinese politics, and they would hold on to it. The communists relied on their army to win them new territory, and to retain what they had got; and they could scarcely trust their old enemy, the Kuomintang, with any recognized power to dispose of this force.

A subtle, concealed, very bitter struggle was resumed between the Kuomintang and the communists. Everybody who was interested in Chinese politics saw the danger of revived civil war taking shape. The Kuomintang, without entirely dropping the mask of the common front, was alert to the spread of communist power, and tried to guard against it by maintaining, as far as it could, an inner blockade of the regions which the communists ruled, including an embargo on all medical supplies. The most competent and orderly section of the Kuomintang army was in fact left permanently at Sian, where its sole duty was to watch and over-awe the communists. The communists directed their fire equally against the Kuomintang and the Japanese.

Sometimes the struggle became too obvious for decency between apparent allies. Each side had its own territory. Sometimes the communists would move into a Kuomintang region: the Kuomintang would drive them out by force. At such times the hollowness of the partnership became plain. There was a particularly flagrant example of this in 1941 when the communist Fourth Route Army was ambushed by patent treachery, and fighting flared up on a large scale. The communists lost several generals in the course of this affair. But even at such times both the communists and the Kuomintang tried to put limits to hostilities. An important part in keeping peace at least formally was played by the communist representative at Chungking, who was Chou En-lai, destined in the next decade to become the prime minister of China. A competition was being fought out between the two governments, to determine which of them, in the harsh conditions of war, had the better spirit to endure. The war was proving a hothouse, and had brought on the decision which otherwise might have taken half a century to deliver. All the data were to the discomfiture of the Kuomintang. The communists, which began as very much the weaker, became a steadily greater force.

Meanwhile a part of the horrors which had overtaken the Chinese people became known to the West—to a West which was bracing itself to face its own agony. The full terrors of war broke over the Chinese towns and countryside. They had gradually become accustomed to civil war during the thirty years of breakdown of ordered government. In much of the country, the old magistrates had left. The armies of the war-lords had harried the villages, seized their grain, and sometimes carried off the young men and women. But all this was very little compared with what befell in the years after 1936. One estimate puts the number uprooted from their homes by the war as 50 million. The Chinese are as a rule greatly attached to their villages, and will not forsake a home which contains the graves of their ancestors. Many of the cherished customs of the village—the sweeping of the family graves, ceremonial meals eaten over the tombs

—are connected with tomb-rites. Now a great wrench had loosened the population from its hold. China dissolved from people living in orderly, extremely conservative patterns of life, into a maze of people wandering aimlessly from village to village. They sought food, protection, shelter. All China seemed to be restlessly on the move. Any representation of its people at this time shows them trudging from place to place, carrying their belongings with them. (A similar nightmare befell persons who were compelled to see the sights in post-war Germany.) How many perished in this time will never be known. Their plight made them powerless to escape the scourge of famine and the scourge of the other terror of the Chinese countryside, flood. One by one, the very ancient annual ceremonies in the villages, which gave Chinese life its admirable quality and its deep sense of continuity, were given up. Life became especially hard for the old, the class which Chinese civilization was notorious for revering.

Colour, richness and elegance disappeared from China. Everywhere people went dressed in simple cotton clothes, either because they had been impoverished, or because the slightest display of luxury was an invitation to plunder. The pleasantness and decorum of the life of the Chinese upper classes, which had already been much shaken for a hundred years due to the impact of the West, descended to a new calamitous level, as society gradually disintegrated. Only in such protected centres as Chungking was the attempt made to live in accustomed Chinese style.

A similar break-up of society had taken place in France at the end of the Hundred Years War, and in Germany during the Thirty Years War.

*

Early during this period there had taken place one of the most unlooked-for emigrations in history. As we have seen, the universities of China had a precocious development. In wealth, in their standing in society, by the personal eminence of their staff, both Chinese and also the core of expatriate foreigners, they were ahead of the standards which universities might have been expected to reach in the country, and were suited for a society such as China might have evolved two or three generations later. In consequence of this, much of the most advanced, the purest, and certainly the most disinterested nationalism of the day was nursed to life within their walls.

Most of the universities were on the seaboard in the path of the Japanese invasion. They were one of its special targets, because the Japanese, being themselves Far-Eastern people, understood (though Japan did not share in this peculiarity) the extraordinary influence which the Chinese intelligentsia had over the rulers of the nation. The Chinese student was alone among the student class of the world in not feeling, or feeling much less, an acute sense of frustration. Why should he? The nation hung on his moods, was willing to follow him in his attitudes to Ministers and public affairs. Since he was so influential, the student buoyed himself up: and the conditions he put up with in the student life, the squalid poverty, were felt to be the necessary price of privilege. Besides it was spread equally over the whole student body. Let them reduce the pride and aspiration of the intelligentsia, the Japanese told themselves, and they would have gone a long way in subduing Chinese nationalism. Under Japanese domination, the universities knew that they would face a purge, and the conditions of the new life would be quite intolerable to them. Rather than suffer it, many of the university communities moved off by spontaneous resolution, and trekked from the coasts to new sites far in the interior.

Chinese learning was pulling up its stakes and was seeking out a territory where it might exist in freedom; and, as the price to be paid for this, live a life less gilded than before. The professors and their assistants, the student body, and university servants, all sought a home where they could continue their life with less harassment. Previously, Chinese scholars had not taken kindly to manual work; now they voluntarily undertook the hardship of the journey, the uncertainties of what awaited them, and a life of toil. It was the more surprising because these learned societies had to leave palatial premises, which had been given them by millionaires and foreign philanthropists, and had to fit their academic life into camps which had been made available to them as exiles. Throughout their vicissitudes they had safeguarded their libraries and the equipment of their scientific laboratories. Many of them transported these across the rivers and mountains of inland China.

During the war years the Chinese intelligentsia continued their studies diligently. In view of the way in which learning was regarded this turned out to be the most useful thing which they could contribute to China's war effort. They had firmly aligned themselves with China's decision to resist Japan, and by their action in seeking voluntary exile they increased their prestige in the eyes of the people. The scholars and the mass of common people came closer together.

The universities, in deciding on their odysseys, were influenced by the example of the Chinese communists on the Long March. From this time there began to grow up the great sympathy of the Chinese scholar class for the communists. The scholars felt themselves being blown along by the same hurricane which had swept together the communist insurgents throughout China: and as the leadership of the Kuomintang began to falter, they began to look to the communists for an alternative. They did so with more eagerness because when they had migrated in the cause of freedom, they found that, when they eventually reached the security of the interior, they were regarded with suspicion by the Kuomintang, and that their freedom was interfered with by an irksome secret police. The campus was invaded by an army of spies.

The reliance on the secret police by Chiang Kai-shek to maintain his exaggerated political role was a departure from Chinese tradition. Before Chiang, China had known periods of despotism; but the despot had, to a remarkable degree, avoided the organization of a secret police as the instrument of tyranny. Even in the last years of the Manchus the government, though repressive, had avoided the creation of an organ specially for intelligence and coercion. Therefore the collisions which now became frequent between the literati and the secret police offered the more provocation because the Chinese had not been accustomed in the past to think of the police as a necessary evil.

The writings of Chinese academics became full of woe; they had exchanged the persecution of the Japanese for the supervision of the police. It was less efficient, less rigorous, but it was deeply offensive. The grievances thus sown were to bear fruit at the end of the war. Without the moral approval of the scholar class, the Chinese communists would never have been able to impose themselves so successfully on the Chinese nation.

*

The setting in of the war in earnest brought a decisive change in attitude of the westerners. Sentiment, which among some classes in Britain, for example, had for some time been anti-Japanese, hardened; and it spread throughout most sections of the people, at least of those, admittedly a minority, who thought it necessary to take a view about such a distant part of the world.

The change was marked in the early period of the Japanese adventure. Westerners with foreign contacts, especially the businessmen resident in the Far East, had on the whole been well disposed to Japan. Japan professed to be the champion of foreign business interests. It claimed to be taking steps—in putting down bandits, in removing the Chinese officials who were the bane of traders—which the other countries would have followed if they had had the resolution to stand up for their interests. Chinese xenophobia was the enemy of all who had to do with China. And, for a long while, Japanese action received a great deal of sympathy from certain sections of westerners.

This view continued to be held, at least until the war became merged with the Second World War. A section of businessmen, progressively smaller in number but still powerful in influence, maintained their regard for Japan. They thought that no comparison was possible between the Japanese, clever, energetic, industrious, above all disciplined and punctual, and the Chinese, who, if they were clever, had all the faults which went with political impotence; who were corruptible, were voluble in justifying the inexcusable, were argumentative without being convincing to the not very admirable representatives of the West. These liked the Japanese way of life, Japanese discipline and Japanese customs: though it should be noted that most of the things they admired were regarded by educated Japanese, who had kept some standards from the past, as vulgar. They liked the solidity of the buildings in western style which the Japanese had put up. Some of the westerners felt that the Japanese had very sensible ideas about the status of women. The comic side to this is that very few of its would-be admirers understood correctly the genius of Japan, which is aesthetic, non-intellectual, and not acquisitive, is swept by temporary enthusiasms, and taking the culture as a whole, does not admire the use of force.

But this view was not unchallenged. A rival section of western residents in Treaty Ports had backed the rise of the new China. From among these, there was, it is true, not at first a strong condemnation of Japan. Most of these people felt, secretly if not openly, that China had been moving too fast and too far, and that chastisement by Japan would bring it to reason. A series of murders and outrages had occurred in previous years: and Nanking did its cause no good by obvious deception and the pretence that it could not unravel the circumstances.

Western businessmen were less far-sighted, less impersonal than their governments. They had also a sense of racial superiority, which they had abandoned in the case of Japan, which had demonstrated that it could not be pushed around. Business was conscious of the great advantage of living in concessions under an extra-territorial régime. It lamented the fact that negotiation had begun for their abolition, and that many concessions had already been surrendered: it saw itself vitally threatened. There were some men of vision among them, who looked ahead and saw the future; but these men were rare. Americans, in spite of their general liberalism and of the pro-Chinese sentiment of many of their countrymen, were of the same temper as the others.

However, as the great offensive of the Japanese began to take shape and its direction passed from the Japanese civilian, whom the western businessmen used to know, into the hands of arrogant generals, with whom they did not feel at home, they began more and more to change their minds. The fear grew up that it was the Japanese, not the Chinese, who would chase them out of the concessions. Japan was spending its blood and treasure to make China into a place fit for a man to live in; but it was to be a Japanese businessman, an agent of the Mitsui and the Mitsubishi, not the foreigner whom the Japanese regarded as more undesirable than the Chinese. The western traders or industrialists saw that if they lost the protection under which they were living, they would not have a very long tenure of life. By controls, by subsidies, by taxation, by withholding permits to move their capital and profits out of the country, Japan would be able to drive them away in a brief time, and in less than ten years' time the concessions would be no more.

Thus the change of attitude had become almost universal, and the businessmen were as anxious as the Chinese when in July 1937 the fighting began in earnest. At least they could console themselves that there was an end for the time being to the negotiation for the return of the concessions. The Chinese defence of Shanghai happened before their eyes, and the rape of Nanking was near enough to cause acute discomfort, however cynical the businessman might be.

The Chinese did not lose hope of entangling foreign powers, including Britain, in the war at various of its stages. In 1937 the Japanese, perhaps unaware of who was their prey, had machine-gunned from the air a motorcar on the way from Shanghai to Nanking. In it was Sir Hughe Knatchbull Hugessen, the then British representative in China. He was seriously wounded, and for a few days this nearly fatal accident caused an electric tension. But the British could do little more than protest, and the incident was closed by an exchange of notes that were meant to save everybody's face. (Sir Hughe thus goes down in history as a diplomat who was nearly murdered and started a war. He is remembered also as the Ambassador in Turkey who had the plans of the Second Front filched by his valet who gave them to the Germans. The incident is described in the book *Operation Cicero*. Fortunately the Germans could not credit their good fortune, and assumed that false information was being planted on them.) Though feeling was shifting among even local businessmen from being pro-Japanese to being pro-Chinese, the British were resolved to go to great lengths to preserve their neutrality. All eyes in Britain were on the European continent; from 1938 there was almost constant crisis in Europe; Britain was not ready to allow any of its armed strength to be engaged in the Far East when every ounce of it was required in Europe.

There was a certain comedy as the British Ambassador in Tokyo, Sir Robert Craigie, fought out the battle on what should be British policy towards the war with Sir Archibald Clark-Kerr, the successor to Knatchbull Hugessen in China.

Clark-Kerr had pronounced left-wing views, which were in favour of Britain supporting China on grounds of plain international morality. China was weak, was being bullied, and, he thought, should be protected. Craigie, in Tokyo, was fully convinced of the benefits which Britain had derived from the Anglo-Japanese alliance as long as this had existed. He saw the best hope in working for its revival. The pro-Japanese views of the British Embassy were reinforced by the peculiarly romantic view of Japanese history held by the British Military Attaché, General Piggott. The divergent views of the two representatives, at Chungking and at Tokyo, clashed with vigour in their telegrams and reports. Those who took part in this conflict were convinced that the issue was of first importance. They failed to recognize that the attention of London was otherwise engaged, and their respective views were not treated very seriously.

Similarly, the Americans in the area were divided about their policy. There were incidents between them and the Japanese, which stirred up American hopes, but nothing came of these. The war was fought at Shanghai in a vastly overcrowded space, and inevitably the bystanders were hit. The USS *Panay*, an American gunboat in the Yangtse, was bombed and sunk. Whether some of the Japanese commanders desired to frighten the United States away, or the bombing was a mistake, was not known. The United States was in the heyday of its neutrality, took no action and patched up an agreement. But privately, the Americans were strengthened in an anti-Japanese frame of mind. The tide was running in support of the China lobby which was made up of businessmen, scholars, philanthropists, former missionaries, and other specialists on Asia. The China lobby was to become one of the powers of the land.

By 1939, when the European war began, many businessmen in the Far East recognized that their bright day was over: and that, once the Treaty Port system was disbanded, it would not be set up again. In this year there was the humiliation of the businessmen of Tientsin. A Chinese collaborator had been murdered in the British concession, and the Japanese demanded that two suspects, who had been arrested by the police of the British concession, should be surrendered to them. Pressed to accept this radical demand the British refused: and in consequence the Japanese blockaded the British concession. People still went in and out but at the cost of an exhausting wait and a humiliating bodily search. A smile of appreciation went through Asia, even among countries which approved of China and were against Japanese militarism. The Japanese, it seemed, were effectively putting down the mighty from their seats, and scattering the proud in the imagination of their hearts.

The Taipans, as the heads of firms were called, saw the clouds darken steadily, and could not see their way ahead. The European war was beginning. The British government was preoccupied with that, and there was little hope that they would do much for their countrymen at Shanghai or Tientsin.

Meanwhile Japan had been making itself conspicuously disliked by the classes which had no interest at all in residing in the Far East, but made their living at home in trade. For them, Japan mattered simply because of its commercial policy. In the thirties this became increasingly competitive. Japan felt an increasing need to increase its exports or to starve; and, under this compulsion, it became notorious as the country hunting for markets, successfully snapping up the old markets of older countries, ruthlessly underbidding, successfully dumping.

Japan, in short, was feared and disliked by everybody in an established position in world trade, who saw its activities with dread. This dislike of Japan for commercial reasons was carried over into an irrational anti-Japanese prejudice. Feeling tilted over and became pro-China and anti-Japan; it was reinforced by a modish fashion amongst the intelligentsia for all Chinese things. Nevertheless, commercial competition was at the root of the sentiment.

8

India and the Conflict

AT the time of the clash between China and Japan, the surprising fact in the rest of Asia was that most of it was under western government. Much of India, for example, had been under British rule for 150 years. Nearly all the rest of the region had also passed into the empires, or spheres of interest, of one European power or another. Two ancient, but comparatively small, countries, Persia and Thailand, were the only exceptions. They owed their preservation to uncommon adroitness, aided by the fact that in each case two foreign powers were competing for dominance over their territories.

From the beginning of the 1920s India, the heart and core of this series of subject countries, had made a resolute and persevering effort to throw off western rule. It was a fair deduction that, if it succeeded, an end would be put to the lesser imperialisms of Europe in Asia. Their circumstances were in some respects dissimilar: their end would be the same. All Asia would be free. Moreover India had so central a position in Asia, was a country with such prestige and resources, that the way in which it reacted to the issues of the time would have the deepest consequences for its neighbours. An account of the war requires therefore that the affairs of India should be followed, that its quarrel with Britain should be recorded, that the degree at different times of its pro-Japanese sentiment should be remarked, and its role in Japanese strategy examined. It demands also an inquiry into the different quality of British imperialism from

Japanese which made the British Empire, even in its decay, by contrast so durable.

*

The major part of India was conquered by Britain between 1757 and 1820. The form of conquest was straightforward military annexation, but of a somewhat unusual kind. The conquest was not premeditated by Britain. A British trading company, the Honourable East India Company, had begun to trade peaceably in India. It was sucked into intervening in the management of Indian affairs by the anarchy which followed the downfall in the eighteenth century of the Moghul empire. Out of its activities, the British government, which had gradually assumed control of the political responsibilities of the company, eventually found itself the master of a great military empire.

The British Raj was unique in having been set up by a people which used no large standing army of its own countrymen for the purpose. Alone among governments which pursued an active imperialist role Britain operated with such a small army of its own that its aims seemed derisory. It was much too small for Britain to have played any notable part on the continent of Europe, and it might have seemed too small to undertake operations on other continents. The empire was won, not by British forces in the main, but by dexterous political manoeuvre, and by the Indian forces who chose to fight on the British side in a situation where there were several claimants for their arms. The East India Company, which was in India for trade, became, to all intents and purposes, one of the native powers between which India was divided; and from being one of these native powers it became gradually the paramount native state. It raised and paid for native armies which won for it territories for which it had to provide an administration: and this, though informed by British concepts, continued in many respects the traditional administration. The predominance of the company was due primarily to the coherent political organization which it imported into India. It was also due, initially, to superior military technique, but when other native powers through foreign advisers imported the technology, it was due to superior discipline and organization.

Those statesmen of the company who had conceived the policy, and saw where it tended, had usually to draw along their reluctant colleagues, who were always saying that a trading company had no right to be considering policies which would thrust upon it unwelcome political responsibilities. Nevertheless the bolder spirits prevailed, and they succeeded in their manoeuvres with startling ease. Thus Britain, which was five thousand miles away, found itself with an empire which it had never, in its deliberate moments, set itself to acquire. It had gained it with the minimum military force; and it held it by the stiffening effect of a garrison of British troops which, in normal circumstances, amounted to no more than 60,000 men. It would have been impossible with such a puny force to have held down a genuine national movement, and to have ruled India by the sword. British government thus rested, in the deepest meaning, upon the consent of the people to be governed. Its continuance depended on the tacit ballot that this government afforded benefits which the majority of the people accepted, either from apathy or from general appreciation of it.

The reason why the British had made such an easy conquest of the country was that for the most part a stubborn defence was never encountered. The country changed hands while the peasantry, from which a popular army would have to be recruited, looked on. This followed an old tradition of India. Observers of the country from earliest historical times had often exclaimed with wonder at the detached attitude of the peasantry, who went on with their agricultural tasks, ignoring a pitched battle of their betters which might be taking place a few hundred yards from them, and on which their destiny depended. Not all the conquests were as easy as this. The East India Company had to fight hard, for instance, against the Marathas and Sikhs, who both had organized military kingdoms of a formidable nature. But even with them, the kingdoms were the armies: once these were defeated the East India Company had no more to do: there was no great popular resistance to wear down. Popular feeling against the foreigner interfering in the political affairs of the country is mainly a product of the twentieth century.

*

In this take-over of India there was no intention on the part of the British to produce a social transformation. As regards forms of society, the British were willing to leave things put. This was in some part due to the fascination and esteem which Indian life, in all its astonishing variety, exercises over the spirits of those who encounter it. It was also due to the realization that any interference with existing customs was likely to cause trouble. For example, the British were at first reluctant to give any countenance to Christian missionaries. Later, with the growth of evangelism in the nineteenth century in England the resistance to missionaries was partly eroded; but the mutiny of 1857, which stemmed from the mistaken belief of Indian soldiers that the British intended to force Christianity upon them, demonstrated the wisdom of non-interference. Thereafter social change was on the whole carefully refrained from. Profound social changes did, in fact, take place, but these were the inevitable result of the impact of a modern, highly industrialized society, such as Britain became, on an archaic, predominantly agrarian one. They were part of a world-wide trend, and not peculiar to the relations of Britain and India.

It was in the sphere of politics and administration that the struggle for sovereignty developed in India, and it was here that interesting forms were evolved. Nearly all the strains of thought in political philosophy in Britain during a century and a half found at one time or another reflection in the institutions of India. At the end of the eighteenth century the main preoccupation was to protect the individual citizen against arbitrary power, and to put government in the shackles of regular procedure controlled by courts. Then for a while the dominant interest was the philosophy of utilitarianism. One Governor General, Lord William Bentinck, was a close disciple of Bentham, and for forty years James Mill, and his son John Stuart Mill, held key positions in the office of the East India Company. Certain questions were endlessly discussed, for instance, the case for direct administration by the British and the case for indirect administration; the duty of the government to promote change, and its duty to shield people against too rapid change; the virtues of control from above and the virtues of self-government; and the discussion resulted in action, or in some cases inaction—for instance, after the mutiny of 1857 there was no extension of direct British rule. Some of the shrewdest minds in Britain, from Victorian times to the late 1930s, found the Indian government more malleable to ideas than society in the West. A philosophically inclined visitor to India towards the end of the nineteenth century said that a trip there was like re-living his life as a student of politics at Oxford.

The civil service in British India became remarkable for its quality. In the kingdoms and empires of the sub-continent in the past, the central governments found it traditionally very hard to get anything done. Their acts might be sporadically vigorous and imaginative, but the sum total of their deeds was slight: it disappeared quickly in sand. The Indian Civil Service, first instituted by the British, and then increasingly operated by both British and Indians, gave India for the first time an instrument by whose means government could carry out reforms which were pushed through to the end. Such was the prestige, the intelligence, and the standard of service to the community of this body of men that, even when the freedom struggle was at its height, distinguished Indian families, including the Nehrus, sent some of their sons into government service while others were operating in the opposition movement. The ideal of the Indian Civil Service was to gain willing acceptance of the policies and actions of the government. To be compelled to use force at all was, therefore, regarded as a mark of failure; and its excessive use was rarely forgiven. This was a reflection of the fact that from the beginning of the Raj the number of Englishmen in India was far too small for them to govern the country arbitrarily and with incessant use of force. In the last years of British rule the British members of the administrative class of the civil service numbered less than a thousand, and in the subordinate services they hardly existed, whereas the population of India by the beginning of the war had swollen to three hundred and fifty million, or one sixth of the population of the world.

Although, through the British period, government was carried on chiefly by the civil service, India was also by stages equipped with free institutions. Because Britain, in the grip of nineteeth-century liberal ideas, knew only one way of being politically constructive, it instinctively introduced into India representative councils and assemblies and the whole apparatus of liberal democracy. At the beginning these councils were largely consultative, but they contained seeds which grew, and which decided that the struggle for freedom in India would take the form of a demand for parliamentary rule.

Constitutional reforms in India were partly a response to, and partly they stimulated the Indian national movement. That the transition from subjection to independence in India came in the end with such remarkable ease and restraint on both sides was due chiefly to three things: the liberal institutions set up in India by the British: the genius of Mahatma Gandhi, for many years the leader of the national freedom movement: and the quickening of a new age in Asia, and new ideas and a new type of British personality in India, as a direct result of the Japanese war.

*

On the Indian side, a vital factor in the struggle for independence was the emergence of a new Indian middle class. This class adopted English as its language, and owed its existence to the mass of institutions which the Raj fostered. Some members of it adapted themselves so phenomenally well to English culture that they became, to all intents and purposes, Englishmen. They lived in English style. They spoke English in their homes. Perhaps there is no comparable case in modern history of a class taking over so completely and with such ease the culture and language of another people: the parallel in the past is the assimilation of Latin culture by the provincials of the Roman Empire. Not that these families lost all touch with India; the women especially carried on the old Indian tradition, and in the deeper layers of the mind, the Indian structure persisted. But in practical action most of the men thought, felt, acted like Englishmen, and made very much the same value judgements. This victory of an alien personality was seen at times as a doubtful advantage to India; its psychological effects were frequently lamented by the social group in which it took place; but in the long run such fusions of culture are prized by the countries in which they occur, provided the assimilation is complete. The most surprising instance of this deep westernization is usually masked. Gandhi, the man under whose leadership the independence of India was achieved, a man who always stressed that he was a Hindu, the heir of the Hindu tradition; who wore Indian clothes, or very few clothes at all in the manner of Indian holy men, was nevertheless profoundly influenced by ideas from Britain. Equality of citizens, non-doctrinaire socialism, his apotheosis of the individual conscience, his social experimentation, prohibition, feminism, nationalism itself—this was the British tradition, not perhaps of government, but of radical non-conformism. Here, it might be said, was an example rare in history, of Rome making Greece its captive, not vice versa.

This westernized Indian middle class, though numerically very small, became immensely important, and in the eyes of the rest of the world, it *was* Indian, spoke for India, represented India. As it matured, it inevitably took to nationalism, and the Indian patriot became the most typical example of the nationalist in his time. He was the most eloquent in denouncing imperialism—often in admirable English prose. He demanded the most fiercely to be liberated. He was the most confident, and with reason, of being able to operate by himself the institutions amongst which he had passed his life. Some years before the First World War, Indian nationalism was already vigorous. At first the nationalists had been divided between revolutionaries and constitutionalists. The revolutionaries, who carried on old Indian traditions of romantic protest, wanted root and branch overthrow of British rule, and terrorism seemed to be their best instrument. By contrast, the constitutionalists did not expect to end British rule by a lightning stroke; but by forming political parties, by entering the representative assemblies, by propaganda, and by accepting and operating the political systems which Britain was setting up, they expected to be able to bring enough pressure on the government to make their voice felt in its decisions. They were buoyed up and encouraged by the support which they received throughout from radicals in Britain. This active lobby in Britain for Indian independence was an important factor in convincing Indian nationalism that constitutionalism would give results. After a time, terrorism lost its glamour, and the majority of nationalists

opted for constitutional action, or only mildly unconstitution-
al action; and, with aberrations at times when crises came
to a head, they remained faithful to this course.

On the British side there were, at times, explosive strains.
There were, occasionally, violent men in the civil service
and in the army, and until the end the danger existed below
the surface that in an emergency they might react brutally.
Once violence had started it would have grown by its own
momentum and both sides might have drifted into open war.
An outrage occurred shortly after the First World War in
the massacre at Amritsar. This town in the Punjab was
the scene of demonstrations in which mobs got control of
the city and martial law was proclaimed in the area. An
Indian assembly convened in defiance of an order, was
caught in a walled space, with inadequate exits, and a British
general, General Dyer, ordered troops to open fire. As a result,
nearly four hundred unarmed people were killed. That this
atrocity should have taken place, and even been approved by
a section of British opinion, was a shock to Indian leaders.
But there were denunciations in London; those in parliament
were led with much force by Winston Churchill. The repudiation by the British government of General Dyer was one of
the factors which strengthened Indian nationalism in its belief that it could win freedom by relatively restrained means.

The chief organ of the freedom movement, the Indian
National Congress, was led during the crucial years by one
of the most extraordinary figures of history, Mahatma
Gandhi. Gandhi's outstanding qualities were a combination
of a peculiar gentleness with inflexible determination: his
religious temperament, natural in an Indian, was allied with
a practical ability, unusual in seers, to shape events to some
extent in the light of his understanding. Gandhi made Indian
nationalism self-confident: he fed it with imaginative ideas
and moral fire. Avoiding the dreary tactics of terrorism and
guerrilla warfare, he perfected the weapons of civil disobedience and non-violent resistance. Some of his methods,
at first, struck his lieutenants in Congress as too ingenuous;
for instance, Gandhi proposed a famous march to the sea, to
defy the law and make salt, on which there was a very light
tax. Congress regarded it as a useless demonstration and
agreed to it only in order to humour him. But it set India

alight, and demonstrated a method of inducing popular up-risings which was to be of first importance to Congress in their later campaigns. He pursued his ends undeviatingly, but discriminated about means: thus, in the greatest of human traditions, he made politics a branch of ethics. The moral reason for all his major decisions was clearly laid in view, and even if a sophisticated onlooker might sometimes think that he deceived himself, and that the moral judgements on which he based himself were sometimes the flexible hand-maids of political experimentation, his concern with principle was authentic, never hypocritical, and it affected those who dealt with him. An English judge, sentencing him on one occasion to a prison term 'for sedition', addressed Gandhi, as he stood before him in the dock, in words which illustrate the effect he had on his political opponents:

It would be impossible to ignore the fact that in the eyes of millions of your countrymen you are a great patriot and a great leader. Even those who differ from you in politics look on you as a man of high ideals and of noble and even saintly life . . .*

The whole character of Indian history in this period is the collusion, unspoken and hardly admitted, between the British power and Gandhi. For thirty years they fought each other, but cooperated tacitly in preventing the fight from getting out of hand. Both acted as if guided by the maxim of Machiavelli that you should treat your enemy as if he may one day become your friend. Because of the phe-nomenon of Gandhi's personality, a momentous struggle for freedom was fought, resolutely on both sides, but with an almost cheerful cordiality on both sides, and in a way which enabled both sides to be reconciled and to cooperate when it was over.

The climax of the struggle before the war was the civil disobedience campaign of Congress of 1930. Civil disobedi-ence covered a variety of activities aimed at bringing govern-ment to a standstill—strikes, boycotts of British goods and services, and especially of foreign cloth, non-payment of

*B. R. Nanda: *Mahatma Gandhi,* Allen & Unwin, 1958.

taxes, and massive demonstrations, which were remarkably non-violent in the main, but on a scale large enough to alarm the authorities. The police arrested prisoners on a large scale: the prisons were overflowing, and special camps had to be organized. By these means the British government in India felt that it had been able to prevent revolution and to maintain its power. But the years 1931–2 marked a watershed. The government realized that although a rebellion had been broken, it could not repeat the operation, and that, if it tried to do so, it would strain too far the allegiance of the Indians among the civil service and the police. The issue from this period was over the timing of the programme for self-government. While some of the diehards among the British were holding back on grounds of prestige, in other quarters in England and in British India there was anxiety on the more reasonable grounds that India was full of centrifugal and communal strains, and too hasty a withdrawal might lead to breakdown of government.

Congress, on the other hand, regarded the Government of India Act of 1935 as insufficient, although they were about to give it a trial. This Act had been thrashed out in a series of monumental deliberations in London, in which Mahatma Gandhi had taken part as the representative of Congress. It provided for parliamentary government and democratically elected Indian Ministers both in the central government at Delhi, and in the provinces. It retained, however, a British authoritarian element in two vital subjects: foreign affairs and defence. The demand of Congress at this time was for full Dominion status.

*

On 3 September 1939 the war began between Britain and Germany, and India was declared by the British government to be also at war. It had no adequate cause of dispute with Germany to justify this declaration, and the Indian leaders said so forcibly. Nehru, it was true, and the more liberal leaders of Congress, shared the sense of outrage at Nazi misdeeds which was experienced by similar leaders in Europe. Nehru, while visiting England in the previous year, had written in the *Manchester Guardian* criticizing the policy of appeasement towards Germany. Gandhi, writing in his own newspaper, *Harijan,* after war broke out, expressed condemnation of Hitler and moral support for Britain and France, although as a pacifist he also condemned the fighting. The more reactionary Indian leaders were indifferent: not that they would have condoned Germany's brutality had they created them: they wrote them off as inventions of British propaganda. But since no attempt had been made to consult Indian opinion through any representative institutions, how, asked the Indians, could there by any sincere talk of a war for democracy when the war was begun in such an undemocratic way? As a result, the Congress Party resigned from the government, withdrew from the eight provincial Ministries which it held, and recorded its extreme disapproval of all the acts of British officialdom.

Yet India did not protest very effectively against the German war. Several divisions of its army fought in the Middle East, gaining battle honours at which even Indian nationalists were, paradoxically, rather proud. In one province of India the war was genuinely popular. This was in the Punjab, which was traditionally the chief recruiting ground for soldiers, and where the provincial government had not considered resigning. The Punjab actively demonstrated in favour of the war, and regarded as enemies those who were lukewarm in its service. Surprisingly accurate knowledge of the ups and downs of war strategy began to circulate in Punjab villages. Elsewhere the war, simply as war, began to appeal to the so-called martial classes. Anything to do with it—news about it, the social and economic changes consequent on it—interested them as trenching on their monopoly in life.

But by the rest of India the war was treated with indifference: with neither the excitement caused by the sense of genuine change in the air, nor with the alarm caused by the knowledge that India was compassed about by real dangers, some of which might soon hit India very hard. The fact that the war was to be enlarged, that a new enemy was at hand by means of whom the war would be transformed, that through no initiative of its own India was to be placed in its vanguard, and that invasion was to be a very near possibility, would jerk it out of its previous apathy. It would go to bed at night and get up in the morning with war at its elbow, instead of viewing it academically at a safe remove. The extension of the war would be the signal for a new phase of the freedom struggle to begin.

II

OCEAN CLASH

9

The War changes its Character

THUS far the war had chiefly concerned China and Japan. Japan was aggressive towards China; considerations of how far this affected Japan's relations with other countries were peripheral. But from this time onwards, Japan's relations with the Great Powers became the prime concern of its government. The war between China and Japan became increasingly difficult to limit to a private war; Japan was faced with problems, rising out of this war, each one of which caused it to consider afresh its policy towards other powers. Sometimes it experimentally remoulded its policies towards them, only to change them again, with all the repercussions which such instability led to. Japan's policies became very uncertain. No settled principles guided its action.

Actually, since the days of the Anglo-Japanese Alliance, Japan had pursued a wavering foreign policy, spreading everywhere a diffuse suspicion. It had no sure base in a firm agreement with a Great Power. But until a late period, it seemed that its special, inexorable opponent was Russia. Suspicion of and hostility towards Russia governed its designs. One product of this attitude of mind had been the signing by Japan of the Anti-Comintern Pact with Germany in 1936. This was an alliance which somewhat nebulously pledged the partners to resist the infiltrations of Communism, and, in a secret clause, bound them to withhold aid from Russia should either party be involved in hostilities with the U S S R.

Since even before Commodore Perry's expedition in 1853, which marked the opening of Japan's modern period of history, there was special meaning in Japan regarding Russia as its hereditary enemy. Russia, as the perpetual threat, had penetrated into the folklore of the people. Ever since the end of the last century, it had regarded Russia as the Great Power against which it was destined to fight for survival. In 1904–5 it had fought the first round; it was convinced that it would have to fight again. When Russia was stricken by the Revolution, Japan seized the chance and took part in the allied intervention against it. For a time it occupied a large part of eastern Siberia. Its army was persuaded finally to withdraw, but as a result relations between the army and the civil government became seriously strained. It was an example of the situation that was often to develop in the future, but this time the civilian government, using one of the anti-imperialist swings in public opinion which at the time alternated with moods of aggressive nationalism, had prevailed in restraint of the military. The army felt that it had been ordered to drop its prey when it had been certain of it, and the sense that the civilian government could not be trusted continued to weigh with it.

After Manchukuo came into being in 1932, Japan stationed there a large part of the Japanese army. This did not disguise the fact that its eyes were on war with Russia; all its training and manoeuvres were made with Russia as the certain adversary. Exchanges between the two countries became increasingly explosive.

In July 1938 Japan deliberately picked a quarrel with Russia in the Far East and systematically set out on the task of trying out the Russian defences to see whether Russia could be made to vacate its forward positions on the frontiers of Manchuria by a show of force. It selected a spot where the frontiers of Korea, the U S S R and China meet. It demanded that Russia should withdraw its forces from the area. In spite of a convincing Russian argument, from a treaty map of 1886, that it was in the region by right, the Japanese attacked with a division and took the hill called Cheng Ku Feng.

The next week Russia replied. The area disputed was visited by General Zhukov, later to be covered with many laurels. He moved up heavy formations and overwhelmed the Japanese in a prolonged pitched battle: and the Japanese for a few months were quiet.

It is an interesting fact, showing in what a desert the war was fought, that this incident, which involved tanks, artillery and aviation, was reported in the British press in a quite inadequate way. Very few people heard that there had been large-scale fighting. All eyes were on Europe: Asia was licensed to be in upheaval, and not to be noticed. Nevertheless, it is surprising that with the probable conduct of the Red Army in war still an enigma, more regard was not paid to its striking success against the Japanese. Russia fought this action under the handicap that its army, especially the officer corps, was under the strain of being visited by Stalin's purge. The Russian commander in the Far East, the celebrated and experienced Marshal Blucher, was one of the victims during this time.

Next year, there was a repetition of these incidents. Japan considered that it was progressing. It was satisfied in part with its exploration of whether Germany was fated to be its sure and certain ally—the successor to Britain. In preparation for this it allowed it to become known that it relied on the Germans to handle Russia. This time the place was Nomonhan, on the Outer Mongolian frontier. In the middle of May the Japanese attacked unexpectedly and drove away the Mongol frontier guards. The Russians issued an official warning that, by virtue of its defence treaty with Mongolia, it would treat any further incidents on the Mongolian frontier as if it were aggression against the Soviet Union.

Japan decided to test whether Russian deeds would match Russian words. In July it sent an expedition of 30,000 men to Nomonhan: artillery, tanks and planes. The Russians replied resolutely. There was fierce fighting for well over a month; a whole division of the Japanese force was annihilated. While the fighting lasted, the Russo-German non-aggression pact, the pact which surprised Europe and was the signal for European war, was announced. This shocked Japan. It was regarded by Japan as a betrayal of its experimental advances with the tighter links with Germany, the more audacious disregard of Britain and the United States. Its immediate effect was to bring back to positions of influence in Japan the representatives of the more old-fashioned groups which looked back with nostalgia to the old days of the Anglo-Japanese Alliance, and who felt that no confidence was to be placed in new friends. There was a tendency to walk more cautiously for a period. Partly because of this, Japan was willing to wind up the Nomonhan incident, even though it was by an agreement which was interpreted by all concerned as a Japanese concession of a reverse. Moreover, it became known that Japan was feeling shock and anger at the lack of reliance it could place on its new friend, Germany.

There was no more fighting. The frontier gradually fell quiet. Even the small-scale incidents, the constant shooting and skirmishes, the espionage and incitements, which had from the start seemed natural to the relationship between these two powers, dwindled. There was plenty of rumour, and the outbreak of war on the frontier was still regarded as a very natural possibility by the Japanese. The psychology had not changed: Japan remained malevolent towards Russia. Russia was still regarded, with deadly cold hostility, as a national enemy, in a way in which China, even at the height of the war between the two governments, was not. But it became clear that in one way Japan had changed its behaviour. Unless it was attacked in Manchuria, it was content to do no attacking.

An unnatural peace slowly spread throughout the border. In this region not a shot was fired, while, in other parts of the world, fighting broke out with great savageness.

*

The key to Japan's policy was still the Sino-Japanese war. With this overwhelmingly in mind, it approached the matter of its relations with the western countries in the war which was beginning in Europe.

When the Japanese found that Chungking would not make peace with them, they became convinced that it was enabled to continue fighting, and was encouraged to keep up a hopeless resistance, because of the aid given to it by the western powers. In fact, China was complaining desperately because of the shortage of war supplies. The aid that it received was a trickle, which the Japanese greatly exaggerated. They became convinced, however, that only the severance of the link with outside powers would bring an end to the China adventure. The war was telling upon the Japanese, and most groups were anxious to be free of it. Some of them had begun to think that it had been too lightly embarked on.

The outbreak of the war in Europe in 1939 seemed to give Japan its opportunity to bring pressure to bear upon the countries which persisted in maintaining relations with China. Japan, on the world stage, found itself in much the same position as it had been in the war of 1914–18. The direction which it might take had suddenly magnified its value very greatly. For Britain especially, whether it remained strictly neutral or sided with the Axis powers was a life or death matter. Japan saw that a new bargaining opportunity had opened up. There was an unfamiliar flexibility in its international relations. Out of the international situation, by blackmail or cajolery, Japan could expect to bend the attitude of other powers in such a way as to tilt the whole of the Far East under firm Japanese hegemony.

Already from 1938 Japan, partly under the impetus of patriotic parties which increasingly dictated its policies, partly because of the weakening position of its rivals in the Far East, drifted into a steady widening of its powers in the region. The stage was being set for its collision with the U S. It became convinced that it was practicable to clear the Far East of American influences. The United States, while avoiding aggressiveness, had no intention of vacating.

First, however, Japan sought to apply its growing power to complete the isolation of China, and thus to compel it to bring the Sino-Japanese war to an end. Japan's force had, as immediate object, the task of cutting off the links which enabled China, though beaten in the field, to refuse peace.

Chiang Kai-shek, in his retreat to Szechuan, had two lifelines to the West. There was a road through north-west China, occupied by the Chinese communists, down which there filtered a little oil from Russia, and some Soviet personnel. But it was clear to anyone who was at Chungking at this time that the channels of communication which were most valued were those with the Anglo-Saxon powers. It was on these—first on a railway through Indo-China which had its outlet at Hanoi, and later after it was wrecked by bombing, on an earth road through Burma, and still later on an air lift from Calcutta direct to Chungking—that Kuomintang eyes were riveted. The Japanese were right in supposing that as long as these remained open China would feel that it was not cut off from support from the West. However little was flowing at the moment, as long as the communication remained open, the hope endured that more might be made to flow. Especially if they put their trust in a turn in events making it appear more a matter of material interest to the West that they should put out aid to China. But always the hinge of China's fate depended on these communications remaining open. Always Japan saw the most immediate way to force an end to the war lay in interrupting these tenuous lines of communication.

The outbreak of war in Europe in 1939 gave Japan its opportunity. In the middle of 1940, after the fall of France, when Britain was in its most desperate condition, it demanded that Britain should close the Burma road. Britain was in no condition to refuse. Churchill demurred but in the end gave way. But he agreed only for a three months period, at the end of which the aid again flowed, though in minute quantity. It was enough to give China hope.

*

Japan came increasingly to collide with the other Anglo-Saxon power, the United States. The clash with the United States, which at first had seemed a passing incident of its China policy, swelled up until it came to dominate all Japan's foreign relations. The need to free itself from American pressure in its plans for the future of the Far East became an obsession with Japan.

Japanese relations with the United States had been worsening for years. They had taken a steady decline from the days of the Russo-Japanese war, at which time the United States had been very sympathetic towards Japan, and relations had been cordial. In those distant days the United States had the characteristic of not basing its sentiments in foreign relations so solidly on self-interest as did the other Great Powers. It gave more play to national feelings in favouring and disfavouring countries. America was temperamentally drawn to the underdog; Japan seemed to be a small Goliath.

Afterwards the relations became less good as Japan became a great naval power and a threat to the American domination of the Pacific. Simultaneously, the American policy in 1924, forbidding emigration to the United States, which it pursued with the maximum resolution and the minimum regard to sparing Japan's feelings, made Japan reconsider its sentiments towards the U S. To Japan the United States was the insensitive Great Power, blocking Japan's progress, and exhibiting a dynamism which propelled them both towards an inevitable collision.

When the Manchurian affair happened, the United States quickly disclosed a policy which it was to follow with remarkable consistency. It would have nothing to do with the League of Nations or with collective attempts at restraining Japan as an aggressor. That was ruled out by the overwhelming strength of American isolationism. American opinion was behind isolation as the only way of preserving the United States from involvement in war: and it recognized that in isolating itself, it was cutting itself off from the possibility of influencing the course of world affairs. Many enlightened Americans chafed at this. But it was accepted by most realist Americans that the United States had no alternative in the state to which it had been brought by the many-sided propaganda to which it was subjected.

The United States was unwilling to draw the conclusion from its inactivity that it would acquiesce in the map of the world being redrawn by force. It declared that it would never recognize changes which were brought about by aggression. There was, it must be admitted, something slightly ridiculous in the spectacle of the United States refusing to recognize the facts brought about by war, but declining to do anything to prevent these changes. It was living in a fool's paradise. But the policy was calculated to bear fruit in the future: as in fact it did. By persistently refusing to recognize Japan's coups in defiance of international law, by obstinately declining to regard Japan as ever succeeding in closing a door, by leaving open every issue for regulation in the future, the United States managed to undermine, with surprising success, Japan's various steps at building its empire.

The United States, however, was peculiarly self-distrustful. It had had, in the First World War, the experience of being drawn into the fighting partly, as it decided afterwards, against its better judgement. Probably, when the war was over, a majority of the people, if their opinion had been tested in a plebiscite, would have opined that the war was a mistake. If they had had a second chance, they would have kept out. They believed that America had been over-persuaded by subtle propaganda. They were intent on warning their fellow countrymen to beware of all plots to make them go further than they meant.

So, when the second war broke out, most Americans, though their sympathies were for the most part engaged against Hitler and his supporters, were firmly against American participation in the war. They were bent on saving the United States from itself. Just because they wished for Hitler's defeat, they were suspicious that the United States would come under pressure to depart from its neutrality: they therefore sought to provide against American force being employed in his overthrow, and that the United States should not be officially engaged in war. They went to extraordinary lengths in devising laws which would tie up the American executive, and prevent it from drifting into war. Of the fetters by which the United States bound itself, the most remarkable was the Neutrality Act: a law which aimed at prohibiting the United States from engaging in commerce with either of the belligerents which might involve the country in warlike attitudes. The Neutrality Act had been passed by the U S Congress in the teeth of opposition by the administration. It was made possible by the American constitution, which sharply divides the legislature from the executive.

Because of this resolution to maintain the peace, because of the peculiar institutions by which the American resolve was enforced, Japan was to a large extent protected from the consequences of its actions. The Neutrality Act was a product of the fear of war with Germany, but Japan derived the benefit of it. There had never before in world history been such a peculiar case of a Great Power deliberately tying itself up, and ensuring that in no circumstances should it act as it would have been natural for it to do. The consequences, the way that the United States responded to pressure from Japan were curious. True, it was possible for the American government to thwart in various ways the intentions of the American Congress, but the laws were rigid, and there were limits to the degree to which they could be transgressed.

All the time, some powerful American personalities and groups were warning the country that Japan on the march was a threat to the security of the United States. Each Japanese thrust—the rape of Manchuria, the rupture with the League of Nations, the war with China which had set in in earnest in 1937, the blowing of the wind in Japan of a revolutionary assertiveness—caused the warning to be louder. American opinion became troubled. It had reacted with little force to the beginning of the crisis in 1931 when Japan had seized Manchuria; ten years later, Japan's moves were followed with tense interest by many people in the United States. At first the concern over Japan was largely regional, being found especially on the West coast, which had trading connections with Asia. Gradually it became more widespread.

Fortifying this group of people who would have liked the United States to take an active role in Asia was the China lobby. This became for some years an influential pressure group in American politics. The active and practical minded found themselves in an open conspiracy for bringing pressure to bear in Congress upon all matters in which Chinese interests were engaged. The curious thing was that in the United States this group was so intent, and generated so much emotion. Other countries, Britain for example, had had sectional groups which, by the accident of their history, had been equally exposed to the lure of Chinese civilization, a force which habitually proved attractive to minds of a certain type. But a Chinese lobby, in the sense in which it was known in the United States, never operated in British politics.

Japan probably failed to give due weight to the importance of the China lobby in the United States. It always mistook American politics: that was one of its features. Japan had, it is true, some experts on the U S who were well-informed: but they were not attended to. The Japanese, especially those who made Japanese policies, believed, and acted on the principle, that the United States, whose soul was given up to commerce, could not prevail over a nation of Samurai warriors, whatever material advantages it seemed to possess. They misread American history. They took no account of the fact that, after the compromises and the prevarication of the democratic system, the United States had shown itself able to go to war, and to wage it with an obsessive stubbornness until its objects were achieved.

*

From September 1940 to July 1941 Matsuoka Yosuke was the Foreign Minister of Japan. It was a critical period in Japan's foreign relations; and he was a new and unusual man to handle them. He came from a different background from those who were normally appointed to that office. He had made his reputation as a business executive, working for the South Manchuria Railway. By temperament he was rather like the type of man who, in an earlier generation, had made the Meiji Restoration. He was abrupt, conceited, gauche, and impatient of the respect for old men which Japanese civilization, being partly Confucian, has usually shown. He was exaggeratedly westernized, or at least he had adopted wholeheartedly the characteristics which he thought to be the essence of western culture. At the same time, he was exaggeratedly xenophobic, and opposed the United States and Britain to the limit.

He began by negotiating Japan's adhesion to a Triple Alliance with Germany and Italy. The treaty, which was signed in September 1940, was subtly conceived. It was primarily directed against the United States: it was intended chiefly to immobilize the United States and to deter it from too active intervention in the Far East and in Germany's wars in Europe. It stipulated that if any power—and the United States was particularly intended—attacked one of the three signatories, or should, by giving economic aid, threaten to affect adversely to them the conflict then taking place, the other two should come to its aid. The United States rightly interpreted this as an attempt to put fetters upon its freedom of action, and a Japanese withdrawal from the pact became one of its demands upon Japan. The pact was aggressive: but on the whole, it could be regarded as operating to prevent the spread of war.

Matsuoka conducted his foreign policy on the principle of *sacro egoismo*. In the spring of 1941, filled with this spirit, he made a tour of Russia and Germany. Before he went he had been in favour of committing Japan up to the hilt for

Germany, giving it his warm support and leading it to suppose that it would have Japan's military backing if it attacked Russia. He was convinced that Germany was the winning power, and that only by being among Germany's associates would Japan gain in the eventual share-out of the world at a peace settlement. He was restlessly aware that Japan could pluck great profit from the disorders of the world, and he feared that if it sat still it might fail to gain them. The world would have shaken itself to pieces—to no avail, if Japan did not set itself to win advantage from the outcome.

In his travels, however, his natural cynicism found the cynicism of Stalin irresistibly congenial. Conversation with him left Matsuoka convinced that Stalin was the wily man who would sit by Hitler's grave, and was the statesman whose combinations of policy were the most impressive to be met. The meetings of Matsuoka and Stalin were specially fateful. They resulted in a genuine change in policy by Japan, one of the Great Powers of the world. Matsuoka, behind his front of self-assurance, proved more volatile than is usually the case with Foreign Ministers; and he was able to communicate his erratic intentions to the Japanese state. So impressed was Matsuoka with what he deemed to be Stalin's superior power that he proposed that Japan and Russia should sign a Non-Aggression Treaty. Stalin, who was already alarmed over the German intentions towards himself, and would in the coming days find Japanese neutrality a pearl beyond price, was much gratified, and closed with the offer at once.

Stalin played on the rather crude imagination of this brash man. When Matsuoka left Moscow, he surprised everyone by coming to the railway station to take farewell of him. Stalin hugged him, and used a phrase about their both being Asian which was taken to mean that, as a result of the western countries' suicide in the war, the future hegemony, at least in Asia, belonged to Japan and Russia.

The non-aggression pact of Japan and Russia caused surprise. It was one of the sensational events of the war. The Japanese government, confronted with this astonishing decision of its Foreign Minister, had to take stock of the new position. Events—the dying down of tension on the Russo-Japanese border—had, it is true, been running in this direction; but it was a different matter for the Japanese government to recognize that its antagonism to Russia, the most cherished and traditional part of its foreign policy, should be formally suspended.

There are in existence the minutes of the Liaison Conferences and the Imperial Conferences held during 1941, at which the new situation was exhaustively debated. These conferences were a unique feature of the Japanese constitution. The Japanese government had been so much split up, particularly the Service Ministries which had been freed from civilian control, that special conferences were needed to achieve any kind of unity. The Liaison Conference became the centre at which the vital decisions of policy were made: there were present the Prime Minister, the Foreign Minister, the Service Ministers and the Chief of Staff. The Imperial Conference, which was held more rarely, was a meeting of the Liaison Conference together with the Emperor and the President of the Privy Council who acted as a spokesman: it was held when especially momentous decisions were being placed on record.

The notes of these meetings during 1941 are fascinating to read. They show the bewilderment of high Japanese officials at Matsuoka's radical new policy—which was the virtual designation of Japan's hereditary enemy, Russia, as the successor of Britain as the traditional friend of Japan. They show their constant bewilderment in the kaleidoscope of the contemporary world, always casting round for a dependable ally, always disappointed in their search. They reveal their experimentalism, which is very Japanese. The discussions took place under the urgent sense that at the time the world map was being re-made, and that a golden opportunity had arisen for Japan to share in the general loot—an opportunity which Japan, by its ineptitude, might lose.

The sense is conveyed that the Japanese have got out of their depth. Here are generals, admirals and high diplomats ruthlessly planning how to further Japan's interests at the expense of the rest of the world: and, though later it was to be found that this ruthlessness could bear heavy consequences, their deliberations seem oddly light-weight.

For the immediate period, the main preoccupation of the Japanese government was to get rid of Matsuoka. Clearly they felt an embarrassment in this colleague, who spoke with such an unaccustomed and uncomfortable directness, not taking advantage of the ambiguities and vagueness of the Japanese language. The Japanese are accustomed to convey their meaning by indirect hints and innuendoes, and the whole of life is in consequence strangely inexact, as if the Japanese did not dare to face the truth. In the case of Matsuoka, the Japanese dignitaries, already thinking of an enterprise which was so audacious that they hardly dared acknowledge it, were constantly embarrassed by a Foreign Minister who called a spade a spade. In the end, to get rid of him, the Prime Minister Prince Konoye, and the whole cabinet, had to resign; and it was thus reformed without him, but with a Foreign Minister who spoke the diplomatic language, and rescued his colleagues from contemplating too directly the stark realities of the world as it was being made by their policy.

*

By the summer of 1941, opinion in Japan had veered round to the view that Japan should strike south. To the south lay the vastly rich resources of oil, tin, rubber, and other valuable commodities. This was the area of colonies: British, Dutch, French and American. If it seized them, Japan could hope for three results. First, it would make itself free from the economic pressure of the western countries, which had the temerity to threaten it with economic sanctions in an effort to control Japanese expansion. Second, by making deadly war on these powers, it would finally crush the hopes of Chungking and make it sue for peace. And lastly, out of the defeat of these western adversaries, it would build up a great Japanese empire overseas, which would be the principal monument of the war. It would not have to take account of the feeling of its allies in Europe.

The birth of these new conceptions was guided by the plan being presented, not as a military operation or crude imperialist activity, but as being a beneficent, world-regenerating liberating empire in the East which was to be called 'The Greater East Asia Co-Prosperity Sphere'. It was to be a great enterprise, summoning under the Japanese flag the people of South-East Asia and of China, in which justice would reign and the needs of each would be promoted by what was done for the whole. The pride of Japan, the welfare of the world, would be satisfied in equal measure. The mixture of moral ideas reinforced by a popular Confucianism, with a dash of Buddhism and of hard-headed military strategy, made a powerful appeal to the Japanese mood of the hour.

These ideas had been for some time in parturition. As early as 1938 Prince Konoye had proclaimed solemnly that the aim of the Sino-Japanese war was not to conquer China but to win its cooperation. Looking at East Asia, seeing it threatened by communism, he said that Japan hankered after a 'new era' in the territory: an order marked by harmony, universal cooperation, and, it was taken for granted, by the benevolent, orderly presence of Japan. Individualism, materialism, the power struggle, everything to do with Communism, were to be ruled out.

The ideas fructified in the next years: and came to apply to a steadily widening territory. The 'New Order' was enlarged into the 'Greater East Asia Co-Prosperity Sphere'. In this the countries of Asia should be governed by what were thought of as essentially the ideas of Eastern civilization. This meant an end to the long night in Asia during which western ideas had prevailed. It meant that an end would be put especially to everything which favoured American ideas and the American business presence. East Asia would in future be under Japanese hegemony; and everyone who accepted the New Order accepted this. It was marked by a recognition of the arrangements which Japan had organized, such as the state of Manchukuo, and the special zone of close Sino-Japanese collaboration.

One of the fascinating things learnt about the war by inquiries afterwards is the butterfly-mindedness of many of the imperialists in Tokyo. They were not dogged, implacable men, tied down to a single idea. They were resilient and receptive. Contrary to the general opinion, they did not make their plans far ahead, and they were not unwilling to shift their enterprises and to change the details. So, in 1941, there took place the great movement which determined the course of the war: the shift of mental concentration from a land campaign against Russia, with armies locked together to see which would prevail, to a sea strategy, a joint operation of army and navy, which should have as its object the putting of western imperialism to its death, and which would be directed against the Anglo-Saxon powers, not against Russia.

In 1941 the decision was not taken: what had happened was that the willingness had appeared to take a decision when a great crisis should happen. A great mental revolution was lived through. New possibilities were envisaged and welcomed. For the present, Japan would press on as before.

The Japanese people responded to this policy. Quite honestly and sincerely, they saw themselves, in opposing western activity in Asia, as fighting a battle against imperialism. Sincerely they believed the Japanese government was altruistic, and that the Asian people, who objected to being saved by Japan, were simply misguided. There was little need for propaganda to prepare Japan for the war which Japan was risking with the United States. If ever a people has gone to war thinking it a just war, if ever a war has been thoroughly popular, so it was to be in 1941. There was little trace of an elaborate misleading of the people.

The first territory which Japan was tempted to bring in to the Co-Prosperity Sphere was Indo-China. Its government had been left helpless by the collapse of France. The only power to which it could have looked for aid was Britain, but Britain, especially since Dakar, had become the enemy of France. Thailand was incited to present ultimatums. Throughout 1940 and 1941 Japan was able to extract larger and larger concessions for not swallowing it up entirely. In 1941 it had reduced the northern part of Indo-China to a protectorate; Japanese garrisons were admitted to the key areas; they occupied the centres from which they could strike at Malaya and the Philippines.

*

Japan pressed on with this new policy regardless of the fact that on 22 June 1941 the war started between Russia and Germany. The German attack on Russia certainly did not take Japan completely by surprise; but Germany, in this as in several other matters of great consequence to Japan, acted without any consultation with the country which, since it had signed the German-Japanese anti-Communism pact in 1936 and the Tripartite pact of September 1940, was formally its ally. Seldom had an alliance been operated by a country with quite such painful, humiliating lack of confidential deliberation.

Germany now began to press Japan to throw in its forces against Russia. It had previously indicated to Japanese diplomats, in boastful language, that should it at any time attack the U S S R, the campaign would be largely a police operation since Russian resistance would be swiftly overcome. The Japanese government was inclined now to wait and see. The Kwantung Army, bogged down in China, was not in a mood to venture further afield without the prospect of specific advantage in the overriding aim of bringing China to its knees. Moreover, the pull of the Asian Co-Prosperity Sphere was now being strongly felt. Japan the imperialist, among the other imperialist nations of the world, had suffered mortifying checks. In south Asia now seemed to lie its opportunity and its natural sphere.

10

The Negotiation preceding War

IN December 1940, the American government, disturbed by
the increasingly belligerent tone of the Japanese, had imposed an embargo on the sale of scrap iron and war materials to Japan. Hitherto it had put no hindrance in the way
of trade with Japan, and China was able to argue, with
reason, that Japan's operations, in the first three years of
its warfare, had been made possible economically because
of United States' policy. The American government took
advantage of the rising temper of the U S to act resolutely,
but it still had to move cautiously. Its action was an attempt
to halt Japan's military activity against China.

A new way of conducting diplomacy was being tried out:
the method of using economic pressure to effect political
ends. Ever since the covenant of the League of Nations was
drafted, the efficiency of ecnonomic sanctions had been in
dispute. They were tried out against Italy, unsuccessfully,
and deliberately with so many imperfections that they were
bound to fail (because that was the intention of some of the
Great Powers which had been coerced by pressure of their
electorates into taking part in the operation) at the Abys-
sinian crisis. But, as enforced against Japan, in the peculiar
conditions of the time, they had an indisputable effect. They
suggested to President Roosevelt the line of government
action which, because of the caution of public opinion, he
would not have dared to propose that America should take
by more political means.

In July 1941 the Japanese extended their political control

of Indo-China from the north to the south. Their motive was plain: the places Japan had demanded to occupy were those which the military experts regarded as essential for an operation to reduce South-East Asia. Japan had seized the opportunity of the desperate situation of the French in Indo-China, and of the inability of France, following its collapse, to give the local French government any decisive aid. The American press digested the facts, debated them, and had seen that the damage, which might or must result, to the security of the United States, was put before the American public. Even now the American will to peace, and the concern over its neutrality sentiment, remained strong. Its propagandists continued to warn that the United States was being led along the path to war by appeal to fear and sympathy. Many of them feared that the United States was being led by the back door of war with Japan into the war which they feared and opposed: war with Germany. In spite of the alarm which they expressed, President Roosevelt responded firmly in the crisis over Indo-China. He tightened very greatly the economic war which he had begun against Japan. He froze Japanese assets. He proclaimed what amounted to an embargo on Japanese trade in oil and steel.

This was a vital stage in the development of the crisis. The American government had suddenly stiffened its policy. It did so to the surprise of many of the parties concerned, including the Japanese. It had moved somewhat in advance of the change in the mood of the country. It had taken steps which it knew to be desperately inimical to Japan.

The effects on Japan were immediate. It was especially susceptible to pressure from the oil sanctions. Japan had stored enough oil for two years of war. Denied the opportunity of replenishing it from the U S, it had to recognize in the circumstances of the time that it could not gain oil from alternative sources of supply. The U S was immediately followed in its embargo by the British Empire and the Dutch in Indonesia: and Japan discovered that there was no possibility of driving a wedge between them. Each month brought the prospect of the exhaustion of its supplies that much nearer. It knew that its aggressive policies, Japan itself, must wither away when the time limit arrived—because the vital fluid which sustained them would no longer flow.

The United States during these months was in an extraordinary state. Roosevelt steered it resolutely on a course which must result in war. But he did not make the decision publicly: and the majority of the American public, though more deeply stirred by Japan than in previous years, still wanted peace, not war. A certain amount of the exchange of view with Japan was behind the scenes: but much of it leaked to the public. In the last period before the final catastrophe American feeling had moved towards greater caution, so that an impartial observer, if he believed that the great decisions followed the popular will, would have said that the chances of the United States going to war were lessening, not increasing. But the country had the sense that it was in the grip of uncontrollable necessity. Like a sleepwalker, it moved towards war.

The President, though he believed that war was inevitable, was willing to test the possibility of curbing Japanese expansion without fighting: he would have abandoned larger projects if he could have gained acceptable guarantees of a reversal of Japan's policies in China and Asia generally. The outcome of American economic pressure was not certain. The United States might indeed have forced Japan into belligerent action, but war against the British in Malaya and the Dutch in the Netherlands East Indies, and not against the United States itself. The American administration could have been helpless before the Neutrality Act, and have had to stand by while its allies in South-East Asia went down before Japanese attack.

When Japan proposed a final exertion to come to terms which would make war unnecessary, Roosevelt, and his closest advisers, entered with some hopefulness on negotiations. They did so with the more readiness because they knew (and nobody else knew) that they had the great advantage of seeing into the mind of their adversary. The United States had got possession of the Japanese cipher (one of the most notable feats of code-breaking in history), and during these weeks no communication passed between the Japanese Embassy in Washington and its home base in Tokyo, but the U S government was aware of it. The putting of the Japanese war machine into readiness, its dispatch into action, all took place under the eyes of the American government, which knew that it was provoking Japan unendurably.

Unhappily, so highly did the Americans value this means of overhearing the conversation of its adversaries, so resolute was it to defend the secrecy of its knowledge, that the circulation of this intelligence was rigidly circumscribed. Extremely few men were privy to it—President Roosevelt, the Secretary of State, the Secretary for War, and General Marshall—and these, to guard the secrecy, read the messages and destroyed them on the spot within sight of the bearer. Whether full advantage was taken of this unique knowledge is questionable. Possibly the intense precautions to guard security prevented it from being properly digested, and opportunities may have been missed.

In these negotiations, the United States rightly perceived that the interests of friendly powers with Far-Eastern involvements were engaged. It informed Britain in particular step by step of their progress. Churchill, for his part, offered no resistance. Churchill, indeed, was less than clear-sighted about Japan. He tended to discount the conviction at Washington that war was imminent. Down to the last he believed that Japan would probably back down. It must be said that the war surprised him.

*

The vital negotiations were started through the initiative of some gifted amateurs of diplomacy, the clerics of the Catholic mission in the Far East known as the Maryknoll Fathers. Their intervention is an interesting story. On the one side they misunderstood and immensely over-simplified the complexity of the issues dividing Japan and the U S. They viewed the imminence of war with horror, and were convinced that, by taking diplomacy out of its accustomed rut, they could give men of goodwill on both sides the opportunity to turn their natural benevolence to useful account. In their opinion, in the new atmosphere which they tried to generate, matters which had appeared as great obstacles, matters which had in them the seed of war, would be found unexpectedly tractable and would shrivel away.

On the other side, their over-simplification of the issues, which they minimized for lack of adequate appreciation of them, led in the long run to increased confusion, and had the effect of making agreement harder to reach. They roused hopes in both sides by representing the exact nature of the demands to be other than what they were. Thus they roused the hopes, and stirred up the expectations of a settlement which was found impossible when the exact terms of the other side were clarified. The possibility of an accord receded. It left disillusionment, and made the situation seem more hopeless than before.

The contribution which amateurs can make in complicated dealings between Great Powers is always apt to run into this difficulty. The work of experts is written off, and it is assumed that the fresh approach by fresh minds is likely to succeed: in the end it is found that the expert has a dreary and hard truth on his side. In the present case, the Maryknoll Fathers undoubtedly for a time raised hope in certain quarters in the U S, and in Japan also, of being able to draft a kind of Monroe Doctrine for the Far East which would be acceptable to those circles in the United States which were anxious before all to secure peace. Determined men in Japan seized on this, and translated it into a draft agreement between the two powers, which they sought constantly to put forward as the basis of negotiation. But their draft treaty revealed the insubstantial basis on which they proceeded. They would have been better advised to realize that in seeking an agreement of this kind they were bashing their heads against a stone wall.

The enterprise of the Maryknoll Fathers was a little like that of Swedish philanthropic interlopers who tried to come between Germany and the West in the years before the European war. They were prompted by goodwill: but their initiative did not achieve much.

*

The Maryknoll negotiations led on to official negotiations which began in July 1941. By November they reached their climax.

Japan had begun them out of desperation, but it hoped little from them. The sanctions were pressing hard. It is true that there were powerful influences in Japanese government circles which dreaded war, which were opposed to all the tendencies which Japanese foreign policy had given rise to, and which snatched at Japan's peril to recommend that safety lay in retreat: these men were quite sincere in wanting a rapprochement with the United States. But Japanese foreign policy was made now chiefly by generals and admirals, many of whom had come to the conclusion that war was the only policy which offered hope. They were being egged on by their exchanges of view with Germany, which in these months was urgent that they should embarrass Britain by attacking Singapore, and which supplied all kinds of information about how easy they might find this adventure to be. They judged that sooner or later war would be inevitable, and that Japan stood a better chance by having the war then rather than later.

By November, the United States was satisfied that general talks were fruitless. The negotiations had been interrupted by a government crisis in Tokyo: the resignation of the essentially moderate Prince Konoye, the Prime Minister, and his replacement by General Tojo Hideki. He was a military man, not in the highest position of control of the army, but a product of fashion. He had no special political ideas or standing, but represented in general the military ideas: contempt for the United States, willingness to take extreme risks, ignorance of the politics of the world. The government was negotiating, but had decided on war in principle; it was, however, ready to see whether anything would be offered by the United States which would make war unnecessary. Twice a deadline for a breakdown of the negotiations had been fixed, and later postponed. The absolute decision had been made, but, until the end, the fleet, which was to deliver the first blow, had been ordered to leave room for calling off its operations, so that it could return to Japan with peace preserved.

The government of the United States, though prepared for war, still manoeuvring for peace, decided to offer Japan a final bargain. The oil and steel embargoes, which threatened to cut its freedom of action, were to be lifted: in return, Japan would need to give territorial guarantees. But what? Over this there was a great deal of debate: and the United States consulted its friends abroad.

The first attitude was to let Japan down lightly. Withdrawal from Indo-China would suffice. It was hoped that this would lead on to a general withdrawal from the Asian mainland: but this was not to be rushed, and was not to be included in the immediate terms.

But here came in the China lobby. Chiang Kai-shek had been informed of what was to be offered. He was indignant: he reported it as unlikely that China would be able to continue to fight Japan. He telegraphed London, and, as unlikely partner, he enlisted Churchill in representations. All the China lobby was turned on to the President and Cordell Hull, the Secretary of State. In the result they stiffened the terms, and called on the Japanese to evacuate not only Indo-China, but all China as well, including Manchuria. In return for this the United States would rescind its oil embargo.

In the negotiations Cordell Hull took a stiffer line than Roosevelt. The President had been willing to accept an invitation from the Japanese Prime Minister, Prince Konoye, while he was still in power, to negotiate personally: Cordell Hull intervened, and stopped this. Konoye had gone so far as to propose that the two leaders should make a preliminary temporary pact under which Japan would agree not to make war on the U S even if American activities led to war with Germany in the Atlantic Ocean. This meant that Japan would repudiate its Tripartite Alliance with Germany and Italy. The gist of that was to deter the United States from intervention in the German war by the threat of collision with Japan. Apparently Cordell Hull felt that Konoye had been offering an engagement which he would not be permitted to fulfil.

President Roosevelt made a final attempt at peace by appealing over the heads of politicians to the Japanese Emperor, but this action, though it was seriously meant, was misunderstood and resented in Japan.

On 7 December Japan sent a note which recognized that the negotiations had failed. By the time it was delivered, the consequences of the recognition were also clear: the Japanese were bombarding Pearl Harbor, which they had decided to do if the negotiations ended in deadlock. It is interesting to find that General Marshall, when the reports of the bombardment were first given to him, said incredulously that they must be mistaken: Japan would have bombarded Singapore, not American territory. This is perhaps a measure of the failure of the Japanese to wring final advantage out of the United States' preoccupation with remaining neutral.

11

The Bombardment of Pearl Harbor

JAPAN, goaded into decisive action, was unleashing against
the world its other major force, its navy. Hitherto Japan's
army had been the agent of Japan's dynamism: it was the
army which Japan's neighbours feared, and it was the influence of the army upon the Japanese government that kept
the world in anxiety. The navy, which by tradition was pre-
ponderantly officered by men whose Samurai origin lay in
clans different from those which were powerful in the army,
was highly conspiratorial: it had tended to deplore the rash-
ness of the army, and to favour much more cautious policies.
It was conservative: it did not feel the same desire to intervene over the whole range of government: it had less
connection, though it had some, with patriotic societies. In
the navy, the old feeling in favour of the Anglo-Japanese Alliance lingered on, and there was a nostalgic sentiment in
favour of the older basis of Japan's foreign policy.

But the navy, like all other institutions in Japan, was
divided by factions. One faction had been captivated by the
vision of the economic adventure in the South Seas, and
by the empire which it felt lay open for Japan, open to the
touch of the Japanese fleet. This section began to think of
the war with the British Empire, which it would have to overthrow, as inevitable. It thought, too, that a collision with the
United States was certain, for the U S also was likely to block
Japanese expansion in this direction. The navy, or this section of it, gradually came to regard the Anglo-Saxon powers

as the inevitable enemy, against whom war was to be prepared.

This faction identified itself in the vital years with the 'Go South' movement. It naturally saw in this an opportunity to reinstate itself with the army in the public esteem, and to clip the army's wings as the instrument of expansion *par excellence*. The prevailing war, an army-inspired war, between Japan and China, would be transformed and eclipsed by being converted into a predominantly naval war, fought by different instruments, by the navy chiefly instead of the land forces, and with the adversary changed. The war would be in a different terrain, would involve huge distances, vast oceans, distant islands—in all of which, the navy, and not the army, would shine.

In calling into action the second of the great weapons of Imperial Japan, the Japanese government was employing an instrument which had been untested for thirty-five years. The Japanese navy had won its greatest triumph as long ago as 1905, and had, since then, not fought a serious action. As long as the Washington Naval Limitation Treaty had been in force, the West had been able to inform itself of Japanese naval construction: and Britain, making use of old ties, had kept abreast of Japanese naval thinking. But the link had been severed in 1935: the American and British navies felt themselves incompetent at assembling information about interesting new developments in Japanese naval construction: in 1941, it was a matter of speculation how the Japanese navy would fare if pitted against those of the other Great Powers. A great spurt in construction of big ships had taken place at the end of the 1930s.

In the twenties and early thirties, while contact lasted, the Japanese navy had maintained a large battle fleet. It possessed ten large battleships: it was known to have built four more subsequently, though the West was without knowledge of their details. In addition the navy, from the beginning of the 1920s, had been interested in the air, and had built aircraft carriers. This was the specialty, not of the navy as a whole, but of a clique in it, whose most forceful member was a Japanese naval officer, Yamamoto Isoroku, who early on had been attracted by theories of air power. He was openly sceptical about the usefulness of battleships: he thought their value was chiefly prestige, and he compared them to the ancestral scrolls which were hung upon the wall of Japanese houses, proving the piety of their upkeep but not able to guarantee much to the present prosperity of the family.

Yamamoto had, however, a very difficult time in propagating his views. Most Japanese admirals regarded his insistence on air power much as British military officers regarded the use of the machine gun before the First World War. Some made it a point of honour never to fly in an aeroplane themselves, and to discourage flying by their officers. Yamamoto got his way, largely by becoming commandant of a naval school, which trained a considerable number of naval pilots: they were to be the heroes of the coming war. By a characteristically Japanese compromise Yamamoto secured, not the replacement of the existing Japanese navy by one which was governed by his ideas, but the organization of a separate fleet, which was geared to the air, in addition to the orthodox battle fleet. Apparently there was no stringent testing of naval construction in Japan by commissions from the Diet, which might have subjected this settlement to criticism on grounds of economy.

The air development of the Japanese navy was one of the things overlooked by the Intelligence of the Anglo-Saxon countries. In 1938, aeroplanes which had bombed Shanghai had flown direct from Kyushu in southern Japan and had returned without refueling. In spite of the stir which this made at the time, the official judgement in England and the United States continued to be that Japan had made little progress in turning out skilled naval pilots.

Yamamoto had risen high in the navy, by great industry fortified by originality of ideas. In the middle of 1939 he was made Commander-in-Chief of the Combined Fleet, which made him one of the three or four men who were responsible for planning naval operations. As relations with the U S worsened, he became convinced that, in the event of Japan being forced into war by the United States—as the Japanese thought—Japan should begin operations with a surprise attack on the U S Asian fleet, which was stationed at Pearl Harbor. By doing so, the navy would be repeating its attack, before the outbreak of war, on the Russian fleet at Port Arthur in 1904. Yamamoto had himself been present at that famous action, and had lost two fingers. The American plans for war were known to be that, upon its declaration, the Pearl Harbor fleet should advance westwards, and that the war would take the form of great naval engagements with the Japanese fleet in the western Pacific. Yamamoto's plan was to make this impossible by destroying the American fleet, by surprise, before it could sail. As a professional sailor charged with advising his government on great matters, he recommended it to borrow from Japan's mode of action in the past, and to deal a lightning blow.

Admiral Yamamoto, it should be noted, was not a firebrand. For many years he had been associated with the moderate group, and he had risked assassination in consequence. His advocacy of his bold plan was conditional upon the Japanese government concluding that no means other than war was open to it. It was to be the desperate means when the situation was desperate.

For the attack on Pearl Harbor, Yamamoto proposed to use his aircraft-carriers, and to carry out the destruction from the air. No coup of such magnitude had as yet been carried out: it was its boldness which surprised the world. A relatively small operation of the kind had been executed by the British when they had bombed Taranto with twenty-three planes: their success undoubtedly persuaded Yamamoto to proceed. He had the operation studied minutely, and torpedoes were manufactured on the British model which were suitable for attacking in shallow waters: the depth of water at Pearl Harbor was little deeper than it had been at Taranto. The planning of the action to be taken at Pearl Harbor began in June 1941. Yamamoto had the greatest difficulty in getting the consent of the very few naval colleagues whom he had to consult, but whose number was rigidly limited by the need for entire secrecy. An appreciation by the naval General Staff was that success would depend on surprise, and that the chances of sailing a task force within reach of Pearl Harbor undetected were negligible.

Yamamoto, however, was finally permitted to proceed. His skill in advocacy must have been great, and it was one of the qualities which made him so conspicuous in the war. He assembled a task force of twenty-three surface ships (which included six carriers and two battleships) and twenty-seven submarines. In the middle of November, one month before the actual bombardment, this force sailed from Japan to Tankan Bay in the Kurile Islands; from there they approached Hawaii from the north, arriving within 220 miles of it on the night of 6–7 December. Though Yamamoto had supervised in detail the planning and rehearsal of the expedition, he did not accompany it, but remained, wisely, at his post of command near Tokyo.

It was understood that the issue of success and of disgraceful and humiliating failure turned upon secrecy. The United States had been warned many times that the Japanese did not exclude an attack on Pearl Harbor. It was not supposed that the Americans were likely to be as extraordinarily negligent as proved in fact to be the case. Japan took a formidable risk in relying on the friendless and empty seas of the north Pacific in protecting its fleet from discovery. In other ways it had taken security devices which had in some measure deceived the Americans, and were an essential part of the operation. When its fleet sailed from Japan, the fact had been camouflaged by setting up a system of fake radio messages which stilled any American suspicions that ships were on the move. After some time, however, the American monitors realized that calls to and from the aircraft carriers, specifically, had unaccountably ceased. They accepted that the carriers had been moved, but made the wrong deduction that they had been sent to the south. The Americans were already aware, from their interception of the code messages between Tokyo and the Japanese Embassy in Washington, that the Japanese were preparing for war in case the vital negotiations with the United States ended in deadlock; and they assumed that the operations would, in the first case, be directed against Malaya, the Netherlands East Indies, or the Philippines. With this inference, the assumption that the disappearance of the aircraft carriers meant a concentration of force in the South Seas fitted excellently. That the concentration was at the moment against Pearl Harbor never seems to have crossed the mind of anyone in authority.

So the evidence, and plenty was at hand, of a coming coup at Pearl Harbor was allowed to pile up, and no countermeasures were taken. The American monitors intercepted wireless messages between some source in Japan and a Japanese in Honolulu which were mysterious, and should have put them on their guard. After the attack it became clear that these conversations gave minute particulars of the American ships likely to be in port on 7 December. But they were thinly veiled, in a code which was subsequently seen to have been quite plain. All that was done with the messages at this time was to refer them to a language unit for a report on them, without any indication of emergency. The American Intelligence had knowledge of a key phrase which would be used in the Japanese radio programme a few hours before hostilities: it was to be a semi-secret way of conveying information to Japanese agents abroad, Japanese shipping and so on. It was used and remarked on: but the machinery for transmitting this information was tied up with red tape. What was necessary was that Admiral Kimmel, who was in command at Pearl Harbor, should have instituted air reconnaissance of all the seas around him: but this, after weighing the advice, and with the assent of his staff, he neglected to do. He believed that it was unnecessary, even though he had been warned, from the intercepted cipher messages of the Japanese, that Japan was seriously preparing for war.

The American blindness to their danger continued until the very morning of the attack. An outlying radar unit, whose business it was to track aircraft, picked up clearly the traces of two Japanese planes which had been sent out just before the attack, to search for all American carriers. They came on the radar screen at seven o'clock, one hour before the start of the attack, and, if this alert had been acted upon, it would, late though it was, have enabled the battleships to be put in some state of readiness, and the American planes to be in the air. The attack would quite possibly have failed, or the main havoc been averted. But this radar station, which was manned by an inexperienced but enthusiastic trainee, informed Honolulu of what had been observed, and was told not to be alarmed. It was assumed that it must have detected an American flight which was due from the mainland.

Similarly one of the Japanese submarines entered through the harbour gates at 4.50 in the morning. It was reported and hunted: but a general alarm was not given; the significance of the news, the fact that it heralded a full naval assault, was not appreciated.

The United States was amply served by an acute intelligence force. But what is the use of intelligence if there is sheer negligence over its use and interpretation? A dispatch rider, carrying a detailed warning from General Marshall in Washington to Headquarters Command—a warning that had taken an unaccountable time to transmit on the telegraph—was forced to take shelter in a ditch while the raid, which was accurately forecast in the document which he carried, was taking place round him. The warning never reached the authorities who, had it been forced to their attention twelve hours earlier, could have taken effective action.

Thus secrecy was maintained: the Japanese triumph was assured. To do Yamamoto justice, he had doubts about the propriety of what he was doing, and stipulated that the attack should not be made until thirty minutes after Japan had informed the United States that it considered that the peace negotiations were at an end. Thereby correctness would be observed, even though by a hair's breadth. Actually the attack, when it came, preceded the notification, and it appeared as perfidious as Admiral Togo's assault on the Russians had been in 1904. But the Japanese had in fact tried to observe the usages of war. The notification was in a bulky message which it took the Embassy much longer to decipher than had been foreseen in Tokyo. It was in a way symbolical of how often the actions of the Japanese authorities were to be ruined by slovenly or incompetent work in their execution. When the note was delivered, the blow had already been struck.

In the early hours of Sunday 7 December, a last radio instruction came from Tokyo. By a quarter past six, the first wave of aircraft left the carriers. The flagship hoisted the flag which Admiral Togo had carried thirty-six years before in his victory over the Tsars. The operation was the more hazardous because the Japanese possessed very sketchy information about the forces they were about to assail. It is a legend that they were well supplied by their Intelligence organizations, and knew their way about the American defences. They were uncertain to the end, for example, about whether the Americans had torpedo nets to protect their ships. They only had information, which they themselves mistrusted, about exactly what ships they were to encounter. One of their agents in Honolulu had warned them that the four aircraft-carriers which were normally with the Pacific Fleet were away from port that week-end. To catch the carriers was a vital objective. They had had in consequence serious thoughts of calling off the entire adventure at the last moment, or of postponing it indefinitely. Many of the decisions were made by guesswork.

The bombing fleet which the Japanese let loose was divided into squadrons of fighter planes, high-level torpedo-bombers and dive-bombers. The leader of one squadron of torpedo-bombers has put on record the sight which met him. It is quoted in John Deane Potter's book, *Admiral of the Pacific:*

> Below me lay the whole US Pacific Fleet in a formation I would not have dared to dream of in my most optimistic dreams. I have seen all the German ships assembled in Kiel Harbour. I have also seen the French battleships in Brest. And finally I have frequently seen our warships assembled for review before the Emperor, but I have never seen ships, even in the deepest deep, anchored at a distance of 500–1,000 yards from each other. A war fleet must always be on the alert, since surprise attacks can never be fully ruled out. But this picture down there was hard to comprehend. Had these Americans never heard of Port Arthur?*

Actually the mooring of the ships was culpably unsafe. It was odd that their radar protection, though it was in existence, did not afford more effective safety.

The attack lasted two hours. In this short time the Americans had suffered loss or damage to eighteen battleships and auxiliaries, the destruction or damage of 349 aircraft, and had 3,581 sailors, soldiers and marines and 103 civilians killed or wounded. By mid-morning the vast and impressive naval base, which had filled the United States with such confidence, was transformed into a vast ruin with flaming ships, a decimated garrison, and with a monumental disorganization. The base from which the U S had counted on directing the war was a chaos enveloped in smoke.

To effect this massacre, the Japanese had used 353 planes. Of these they lost fifteen dive-bombers, nine fighter planes, and five torpedo-planes. Their total loss in personnel was fifty-five officers and men. It was the most spectacular triumph of the war. The Americans remained unaware

*John Deane Potter: *Admiral of the Pacific*, Heinemann, 1965.

throughout of the source of their attack, and the entire fleet sailed back in safety to Japan.

*

Impressive as were the results of the raid, humiliating as it proved to be for the American navy, Japan fell just short of making it the crushing success it was meant to be. The Japanese, inexplicably, did not destroy the vast oil stocks on Hawaii, or, as far as is known, consider whether it could seize them. America began the war with oil reserves which were almost equal to the entire supplies of Japan. Japan had them at its mercy: why they neglected to fire them remains unexplained. At one stage it had, it is true, been the Japanese intention to try to seize Oahu, the Hawaiian island which contains Pearl Harbor, and in that case the oil would have passed into Japan's hands. But this part of the plan had been quickly given up as, among other reasons, it would have demanded troop transports and landing craft which were needed for the operation beginning at the same time in the South Seas. To have made the operation one which would really have altered the fundamental position of both sides, the Japanese would have needed, not only to destroy ships, but to have seized territory in the middle of the Pacific Ocean.

Japan did not include among its victims any one of the four major American aircraft-carriers which were attached to the Pacific Fleet. These were to prove the decisive weapon in the subsequent struggle in the Pacific, as was well understood by Admiral Yamamoto. Fortunate accidents led to one aircraft carrier being away delivering some planes to Midway Island; to another delivering planes to Guam: another being under repair on the American Pacific coast. The fourth was, as was found out later, trailed for some hours by a large Japanese submarine, but, in the eventual contest with this, the submarine was sunk.

Pearl Harbor contained also one failure of the Japanese which was little noted at the time but which was to have a decisive effect. The plan of Yamamoto had included a submarine attack as well as one from the air: but this was as uniformly a failure as the attack from the air was a success. A special Japanese invention, the midget submarine, a minute

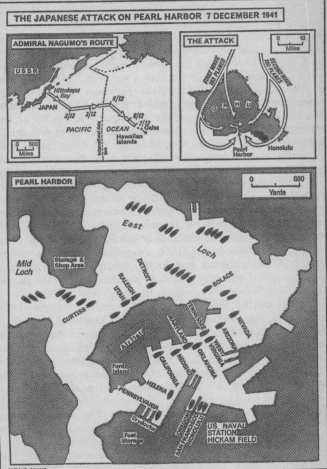

THE JAPANESE ATTACK ON PEARL HARBOR 7 DECEMBER 1941

ADMIRAL NAGUMO'S ROUTE

USSR

JAPAN

Hittokapu Bay

PACIFIC OCEAN

International date line

2/12 3/12 5/12 6/12 7/12 Oahu

Hawaiian Islands

0 500 Miles

THE ATTACK

0 10 Miles

FIRST WAVE 183 PLANES

SECOND WAVE 180 PLANES

OAHU

Pearl Harbor

Honolulu

PEARL HARBOR

0 880 Yards

East Loch

Mid Loch

Storage & Shop Area

DETROIT

RALEIGH

UTAH

CURTISS

SOLACE

NEVADA

ARIZONA

TENNESSEE

MARYLAND

WEST VIRGINIA

OKLAHOMA

Arizona

Ford Island

CALIFORNIA

NEOSHO

HELENA

PENNSYLVANIA

Clydedock

Fuel Storage

OGLESON

EAST TRANSPORT

HONOLULU

U.S. NAVAL STATION HICKAM FIELD

~ ARTHUR BANKS ~

submarine operated by a crew of two, was to be let loose inside the harbour among the battleships, and to work what havoc it could. Five of these submarines, which were transported by large, ocean-going submarines, were inserted through the harbour gates: this was, to all intents and purposes, a suicide mission, for the chances of the crews being picked up again were, though it was just possible, exceedingly slight. In fact all the five submarines were destroyed and only one member of the crews survived, falling prisoner to the Americans. (Contrary to Japanese convention, he proved singularly talkative, and he disclosed useful information to the Americans.) In the subsequent share-out of the honours for the raid, the submarine commanders felt themselves neglected, and all the credit fell to the airmen. Subsequently, the submarine service was at a discount in Japanese eyes. No further plans were drawn up which devolved any great responsibility on it. Though attention had previously been given to the production of the midget, Japanese inventiveness swung away from the submarine and concentrated on other matters. Japan had begun the war with several very large and technically efficient submarines; they were subsequently engaged on colourful, hazardous action on the American coast and in the fighting at Guadalcanal; but they failed to keep their hold on the imagination of the public, which was fixed upon its navy pilots. So, in war, the issues can be decided by the irrational judgement of the public. An inference was that the Japanese navy, though it possessed one incontestable genius in Yamamoto, did not have the staff officers who were capable of recognizing that Japan possessed an asset which it was wasting: who were capable of evolving a strategy which would make use of this instrument; and who simultaneously had the ability to force their views on the attention of the rigid Japanese High Command. What Yamamoto had done for naval aircraft, nobody seemed able to do for the submarine.

Was Pearl Harbor therefore really a success for the Japanese? Taking into account the whole course of the war, this has been doubted. The American naval historian, S. E. Morison, doubts this. He sums up the situation by saying that Pearl Harbor, for all the destruction which it achieved, was really an empty triumph. He looks towards the careful Japanese plan which had been evolved for dealing with the United States' expected offensive by the United States Asian Fleet advancing in the Pacific: and thinks that Japan would have done more wisely if it had waited for the attack, and contained it somewhere in the Marshall or Caroline Islands. By fleet action on these lines, Japan would have gained the best chance of surviving. But such a view is hard to credit. Putting it at its most down-to-earth estimate, Yamamoto had gained eighteen months', or two years' respite for Japan, and, though the long-term prospects remained exceedingly black, he had insured that the typhoon should rage over Japan in two years' time, not rage at once. He gave the opportunity to his own warlike schemes, and to any others which Japan might produce, or, better still, to her diplomats and statesmen in their ability to work out a peaceable solution, to find a way of averting ultimate catastrophe.

One peculiar circumstance aided Japan at Pearl Harbor. It was to continue in some form throughout the war and was to handicap American arrangements repeatedly. This was that the High Commands of the U S navy and army at home were scarcely on speaking terms. The degree of discord varied from place to place, and depended in part on the accident of personalities engaged. But the tension was often an important fact of the situation: as it had been at Pearl Harbor, where there was the minimum cooperation between the air force, which in the United States was part of the army, and the navy. Most of the responsibility for friction lay with the navy. The American navy existed in peculiar isolation from American society. It was self-sufficient and self-contained. It had its own politics, outlook, ethos. In a war it was apt to think that its chief enemy was at home, in the rival services which entrenched upon its own liberty of action. The result was peculiarly catastrophic. It was due to this self-imposed remoteness that the defence machinery creaked so badly.

There were other defects in the American defence machine. All these stood out clearly at Pearl Harbor. The extension of peacetime bureaucratic controls went so far that the anti-aircraft batteries were obliged to indent for every shell which was fired. As the American wartime machine swung slowly into action a great many blunders were discovered which had their source in this over-meticulousness of civilian control. It was the natural consequence of a long period of peace.

If the sights are lifted beyond this war, it must be recorded that, by the shrewd blow delivered to the United States (which was so much larger than Japan) and by the superb secrecy which had been preserved in organizing such a complex operation, Yamamoto had given an increase to Japanese self-esteem, which would bear the people up in future periods of national calamity. One day the Japanese triumph at Pearl Harbor will be regarded in a different light from that in which it was inevitably seen by the opposite side at the time; the memory of treachery will fade: it will stand out as a most memorable feat of arms.

12

The War after Pearl Harbor

AN imperial rescript—the manifesto which is issued at great decisions of the government—accompanied Japan's declaration of war, and read as follows:

We hereby declare war on the United States of America and the British Empire . . . It has been truly unavoidable . . . More than four years have passed since China, failing to understand the true intentions of our empire, disturbed the peace of Asia. Although there has been re-established the National Government of China with which Japan has effected neighbourly intercourse and cooperation, the régime which has survived at Chungking, relying upon American and British protection, still continues its fratricidal opposition. Eager for the realization of their inordinate ambition to dominate the Orient, both America and Britain, giving support to the Chungking régime, have aggravated the disturbances of East Asia. Moreover these two powers, inducing other countries to follow suit, have increased military preparations on all sides of our empire to challenge us. They have obstructed by every means our peaceful commerce and finally have resorted to a direct severance of economic relations thereby gravely menacing the existence of our empire . . . This trend of affairs would, if left unchecked, endanger the very existence of our nation. The situation being such as it is, our empire, for its existence and self-defence, has no other recourse but to appeal to arms and to crush every obstacle on its path.*

*Quoted by Jones, Borton and Pearn: *The Far East 1942-46*, Royal Institute of International Affairs, O.U.P., 1955.

Except for the blame it casts on China for the convulsion, this is an accurate statement of why Japan went to war. Japan states that it enlarged the war because it believed that only by doing so was it possible to wind up a smaller war with China. Its intervention in Indo-China, to which America had reacted so stiffly, had been undertaken for the same reasons.

War on such a scale as Japan now determined had come out of the inability of the Japanese government to find any other means of dealing with a situation which had passed out of its control. It was due in the last resort to a failure of ingenuity. The war was not preceded by elaborate planning. There was no systematic scheme of operations against the United States and Britain, which laid down a timetable for successive undertakings. All the evidence which was to become available to the western allies at the end of the hostilities confirms that the war was a desperate venture, hastily decided on: that it was conducted by a series of improvisations, however brilliant some of these were: that no elaborate plans were made of the assets, military and economic, of the western allies, and that no intelligent scheme existed of how to erode them: that Japan was, quite literally, taking a great leap in the dark, and casting its faith into the keeping of a veiled providence, which it had no reason to think would be kind.

Admiral Yamamoto, the architect of Pearl Harbor, summed up the attitude of those who took the decision to go into the war:

> What a strange position I find myself in now—having to make a decision diametrically opposed to my own personal opinion, with no choice but to push full-speed in pursuance of that decision. Is that, too, fate?*

To his sister, he wrote, 'Well, war has begun at last. But in spite of all the clamour that is going on, we could lose it. I can only do my best.'† And to a fellow admiral he wrote:

> This war will give us much trouble in the future. The fact that we have had a small success at Pearl Harbor is nothing.

*John Deane Potter: *Admiral of the Pacific*, op. cit.
†ibid.

The fact that we have succeeded so easily has pleased people. Personally I do not think it is a good thing to whip up propaganda to encourage the nation. People should think things over and realize how serious the situation is.*

He had, at Pearl Harbor, fought a successful holding operation, which had bought time. But he knew, as well as anybody, that this time would pass, and that, if at the end of it, Japan—and its ally Germany—had not found a way to peace, Japan would be ruined. He had said repeatedly that it was easier to start a war than finish one. However much territory the Japanese took, however many American battleships they they sunk, final victory might elude them.

One way only seemed to offer hope. Japanese strategy should be to win, by the impetus of surprise, as much as it possibly could in the first six months of the war. The only chance of a satisfactory peace would be to follow up Pearl Harbor by sinking the American aircraft carriers: and then, from the triumphal height of that moment, to persuade the United States to negotiate peace. It might hope that it would seem to be in such a commanding position that its Anglo-Saxon enemies would be cast down by the difficulty of dislodging it. Though they had potentially invincible power, they would be unwilling to make the exertion of mobilizing it, the more so since they would have been worn out by the war effort they were making against Germany. Japan, it should be remembered, occupied a naval position of great strength strategically. After the war of 1914–18, it had inherited from Germany the Caroline and Marshall Islands in the Pacific which, by being thoroughly (and illegally) fortified, interposed a screen which hampered the Americans in defending the Philippines. The vast depths of the Pacific Ocean were in themselves a very strong defence. Japan could argue that the United States, confronted with the possibility of either a prolonged, arduous counter-assault, ot with a generous peace offer by Japan—generous in the sense that it would not be against the United States' interest in any part of the world except East Asia—would choose the path of peace.

Of the chances of their ally Germany—who was little more, either then or later, than their nominal ally—they took

*ibid.

a rather similar view: its long-term prospects were black, but it might find salvation in the war-weariness of the western allies. In this titanic world contest, one of the most curious things was the failure of Japan and Germany to cooperate. Their relations throughout were scarcely more than the conventional ones of peacetime association. Their relations were conducted by Ambassadors. The joint planning which essentially made up Anglo-American cooperation was almost totally absent in the wartime partnership of their rivals. When diligent spying failed to discover any joint war plans by Germany and Japan, at first it was assumed that an unusually opaque veil had been woven to hide them. Not until much later did the real and simple truth become credible. No such plans had been brought into being.

Japan, unlike Germany, had no well-considered long-term war aims. In contrast to what Germany planned for Europe, Japan invested little effort in its projects for the Greater East Asia Co-Prosperity Sphere. The direction of the war on the Japanese side was too widely diffused among different hands for a clear national policy to become plain. Japan, even though it had hopes of limiting the war, was easily diverted away from the idea of a defensive war. By Pearl Harbor and Japan's initial victories, the situation had been created which made prudence difficult, and lured the Japanese on. It was as impossible to restrain its generals and admirals from further adventures as it is to prevent bulls from charging in a bull-ring.

In general, Japan followed strategy remarkably close to that by which Mr Micawber governed his life. It was to take violent action, and then to hope that something or other would turn up, enabling it to escape disaster and to reestablish peace.

*

Japan had committed the error of all military powers in dealing with the United States. It underrated grossly the willingness of the US to bear the adversities of war. It despised it; and continued to do so throughout the war. Because in the course of every war the United States armies began badly, because the democratic institutions encouraged crude criticism and loose talk, because its people were not ashamed to harp upon considerations of material interest, the Japanese, like Hohenzollern Germany before them, too easily expected the U S to give up. They scoffed at the American commercial instinct, and they predicted that, in the grim struggle of war, this could never survive against the Samurai tradition.

But the nature of Anglo-Saxon democracy is its tenacity. This the Americans, and the British, have demonstrated clearly in passages of their history. Confront them with a desperate situation, give them disastrous leaders, let their economic policies have been deplorable, saddle their public life with a rising rate of casualties; and they become more stubborn. They are implacable, and seemingly their pocket is limitless. They become pitiless and merciless, alike to their enemies and to the civilian minorities among themselves which protest against the transfiguration of the values of life by the stubborn resolve to continue war. Passchendaele and the battlefields of the American Civil War are a terrible warning, which naturally militant people, but those untouched by the traditions of Anglo-Saxon democracy, have never taken to heart. Once it has taken up arms, and has suffered the blood-letting which warms its temper, the democracy ceases to understand the virtues of a peace which is negotiated, and is satisfied only with the barren conclusion spreading bitterness everywhere, of absolute victory. It sets aside all rules, and, with a mood created by the tempest of the hour, works simply and mechanically, grinding its way to victory. This was the tempest which Japan was bringing down upon itself: more awful than any of its feared typhoons.

It was to discover later that, terrible as a victorious democracy may be, it has at least the virtue of quickly changing its temper when the goad of war is removed. The resolution and implacability, while they thrive during war, are dissolved after a year or so of peace. Hence Japan, if it had dwelt on past history, need not have been so miserably cast down by its total defeat.

If the Japanese despised the United States, Americans no less misunderstood the Japanese. The mutual incomprehension is one of the facts, tragic and at times comic, of the war. Throughout its course, anyone visiting the U S was at once made conscious of the passionate contempt, which was originally based on resentment, for the Japanese. All the discreditable facts about them were remembered. All that made Japanese civilization interesting was, as by system, forgotten. All Japanese were lumped together as a misshapen, ugly, stupid, dwarf people. They were like nothing so much as Mr Tolkien's orcs in the *Lord of the Rings,* creations of a people of sheer malevolence and hideousness.

The British reacted in a less extreme way. On going to war, Churchill wrote quite a sentimental letter to the Japanese Ambassador. The stream of American feeling did not sweep the British along with it; the British had their emotions concentrated on the Nazis, and, except where they had powerful reasons for hatred from personal experience of Japanese camps or other atrocities, regarded the Japanese as a provoking irrelevance.

*

By its fateful decision Japan altogether changed the character of the war.

China, which until then had preserved the fiction that its war was no war but merely an incident, declared war on Japan on 9 December. It rejoiced in the United States being committed and saw the prospect of its operation being enlarged by vast American aid. But the declaration was a voluntary act by China. Events might have taken a different course if China had not thus regularized its American alliance. Similarly, on the same day that it declared war on Japan it declared war on Germany.

Why it did so is not clear. As Germany was under no obligation to declare war on the United States, and did so against its interests, so China was under no obligation to declare war on Germany. Apparently it did so out of a kind of contagion. It might be assumed that the countries were beset by madness.

From this time onwards, the direst, and chiefly decisive part of the war was waged on sea and in the air. In fact the Japanese sea and air operations were probably the most spectacular in human history. It is true that the war with China continued desultorily, but the problems which compelled the attention of the Japanese government had very little relation to those of the earlier period. Pearl Harbor meant a huge increase in Japan's enemies. It had against it the British Empire, in those days still a major power, as well as the United States. It had defied a great part of the world, and though it had at first won prodigious successes, the precariousness of its position was always plain.

In the whole of the latter part of the war, in the struggle of Japan with the western powers, Japan was compelled by circumstance to appear as the liberator of the orient against occidental control. The role of the emancipator, which nationalists everywhere had first hopefully seen Japan as fulfilling in its victory against Russia in 1905, was now firmly wished upon it by the exigencies of the time. In India, in Indo-China, in Indonesia, in Burma, a tide was started which, if the Japanese had rightly worked with it, might have proved irresistible. In this new illumination the presence of the white man in Asia seemed a ghastly insult to the rights of the Asian peoples. Even the classes of people which had formerly been contented to work with the West hailed the new prospect of building the future of Asia upon Asian foundations.

The history of the war is the chronicle of Japan's lost opportunities; of a crusade which never got started: of a Japan which was so hampered by inner contradictions that it was astonishingly unsuccessful in rising to the occasion. As the war went on, Japan allowed it to become plain that it was bent on a simple predatory enterprise of the kind which had been supposed to have passed out of fashion with the passing away of the nineteenth century. It failed to disguise in a plausible way that its interest was no higher than the transfer to itself of the benefits enjoyed by western countries in the South Seas and in Asia. The gloss which it sought to put on this—the ideology of the Greater East Asia Co-Prosperity Sphere, with its picture of an eastern world finding harmony under the protection of the Japanese armies—was too perfunctory to carry conviction.

In three years, Japan, by a series of blunders, disappointed the hopes of Asia that it was the liberator. By extraordinarily insensitive action it convinced Asian nationalists that Japan offered little or nothing to the peoples struggling to be free; and satisfied the national leaders that more was to be had from western imperialists than from the victory of Japan. For this result, a part of the responsibility was due to the conduct, the repeated blunders, the arrogance and stupidity, of the Japanese army. Japan's imperial adventure was always associated with the Japanese army: Japanese diplomats, civilians, and captains of industry were of secondary importance. The opportunities for a genuine new era in the region, which were at first made available by the daring and glittering achievements of Japanese arms, were flung away because the Japanese army went in the teeth of the inhabitants of the region, and came to be odious throughout Asia. It was defeated by Anglo-Saxon powers in military combat, but when this came about, few tears were shed by Asian nationalism because of the result.

After Pearl Harbor, the war, or the Far-Eastern war and the European war, broadened out, and became a world war, in which nearly every country was engaged. It was more universal than the First World War had been. The greater part of the civilized world was drawn in.

There is a distinction, of kind as well as of degree, between a local war and a universal one. In a local war, there are boundaries to the general savagery. In general men can opt out of it: they, or at least some, can go to neutral territory. In a universal explosion, war is everywhere. The shortage of neutrals leaves man without refuge.

Ruskin, in a passage from *Praeterita,* describes the difference between a local war and war which had got out of hand and swept the world: that of Napoleon. Of this war, Ruskin says that it was marked by:

> Life trampled out in the slime of the street, crushed to dust amidst the roaring of the wheel, tossed countlessly away into howling winter wind along five hundred leagues of rock-fanged shore.

He continues:

> The death was of another range and power; more terrible a thousand-fold in its merely physical grasp and grief; more terrible, incalculably, in its mystery and shame. What were the robber's casual pang, or the range of the flying skirmish, compared to the work of the axe, and the sword, and the famine, which was done at this time in all the hills and plains of the Christian earth, from Moscow to Gibraltar. . . . Look on the map of Europe, and count the bloodstains on it, between Arcola and Waterloo.

So with this later convulsion; only the scientific progress with weapons of destruction made the havoc worse. What, in other ages, armies could bring about in a dozen years, they had now the capacity to do in a dozen days, or even hours.

The greater part of the civilized world was at war: little by little, in every country of the world, in all the great cities, and in most of the accessible villages, the sights and sounds of war were to become the commonplace of the age. In North America, in the Asian countries, in Australia, and in North Africa, the progress of the war became a grand preoccupation. In all too many centres of ordered life, centres which for more than a century had been famous for commerce or culture, the distant hum of conflict turned abruptly into the clash and commotion of sudden battle, to be followed often by the long tedium and horror of military occupation by an alien power. In all the world, only central Africa and South America were relatively undisturbed.

*

The whole world moved senselessly in one direction or another, suffered and died in great swaths. Peasants and citizens of the huge Asian towns were caught alike. Many more perished from famine and disease than were killed by the armies.

This huge populace was informed about what was happening chiefly by local newspapers. Other media of communication scarcely touched it. Only the rare Asian village was, at the time, equipped with radio. For the townsmen, the radio set poured out propaganda, but in the towns the people largely discounted this, and put their faith in the printed word. From the newspapers, and from human contacts by mouth to mouth, word was spread, without which the Asian people would have supposed that there was no rhyme or reason in the convulsion of the world. It is hard enough to see how these instruments were sufficient for their purpose. Even though newspapers made their way into most of the villages, into the very remote ones in China and India, the number of people who could read them was very restricted. The war which had engulfed the governments had drawn in a mass of illiterate peasants. Those who could read found their talent even more highly regarded than in the past. They read in the newspaper and told the rest of the people what it contained. They were the agents of the increasing self-awareness of the peoples of Asia during this time. But it is unlikely that many of them came to any conclusion about the events they contemplated more perceptive than that of little Peterkin on the battle of Blenheim two and a half centuries earlier:

> But what they fought each other for
> I could not well make out.

III

THE HIGH TIDE OF WAR

13

Japan's Hundred Days

Hong Kong

JAPAN, following the brilliant start in the new theatres of its war, had the limelight in the times which succeeded. For the next three months it held the initiative in many different sectors. It concentrated on dealing with its new enemies, especially the United States and Britain, and it enjoyed a dashing period of cheaply won triumphs, rolling up the long established positions and colonial territories of the western powers in Asia. Its record was of almost unbroken success in the first hundred days of this war. This was to be a bitter recollection in Japan when its record ceased to be one of uninterrupted conquests, and the country faced the experience of endless decline.

Its first conquest was Hong Kong. That fell almost immediately. A very small off-shore island of China, useful for trade and for political action, Hong Kong had never been seriously prepared by the British for standing a prolonged siege, even in the recent years while the situation had looked threatening. It was ringed by Japan's armies and its fleet; it was without a hinterland of more than a few miles; its water supply was easily vulnerable; it was too far from a British base for there to be any possibility of reinforcing it. It never had a chance to survive, and it was surprising that it held out for as long as thirteen days.

The main feature of its siege was the confusion among the population, which was overwhelmingly Chinese. Many, though loyal inhabitants of the colony, had dual nationality with China, or else were moved by strong Chinese sentiments. These had for the most part been loyal to the Chungking government, and its most active and enterprising members, who in consequence had become marked men to Japan, succeeded in escaping to mainland China; as also did the Chinese politicians who, because they found it safer to operate beyond reach of the Kuomintang, resided in Hong Kong. Many civilians in Hong Kong responded to the call for at least a token resistance. The Japanese, in the use of their political warfare techniques, attempted to set off the Scots in the garrison against the English. Pamphlets were dropped which were full of Scottish sentiment, invoked the memories of Loch Lomond, and inquired whether the Scots were willing to be sacrificed in an English quarrel.

The siege was ended on 19 December when the guns were silenced. There was heartening drama at the finish when some of the spirited young men of the colony, together with a Chinese one-legged admiral who gave a foretaste of the astonishing toughness which the Chinese today display, but did so seldom at that period, got clean through the blockading Japanese, and escaped up country to Chungking. Politically the forfeiture of Hong Kong was a blow to the British; but strategically it was inevitable. It had been foreseen and meant little.

A serious loss at Hong Kong was of several of the Far-Eastern experts which the British army possessed at the start of the war. The number of these was appallingly scanty: the army authorities had caused surprisingly few of its officers to learn Chinese and Japanese at a time when trouble was evidently preparing in this part of the world. Of Chinese-speaking officers, many had been posted in Hong Kong, since naturally it was desired to employ them where their talents could be most immediately used. Apparently nobody foresaw that they would pass, after a few days, into captivity. The army, for example in India, would be crying out bitterly against the famine of China experts, for the interrogation of prisoners, the reading of documents, or for the countless ways in which expertise in language is required in warfare.

The Philippines

On the same day that they attacked Pearl Harbor, Japan had made a similar raid on Clark airfield, the key to the defences of the Philippine Islands. This was an American possession which linked the United States with the imperial systems maintained by the European powers. The United States was expected to defend it tenaciously. It was not, like Hong Kong, regarded as expendable. With this attack, Japan launched upon the serious task of driving the white invader from the soil of Asia.

The Philippines are an island group off South-East Asia which had formerly been the empire of Spain in this part of the world. They had passed into American possession when the United States had defeated Spain in the Spanish-American war of 1898. It was a war which it was hard to justify: at first it seemed to show that the United States had given up its traditional stand against imperialism and was about to start on the acquisition of colonies. Its heart, however, was never in empire: it produced no specialist imperial class of dedicated administrators. No American literature had grown up around the Philippines; no class of Americans (except a small group of West Point army officers) could claim to have the Philippines in their bones.

Thus it had been easy for Americans to compromise when they found that, among their new subject peoples, the Europeanized middle class of Manila was becoming inspired by the nationalism of the day. Americans had engendered no professional imperialists, in their adventure with ruling subject peoples. They could therefore readily conceive a constitution, which was a replica of the United States one, and could foresee that the Filipinos would make a success of this, and of governing their country without disaster.

By the time that Japan attacked, the United States was already well-ahead with grooming the Philippines for liberation. Japan did not find in it a representative of imperialism at its most stubborn. When it struck, the United States had already passed a law which set a timetable for Filipino emancipation. This envisaged, however, that there would be a treaty between itself and the Philippines, regulating their defence.

By this treaty, the United States was to keep a moderately powerful air force, stationed at Clark Field. The rather sketchy chain of airfields throughout the islands was to be at its disposal. The United States also maintained a weak garrison of soldiers. When the war began, the defences were out of date. The communications between the islands were especially poor. The native Filipino army, which was being trained by the United States, was only half ready.

The Japanese bombed Clark Field some hours after they attacked Pearl Harbor. Reports of what was happening there had reached the Philippines by radio. On receipt of the news, the air force—thirty-five bombers and seventy-two fighters—was alerted and had taken to the air. But the Japanese attack was delayed by the dense morning fog. At lunchtime nearly all the American planes were grounded. While they were being serviced, while the pilots were being fed, the Japanese struck. Nearly a hundred American aircraft were destroyed in the air or on the ground.

Thus the war in the Philippines began with recrimination over an unnecessary loss. The American habit of concentrating its aeroplanes in formations which made the perfect targets had before this caused anxiety. Duffy Cooper, who had been appointed a few weeks before as Resident Minister in the British administration of Singapore was horrified at seeing them parked wing by wing at Clark Field and had pointed out to the Americans what a temptation they might be to the Japanese. The loss was nowhere near as fatal as that at Pearl Harbor. Obviously the disaster had no deep influence on what followed. But the disgrace and the material damage had a very discouraging effect.

The raid was followed up by a landing of the Japanese army. It came from Formosa, and the troops had been embarked some days previously. At first there was doubt as to whether the Filipinos, under American command, would resist the Japanese armies, which proclaimed they were bringing freedom. But this doubt was quickly dispelled.

The command in the Philippines was in the hands of General MacArthur. He was thenceforward to play the most conspicuous part of any commander in the Pacific war. A rather older man than most of his contemporaries, a general with an outstanding record in the First World War, a former Chief of Staff of the American army, he had been loaned by the United States government to the Filipino Service to organize the future armies of the free Philippines. He entered with enthusiasm on this task. His father had been the first military governor in the American rule of the island. The relation of trust between him as generous patron of the Filipinos, and the Filipinos as loyal and grateful clients, caught his imagination. He believed that he had the knack and principle to do what other western soldiers and administrators had failed to do: to win the attachment of an oriental people. He was enabled to stand to his own government in the position of a semi-independent power rather than a subordinate servant, a relation which suited him much better than a more regular one.

At the time when the Japanese struck, he had completed six years of a planned ten-year period on this task, and the Filipino army had been brought to a stage of fair competency. Its worst impediment had been the multitude of languages and dialects which were spoken by the soldiers, which made it difficult for them to be organized under a single command. In the months preceding the war, it was, as part of the American preparation against the Japanese threat, reincorporated in the U S army. But when the invasion came, the plans, such as there were, about the defence of the Philippines were sketchy and completely shattered by the events of Pearl Harbor. The American intentions had proceeded from the axiom that the Asian fleet would be intact, and would, at least within months, be able to come to the rescue.

MacArthur quickly appreciated that he could not check the Japanese landings. He met them with a scheme which had something of surprise. He gathered together his force, and withdrew into the historic fortress of Corregidor, on an island in Manila Bay, and into the peninsula of Bataan, on the northern side of the bay. Corregidor was one of the famous strong points in the East. It had first been built by Spaniards in the early years of their rule in the seventeenth century, and was heavy with history. But, though extremely picturesque—like Cyprus in the wars against the Turks or like a Crusader's castle—it had nothing done to it in modern times to make it suitable for modern war. On the other hand Bataan was more serviceable. It was a strip of country covered by jungle and had been prepared by MacArthur for its role by the installation of concealed factories, supply depots and hospitals. In these two centres MacArthur had more than 50,000 troops (of whom only 6,000 men were of the regular American army). He planned to withstand a siege by a Japanese army which numbered about 200,000.

MacArthur was at first optimistic that he would be relieved. Apparently, for a senior officer of the U S army, he was singularly out of touch with the ways in which the U S General Staff thought in time of emergency. He reckoned in terms of a six months' siege, for which he had stored ammunition, though his supplies of food were far less satisfactory. He refused to admit that the United States had been robbed by Pearl Harbor of all powers to relieve and reinforce its protégé. The United States might have lost its battleship fleet, but a great deal could be contrived with cruisers, destroyers and submarines. These ships remained in existence: they might have been used in relation to the Philippines. Actually the American navy fought actively for the next few years in the Pacific without receiving any large new ships. But the will and dash had departed temporarily from the navy. MacArthur, isolated in beleagured Corregidor, did not grasp this fact. He adapted the tactics of strategic defence when they were in fact pointless because the defence, however resolute, could look for no eventual reward in the early restoration of communications with the United States.

When MacArthur in the end faced the facts as they were, he seriously planned that the entire Bataan garrison should attempt a break-out, and should then filter away to southern Luzon, where they should wage guerrilla warfare. But the scheme, transmitted to Washington, was coolly regarded, and was never sanctioned.

The Japanese began their serious offensive against MacArthur on 29 December, when they let loose their aeroplanes against Corregidor. Surprisingly, both Corregidor and Bataan held out. The Japanese met their first check of the war. The resistance, unexpectedly prolonged, began to upset the larger Japanese plan. They had calculated that their forces would be quickly disengaged from the Philippines, and would be free to move on to the belt of coral islands which lay along the northern coast of Australia. From these they would be able to prepare for the invasion of Australia, and the cutting-off of its communications with the United States.

Their delay continued. At one time the Japanese were so badly placed—stricken with dysentery, beri-beri, and other tropical diseases—that the Americans and the Filipinos, had they been able to launch an offensive, could have re-taken Manila. But this did not put hope into the Philippine President, Manuel Quezon. On 8 February he sent a telegram to Washington saying that the Filipinos were nearly exhausted, and proposing that, as the United States had been unable to fulfil its pledges of protection, it should immediately declare the Philippines independent, the islands neutralized, and the American and Filipino armies disbanded. Quezon, though personally loyal to the United States, judged it thus possible for the Philippines to take refuge in neutrality.

At the end of January the Japanese troops were heavily reinforced. Two extra divisions were moved in, together with heavy artillery groups. The Japanese offensive continued. It was marked by none of the brilliant improvisation which the Japanese were showing in Malaya.

On 22 February, the President of the United States sent a telegram to MacArthur, ordering him to leave the Philippines and to go to Australia to organize the war from there. He went unwillingly, half under the delusion, as is plain from the documents of the time, that he would be put in command of a mighty army with which he would return to the Philippines. From this time onwards he developed a monomania about return. 'I will return' were his last words on transferring his Filipino command to General Wainwright.

The American navy had kept four speedboats intact. Mac-Arthur had sent Quezon, the Filipino President, to Australia in a submarine, but preferred to travel in a motor torpedo boat. On the night of 11 March this little flotilla ran the Japanese blockade. The sea is vast; it is surprising how many times a blockade has been successfully broken. The speed-boat in which MacArthur sat found itself at one stage in the shadow of a Japanese battleship, but in the darkness it failed to be aware of its prize. Certainly Japan would have done well to have intercepted this general, who, once away, responded, as if to a magnet, to the powerful drawing force of Japan. But when he returned it would be with an army.

With MacArthur gone, the Filipinos carried on their resistance for a month longer, but the spirit passed out of it. It was one thing to resist under MacArthur's command, and another under General Wainwright, though Wainright was a valiant soldier. On 9 April Bataan surrendered; on 6 May Corregidor. The defenders, the majority of them of the Filipino army, had been still a large force, and, as Japan was in future to show, a Japanese garrison would have been disinclined to surrender. But resistance seemed pointless when the Filipinos heard on the American radio that the United States was putting its energies first into the German war; and that, for the time being, it had written off the Philippines. The Filipino army had fought when there was still reason for fighting and, with that reason gone, was entitled by all the conventions of war to surrender.

The garrison of Bataan and Corregidor met with a terrible fate for having been the first to throw the Japanese timetable out of date. They were shepherded into captivity in a march which earned the grim name of 'the Death March.' Most of the victims passed into the hands of the Japanese military police, the Kempeitai.

The other American island possessions in the Pacific had been able to offer very much less resistance. Guam was taken on 10 December after a spirited defence. Wake Island held out gallantly, but succumbed on 23 December.

Malaya

On the same day that Japan was attacking Pearl Harbor it began its assault on Malaya. This was to be one of the principal theatres of the war, the scene of what was probably its most brilliant campaign, and of disaster and disgrace for Britain which was to bring about the twilight of the British in Asia.

Malaya was a peninsula inhabited by Malay sultanates. Great Britain had extended its colonial rule over them in the nineteenth century while leaving formally intact the machinery of the sultanates; and the territory, with the great importance of its rubber, had become a major part of the British colonial empire. The rich and peaceful country had attracted the Chinese, who became a very large minority.

Malaya had special significance for all the western powers with territorial possessions in the East. At the southern-most tip of the peninsula is the island of Singapore, as large as the Isle of Wight. In the early 1920s, with the ending of the Anglo-Japanese Alliance, Britain had determined to build up Singapore into a great naval fortress, and to make Malaya the vital centre of British power in the Far East. Singapore was to be a dockyard, a naval base, barracks and communications centre. It was to safeguard the communications with Australia and was the base from which the British navy could operate to ensure that the Indian Ocean continued to be a British lake. The British, having decided to rely in the Far East on steel and reinforced concrete instead of on diplomacy, spent £60 million, which at that time was a very large sum, on the fortification of the base. When finished, it was regarded as one of the four greatest sea-fortresses in the world (the others being Pearl Harbor, Malta and Gibraltar).

It would have such obvious military might that, while it stood, it would provide a guarantee of the continuity of British power and thus it would be looked to by all other British territories in Asia; nor was it without significance for France and Holland for the security of their empires in South-East Asia.

The plan was carried through. Singapore was completed. It seemed to double-lock the gateway of the empire so that it was useless for an unfriendly rival power, such as Japan, to dream of forcing an entrance. Japan might have been expected to be daunted by such prestige, and to avoid a direct attack on such an invincible place. It was to prove, however, that the complacency and false security which were generated about Singapore told against drawing up plans for a modernized, flexible defence of the system in case it should ever be challenged.

Almost unbelievably, a totally false estimate of its strength became general. It proceeded from an erroneous view of military reality, which was to prove so eminently disastrous that it is inconceivable how it could ever have been formed, or that, once it had come to determine the fixed lines of policy, it was allowed to continue for nearly twenty years unchallenged. There were two delusions. The first was that, as Singapore lay at the southern extension of 200 miles of jungle, it was militarily impregnable to land attack. Without any serious tests having been made, and as it turned out without any basis of reason, this fortress was given the certificate of virtual invulnerability. It was taken for granted that no enemy could carry on tank warfare in the hinterland of rubber plantations, and it was thought to be impassable, a region exempt from the manoeuvres of modern armies. The actual arrangements for the defence of Singapore were made from this misreading of fact. The rubber jungle was left undefended by human arts. From over-confidence, the garrison of Singapore was lamentably inadequate; the roads were poor; no network of airfields was made which would have been adequate for a great air force; no great air force had ever operated from the Malayan peninsula.

The second fatal miscalculation was that, as Singapore was to be a naval base, it would be threatened only in a great naval war. Singapore was envisaged as the centre of a titanic naval struggle, with a large fleet occupying her to capacity. The eyes of the world would always be on her, and those eyes would always look seawards. All the guns of Singapore would point seawards also. It was prepared with the most modern artillery which money could buy; but the guns were never in a position to fire at an adversary who came by land.

Alas, it was never to play its part in a great war of the seas; its guns necessarily remained silent, for they were not the mobile things of a hundred years before. They were built in concrete and could not in a matter of days or weeks be re-adapted to a new kind of war. Money spent on Singapore was largely useless, for the same reason as was the treasure of France which had been squandered on the Maginot line.

*

In the two years of the war—before Japan suddenly made its nature real and alarming—British people living in Singapore had had time to digest how deadly was their peril. Most of them did not do so. The old myths bore them up. They were cheered by the belief that the British navy, though it was away in other waters, had power to neutralize the Japanese. They could still see the apparent strength of Singapore, which they thought would house its navy, and did not grasp its essential weakness.

Only one British soldier during this time saw the ominous cracks appearing. Colonel Stewart, the commanding officer of a battalion of the Argyll and Sutherland Highlanders, refused to accept the conventions which govern the training of garrison troops. Day after day the soldiers under his command spent their time in jungle training. The Argylls were considered eccentric; but at the end, Colonel Stewart formed the view that Singapore was not in fact surrounded on the north and east by a vast and easily defensible belt of jungle. It was possible for an invading army to use tanks in the jungle; and in a short time the Japanese army, made formidable by all the instruments of modern war, would be at its doors. This was the uncomfortable message which he preached, but nobody attended to him.

It happens that one of the Japanese officers concerned with preparing the Japanese offensive has left a full account of the processes involved. (*Singapore—the Japanese Version*, by Colonel Tsuji.) It was conceived as a rescue operation to free the inhabitants from British imperialism. It was not planned from years ahead, and in great detail, as was wrongly supposed by the British government. The expedition was improvised, and planned on a shoestring. The serious preparation and advance studies began only eleven months before the actual attack, in January 1941, and had started with a monthly budget of no more than 20,000 yen (or less than £2,000). The initial planning was carried out in Formosa, which was then a firm part of the Japanese empire, and it was rehearsed on Hainan Island, which had passed under Japanese control in 1938. The Japanese forces were able to use a mass of photographs and other data which its enthusiastic agents had been busy gathering, partly as a matter of habit and by voluntary initiative. Every town and village had had its Japanese businessmen, Japanese doctors, and Japanese dentists, and these were now revealed as the advance guard of the invasion that was being launched; but it is surprising how sketchy was much of the information. It was discovered that for their coastal operation the Japanese had to rely upon the data furnished by a single master

mariner, who had collected the facts for years in case they
should come in useful.

*

The invasion did not begin with a surprise massive Japanese
attack from the air, similar to that on Pearl Harbor and
the Philippines. The war started with the transport of two
divisions of Japanese soldiers from Indo-China; the overcoming of the weak coastal defences in northern Malaya.
At first, the Japanese were too distant from Singapore to
make effective use of the air; today it is overlooked how
comparatively limited the range of massive air operations
still was. The Japanese landing in the north did not take
the British by surprise. It had clearly been a possibility
ever since the Japanese took Indo-China, and plans had been
worked out, which were in fact forestalled by the Japanese,
for a possible seizure of a part of southern Thailand, as a
defensive move. The British were, however, out-manoeuvred
by the speed and resiliency of the Japanese in moving from
their bridgeheads to a lightning drive on the south.

In the first days of the war the British commanders at
Singapore disposed of two major warships, the *Prince of
Wales* and the *Repulse*, which the government at home, as
the skies blackened in the days before Pearl Harbor, had
been persuaded to detach from other operations and to spare
for the East. These were a powerful reinforcement: with
them, Singapore appeared to be about to play the part intended for it by British planning. In theory, at least, they
would restore mobility to British arms. They were meant to
insure the safety of Malaya, in case the Japanese struck out
during the negotiations at Washington. The battleship and
battle-cruiser would enable Britain to strike at great distances. With sea power, Britain could exercise what Bacon
had described as its natural advantage in all its wars: to
take as much or as little of the war as it desired.

Yet the voyage of these two ships was a perilous excursion
into the unknown, and should surely have filled those who
ordered it with great alarm. Moreover, they were moving
against forces which they could not compute. The Japanese
had a history of waiting for, and dealing with, naval units
sent out from European waters to alter the balance of force

in the East. Admiral Rozhdestvensky had sailed a fleet half-way round the world in 1905 to be destroyed at the battle of the Japan Sea. In like manner, the *Prince of Wales* and the *Repulse* were to be the victims, not it is true of a waiting Japanese navy, but of the new Japanese fleet air arm by which the two warships were sunk on the fourth day of the war.

*

With these warships swept from the chess board, the Japanese advance down the peninsula to Singapore could go forward unimpeded. Troops came in by transport from Indo-China, and nothing availed to stop them; more alarmingly, they were accompanied by tanks, which against forecasts, overcame the natural barriers of the jungle. They advanced south with surprising speed. A clear picture of the Japanese strategy began to show itself. The British army, heavily burdened with its impedimenta, untrained for jungle warfare, resisted as hard as it could by throwing up positions across the roads. Meeting their challenge, the Japanese forsook the main road, advanced through the allegedly impenetrable jungle, and took the British in the rear. The jungle betrayed the British; the jungle which had been in their possession for eighty years and whose possibilities for war they had never learned. By these means, repeated so often that they became monotonous, the Japanese came on, and within six weeks were within sight of Singapore.

The achievement of the Japanese has been glossed over. It was remarkable. The Japanese army had until now acquired its battle experience in China, a terrain vastly different from Malaya: and its battle training had been almost exclusively the steppe country of Manchuria. Its performance in the tropics showed an adaptability and resourcefulness in the Japanese officers, and endurance by the Japanese soldiers which had been insufficiently recognized. Though the imaginative qualities of the Japanese army were not afterwards apparent, they shone in this campaign.

The manner of fighting by the Japanese surprised their antagonists. They showed none of the preference for long-range combat, such as most of the other civilized combatants exhibited. They seemed to exult in struggle body to body.

They produced gestures of defiance and glee and also of fear which, by most other soldiers, were regarded as childish. A skirmish was accompanied by grunts, gasps and blood-curdling yells. Later, when the Japanese film became popular in the West, it was seen that the Japanese soldier had fought very much as Japanese actors traditionally represented him as doing. It made him a surprising and alarming adversary.

As the Japanese assault on Malaya intensified, it was noticed that the Japanese had a string of successes in air raids upon British aircraft. Time and again the British were caught on the ground. Japan's planes appeared in great force just when the British were getting ready to take to the air. Finally the reason for this striking good fortune of the Japanese came to light. An officer in the RAF, a citizen of southern Ireland, was pursuing his country's feud of twenty years back with the British government, and was detected signalling to the Japanese. This affair was kept secret. It had accounted for an unfortunate part of the air losses in the early stages of the campaign.

*

In the confused ill-temper of the retreat—and it was always retreat, without one solid success to restore self-respect—there was recrimination between the British commanders, and the commander of the large force of Australians, which had been a part of the allied garrison and who had shared in the defence. It was reflected in the lower ranks. Many of the Australians had been stationed in the Middle East before they fought the Japanese. As this was largely a time of defeat before the days of Montgomery, they had formed a disgruntled view of British competence. Their transfer back to the defence of the region where Australian interests were more vitally at stake had been agreed to with a rather ill grace by Churchill; this put the Australians in the mood to be touchy partners. By ill fortune they were under a general, Gordon Bennett, who, though a rather dashing soldier, had in addition the qualities which hardly endeared him to the usual type of British officers. He was not of a modest nature, he did not minimize any affronts shown to him, he did not agree with those people who saw virtue in silence.

To the necessary disgraces which afflicted the beaten army, there was thus added the scandal of a dangerous difference of opinion between England and one of the Dominions, which at bottom had always been so loyal to it, and whose feelings were the more ruffled because they had been so warm. The quarrel threatened to widen out into a dispute which uncovered a diversity in war aims. Australia was left with the feeling that it had been betrayed. Its interests were treated as of slight concern. It seemed that England would unfeelingly sacrifice Australian soldiers for its own advantage. It was the type of ill-feeling which sooner or later was bound to cloud the cooperation of England and the Dominions. A considerable effort was needed to overcome the bitterness: Britain was too occupied for the diplomacy needed. Singapore, which was becoming a curse to the empire which it had been called into being to serve, merely added to its demerits that, in the turmoil of this period, it caused London and Canberra to be for some weeks estranged.

In the long retreat through Malaya, the British had suffered much more than a great military reverse. For the first time their administrative system in oriental countries had been exposed, and went down in ridicule. They, the masters of political craft for conciliating the oriental, found that they had used up all their reserves of prestige, and had no comfort anywhere. In Penang, in Kuala Lumpur, in all the centres of administration, the events were disastrous. The institutions built up over decades, the loyalties so laboriously produced, the habits which the British had so complacently regarded as fixed and permanent—all were swept away. The British were not regarded with fear or hatred: had that been so, they would not have been so quickly written off. Their day was regarded as closed. The local Malay population (not the Chinese), giving a lead to other colonial communities of the empire, regarded it as politic to transfer their loyalties as quickly as possible to the Japanese.

When the backward movement of the British began, it was supposed by home public opinion that, with the example of a scorched earth policy in Russia before them, arrangements would be made for the Japanese to meet with a similar bleak reception. But in almost all cases, the government lacked the nerve to demand the sacrifice from the local people, or, more rarely, the demand was made and the people refused to cooperate. The British efforts to build up a resistance behind the rear of the Japanese army, and to create an adequate spying and Intelligence system were at first unsuccessful. Later on in the war, when the Japanese had made themselves detested, the organizations were to begin to function: but this was to be in the future.

It must not be supposed that the psychological atmosphere changed abruptly to contempt or hostility towards the British. There were many warm and compassionate acts of loyalty and friendship by the Malays and the very mixed population of this cosmopolitan peninsula. The British, in defeat and disillusion, often found unexpected shelter.

How news of great and dramatic events transmits itself in Asia, by what means it travels to remote valleys and distant villages, is not clear. At this time there were very few radio sets outside the larger towns. But in these months a great sensation was felt throughout Asia. The British Empire was dying. It had been pushed over in Malaya, and it was found to have rotten roots. Soon it would be treated in the same way in the other countries, and in all parts of Asia where the union flag still flew. Britain never recovered from the deplorable events of these few weeks. The happenings in one small section of its empire were enough to destroy its prestige everywhere: and the life and soul of the British Empire had consisted of prestige.

*

While Singapore was in its death pangs, the British committed one more egregious mistake. Large reinforcements of British troops, complete with equipment, had been spared from the war in Europe and ordered to Malaya. These arrived off Singapore when the siege of the fortress was about to begin. With remarkable folly, and with the idea still prevailing that there would be a final effort to redeem the fortress by undergoing a siege, they were disembarked instead of sailing away to India where they were urgently needed, as quickly as they could. These troops, with all their artillery and stores, were put ashore, never to fire a shot, and were to enter on the long martyrdom of Japanese imprisonment.

On 31 January 1942, the army, defeated, bewildered and demoralized, re-entered Singapore. Their rear-guard was led across the causeway which connected Singapore with Johore by the remnants of the pipe band of the Argylls.

The final defence lasted fifteen days. Singapore surrendered on 15 February. It gave in because its defences crumbled; because its water supply passed out of its control; because the Japanese, again falsifying expectation, managed to infiltrate the island's defences at all points, and, within a week of crossing, were seen to be everywhere; because the troops were disorganized, and no pattern of defence established itself; because it was clear that the civilian population in the city had been paralysed and most of it did not desire that it should be defended; because the enemy, which had penned them up in the fortress, had swollen in their imagination to such a size by a unique series of triumphs that further resistance was not really thinkable. He had sunk two battleships which the English had naïvely supposed would have over-awed him: at Pearl Harbor he had struck away the navy that would have made the Americans an effective ally: he had demonstrated that the jungle, that was feared by all other armies, could be treated as the home of the Japanese, from which Japan could draw strength. When this Japanese army began to follow the British into Singapore, and to infiltrate over the island, the British recognized that the battle for South-East Asia had gone against them. By a local decision the fact was recognized: and Singapore was Japan's.

Yet it remained true that the army in Singapore was twice as large as the besieging force, and, in theory at least, a prolonged resistance would have been possible. Even the fact of the non-existence of prepared defences did not cancel out the fact of the great British superiority in man-power. There have been famous sieges in history that have been carried on long enough to embarrass the besiegers and which have been begun in circumstances as disastrous as those in Singapore. Exactly a year later, Singapore was to be followed in the news interest of the world by Stalingrad, and its defenders were not moved by the civilized sentiments of those who had to make the decision at Singapore. It is true that the defenders, unlike those of Stalingrad, could not have cut their way out to safety: but, in theory at least, they could have put up a notable resistance. The defeat was not gilded by any valiant enterprise, such as the rescue of the British troops at Dunkirk, which in after days made Dunkirk a stirring myth, instead of one of the worst reverses to British arms on the continent. In fact it became known later that General Yamashita, the rather eccentric commander of the Japanese, had outrun his supplies. He would have been in no position to support the troops which he had filtered through to the island; they must have fallen back if the garrison had been determined to make the counter-attack of which it was capable. Thus, to other humiliations, the British added that of being bluffed.

To one man, the decision was particularly unwelcome, to the British Prime Minister. It is a little hard to say how at any one moment the events of the war in the Far East affected him. On the whole they were always secondary to the affairs of Europe. It seems that through all this time of the brilliant hundred days of Japan he never succeeded in getting a grip of what was happening. Before the Japanese attack, he had continually underrated the chances of Japanese intervention. He did not equal the grasp which he had on the war in the Middle East. His speeches and his writings about it have a faint note of unreality, of a theatre of war where his views are not translated into action. The impression is dreamlike, of playing with vast conceptions which are fatally unrelated to fact: there is the occasional tumble into an abyss, which he must have foreseen but could not be reconciled to. General Percival's decision to surrender at Singapore had been approved by Wavell. He took the view that the soldiers had done all that could be expected of them, and that a resistance prolonged further would have been a pointless waste of life. In Churchill's distrust of Wavell, which was to become so painfully obvious, perhaps there was an element of resentment for his part in the capitulation.

Churchill's speeches at this juncture are very curious. They are the comment of a detached observer rather than of a committed politician who had to explain the disaster which had befallen one of his projects. The British had surrendered Singapore: that was the bare fact, which people in Britain must stomach, and which they could not be expected to dwell on with satisfaction.

There departed into Japanese captivity a large British

force and most of the civilian staff which had passed their
lifetime in the administration of Malaya. They had little
further part to play in the war, though the suffering of the
prisoners was very great, and was periodically used by the
British Ministry of Information to stir up public effort, and
to keep the people resolute on their liberation. Given the
chance to resist, these same prisoners, many of whom died
before they could be released, might have preferred to be
sacrificed in making the end of Singapore a little more
creditable than it was.

The Japanese rejoiced, and not without cause. They looked
almost incredulously at the facts of the size of their forces,
and what they had achieved against much larger British
forces. Usually the attacking force has to be considerably
greater than the defenders if it is to have any chance of
success; in the Malaya campaign this was reversed. The
Japanese losses had been extravagantly small. From the time
of their first landing to their occupying the Johore causeway
and beginning the assault on Singapore their casualties were,
according to Japanese official information which need not in
this case be disbelieved, 1,793 killed and 2,772 wounded.
They had deployed a force not greater than 35,000 men, and
from information they afterwards obtained, found that the
defending force numbered 80,000. In the actual assault on
Singapore they lost a further 1,714 men killed, and 3,378
wounded. The Japanese claim that not a single man was
captured. The myth has grown up that the Japanese troops
were helped by having a corps of men trained in Malayan
affairs. This is quite false. The number of Malayan experts
was less than ten.

During 1940 and 1941 Germany had discussed with the
Japanese from time to time the possibility of an attack on
Singapore. But the German estimate was that the initial
campaign would last one and a half years and would need
five and a half divisions. Actually Japan required fifty-five
days; and only two divisions.

Japanese publications since the war have shown a high,
rather theatrical morale among Japanese troops. The telegrams are still extant which Japanese generals sent to one
another; their style is extremely patriotic, conventionally
moralistic, reasonably free of the rivalries between officers
and between services which were so common later in the

war. One of the ceremonial acts which the Japanese performed after their victory was to build a tower which was dedicated to holding Buddhist requiem masses for the British killed in the campaign.

The Japanese, perhaps because they had taken Singapore with such an inadequate force, established there an occupation régime which governed it with extreme strictness, and rather purposeless brutality. They felt uneasy. Soon reports began to circulate of extraordinary Japanese measures against any suspected organization. Singapore was principally inhabited by Chinese, and the Kuomintang had used its citizens to extract funds for the Chinese government. They were determined to stop this. The Chinese, in general, were irreconcilable; some had the reputation of being extremely radical in politics, which Japan also feared. The existence, in a peculiarly ramifying form, of the Chinese secret society, was another thing which provoked them. So, from the earliest days of their triumph, ugly tales of police terror and torture were mingled with a great victory. In the first few days of the occupation of the city, they compiled a list of hundreds of the Chinese and arrested them *en masse*. The beaches near the centre of the city became execution grounds by night where the Kempeitai—the Japanese military police—took their preventive action.

Burma

In Burma, the history of the Malayan campaign repeated itself. The Japanese army invaded it on 11 December from Thailand.

Burma, one of the smaller countries of the British Empire, had had, in the half century of its membership, a comparatively uneventful history. Now it became lurid in the extreme. In the minds of most English people, Burma became known, no longer as an oriental paradise inhabited by a merry, picturesque people, but a fated, evil country, the arena—from no fault of its own, it is true—for some of the most horrible fighting of the war. It was not simply to flare into prominence by the brief experience of being overrun, but was to remain a contested land until the end of the war.

Burma had formerly been attached to India. It had been annexed to it as the result of three wars in the nineteenth century. It was an act of convenience for Britain; by no shadow of claims could it be regarded as an Indian land. Its majority people, the Burmese, were one of the Asian peoples with the clearest national consciousness; their economy was not inevitably linked with the Indian; their language and script had only a distant connection with Sanskrit; their religion, to which they were peculiarly devoted, was the Hinayana form of Buddhism, which ultimately derived from India, but which had practically died out there. Hinduism, which Buddhism had once rivalled in India, had revived powerfully, and had overgrown Buddhism. But in Burma, Buddhism had no competitors, and flourished mightily. This rendered Burmese culture different from Indian.

The unnatural union of Burma with India was resented by the Burmese. Their desire for freedom was two-fold, freedom from Britain and freedom from India. This second freedom they won at the time of the great political recasting, at the time of the Government of India Act of 1935. It was perceived that to continue to enforce the unity of the two countries would impose an unnecessary strain on the problematical machinery of government devised for India. Burma was allowed to settle its own destiny, and the Burmese legislature voted to go on its own way. It had a constitution which half met Burma's growing demand for complete freedom. Its government had the same liberties as a provincial government in India under the Act of 1935. But what in India were to be the federal powers of government were in Burma controlled by the British.

In the days of the union between India and Burma, the British had neglected to build up communications between the two countries. A railway was planned, chiefly for military reasons, but was never made. Its absence was to have a powerful effect on the shape of the fighting now to break out. Shipping interests, powerful with the government, saw in it a threat to their monopoly of traffic with Rangoon, and successfully opposed the scheme.

In the years just before the war, political life developed rapidly. The professional and commercial classes were organized in orthodox political parties, which were willing to pursue their national aims through non-revolutionary means

and within the framework of the institutions already conceded. But the desire for independence was greater, perhaps,
than it was in India, though it was not taken as seriously.
Moreover there were revolutionary parties, notably the
Thakins, which meant the party of the 'masters' or 'gentle-
men', which were ready to seek any aid, and do anything,
which would bring about the end of British rule. These
parties, which stirred up political consciousness in Burma,
had a growing clientèle among students, and among people
who had no limiting restrictions placed on their political
activity by economic considerations.

Japan found the political situation in Burma more suited
to its intervention than in any other country. Moreover
Burma, through the existence of the Burma road, had become a major preoccupation of Japanese strategic plans.

Japan had prepared its action in Burma for several years,
and more carefully than in most other centres. It had sent
there a naval officer who, disguised as a trader, had made
the first contact with Burmese politicians. The results were
so promising that a Japanese consul was instructed to build
up a pro-Japanese network. This, however, had brought the
Japanese Ministry of Foreign Affairs into the picture. This,
fearful of angering the British unnecessarily, demanded extreme caution.

Progress came, not from persons engaged in this part of
the enterprise, but from the coming to Burma of a Japanese
army officer, Colonel Suzuki, who was a natural genius at
all kinds of espionage and subversion. He modelled himself
on Lawrence of Arabia. Until 1939 he had had a career as
a regular combat officer; it ended with Suzuki under a
somewhat mysterious cloud, brought about by an incident in
1939 in the war with China. Thenceforward he was a spy.
He chose Burma as his field of activity, and he was as
little subjected to control in what he did there as was
Doihara, a much more celebrated agent and planner of
subversive action in Manchuria and China. Officers like him
were given much latitude by Japan. They might create a
situation which the Japanese army would be free, when the
time came, to manipulate or to ignore, as circumstances
decided.

Suzuki decided that the Thakins offered promising material with which to work. He was a curious man; he was genuinely interested in promoting the movements of Asian peoples to be free; he took seriously the claims of Japanese propaganda that Japan supported all movements for independence; he was regarded with suspicion and as a nuisance by the more orthodox Japanese, who had no intention of conquering large parts of Asia, and simply transferring them to native hands. In Japanese service, he was advancing views and actions which were not at all favoured. He has been described as a rebel by temperament, a conformist by upbringing. His conversation fascinated the Burmese with whom he came into contact. He would tell them to insist on being independent. If, after the Japanese conquered their country, they refused to grant independence, the Burmese ought to shoot back.

Suzuki set himself to form the nucleus of a Burmese independent army, which could be extended as soon as a Japanese army crossed the borders. He calculated that a Burmese force would prove a valuable auxiliary for bringing about the discomfiture of the British, whether in harrying them politically, in forming a link with the Burmese population, or in straightforward military operations. In 1940 he began to select likely young revolutionaries from the class of political adventurers and arranged for thirty of them to be sent over to Formosa for military training in Japanese schools. The thirty Thakins received this education partly in Formosa, partly in Hainan Island; Suzuki had them well grounded, by strict Japanese discipline, in combat tactics, in methods of civilian cooperation with the Japanese army, and in all ancillary methods. It is clear that he had some difficulty in getting these young men accepted in the various training camps, for he acted as a lone wolf, and he had not fully emerged from the disaster which had temporarily blocked his military career. The Thakins, for their part, objected to the strenuous quality of their training, and contemplated desertion. They had actually got control of a small sailing ship with which they proposed to sail for home. On their fate depended much of the modern history of Burma. The accident of who was chosen among the thirty Thakins, the founder members of the Burma Independence Army, governed the course of Burmese politics down to the present day. Because of personality difficulties, the Thakins tended to fall into factional groups, which were reflected for long after, quite irrationally, in Burmese politics.

Suzuki, together with a staff of adventurous Japanese who were looked at rather askance by the Japanese army, transported his thirty Thakins to join the two division of Japanese troops waiting to invade Burma. By a shrewd move to catch the Burmese imagination, he gave each of the Thakins a new name from Burmese folklore, which was peculiarly rich in such things. He devised ceremonial oaths to link them together. And he revived the old Burmese legend that they had discovered ancient charms which brought them invulnerability. This, which was traditionally affected by Burmese insurrectionists, and had been the sustaining weapon of the peasant leader, Saya Sen, in a rebellion in 1930, was obstinately believed by the Burmese populace. It was to support the Thakins handsomely. The atmosphere in their camp was that of a boy scout jamboree, the same vague high-mindedness, the same enjoyment in devising ruses, rather the same kind of humour. The Thakins, half in terrified awe of Suzuki, half in naïve enthusiasm for him, admired the way he genuinely fought for their interests with his orthodox Japanese colleagues.

*

This Japanese dealing with Burmese politicians was to have interesting consequences later as the history of Burma unfolded. But, in the actual conquest, the principal agent was the Japanese army. This fought the battles, and defeated the British. The British were embarrassed by the Burma Independence Army, but it only contributed marginally to their downfall. They complained of the treachery of the population, the clamour against them by the Pongyis (Burmese monks), the betrayal of their movements to the Japanese, and the false intelligence often given to the army by the villagers. For all these things, the Burma Independence Army, playing the part of aide to the Japanese, was partly responsible. Their experience permanently soured the British troops, and gave Burma a bad reputation as a country to be fought in. Anything to do with Burma was thought to be unlucky, and the country filled the army with great apprehension.

However, for their rout, the British had to blame the Japanese directly. They had invaded at the start with two divisions with which they overran the south and took Rangoon, the capital. As in Malaya, the British had placed their confidence in the natural obstacles to troop movements in the rugged, jungle country of the border. Again it had become axiomatic that tanks could not penetrate this, and again the fact had not been tested. They quickly found out that they had deceived themselves. Unlike Malaya, the country was held by too few troops, badly trained, with a defective air force. From the start, the British were too unevenly matched to have any chance of holding the Japanese advance. After Singapore fell, the Japanese were reinforced by another two divisions, which had been campaigning there, and they advanced to the north, pushing back the British before them.

The British accepted the offer of Chiang Kai-shek to send a Chinese army to assist in the defence. They did so reluctantly because, through awareness of maps which were being published in Chungking, they had reason to suspect that Chiang had designs on the Burma frontier, and that, once they were in, the Chinese troops would be hard to evict. Japan, however, prevented this danger by driving them back into China. On the borderland some of the Chinese were broken up, and also suffered a great defeat.

By the end of April, the British were expelled from the country. They were pushed right out of Burma. Eventually the greater part of their forces escaped into India, marching out through the trackless jungle land which intervened between Burma and India. Only a part of the far north remained out of Japanese hands. It was inhabited by Chins and Kachins with whom British rule was unfamiliarly popular, being, like all British administration of the jungle fringes of their empire, so light as hardly to be noticed. This territory was held by a body of irregular troops, recruited chiefly from the Chins, which was raised by British anthropologists. The exploits of this force, the intelligence and devotion of the Chin people, are one of the subjects which has escaped narration.

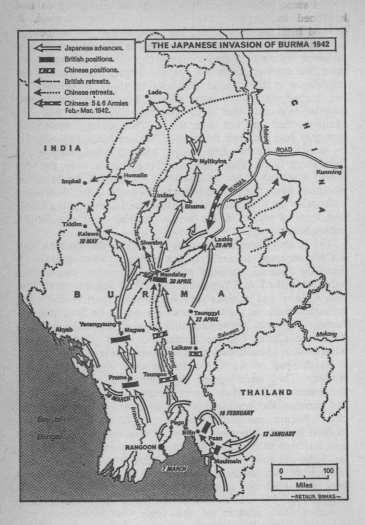

THE JAPANESE INVASION OF BURMA 1942

Japanese advances.
British positions.
Chinese positions.
British retreats.
Chinese retreats.
Chinese 5 & 6 Armies
Feb.- Mar. 1942.

INDIA

Ledo

Myitkyina

Kunming

ROAD

Homalin

Imphal

Indaw

Bhamo

BURMA

CHINA

Chindwin

Tiddim

Kalewa
19 MAY

Shwebo

Lashio
29 APR

Mekong

Mandalay
30 APRIL

B U R M A

Yenangyaung

Magwe

Taunggyi
22 APRIL

Salween

Mekong

Akyab

Prome

Toungoo

Laikaw

30 MARCH

Irrawaddy

Sittang

THAILAND

Bay of
Bengal

Pegu

Bilin

16 FEBRUARY

Paan

12 JANUARY

RANGOON

Moulmein

7 MARCH

0   100
Miles

~ARTHUR BANKS~

The same incidents marked the Japanese advance as had happened in Malaya. The civil government collapsed. It showed itself again and again to be extremely incompetent, its officers were lazy, its resolution was contemptible, its planning was certain to be based on faulty information, its complacency was unlimited. Its poor showing did not come altogether as a surprise. Before the war, the British administration in Burma had been notorious for delays and muddle. When it was put to the test, it perished with the same sense of scandal as the administration in Malaya. The machine of government had been allowed to rust, and its levers broke in the hand when pulled. It was unfortunate because it could not rely upon any machine of popular government to provide a link with the people, or to rouse any enthusiasm on the government side for the war. Shortly before the start of the war, the Prime Minister of Burma, U Saw, who had been on a visit to London, was detected while returning home in making contacts with the Japanese. He was arrested and interned in the Seychelles, but although U Saw was made harmless, the episode did little good to the British sense of security, and brought little change among the politicians who replaced him. (U Saw, a turbulent figure, was the powerful opposition leader in post-war Burma. He came to world notoriety in 1947, when he organized the assassination of U Aung San and half the Burmese cabinet. For this he was hanged.)

The growth of the Burma Independence Army took place as Suzuki had foreseen. By the time that they were able to parade in liberated Rangoon, they numbered 5,000 men, and claimed to number 10,000. Their appeal had been great. But their methods of recruitment were deplorable. The Burmese villages, partly because of the peculiarly rapid tendency of the Burmese to resort to violence, had always had a higher proportion of criminal types than was usual in the East. As the Burma Independence Army advanced through the country it proved to be irresistibly attractive to this sort of recruit. An armed force, with licence to rob and pillage, provided the ideal shelter behind which it was possible to hold the whole country to ransom. The army spread a reign of terror behind the Japanese advance. Its original Thakin leaders found that the control of their troops was passing out of their hands. For seventy-five years Burma had experienced deep and unfamiliar peace in its rural life. The exploits of the Burma Independence Army abruptly destroyed this peace, and, to Burma's cost, it was to prove impossible to restore peace in this generation.

The population of Burma consisted of a Burmese majority, and many non-Burmese people, organized with different customs and religions. Under the long British peace, these had relaxed their suspicions; the different peoples had mellowed, and their government had seemed easy. But the exploits of the Burma Independence Army stirred up the feeling of the Burmese that they ought by right to be dominant, and raised a consequent feeling among the minorities of great insecurity. In panic, the minorities organized for self-protection: where a minority possessed the remains of tribal life, its institutions were rapidly brought into play. In no time, civil war was provoked and was spreading, especially between the Burmese and the Karens, the Burmese and the very large Indian minority, and the Burmese and the hill people, the Kachins. As a result, there took place a terrified mass migration to India, and it is estimated that India, in the midst of war, had to receive half a million refugees. For every refugee to cross the Indian frontier, there were several others who starved and died on the way.

The Japanese became aware of the chaos which was being provoked. Having driven out the British from the whole country, except for a comparatively small corner which was inhabited by Chins, they were looked to by the law-abiding part of the population as the only power able to secure basic order in the country. They had been manoeuvred by Suzuki into giving countenance to Burmese revolution, but it had served its term, and they had really no sympathy with its explosive purposes. Japan, whatever its propaganda might declare, was never a revolutionary power, and generally was on the side of property and privilege. In the middle of June it applied itself to the problem of providing a government for the country. It was not willing to proclaim Burma's independence, but established a provisional government, made up of politicians of the orthodox parties. The Burmese cabinet could only rule the country through the civil service structure of the British, and this the Japanese sought to preserve. Burmese civil servants were promoted to take the part of British officials.

Stability, however, could not be expected as long as the Burma Independence Army was allowed to roam the country, doing its will by sheer force. The decision was therefore arrived at to suppress the army. Colonel Suzuki was to return home to Japan. He sought to stay, claiming that he held a commission for what he had done from Prince Kanin, and therefore came directly under the imperial house, of which Prince Kanin was a member; he asserted that this freed him from control by the Japanese army. But he argued in vain. In place of the Burma Independence Army, a new force was raised, much more regular in its structure, more firmly placed under the control of the new government.

This was a natural, merely prudent step of the Japanese government. It was a decision which any responsible government was bound to take: the Burma Independence Army had stirred up so much feeling that any orderly administration was really impossible so long as it persisted. But the apparent repudiation of Burmese revolutionary nationalism by the Japanese was held by nationalists all over Asia to be difficult to square with Japanese propaganda claims; the more so since the Japanese were at first unwilling to satisfy the Burmese with any talk of independence. In Burma it caused the start of a long-drawn-out quarrel between the Japanese and Burmese nationalism, which was to play a part in the Japanese downfall at the end of the war.

The Dutch East Indies

The fate of the Dutch empire was the same. Because of oil, the territory was especially attractive to Japan. The first Japanese landing in Indonesia had taken place on 6 January. On 6 March, Batavia, its capital, fell. A large-scale naval battle had been fought between 27 and 29 February and resulted in the destruction of five Dutch cruisers, and of the few British cruisers which still were afloat in these waters. By April the fighting was at an end.

The experience of the Dutch was generally similar to that of the British. They had a considerable army in Indonesia; 98,000 men surrendered, almost without fighting, and were interned. Apparently the Dutch could not rely sufficiently on their Indonesian troops to risk combat. A feature of Dutch colonialism was the far greater number of Dutch residents in their colonial territories. The number of internees was therefore greater.

The impressions formed by the Dutch of the victorious Japanese army were interesting, since they come from people who formerly had less to do with the Japanese than the British or Chinese. Their first feeling was one of unwilling admiration. The Japanese marched in, in perfect discipline. For whatever reasons, the disorders of the Japanese occupation, which had been reported in the Philippines, Malaya and Burma, were avoided. There was no deliberate relaxing of discipline while the troops ran wild. Plundering and unlawful high-handedness by the soldiers were prevented. Before long, these first impressions were found to have been much too favourable; but in the early days were unquestionably widespread.

The Dutch noticed that the Japanese carried very little impedimenta, and went without demur, wherever their officers ordered them. It is usually reckoned that, in modern armies of the West, for every fighting man there are eight supporting soldiers; among the Japanese the ratio was said to be as low as one to one. The Japanese continually demonstrated before the eyes of the Dutch that no obstacle could deter them. And there was no sign that the Japanese private soldier, or junior officer, murmured against the savage discipline which was used against them.

*

With these conquests, there came to an end the extraordinary hundred days of Japan. The army and navy had raced ahead, and, after a period of rattling and shaking down the empires of Britain, Holland and the United States, they needed time to rest, and to make new plans. The extent of the territory which had fallen into their hands bewildered, while it exulted them. They had to provide for its administration. They had also to fill out the contents of the extremely vague and propagandist plans for the 'Greater East Asia Co-Prosperity Sphere', which had come into being long before it was planned as a reality.

Meanwhile the Japanese population would have been more than human if it had not given itself up for the time to

the spectacle which was fed to it by all the propaganda
machines of the modern state and was meant to generate a
profound mood of self-wonder. The streak of exhilaration
came after a long and anxious period which preceded Pearl
Harbor, a period of grave economic anxiety, of regrets over
the interminable war with China, of fears that it was getting
out of its depth in international relations, and of perplexity
over the disorders in its political life.

The great outburst of Japanese victories had lifted the
reputation of the Japanese soldier to unexampled heights.
He was suddenly regarded as superhuman and invincible:
his military virtues were so stupendous that it struck wonder
that they had not been noticed adequately before. It seemed
to be useless to struggle against them: they had eclipsed the
virtues of the white man, until then incontestably the most
formidable in the imagination of the Orient. As the Japanese army went to war in 1941 it sang a song called 'Umi
Yukaba'. One of its verses, in translation, is as follows:

> Across the sea,
> Corpses in the water;
> Across the mountain,
>
> Corpses heaped upon the field;
> I shall die only for the Emperor,
> I shall never look back.

No British or American troops ever sang such lugubrious
or unsophisticated words. But the Japanese sentiment was
precisely that of the song. It contains much of the meaning
of war between the western world and Japan; Japan found
hard to understand the cryptic, quizzical, and somewhat
ambiguous songs of the western allies: the simplicity of the
Japanese view gave them strength.

The downward turn in Japan's war fortunes set in the
autumn of 1942, and thereafter its way was steadily towards
disaster. Day after day there was only bad and worsening
news; nowhere, either in its own fortunes or by rescue
through possible triumphs of its European allies, did there
appear any rift in the clouds.

Meanwhile, in the brief moment of joy in Japan, it is
vain to look for any monument of Japanese achievement in
art, music or letters. The Japanese spirit remained strangely

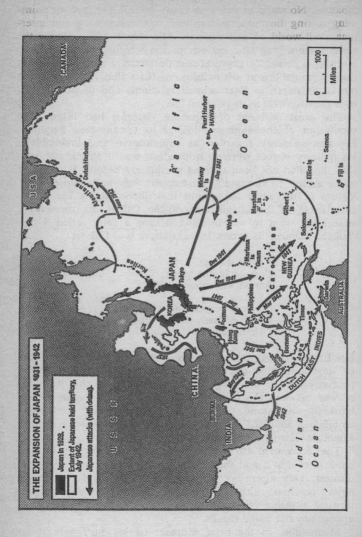

THE EXPANSION OF JAPAN 1931-1942

- Japan in 1928.
- ☐ Extent of Japanese held territory, July 1942.
- → Japanese attacks (with dates).

barren. No works of poetry, philosophy, architecture, or paint-
ing during this time had come to the notice of the international world of cognoscenti, or have won sympathy for the
civilization which was about to endure such ravage and destruction. No sounds of natural gaiety came from Japan: it
was a world now devoted to material advance: it was devoid
of lightness, wit, romantic lyricism, the cultivated intelligence of women. In politics there was no originality: in
science, having borrowed from abroad, Japan was ingenious-
ly adaptive, but was without a creative impulse; in sociolo-
gy, it was unimaginative. The Japanese pursued their war in
a grey atmosphere of the human spirit. Victory, if that
had been possible to them, would not have conduced in any
way to human enlightenment.

14

The Storm in India

WITH Singapore and Burma lost, the storm was breaking on the edge of India. There the consequence was not at first military action, but an intensification of the political crisis which had lasted thirty years and which was compendiously called the freedom struggle.

A great excitement swept India. The British in India had the mortification of being made to realize that the military crisis did not signify for most people there a time of mortal danger, but was a time of opportunity and interesting uncertainty. The news of the rout in South-East Asia had the inevitable effect. Britain imposed only a very slight censorship on news, and it was in consequence possible to form a clear idea of Japan's military prowess. Under the influence of this situation the Indian political situation changed rapidly. The war, and its consequences, was suddenly at its gates: India was no longer to be the distant spectator of events: they were at hand.

By the time of the outbreak of war, it had been obvious, to all who chose to look, that India was nearing a period of deep change. Delhi, its capital, at this time was a place of unusual interest. The last days of the old order were bathed in a rather unreal light. They were touched by a sunset. This revealed possibilities and beauties of the scene which had never been noticed before. The British, who were about to put up the shutters on their period in India, suddenly discovered, as they were on the edge of terminating their role, the enchantment of the country, which most of them had ignored as long as they were in secure occupation. India was in the condition typical of countries which are approaching revolution. Only the first rustling of the storm could be heard. It was not yet disturbing because the politics were still interesting and had not yet become lethal.

New Delhi, built chiefly by Lutyens, was then at the height of its brief but real beauty. It had matured and had been sufficiently lived in to have the atmosphere of a city rather than a camp, as it had been only a short time before; but it had not been sufficiently encroached upon by planless building to be spoilt as it is today. Unlike most capitals which have played a part in this chronicle, it had remained outwardly at peace. It was full of talk, and uniforms, and war; but it remained unravaged. The war had brought a flood of new men to the city for the first time, especially young Englishmen of the citizen army of the war years: these were often intelligently attentive to the qualities of Indian life, and they refused to be bound by the restrictions of the colour bar—that fatal barrier which had done so much harm to race relations in the past, and also cut across the natural enjoyment of the country by British visitors. Though there was more political controversy than ever, there was a distinct thaw in the relations of the British and Indians. The old barriers were falling one by one. Life, in the capital though not in the backwoods, became more normal, relations more relaxed. Even while they were engaged in hot dispute, Indians and British alike began insensibly to sun themselves in the climate of emotional debate, which they enjoyed as the most engaging pastime in the world.

In the political arena war speeded up the struggle of Indian nationalism against the British. But the war had the effect of inflaming even more intensely the divisions within Indian nationalism: between Hindu nationalism, which stood for a united India, and Moslem nationalism, which envisaged a British withdrawal from the continent leaving the predominantly Moslem part to become the independent state of Pakistan. The Hindu-Moslem crisis was the heart of political India. In the critical war years, politics turned chiefly on this, and it was the key to almost everything which happened.

*

The issue between Hindus and Moslems was relatively simple. Over a part of north India, the Moslems, chiefly as a result of past invasions, were in a majority. This was limited to certain regions: over the country as a whole, the Hindus were in a substantial majority. They were, moreover, the more advanced community in political activity.

When Hindus raised the cry of Indian independence, they had assumed that the Moslems would support them, as following the most advanced political leadership, and, at the start of the national movement, most Moslems had done so. At this period, those Moslems who were politically interested, had been attracted by the parties, which, though predominantly Hindu, claimed to be national, transcending both Hindu and Moslem. But, as politics set light to ever-widening circles of people, the Moslems began to draw apart, and to question whether they would have any benefit from independence, if it were won by Hindus.

The issues thus opened up were plain. Could Hindus and Moslems, by a compact between them, still agree on a common plan? Or, when independence came, should there not more properly be an independence for a Hindu India, and another independence, involving the creation of a new state, for a Moslem India? It took time for this conception to spread among the Moslems, but when it had taken root, it was plain that from the Moslems would come a fierce demand for secession. The Congress claims for independence, which the Moslems represented as a plan for transferring British sovereignty over India into Hindu sovereignty over Moslems, lost its shine and became a matter for controversy.

The Moslem community was at first widely regarded as more backward than the Hindus. At first the Moslems had not taken the same advantage as the Hindus of the opportunities of adopting modern style institutions. This was partly because the collapse of the Moghul power at the time when the British first arrived in India was a psychological blow from which it took the Moslem upper classes a long time to recover. Initially they had stood stubbornly aside from innovations and educational opportunities offered by the new Raj which, they felt, had displaced them. There was also the fact that Islam half a century ago was opposed to modern education: Moslems were more shackled by their

1 Italian partisans near Ravenna

2 Soviet partisans returning from an operation in the Pinsk bogs

3 Czech resisters printing illegal leaflets

4   French resisters mining a track

5   The 'Anderson' shelter on display at a factory, February 1939

6   A rehearsal for dealing with gas casualties

7   Interned aliens lining up for accommodation on a housing estate
in a northern estate in a northern town

8 British factory workers making anti-aircraft guns

9 Russian women making bombs

10 Japanese boys hail Pacific victory

11 Lieutenant General Sakai heads
Japanese entry into Hong Kong

12 Russian tanks preparing to attack: Outer Mongolia, July 1939

13 Japanese troops in China

14 Burma: Chinese troops

15 Burma: British troops

16   Gurkha soldier crosses the Irrawaddy, 1945

17   U S aircraft flying to bomb Japan

18 U S Marines establishing a beachhead on Guam

19 Guadalcanal

20 Iwo Jima: U S Marines begin to attack, February 1945

21 Marshals Rokossovsky and Montgomery after the meeting of East and West: Cossacks salute the British Field Marshal with their battle cry

22 Part of the D-Day fleet of 2,000 ships

23 Normandy, 1944: first landings

24 Normandy, 1944: first landings

25 The Soviet flag raised over the Reichstag

26 Grenoble: youthful members of Darnand's fascist militia executed after the liberation

27 Warsaw: hostages hanged after the rising

28 The fate of a French collaborator

29 Dresden: immolating the thousands of victims of the Anglo-American air attack, February 1945

30   Von Papen prisoner

31   Laval taken into American custody at Linz

32 In Saarbrücken, 1,000 survivors of a population of 135,000 salvage their belongings

33 In Yokohama survivors set up home in the open

34   Berlin after the capitulation

faith at this time than were Hindus. The simplicity of the Moslem outlook commended itself to some temperaments among the British, who were mystified and repelled by the more subtle and exotic Hindu character: but some people sensed in the Moslem mind a greater confusion in the response to the modern world than was to be found among Hindus. The Moslem who fell back on Moslem traditions for guidance in the maze of the modern world often found himself afraid. The Islamic institutions were inadequate; they could not be brought up to date. Moslems tended to live in a world of the past, and, being called on to live in the present, were left with ways uncharted and with reactions for which there was no precedent. The Moslem response to the new life was often unpredictable, unreasonable, and, too often, violent.

The question turned on whether the Moslems were right in declaring themselves to be a separate nation from the Hindus, or whether both were fundamentally Indian, divided only by religion. Both Hindus and Moslems had shared a common Indian state for many centuries: at times the Hindus were dominant, at times the Moslems. Was religion alone sufficient to turn them into irreconcilables?

The Moslems argued that it was emphatically so. No common life for the two people was really possible; to hold them together was too artificial. Each community, though they had been joined under foreign rule, lived in isolation from the other. Each had a separate law, its own customs, wore its own clothes, had its own literature, preserved its own way of eating. Sometimes, after prolonged periods of ordered government, they would somewhat unbend and lower their guards. The natural affinities of neighbourliness would prevail to a limited degree over the divisiveness of religion. The common language would inevitably bear some influence in mingling the two peoples. But of a genuine merger of the two societies, there was no sign. Cases of intermarriage between the two communities were very rare, and free intermarriage is the best sign of the fraternization of communities.

The Hindus replied that this was a gross misrepresentation of the position. They could argue that in previous generations the Hindus and the Moslems had felt no such separateness, and automatically regarded themselves as forming a single people. Most Hindus were willing to concede that in recent years the relationship of Hindus and Moslems had often been bad, but this they attributed to the deliberate attempt of the government to play off one community against the other. To divide and rule was, they held, the first principle of the administration. They argued too that the difference between the communities was largely one of economics, and that, if the economic processes were given free play, these would be enough to break down the communal differences and mould the peoples into a single great society.

*

As the political situation became more fluid, with signs from the British that they would contemplate withdrawal, there was deadlock between the two sides. The arguments of both appeared to be conclusive. Attempts at mediation proved always in vain.

The coming of wartime tension gave a great impetus to the deterioration. The Moslems, in the fevered atmosphere of the times, set themselves, under the lead of their principal nationalist party, the Moslem League, to mobilize their forces. In all the provinces of north India they agitated formidably, concentrating on drawing back all the Moslems who still supported the nationalist Congress party. With an ever-increasing show of force, they intimated that they would resort to civil war if any attempt were made to surrender British power to Hindu hands.

The achievements of the Moslem League at this time are due chiefly to a single man, Muhammad Ali Jinnah. He had two distinct careers. Before 1930 he was an all-India leader of the Congress. The interest of Indian nationalism possessed him and the interest of the Moslem community semed to be reconcilable with the ascendancy of Congress. In other words, he, though personally a Moslem, was very much like Motilal Nehru, the father of Jawaharlal Nehru, who, though a Hindu, assumed that Hindu interests would always be subordinate to Indian nationalism. In the beginning of the thirties, he had retired to England for some years, where he had a flourishing legal practice. During this time he reflected, brooded, thought about his previous career and meditated on the ways that his willingness to subordinate specific Moslem interests to national interests had not been met by a similar disposition in Hindu leaders. He returned to India, broke entirely with the old all-India ideas, and ceased to be in any sense a co-worker with the Congress leaders. Instead he challenged them, and on the whole outwitted and out-manoeuvred them. He denied their right to speak at all to the Moslems; his first major enterprise was to dislodge the Hindus from the foothold they had obtained in the Moslem community. Next he built up the Moslems as a formidable striking force which demanded a state for its expression and existence.

His achievement was to inform it with something like the questing assertive feeling of the poles when for more than a century they had been deprived of a state. Eventually, in 1919, they succeeded in breaking through, and forced themselves on the map of Europe. In the same way the Jews, deprived of a state for many centuries, at last completed its reconstitution. Similarly the Indian Moslems had the will, at the time still partly subconscious, to carve out for themselves an independent state in the Indian sub-continent. Jinnah's contribution to history was to recognize the will in advance of anyone else, and to place himself in its service.

All his successes Jinnah won by the force of his character, by his iron will, and by his clearly marked intellectual superiority. He came to his ascendancy late in life. He had been obscurely born—he was a dentist's son in Karachi—and had had the handicap that he was hardly a true Moslem at all, but, according to local gossip, was the grandson of a converted Hindu. Gradually he made his career, and owed very little to any help which he received from any quarter. The unemotional single-mindedness of his character did not go with any of the amiable qualities which make a man the darling of the crowd. Nevertheless, his way forward was made in full view of the world. There were no secrets in his career: it could be discussed, analysed, appraised, and judiciously respected.

It was characteristic of the Moslem community that his worldly success won him solid esteem; as much as did Gandhi's unworldly conduct prevail with the Hindus.

At the beginning of the second chapter of his life history, his phase as leader of the Moslems, he began by taking over the leadership of a weak party, with a very vague ideology, representing every section of a deeply riven society. He hammered it together to be an exceedingly effective political instrument, to which he then, relying for persuasion on intellectual power, dictated policy. He was the new force of Islam incarnate. As such he was indisputably one of the great actors of the time in the war years. He was one of the few individual architects of the great changes which were coming about.

*

With the Japanese at the gates of India the British government felt that something must be done to rally the country to its own defence. The Labour party had at this time increasing influence on the policy of the British government towards India, and they succeeded in persuading the cabinet that the wisest course was to renew its attempt at conciliating Congress. The principal author of this policy was Sir Stafford Cripps. He was a peculiarly able lawyer, a masterly advocate, and firmly convinced of the benefits of democracy, which, he believed, was a suitable government for any territory, whatever might be its circumstances. He had devoted himself to the study of Indian problems. He was convinced that, if Congress demands were satisfied, it would be ready to take its share in the conduct of the war, and that, by a kind of political miracle, the Indian scene would be transformed.

Cripps was mistrusted by the more conservative influences in London. They believed that, in spite of the evidently superior quality of his mind, his judgement of reality was less than shrewd. They were convinced that his appreciation of India was wrong. The situation in India could not be transformed by eloquent appeal to Congress leaders; Congress support, they knew, might be bought at a price, but at a price which would worsen the situation, since it would bring about a revolt by the Moslem population, and would cause such chaos in India that it would be useless for the prosecution of the war and would drain off large forces of troops from elsewhere for internal pacification. At the same time Congress, if it were won round, could make no difference to the military circumstances. If Congress were given a free hand in war administration, it would, argued these critics, mismanage it. By its participation it would alienate a large part of India which, as the result of various appeals, was showing wartime zeal. There was a strong likelihood that Congress, having made a deal, would take the first opportunity of leading India out of the war altogether.

In spite of these doubts, Cripps was personally trusted with the mission to conciliate Congress. The situation for Britain was at the time so bleak, and the cabinet was so preoccupied with other matters, that his confidence that he could reason with the Indian leaders was contagious, and his offer to go out to see what he could do was welcomed. On 11 March 1942 he arrived and spent three weeks in the country, as a kind of ambassador from Britain.

Cripps, as the chief motive of his tour, carried with him a specific offer to Congress from the British cabinet. It proposed as the long-term part of the scheme, that at the end of the war a constituent assembly should draft a constitution for India, and no limitation should be put upon its work. Though it was hoped that India would stay inside the Commonwealth, it would be free to secede from it.

To most people in London, it had seemed that Congress could scarcely have asked for anything more complete or more explicit. Next, as a short-term measure, as something on account, Congress was offered immediate admission to the Indian central government, but on terms. The government would be a diarchy, partly British controlled, partly Indian nationalist in composition. It would continue to be under the chairmanship of the Viceroy. On its side Congress was to approve the war effort.

Bargaining on these terms had been what Congress had had in mind, when, in advance of the Cripps mission, it let it be known that the Labour party pressure for a new initiative was welcome to it. But politics had moved a long way since the world had been at peace in 1939. In India they had become purely communal: the conflict between Hindu and Moslem, Congress and the League, had put all else, even the conflict between nationalist India and the British, in the shade. The Cripps offer, being drafted in part by civil servants in London, had included matter to conciliate the Moslem League as well as Congress. A sense of realism dictated this. It would have been folly to win over the Hindus at the cost of causing inflexible hostility from the Moslems. In the midst of war, the British government could do nothing which would provoke a civil war in India. Nor could it overlook the fact that a high percentage of the Indian army was Moslem, and, in event of a Moslem rebellion, would have dissolved in its hands.

This explains why Cripps was equipped with a fatal document that came to be known as the 'Cripps Offer'. In the eyes of the Hindus, the proposals had the mortal defect that they were conciliatory to the Moslem League demand for Pakistan. The Cripps Offer included a provision that, if the Moslem parts of India declared their firm intention to be separate—by a plebiscite in the areas concerned—they should be permitted to secede and to form their own constituent assembly. This was a permissive clause; it was not a definite award; what was to be decided in fact was to remain open until the war was over. But though the plan was hedged round with limitations, and was only to be looked on as one among several possibilities, the putting of it forward was a bitter shock to the Indian nationalists, who had not yet been taught by frustration, disappointed hopes, and blows of fate, to adjust themselves to realism.

This was the point of major controversy. It was the reason why the Hindus felt they had nothing to gain from the offer. They could not bring themselves to complicate a negotiation with the British over what they considered the national demands of India by introducing into it a solution, though only a possible one, of the Moslem problems; the more so because of their suspicion that the problem had been distorted by the British as a device to counter the national movement.

This was the reason for the breakdown of the negotiation for the long-term settlement. No less completely did Congress reject the short-term offer by which this was accompanied; this was the invitation to join the central government at once. Congress could argue, with some reason, that its Ministers, if it had supplied them, would have been installed in a subordinate position in the central government, from which they might have been again ejected; and, for this, they were asked, for the first time in history, for a solemn undertaking that, if the Moslems persisted in this demand, Pakistan would be conceded. Congress was quite sure that the Moslems would persist if they were encouraged to do so by the attitude taken up by Britain.

The Congress decision was not so unreasonable as it appeared at the time in London. The negotiations were not entirely straightforward. For tactical reasons, Congress preferred that the break with Cripps should come about over the powers which were to be offered to Congress Ministers if India threw in its lot with the war effort. These were to be limited in the army itself to various matters of administration and supply, which the government felt it would be safe to delegate; and it was made woundingly clear that from matters of the higher direction of the war, allied strategy and the organization of intelligence, the Indian leaders would continue to be excluded. Nehru, after an exploratory session with Cripps, said that the offer boiled down to Indian Ministers being given control of the army stationery and of canteens. In spite of exaggeration, there was some truth in this.

An American attempt to mediate in the negotiations was unsuccessful. The United States had become deeply disturbed at the situation. It saw a real danger that national India would secede from the war, and, for military reasons, greatly feared the loss of Indian territory as a base. It feared also the effects upon its ally, China. Few Americans understood the complexity of Indian problems, or the reasons which prompted the British government. For them the situation in India was simplified in terms of a repetition of the American War of Independence, and naturally their sympathies were strongly on the Indian side. The United States was embarrassed that, in a war which it increasingly advertised as a war for democracy and freedom, it should be tied in alliance with Britain, whose past role in India ran so counter to the principles of the Atlantic Charter. It therefore regarded itself as vitally interested in the outcome of Cripps's negotiations. But its endeavours to help them on, and to ease out difficulty, did not achieve their purpose.

*

Yet it was Gandhi who was ultimately responsible for Congress rejecting the British offer. Gandhi was still in effective command of Congress when Cripps came to India.

Nominally he had for a long while stood aside from holding office in Congress. But in fact he, as Congress adviser, had the overriding influence—though it was never quite an uncontested influence—on Congress decisions.

This was understood by the British. Cripps knew that he must convince Gandhi before anyone else. He had long interviews with him. At the end of one of them, it happened that Sardar K. M. Panikkar, an extremely able politician of the Indian princely states, was seen to be going from the sweepers' colony, where Gandhi was staying, on his way to report to his masters, some of the Indian princes whom the excitement of the times had brought to Delhi. He was asked what view Gandhi took of the Cripps Offer. Actually, Panikkar did not know: his visit had not been directly to Gandhi. But from a knowledge of Gandhi's mind, he was certain, and he expressed the opinion in an epigram which has the accent of the Mahatma. It was, he said, a post-dated cheque on a failing bank.

Gandhi later repudiated the latter part of the epigram; he said that he in no wise wished to impute failure to Britain in the war, or success to Britain's enemies. On the other hand, it was clear that his attitude towards the waging of war differed from that of the belligerents. He proposed that resistance to the Japanese on Indian soil should be non-violent. In a letter written to one of his followers in 1942 (quoted by Shri B. R. Nanda in his book on Mahatma Gandhi) he said:

> Remember that our attitude is that of complete non-cooperation with the Japanese army. . . . If the people have not the courage to resist (non-violently) the Japanese unto death and not the courage or the capacity to evacuate the portion invaded by the Japanese, they will do the best they can. One thing they should never do—to yield willing submission to the Japanese.*

However, Gandhi realized that the British in India, and a large element in Congress, could it have been brought to cooperate with the British by the ironing-out of their political differences, would not employ non-violent tactics in resisting Japan. He had, therefore, no wish to see a compromise be-

*B. R. Nanda: op. cit.

tween Britain and the Congress which involved the issue of
waging war. He was, furthermore, possessed by the idea that
if the British left India, Japan would then leave India alone,
and it would be spared the fate of Burma and Malaya. Accordingly, his influence was thrown against the Cripps Offer,
and, in the circumstances of the time, was strong enough to
kill it.

*

In April, soon after Cripps had failed, Gandhi, by one of the
daring simplifications of issues which were a part of his
strength, began to use the slogan 'Quit India'. The precipi-
tating cause of his decision was his foreboding of a coming
crisis, should the government take steps to compel the peasantry to adopt a scorched earth policy in the case of an
invasion. Gandhi said that it was one thing for the Russians
to adopt this policy voluntarily; it was another for a government to impose it on a confused people, too poor to endure
it.

The British protested that, as politically responsible beings,
they could not, in the middle of war, walk out of India,
without making arrangements for the orderly transfer of
British power. The suggestion that they should go seemed
self-evidently absurd, and the fact that it was made seemed to
the local administration either to reflect on the political sense
of the opposition, or to proclaim that the demand was made
for objects of whipping up national feeling, and it was not
expected that it would be considered seriously. The British
had been willing to promise, in a series of policy statements,
which gradually eroded their position, that British power
should eventually be wound up. Most of these were sincere.
They felt injured when Congress doubted their word. They
argued that they must have time: essentially it was impossible
to set about the hazardous political experiment in wartime.
The British side, although under pressure of the social radicalism which was mounting at home—increasingly liberal in
statements and assurances about long-term intentions—remained adamant against immediate radical changes until they
judged that the war should have been won. The day-by-day
pressure of the events of war at home was too great to allow
the liberal forces in the Westminster parliament to give very

much consecutive attention to events in India. It was upon the constant distraction of the British government in London that British bureaucrats in India chiefly relied; it saved them from having their hands tied.

*

Congress, in facing a renewed rebellion, had the experience of its two major collisions with the British to work upon. It had learned much in these. In 1942 Congress was better organized than it had been ten years earlier.

The traditional Congress method in working against the government was to use the method of 'open conspiracy'. That it conspired could not be doubted: but it avoided anything in the nature of a secret plot, since by doing so it strengthened its moral force. Politicians who plotted secretly drew on themselves some of the odium that terrorists are never entirely free from, even when the government, as in India, was unpopular. Congress seldom made any secret of its plans; it carried them out in daylight.

Thus, when Gandhi turned from patient agitation and persuasion to direct action, he openely proclaimed it. Success in what he intended would depend on the willing cooperation of masses of the people. Therefore, after giving his ultimatum in late May, all through June and July he worked up the feeling of the country by explaining in every possible way what Congress, under Gandhi's direction, meant to do. He hoped, by summoning the people, to induce so many men at all levels to withdraw their support from the government—while taking care to be non-violent—that the business of carrying on the government would become impossible, and the British would evacuate. The army would have a large number of deserters; so would the police; the workers in the towns, by going on strike, would halt the production of war materials; chaos would set in in the civil administration. And all would be done without violence. Gandhi, even at a great crisis was enough of a lawyer to frame his own statements, and to persuade most of his colleagues to do the same, in such a way as to ensure that this point was clearly made.

Gandhi was waging a war of nerves. The British were bent on giving no provocation. Their interest was to prevent matters going to extremity. Though by the mid-summer, Japan had passed the peak of its war, though the battle of Midway Island was recognized by experts as having been a decisive test of strength, though Japan's *élan* was slightly drooping, the British government had still only a very slight margin of safety to play with. The danger of invasion was still very real, and a Congress rebellion would be found to add to the emergency of the war; it would threaten the Allied use of India, which, geographically, seemed likely at this stage, before subsequent successes of the United States in the Pacific, to play a major part. To contain the outbreak of national feeling, which Gandhi knew he could command, required great coolness and discrimination on the part of the government in deciding the precise moment for contending it.

The man who had to combat Gandhi, and who at this stage flared into prominence, was Lord Linlithgow. He had been Viceroy for five years. On the whole he had not had an impressive term of office. He had arrived with the reputation of being an expert on agriculture, having been chairman of a commission which was expected to do something about this flagging but vital Indian industry; but he had totally disappointed the country by taking no initiative. By the time of the war he had shown that he entirely lacked the common touch, the ability to communicate with the masses, and, if he was sympathetic with anybody, it was with the bureaucrats. He may have been unlucky in this; but though there were men who affected to find human feeling in him, few if any of the politicians ever established rapport with him. He had neither an evident enjoyment in the discharge of his great office nor a knack of handling the politicians of varying and often irreconcilable opinions who were his necessary acquaintances. He seemed totally to want imagination, and could not fire others with a vision of the importance of what he had to do. He had great industry without a capacity to turn this to account in ways which caught the imagination, considerable public spirit without it being able to gild any of his actions. Politically his main task had been to preside over the constitutional reforms which were meant to convert India into a Federation and to bring the Government of India Act of 1935 into operation; but in this also he failed to achieve anything. The Federation never got off the ground, and it was widely believed that its failure was partly due to Lord Linlithgow's willingness to let matters drift. He had allowed himself to be weighed down by the Indian realities and concluded, on seeing them at close quarters, that the proposed constitution was not really prudent.

There is no need to see Lord Linlithgow as an essentially fascist type, as was apt to be supposed by some Congressmen. In calmer times he would have been perfectly happy in presiding over a democratic and constitutional India; he was not a permanent adversary of liberalism. But in the conditions of war, he judged it clearly crazy to hand over political responsibility even in part, to politicians who were untested, and whose statements had aroused a strong suspicion that they were opposed to the war. Lord Linlithgow's view was that of British common sense at the time. He had the strength of seeing the situation in the same light as Churchill and the majority of the British cabinet, and therefore was given their confidence in taking the steps which he proposed. One needed to be a man of exceptional political vision to see that Indian national feeling might still be enlisted for the war, and that political boldness might still achieve what it set out to do.

Linlithgow's lack of imagination had allowed the initiative to pass to Gandhi. The government only prevaricated and played for time; Gandhi promised action. Now Gandhi was about to use his opportunity, to take the steps which many men feared to tread but which their mood would support, and to commit Congress to the greatest gamble of its career. The expectation of action set in strongly among the people, so that Congress, though the organizers of the mood, found themselves finally swept along by it. Linlithgow had cool nerves. That which made him incapable of giving creative leadership and made him dull to the distressed conditions of all around him, served him well in this crisis.

In the first week of August, Gandhi summoned the Working Committee of Congress to Bombay. He made no secret of the fact that his intention was to speak the words which would set in motion a new civil disobedience movement on a grand scale.

Late at night the police pounced and arrested Gandhi and all the Congress leaders. They were transported to carefully arranged and not uncomfortable prisons. Gandhi himself was interned in a requisitioned palace of the Aga Khan. The operation had been carefully planned, and, unlike most actions of the Indian government at that time, had been kept carefully secret. The success with which it was executed helped to restore the self-respect of the government.

*

For the rest of the war, Congress was inactive. Most of its leaders continued to be in prison. The government, which had been anxious about the extent of their popular support, discovered that this had been exaggerated; but exercised a perhaps understandable prudence in keeping in the leaders until Hitler was defeated.

The continuing incarceration of the Congress leaders left the way clear for Moslem agitation. By the time that Congress orators were once again free, they found that the Moslem leaders had organized the Moslem community fairly solidly, and that Congress opposition counted for little. One of the unforeseen consequences of Gandhi's 'open revolt' had been to let in Pakistan.

The British authorities were relieved at the passing of a crisis. But, though they might have been expected to revise their general attitudes in the light of a proved weakness of Congress, they did not do so. Their policy followed very closely the official and unofficial statements of it. This was that time was nearly up for the British in India, and that at the end of the war Britain would do exactly what it had said it would do: make a sincere attempt to set up a government, or governments, in India and leave the sub-continent. Most of the politicians in England, even the less enlightened ones, and most civil servants in India, even the more elderly ones, were in agreement about this. For the present India's war-effort was still needed, and nothing would be done to rock the boat. But as the war went on, the government gradually ceased to have the feel of certainty and stability, and took on the style and temper of a provisional government. From London a strong breath of discouragement was blown at anyone who played with other concepts of the future.

Gandhi, the man of peace, who had been obliged by political circumstance to play such a large part in wartime politics, ceased to be a determining figure of the war. Indeed, never again was he to have the personal dictatorship which he had had of the opinion and actions of Congress. His decisions in 1942 marked his passage from supreme authority. After the war, though he had great influence, and though for a time a great deference was used towards him by all who sought to mould events in India, new forces had appeared, and he had to bend before these.

Gandhi's eclipse for the rest of the war, and the eclipse of Congress, removed from India the feature of its politics which had made India fascinating for so many. In a world given up to the contest for brute power, and, worse still, for military power, the claim of Congress that it was striving for higher things was refreshing. Congress politics were intensely histrionic; drama was the essence of them. They were also steeped in arguments over political and secular morality. It was breathtaking to find Congress, in the middle of the war, calmly demanding on moral grounds concessions which no government could have made, least of all a government which possessed a still unbeaten army; yet it had the authority to compel the rational discussion of its demands. All this was now given up. The politics of India were deflated; they followed more practical, limited, lesser ends; greater vision had been dispersed by contact with reality. Yet never again were Indian affairs to be felt as touching the heart of humanity generally as they were when the arch prophet of them had moved around with his strange entourage which recalled, in manners and circumstances, that of St Francis of Assisi and the other compelling figures of the past and perhaps the future.

*

Gandhi's adversary, Lord Linlithgow, also stalked out of the picture. Immensely tall, gaunt, awkward, he had been out of place in Hindu India, which liked to discuss with passion those ideas which seemed to mean little to Linlithgow. His final actions were not much to his credit. In the summer of 1943 there took place a frightful famine in Bengal. For the first time for thirty-five years this dreaded event had recurred in India. It was an ugly fact that this spectre, to exorcise which had been one of the claims made for British

rule, had again appeared. This particular famine was man-
made. Throughout the episode there was no actual shortage
of food supplies in India. But these were allowed to remain
hoarded because the railways, under pressure of wartime operation, had broken down, because the civil servants, also
under wartime pressure, realized too late what was happening. It did not adapt the famine code, which kept the country
from starving in normal times, to the changed circumstances
of war. It was too much harried by urgent and unfamiliar
problems of administration.

In Bengal a great exodus took place from the countryside
to the town, the opposite to the direction of population flow
in the previous year when the panic set in that India was to be
bombed. More and more frightful tales began to circulate of
a population driven by hunger to roam until they fell dead
from emaciation. The streets of the great modern city of
Calcutta were strewn with corpses, and such sights began to
appear there of the juxtaposition of extreme wealth and of
stark hunger as had before the war been notorious of eastern
metropolises such as Shanghai. Another blow had been dealt
to the credit of the British government in Asia.

As reports of what was happening began to come out of
Bengal people expected that the Viceroy would tour the
famine area, to bring what help was possible, to be seen
communing with the people, and to inquire into what was
evidently a failure of administration. To visit the scene of
disaster was a tradition of the Viceroy. But, inexplicably,
Linlithgow on this occasion departed from tradition. Week
after week went by, and he spent the last days of his term of
office in Delhi and Simla.

His successor, the new Viceroy, promptly reversed this behaviour. The solid benefit which by his immediate visit he was
able to do the administration struck the country as a rebuke
to his predecessor. It was evident that more could have been
done by energy, imagination and improvisation. Wavell called
in the army to relieve the miseries of the people, and for a
period this enjoyed a very real and unusual popularity.

Yet Lord Linlithgow, reluctantly though he may be
praised, played a great part in guiding Indian affairs so that
events took one shape and not another. He was given much
latitude by the home government. After the failure of Cripps,

his judgement prevailed on most matters. He handled the open rebellion of Congress almost under the eyes of the would-be invader. That so few lives were lost, and that India continued belligerent, was due to his calm and to his sense of proper timing.

15

---◆---

Midway Island's Battle

THOUGH the attention of the western allies was fixed uneasily upon the territorial gains of the Japanese, that of the most influential Japanese strategists continued to concentrate upon the war at sea. It was to be the greatest naval war in history. The great prize of war would be the mastery of the Pacific Ocean, and this would go to whichever navy proved to be the stronger. The Japanese war planners, in the months after Pearl Harbor, had kept a very flexible outlook. Some favoured a blow in the Indian Ocean, which would open the way to military operations in the region. There was even talk of a naval sweep of the Indian Ocean, which would end with the Japanese making contact at Suez with the victorious German armies. Others wanted an attack in the southern Pacific which would isolate Australia; others a renewal of the attack on Hawaii which Pearl Harbor had begun.

Nearly all sections agreed that Japan must continue to be aggressive. Only by exploiting the impetus gained by Pearl Harbor could Japan even seem to prosper. The long-term odds against Japan were so desperate that the conversion of the war into a defensive one would have been half to admit defeat. The best course lay in a constant series of surprises, which should divert attention from the sombre reality of Japan's true position.

During all this period, the Japanese army showed little willingness to embark on joint plans with the navy. At this time the situation and prospects of Germany were very uncertain: it was in the middle of its great adventures against

219

Russia, which, if they had been successful, would have altered the complexion of the war: the Japanese army was therefore anxious to keep its hands free, so that it could be ready to strike whenever this might, by the unfolding of events, become desirable. Although, by its southward move, Japan had turned its back upon Russia, and was genuinely anxious to make its non-aggression pact with Russia a reality, it could not ignore the fact that Russia was reeling. If it were to be defeated, or to be in obvious danger of defeat, a new situation would come into being, and Japan would be driven to interfere in Siberia. Its divided attention during these months probably accounts for the salvation of India, and perhaps of Australia, from invasion.

The centre of initiative in the months between Pearl Harbor and June 1942 was the brain of Admiral Yamamoto. It is true that, as Commander-in-Chief, he was still technically subordinate to the naval General Staff. But he was regarded by everyone as the author of the victory at Pearl Harbor; and he used the prestige which this gave him to impose his concepts upon the more conservative Japanese admirals. In Yamamoto, Japan had produced its only undisputed genius of the war: a man whose ideas gave a new turn to naval strategy, and who had the capacity to translate the ideas into action.

As a next move, Japan sent a fleet of five aircraft carriers and three battleships, six cruisers and twenty destroyers, into the Indian Ocean in the direction of Ceylon. It was in the command of Admiral Nagumo, who had had the operational command at Pearl Harbor. It was a task force very similar to that which had raided Pearl Harbor, and its objective was to bomb Colombo and a naval base at Trincomalee in the same manner, though of course it could not hope for the same element of complete surprise. It was seeking out the eastern fleet of the British navy, and would try to put it out of action in the Far East by dealing it the same crippling blow that had been inflicted on the American Asiatic fleet.

On 1 April 1942 the British Admiral, Sir James Somerville, was alerted to the presence of Nagumo's fleet, and concentrated his available force to meet him. Somerville had a fairly large fleet, five battleships, seven cruisers, and three aircraft carriers and sixteen destroyers; but the battleships were chiefly obsolete. He had the enormous advantage that he held the

Japanese naval cipher; and the Japanese did not suspect this. No major shift took place in the Japanese disposition but he was aware of it as soon as it happened. The eyes which this gave him were probably the decisive thing in the action which followed.

On 4 April the Japanese made what was intended to be a major air strike at Colombo. They found the British alert to the attack; no warship was in harbour; the air force was already in the air, and gave the Japanese a fair fight. The Japanese, denied the advantage of surprise, broke off the attack to bomb, and sink, two British heavy cruisers, which had approached dangerously near to the Japanese aircraft carriers from which the bombing planes had come.

Somerville had in the meanwhile discovered that Nagumo's force was larger than he had at first supposed. He recognized that he was hopelessly outclassed; his old and very slow battleships were no match for the enemy. He was therefore forced to take evasive action by day, and attempt to engage the Japanese at night, although in fact no naval engagement took place. On 9 April Nagumo made an air strike at Trincomalee, the British naval base, but again failed to take it by surprise. The anti-aircraft and fighter defences were formidable: nevertheless the Japanese bombers did more harm than they had done at Colombo. They ended the raid by locating and sinking one of the British aircraft carriers.

With that, the Japanese raid into the Indian Ocean came to an end. Their total loss had been five bombers and six fighters. They had sunk an aircraft-carrier and two heavy cruisers, with naval auxiliaries and a quantity of merchant shipping, and they had destroyed thirty-nine British aircraft. In conjunction with the Japanese casualties at Pearl Harbor, their losses were absurdly low from this initial combat with the American and the British navies. In ships traded, Somerville came off decidedly the worse. But he had saved the bulk of his fleet from the destruction that might have overtaken it from the Japanese aircraft carriers, and for this he had to thank the decipherers of the Japanese code.

The Japanese were planning the capture of Port Moresby. This was in New Guinea: from its occupation Japan counted on being able to menace Australian ports and airfields. Its capture, as some optimistic Japanese appreciation asserted, might even force Australia out of the war. The military force needed for this operation appeared to be so small that, for once, the navy had the ready cooperation of the army; and was to convoy a Japanese landing force. The Americans and the British agreed with the Japanese appreciation, and decided that, though still far from ready to offer serious opposition to the Japanese, the operation must be resisted. They mustered the forces available to them: these were built round the American aircraft carriers, the *Yorktown* and the *Lexington,* together with an Australian cruiser squadron, a British battleship and smaller craft. To deal with this concentration, Nagumo's fleet, on its way back from its operations in the Indian Ocean, was ordered to detach two of its aircraft carriers, which reached the Japanese base in the Coral Sea late in April, and joined the light carrier and six cruisers supporting the Japanese transports.

For the first time in the war a battle was fought between Japanese and American aircraft carriers. This action, the Battle of the Coral Sea, lasted from 6 to 8 May. It was a drawn action. The rival forces were never in sight of one another, and the battle resolved itself into a hunt for one another by their planes. One of the American carriers, the *Lexington,* was sunk, and the second so severely damaged that it was put out of action. But for the first time in the war, the apparent Japanese invincibility was checked: both Japanese carriers were crippled, and the light carrier was sunk. The heavy aircraft carriers were able to return to Japan, but in a condition which put them out of use for several months; their absence in the impending engagements was probably of decisive consequence. In the air combat, the Japanese airmen, among whom the losses had at last been severe, had shown faults in tactics and intelligence which surprised naval observers generally. They were unused to night operations, and out of their element in making night landings on their carriers. It became plain that the high standards of precision which had made Pearl Harbor possible had been gained by a very few fliers, and the majority of them were far below these. As the result of the operation, the aircraft carriers lost three quarters of their bombing planes and their pilots. Yamamoto, it began to be plain, had allowed his methods of warfare to outstrip the personnel which would have made these decisive. As a result of this first naval reverse, the attack on Port Moresby was called off, and this was to prove of great significance for the future development of the war.

The Americans, though they were concerned about their losses in carriers, were not entirely displeased at the result of the battle. They had brought to an end the run of easy and almost insolent successes by the Japanese. As the result of the air battles, they drew various tactical conclusions, and strengthened the force of fighter planes on their carriers.

These two operations strengthened Yamamoto in his belief that the further acquisition of territory was not of consequence, and that any action which frittered away the Japanese power from its main preoccupations was dangerous. Under his insistent pressure, it was decided that Japan must concentrate its efforts on the destruction of what was left of the sea power of the western allies, especially of the American Pacific Fleet. He, who had designed the raid on Pearl Harbor, was in no illusion about Japan's hopeless position if the war was prolonged, or until Japan had gained the full advantage which had been hoped for in that bombardment. At the moment when Japan at home was still exulting in the mastery of the lands in the South Seas, he saw only the danger preparing for it in the American dockyards. If the United States had the time to bring its economic strength into play, and to translate this into warships, the United States would be irresistible. Japan could find safety only by striking again, and at once.

Yamamoto therefore urged, and after some dissent from the naval General Staff got it accepted, that Japan's next move should be a conquest of Midway Island. This island is 1,100 miles north-west of Pearl Harbor. If it fell into Japan's hands, it would be ideal for mounting a Japanese offensive against the Pacific coast of America. Yamamoto counted on the United States accepting that its defence was of vital interest, and that it would bring out what was left of the American navy in its defence. In the battle which would result, he reckoned on sinking the American carriers; and this was the main objective of the expedition. The force which chance had put beyond Japan's reach at Pearl Harbor he would now succeed in driving into action.

Another motive which also weighed with him was to deprive America of the possible use of Midway Island as the airfield for the bombardment of Japan. Japan had been warned of the danger of bombardment because in April President Roosevelt had authorized a spectacular raid upon Tokyo, primarily for the effect of morale building in America. The raid, under the command of Lieutenant-Colonel James H. Doolittle, had been from land bombers released from American aircraft carriers which, after their attack, had flown on to land in China. Though Midway Island had played no part in this actual operation, it was clear that in fact it might do so in the future; Midway was only 2,500 miles from Tokyo. Yamamoto felt himself heavily burdened by the duty of protecting the capital of his master the Emperor from the indignity of bombardment. Everything pointed to Midway Island as the target at which he should strike. If he succeeded there, he planned to press on Tojo, the Prime Minister, the need to seek a negotiated peace with the United States, even to the extent of proposing terms which seemed plainly disadvantageous to Japan.

The United States had been in occupation of Midway Island since as long ago as 1867; but it was only in 1938 that it recognized its importance. It began to spend large sums of money in fortifying it as a kind of outpost of Pearl Harbor. It was to prove one of the chief theatres of the Pacific war. It was a small coral island; the colours, in the dazzling sunshine, were so bright and assertive that they wearied the eye. In the years just before the war the Americans had built a small but very up-to-date hotel. Its public rooms had, uncannily, the feeling of mountain hotels in, say, Austria; it was strange because the nearest mountains were thousands of miles away; the illusion was heightened because the views from the hotel rooms might have been alpine. The vivid white of the ubiquitous coral might have been from snow. The strangest phenomenon of the island was its prehistoric appearance. On all sides were small, gnarled, dried-up, gaunt trees, of stilted and incredible shape, looking like fossils. The whole place was unnaturally silent. There were noises of traffic and motor cars; but behind this a great hush prevailed. The impression was unreal and nightmarish. This was now to be the scenery for one of the very great battles of the war.

The Japanese assembled a huge fleet. It consisted of eight aircraft carriers, of which four were very large, eleven battleships, twenty-two cruisers and sixty-five destroyers and twenty-one submarines; it was the greatest fleet concentration which had been known in the history of the Pacific. The fleet was divided into three parts. The main striking unit, in which were the aircraft carriers, was to make for Midway. Following this, three hundred miles in the rear, were the battleships. Very oddly, Yamamoto, who this time did not confine himself to making the general plan of action and supervising it from his headquarters in Japan, placed himself in command of this section. It was held in reserve to take whatever action was required after the aircraft-carriers had attacked at Midway. As Yamamoto imposed a radio silence throughout the battle, he was virtually a spectator of the action which was imminent. Thus Yamamoto condemned himself to impotence in the type of battle which he had for so long preached as the typical one in the stage which naval strategy had reached at the time. There was a convoy of eleven transports with the necessary landing party from the army. The third section of the fleet, grouped round two carriers, was to detach itself from the main body and to move up to the Aleutian Islands, attacking and landing on some selected places. This was included in the general plan as the complication and the feint which nearly all Japanese plans contained. The concept was that the United States would divide whatever forces were available to it, and one force would sail for the North Pacific in search of this decoy.

From the start there were grave doubts about the expedition among the Japanese naval staff. There was anxiety about the deficient preparation of officers, about their inadequate briefing, about the speed with which the expedition was launched, about the lack of time for adequate digestion of the lessons of the Battle of the Coral Sea, about the wisdom of the tactics which had been used in that, about the security which had been observed, even about the morale of some of the fleet. The senior officers were despondent at the boasting and indiscipline of some of the younger men. The navy pilots, whom Yamamoto had trained, were held in suspicion by the rest of the navy, and this was not relieved by their tendency to regard themselves as a race apart. Especially by the more responsible officers, Yamamoto was criticized for the speed which he demanded. This required that the two powerful aircraft carriers, which had been badly damaged in the Battle of the Coral Sea, could not take part; they had to be in dock under repair for several months. Their absence was severely felt. But Yamamoto felt that the political situation required immediate action, and everything was subordinated to this.

The sailing of the fleet from Hashira on 21 May was one of the most spectacular sights seen in any country during the war years. There were cheers and enthusiasm from the considerable crowd who witnessed it. The Japanese, though they lived with extreme frugality on all their expeditions, contrasting spectacularly in this with the standards of well-being required by British and American forces, observed ritual and ceremony for commemorating the start of such a major operation. On this occasion, the sailing of a fleet, which was intended to complete the work of Pearl Harbor, and sink the remainder of the American Asiatic navy, was blessed by all the forms of Shinto, the Japanese state religion, and also, though less wholeheartedly, by Buddhism. Cups of saki were drunk which were a present from the Japanese Emperor. Western scholars, reading of these scenes, may find their memory jogged to remember the account by Thucydides of the sailing of another fleet on what was meant to be the culminating operation in a war 2,300 years before.

> The ships being now manned, and everything with which they meant to sail being put on board, the trumpet commanded silence, and the prayers customary before putting out to sea were offered, not in each ship by itself, but by all together to the voice of the herald; and bowls of wine were mixed through all the armament, and libations made by the soldiers and their officers in gold and silver goblets. In their prayers joined also the crowds on shore, the citizens and all others that wished them well. The hymns sung and the libations finished, they put out to sea, and sang. The first ships then raced each other in columns as far as Aegina.

The battle came on 4 June 1942. The Americans had been better informed than the Japanese Intelligence allowed for, and had again been admirably served by what they were able to learn from cracking the Japanese naval code. They were aware of what Japan had gone to ingenious lengths to hide: that their main objective was Midway, and that the assault on the Aleutians was a diversion. Yamamoto was right in supposing that the Americans would fight, even though their navy had not yet recovered from Pearl Harbor, and was manifestly not ready; he was wrong in thinking that they would divide their inadequate fleet, and would send a part to hunt for the raiders in the Aleutians. The Americans could assemble on the spot three aircraft carriers: in the whole American navy at this time there were seven. One of these carriers was the *Yorktown,* which had been so heavily damaged in the Coral Sea that the Japanese believed it sunk, and had accredited themselves with a groundless victory. In fact it escaped to Hawaii, and, while the Japanese ships in a similar plight had entered the Japanese shipyards for thorough repairs, and were out of action for some months, the Hawaiian shipyards, under pressure of the news from Midway, made the *Yorktown* fit for fighting again in three days, though their first estimate had been that it would take a matter of weeks. The Americans also assembled eight cruisers and fifteen destroyers. The Japanese had therefore a more formidable resistance to overcome than they had thought it possible for the United States to assemble, especially as they also underestimated the American strength in planes and troops on Midway.

The Japanese navy had no radar. That Japan, and that Admiral Yamamoto, who had espoused everything to do with the air, had neglected to acquaint himself with this invention, is astonishing. The fact must detract something from Yamamoto's reputation for alertness. Radar had already been widely used in Britain for more than two years, and a form of it was also known in Germany. The Germans sent the Japanese two radar sets by submarine, but either they did not send technicians with the apparatus, or these lacked the quality to make themselves attended to. This incident shows how slight and ineffective was the technical cooperation of the two powers. In the present case the deficiencies of Intelligence, working without adequate equipment, was to exact a price.

The first that the Japanese admiral commanding the aircraft carrier, who was again Nagumo, knew of the proximity of the Americans was when, about 9 o'clock on the morning of 4 June, he was surprised by an American raid when he had his aircraft assembled on deck for a raid on Midway but when they had not yet taken off. As it appeared afterwards, the fate of the mighty armada, of the Midway expedition, and of the possibility of a future descent on the American coast, was decided in five minutes. Nagumo's carrier was torpedoed at this time, and three of the four carriers were mortally struck. The battle continued all that day, very similar to the Coral Sea, with the two navies out of sight of each other; this time the Japanese pilots, in contrast to the Americans, proved definitely inferior. The action was a confused affair of planes from each side which savagely attacked the others, and then pounced on each other's carriers when they were inadequately guarded.

The Japanese had more than their share of mischance. Radio messages were received five minutes too late; cloud movements happened in such a way as just to obscure the movements of the enemy. But in all the confusion, it stands out that on this occasion the high commanders, and the Japanese navy as a whole, did not display the professionalism, the power of rapid adaptation, the coolness amid the horrors of an air combat at sea, which were necessary to bring victory in this kind of action.

Except in the apparatus to facilitate information about what was happening, the defects in the Japanese fleet were personal rather than mechanical. Japan did not lose the battle because of the engineering superiority of the United States. In the actual fighting, the Japanese aeroplane, the Zeke, an improvement on the Zero fighter, which was first tried out in this encounter, was the best plane on either side.

The American fleet, as it appeared later, did not realize for some time how complete and profound their victory had been. In the confusion of the conflict, they assumed for some time that two of the carriers, which had in fact been sunk, had escaped and were on their way back to Japan. Ultimately the facts were established and they were these. Japan had lost all four of its largest aircraft carriers (the fourth was lost later in the day) and a heavy cruiser. It had lost 322 aeroplanes, and 3,500 sailors. The American losses were the *Yorktown*, which was finally sunk, and a destroyer; 150 aeroplanes; and 307 lives.

Admiral Yamamoto, with the main force of battleships, made some effort at retrieving the disaster. He recalled the aircraft carriers which had been sent to the Aleutians, and resumed the hunt for the American carriers, which had destroyed his own fleet. But, in the end, he broke off the battle, partly, it seems because he felt he could no longer rely on the Japanese Intelligence, and because he decided not to risk his battleships further.

The subordinate operation, the one against the Aleutian Islands, had petered out in aimless sailings. There were no serious Japanese losses. But there were no successes either to set against the losses at Midway.

The Japanese government, very prudently, did not risk the shock of the defeat and the collapse of hopes becoming public. Its first aim was to hush up the defeat. One of the Japanese admirals (quoted by John Deane Potter in his book, *Admiral of the Pacific*) said: 'Our forces suffered a reverse so decisive and so grave that details of it were kept as a secret to all but a limited circle, even within the Japanese navy. Even after the war, few among high ranking officers were familiar with the details of the Midway operation.'* A Japanese naval captain complained of the way that the returning sailors were held incommunicado. The wounded were brought ashore after dark, and taken to hospital through the rear entrances. He was himself among those who suffered. The experience is described in *Midway: the Battle that Doomed Japan* by Fuchida and Okumiya.† 'My room was in complete isolation,' he says. 'No nurses or medical attendants were allowed in, and I could not communicate with the world outside. All the wounded from Midway were treated like this. It was like being a prisoner of war among your own people.' After the Japanese surrender in 1945, all the papers about the defeat, classified as top secret, were burned. The extent and the gravity of the disaster which Japan had suffered did not become plain to the Japanese public until publication by the survivors in the course of the 1950s.

The long run of sensational Japanese victories, bought at such little cost, had come finally to an end. The crippling of the U S Pacific Fleet at Pearl Harbor, and the blows at the Royal Navy, had all been made at the ridiculously small expense of the loss of four destroyers. This time was over. At Midway a technically smaller American fleet had challenged

*John Deane Potter: op. cit.

†Fuchida and Okumiya: *Midway: the Battle that Doomed Japan,* U.S. Naval Institute, Hutchinson, 1957.

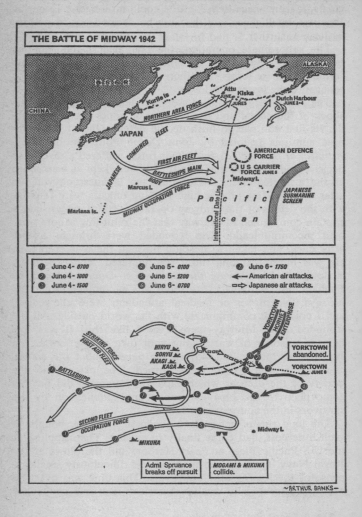

THE BATTLE OF MIDWAY 1942

ALASKA
CHINA
Kurile Is.
Attu
JUNE 5
Kiska
JUNE 5
Dutch Harbour
JUNE 3-4
NORTHERN AREA FORCE
JAPAN
FLEET
COMBINED
FIRST AIR FLEET
AMERICAN DEFENCE
FORCE
JAPANESE
BATTLESHIPS MAIN
BODY
U S CARRIER
FORCE JUNE 3
Marcus Is.
Midway I.
MIDWAY OCCUPATION FORCE
JAPANESE
SUBMARINE
SCREEN
Mariana Is.
Pacific
Ocean
International Date Line

❶ June 4 - 0700	❹ June 5 - 0100	❼ June 6 - 1750
❷ June 4 - 1000	❺ June 5 - 1200	⟵ American air attacks.
❸ June 4 - 1500	❻ June 6 - 0700	⇨ Japanese air attacks.

STRIKING FORCE
FIRST AIR FLEET
HIRYU
SORYU
AKAGI
KAGA
YORKTOWN
HORNET
& ENTERPRISE
YORKTOWN
abandoned.
BATTLESHIPS
YORKTOWN
JUNE 6
SECOND FLEET
OCCUPATION FORCE
Midway I.
MIKUNA

Adml Spruance
breaks off pursuit

MOGAMI & MIKUNA
collide.

~ARTHUR BANKS~

the passage of the Japanese Imperial Navy, had defeated it, had turned it back. It had lost prestige hopelessly, it had lost the *élan* of victory, and the margin of its losses turned decisively against it. It had forfeited its ability to strike where it chose, and to govern the course of the war. Having lost this initiative, it had condemned Japan to convert the war into a holding operation—this, as Admiral Yamamoto had warned, condemned Japan to be overwhelmed by the United States as soon as the American economic mobilization was complete.

16

MacArthur in the Pacific

THE naval war between Japan and the United States was to
be waged henceforward with the utmost ferocity in the crucial theatre of the south-west Pacific. Japan had not foreseen
that its action there would become so critical for its fate: but
it had lost the freedom of action at the Battle of Midway
Island. The United States set itself to wrest the south-west
Pacific from its hold, and Japan, which had committed itself
heavily in the region, set itself doggedly to oppose it, first of
all trying to enlarge its position, and later selling its territory
inch by inch, and with such grimness that it hoped that the
United States would become tired of its enterprise.

As the fighting grew in intensity, it gradually became plain
that, in this Pacific theatre, the war against Japan could be
won. The Pacific offered the path to Tokyo. Interest fell
away from the other theatres and other activities, from India and from China, and was concentrated on two American
commanders, General Douglas MacArthur and Admiral
Chester Nimitz, who shared the direction of events in this
region.

General MacArthur, in whom burned most clearly the
determination to restore the United States' position, and
whose skill, confidence and military genius made him the
most effective commander for the purpose, had in March
1942 been ordered to withdraw from the fighting in the
Philippines. He began his duel with Japan under something of
a cloud. His withdrawal from the Philippines, though it had
been ordered by Roosevelt, and though it was common sense,

had, in the hectic atmosphere of the time, been criticized by the American army, especially by the troops he had left behind. MacArthur was a general who in the ways of behaviour often did not conform to the conventions of his day, but flaunted them rather positively. In the Philippines he had won disapproval by insisting that his wife and family should remain with him: he was able to do so because he had been under Filipino regulations and was free of American army discipline. This singular man was to impose himself on the American and Australian armies, who were almost fanatical in their dislike of privilege, and to make himself respected by virtue of his superiority.

On his escape from Manila in a speedboat, he had had an adventurous voyage to the southern tip of the Philippines. When he got there, he found difficulty in going further. Rivalry between the American services made the American admiral in command in the region unwilling to spare any aeroplane for his rescue. Application had to be made over his head through Washington to transport MacArthur to Australia.

It had been agreed between President Roosevelt and Churchill that operations in Australia should be under an American command, and to this post MacArthur was designated. The forces of Australia many of them battle-trained in the Middle East, passed under his control. On taking over, MacArthur found the Australians thinking in terms of defence. Their morale had been shattered by the events in Singapore: they had been accustomed to thinking of this as a sure guarantee of Australian security, and they did not quickly adapt themselves to its overthrow. Psychologically they were in the position of France after the loss of the Maginot line. The Japanese appeared to be unstoppable, and were heading for Sydney and Melbourne; and the Australians looked round in despondency for a remedy. They aimed at holding the southern part of the continent on a line which passed through Brisbane. All to the north of this they had virtually reconciled themselves to losing when the Japanese invasion, which was expected in a matter of weeks, should begin.

MacArthur's initial success was in changing this attitude. He infused the Australians with confidence, and with the offensive spirit. His command was extremely short in manpower: it was poorly equipped, and air power was deficient. But within three months the counter-offensive started.

The area which was the scene of the fighting was the chain of coral islands which lies to the north of Australia and curls around to the north-east. The pressure of the original Japanese offensive had nearly carried them to this region. But it had begun to flag before Japan had occupied the whole system. If Japan had overrun the islands, it would have been able to set up bases there from which it could have interrupted communications between Australian ports. The chain of islands was half-held by the Japanese, but their firm occupation came to an end in the Solomon Islands, and did not extend to the New Hebrides or New Caledonia. The objective of their next offensive, with a dangerously extended line of communication, was the Australian outpost of Port Moresby in the south of Papua, which was the Australian extension of New Guinea. This lay just to the south of the islands occupied by Japan.

MacArthur's first move was to scatter the Japanese forces, which were preparing to take Port Moresby. The initial event was the drawn naval battle between American and Japanese aircraft carriers off the coast of Papua: the battle of the Coral Sea. It was drawn because the losses on both sides had been roughly equal; but the Japanese had been convoying troops, which were intended for land operations against Port Moresby, and these were turned back and never came again. Thus the issue of the battle was really in America's favour.

The Japanese were, however, favourably placed. From their bases they bombed Port Darwin, on the Australian coast, and severely damaged it. MacArthur moved to the attack, inadequate though his force was. He sent his troops to wrest Papua from the Japanese, and, in a painful struggle which took up a whole year, they prevailed. The backbone of the force was an Australian division which had won distinction at the battle of Alamein, and had been among the Australian forces in the Middle East which were shifted to defend Australia. The fighting was largely a series of savage hand-to-hand conflicts, and there was less skill in manoeuvre than was to be usual in the campaigns designed by MacArthur. It was notable for the endurance of the troops; for their overcoming the vast difficulties of nature; for the skilful use of aircraft, themselves largely improvised for supplying troops. An example was given of the maniacal tenacity of the Japanese which was to be a feature of the entire campaign: of 13,000 Japanese losses in action in the final stage, only thirty-eight men were taken prisoner.

This operation in eastern New Guinea was quite a small one, and, with so much happening in the rest of the world, not very much noticed. But in the record of the whole war, it was significant. It marked the end of the Japanese being on the offensive. It was the start of expeditions, which were desperately hard-fought, but in the end universally successful, to force Japan back across the sea on which it had sailed out to dominate so spectacularly. But MacArthur, surveying the tasks which still lay before him, was painfully aware of all the difficulties which lay ahead.

He was fighting over a vast area, large parts of which were still unmapped. This was a handicap which has been little recognized, but was very grave indeed. For an American general to plan a troop landing in Europe with maps and charts showing the tidal movements was one thing: to plan the same operation for coral islands, where all that was available was guess-work by natives, was quite another. He was short of ships; he was given only medium-range bombing planes, when he needed essentially long-range bombers; everywhere he went, airfields had to be constructed, often hacked out of the jungle by indigenous labour. For his supplies he had to compete with seven or eight rival theatres of war, and, as it seemed to him, invariably came out worst. Disease, especially malaria, was a still more deadly enemy than the Japanese, and the means of overcoming it could only be found by experimenting—and by exposing his armies at first to its ravages.

Nevertheless, from Port Moresby and the operations which he conducted for its relief in the encircling Owen Stanley Mountains, he was led on to the steps which, laborious operation after perilous initiative, in the end resulted in the reconquest of all New Guinea from the Japanese. From this position, he prepared to leap ahead, and he made havoc among the forces guarding the Japanese Empire.

In retrospect, it is plain that the Japanese, from the point of view of their long-term interests, would have done well to limit their offensive; to avoid overlong lines of communication; to have declined combat when this could be avoided;

above all, not to have been lured into a contest for the possession of islands, which could only be of use to them marginally. This was the view of many of the Japanese generals, and if it had prevailed in shaping the strategy would have greatly increased the difficulty of the Americans in coming to grips with the Japanese Empire. But the Japanese navy, still determined to conduct the Pacific War as a naval war, still over-confident in spite of the Battle of Midway, still with an abundance of battleships and cruisers which it could safely risk, overruled the Japanese armies. Little by little the scope of the war enlarged, and eventually spread through all the intricate chain of coral islands in the Pacific. There was little rational planning behind the operations.

*

From the start the Americans had had a second headquarters command in the Pacific Ocean. In March 1942 the Pacific, by a decision of President Roosevelt, was divided formally between General MacArthur and Admiral Nimitz. MacArthur's command included Australia, the Philippines, the Solomons, and most of the Dutch East Indies. The rest of the Pacific fell to Nimitz. But it was not a clear-cut geographical division of responsibility. Each of these officers was entrusted formally with the command of all armed forces in his area, whether on land, sea or in the air; but, by the instrument providing for the division between the commands, it was provided that Admiral Nimitz should have general control of all amphibious operations, whether these took place in his own zone or MacArthur's.

This rather peculiar division caused trouble about the demarcation. It was against logic, and ran counter to the teaching of experience in other theatres of war. MacArthur wrote:

> Of all the faulty decisions of the war, perhaps the most inexpressible one was the failure to unify the command in the Pacific. . . . It resulted in divided effort, the waste of diffusion and duplication of force, and undue extension of war with added casualties and cost.*

*Charles Willoughby and John Chamberlain: *MacArthur 1941–51*, McGraw-Hill, New York, 1954.

The division was difficult to stand by. For example, Mac-Arthur's operations in clearing the menacing Japanese from Port Moresby were on various occasions more amphibious than military, but he succeeded in keeping the campaign to himself. MacArthur wrote with a personal interest about the danger of divided aims. It galled him that it was freely suggested that he, though he was celebrated for his caution, could not be trusted with the safety of the navy's precious ships. A further limitation on him was that the charter setting up the respective commands laid down that Nimitz was from the start to be offensive in his operations; MacArthur, by contrast, was to fight defensively. This grudging attitude was to run, as a discordant thread, throughout the early years of the American counter-attack.

In this issue, MacArthur set himself, not for the only time in his career, to oppose the general political plan of Washington, on which the plan of campaign eventually depended. The navy had for long looked forward to a war with Japan. War in the Pacific must essentially be a naval one: the principal interest with which it was fought must be the aircraft carriers and battleships and the commander of these must be an admiral. The plans according to which it was fought had for two or three generations been the basic manuals for American naval training. This was the prevailing conception among the service chiefs in Washington; MacArthur was a general, and that was fatal to him. American naval officers form a curious, exclusive caste in American society; the war was an opportunity for this caste which must not be neglected. It is true that in the European war the navy took second place; circumstances had taken charge and had directed a land strategy. It seemed only compensating justice that in the Far East, where geography restored primacy to the sea, the navy and its traditional ancillary arm, the marines, should be the main protagonists.

The arrangement of the two commands had further consequences. It had been agreed between Roosevelt and Churchill that the United States should have a large measure of independent initiative in the organization of military affairs in the Pacific. As Britain had the lion's share of the initiative in the Middle East and in the Indian Ocean, so did the United States rule the Pacific war. The convention there was in contrast to that of Europe and the Atlantic; there the planning would be a matter of joint British and American responsibility; in the Pacific, any British initiative came to be headed off. Through this tendency, the United States to some extent evaded the main political directive, which had been laid down very soon after Pearl Harbor, that the war in the Pacific was to take second place to the war in Europe. In 1942 the Americans systematically built up their war-making capacity in the Pacific through the sympathetic connivance of the Chiefs of Staff in Washington. MacArthur might groan that he still had ridiculously inadequate supplies, but they were very much larger than had been envisaged by the directive. Twice as many supplies were sent across the Pacific in the first six months of March 1942 as were sent to the European theatre of war. By the end of 1942, the United States had reinforced its stations in the Pacific by more than 15,000 troops in excess of what was originally intended.

In August 1942 the navy had its first chance to take charge of amphibious operations on a large scale. These were in Guadalcanal, a tiny island in the Solomons: it was in MacArthur's command area, but the campaign there was directed by the naval Chiefs of Staff and played little part in his biography. Once more, the area of combat was in the disputed coral islands which ringed Australia. Guadalcanal was very little known or explored; before its conquest by Japan, it had been a British colony; the local people were extremely primitive; a few traders were like characters from a novel by Joseph Conrad. The colony, which is only ninety miles long and twenty-five miles broad, is the essential idea of a tropical island. Along its sandy beaches are coconut palms; abruptly behind them there rise jungly mountains and extinct volcanoes to a height of seven thousand feet. The flat ground is dark, steamy, rotting jungle, the perfect terrain for breeding the malaria mosquito.

The Japanese nearly forestalled the Americans in gaining possession of it. They had occupied it with a skeleton force, and American air reconnaissance showed that they were building an airfield on it. They were interrupted by a counter-invasion: the Americans landed a force of 11,000 men. At first, both sides supposed that the fate of Guadalcanal would be settled within a week. Actually a savage and terrible struggle developed there which lasted until February 1943, when

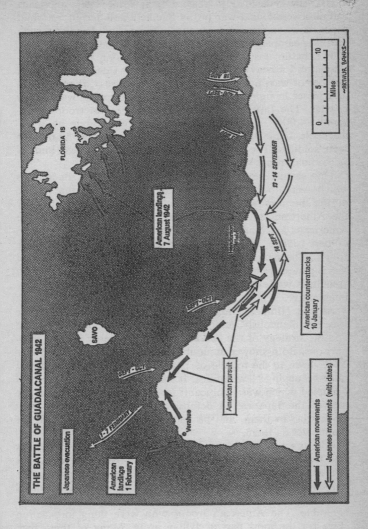

THE BATTLE OF GUADALCANAL 1942

FLORIDA IS

SAVO

American landings,
7 August 1942

13-14 SEPTEMBER

14 SEPT.

SEPT-OCT.

SEPT-OCT.

1-7 FEBRUARY

Verahue

Japanese evacuation

American landings
1 February

American pursuit

American counterattacks
10 January

American movements

Japanese movements (with dates)

Miles

0   5   10

—ARTHUR BANKS—

the Japanese decided to release their grip. The Americans had discovered what war in the Pacific amounted to, and had done so at horrendous account. There had been no such gruelling campaigns before in the history of the war.

The battle cost the Americans six major naval engagements, and a heavy toll of shipping. Both sides lost an equal number of warships (twenty-four of all classes), though Japanese losses in supporting ships, such as transports, were much heavier. The Japanese dead among the ground troops numbered 24,000: American losses were lighter, but by a remarkable feint the Japanese managed to rescue 12,000 of their soldiers. The Japanese troop commander killed himself as the final troops were withdrawn.

This savage battle marked out the pattern of operations which were to be repeated again and again in the Pacific during the next few years. Careful and skilful preparation by the American staff had been the main factor in giving the Americans a victory; and so it was to be at Tarawa, in the Gilbert Islands, at Kwajalein and Eniwetok and Bougainville Island. The navy concentrated upon the islands and pushed the Japanese relentlessly back. This strategy was a head-on assault. It was effective, and remoreseless; but it was not very imaginative.

As the Nimitz campaign developed, General MacArthur was simultaneously attacking in his corner of the Pacific and the strategy of the two campaigns inevitably invited comparisons. Both showed undoubted successes. From September 1942 down to the middle of 1944, MacArthur was employed in re-occupying New Guinea. It was not the extent of the land occupied which was significant; MacArthur had overcome the arts of the Japanese in defensive warfare, in territory very favourable to them, and he had inflicted enormous losses of manpower on them.

Nimitz's war machine had rolled over the Gilbert Islands and the Marshalls. Little by little the Japanese gave way at the edges of the vast empire they had seized; but Nimitz gained his successes by weight of assault and as a result of the endurance of his troops. His casualties were usually considerable. The American troops who were flung into action were for the most part a civilian army. Many of them had, however, been harshly prepared in the rather barbaric circumstances of the training grounds of the American Marines in the Carolinas. Stories which seeped out of these during the war seemed to have been well founded. Some troops had been less well prepared, and this accounted for some of the reverses which the Americans suffered in this campaign, which was the most sanguinary of any which were fought during the war. The American advance proceeded atoll by atoll. It was a war fought among tropical islands, with the same unreal beauty as a background, the same madness of non-surrender affecting the Japanese, the same monotony of desperate attack and desperate defence. It became taken for granted that the Japanese did not surrender, but were killed. Often those places which occasioned the worst slaughter were incredibly small. MacArthur, on the other hand, won his battles by sheer artistry. No other captain of the war had based his strategy so consistently on principles. He commanded with style. He was conscious of history, and of the examples of other generals. The ghosts of all the battles of the world walked in the combats for which he was responsible. In the map rooms of his headquarters there was an atmosphere of erudition which was unfamiliar in the war. The bloody patterns of assault on these remote coral reefs were studiously compared with Napoleon's famous victories, and even on one occasion with the victory of Hannibal at Canae in 204 B.C.

MacArthur despised brute strength. He sought, in a way which was rather like the principle on which the Japanese system of judo is based, to bring his force to bear on the enemy in places and at times that would find his opponent off balance. In this way he could hope to succeed with weaker strength, as was usually the position in which he found himself, and to succeed with the minimum loss. In this island warfare he eschewed the practice of Admiral Nimitz of reducing the Japanese strong-points one by one. Nimitz modified these tactics as time went on, and employed a limited plan of by-passing small islands which would have made an inconvenient defence. MacArthur, on the other hand, practised a strategy of envelopment. He refused to assail the Japanese head-on in one of their prepared fortresses, and thought out ways of isolating it by operating upon its exposed linear communication. The by-passed stronghold proved in the end to be his victim, but it had been left to 'die upon the vine'. General MacArthur then shifted his base forwards by some hundreds of miles, when the process was repeated with care never to expose his forces beyond the reach of protective air cover. He described as follows the system which he pursued:

> The system is as old as war itself. It is merely a new name dictated by new conditions given to the ancient principle of envelopment. It was the first time that the area of combat embraced land and water in such relative proportions. Heretofore, either the one or the other was predominant in the campaign. But in this area the presence of transportation of ground troops by ships as well as land transport seemed to conceal the fact that the system was merely that of envelopment applied to a new type of battle area. It has always proved the ideal method for success by inferior in number but faster-moving forces. Immediately upon my arrival in Australia and learning the resources at my command, I determined that such a plan of action was the sole chance of fulfilling my mission.*

The concept that success lay with a commander who best cooperated with nature was ever-present to him. One of his maxims was: 'Nature is neutral in war, but if you beat it and the enemy does not, it becomes a powerful ally.' A part of his success was due to the American army becoming more at home in the coral islands than the Japanese: which reversed the experience of the Japanese and of the British army in the Malayan jungle at the start of the war.

In his campaigns, MacArthur relied to an exceptional extent on spying. He was fortunate enough to discover an Australian, Commander Long, with a great gift for attracting information and for sifting it. This was a new art in Australia, and Long organized a service which was free of the traits—the elaborate games and the affectation of policy making—which proved so constricting in other countries. The most valuable information was given by a force called the 'coast watchers of the islands'. These were a fifth column which had been left behind in the islands when they were overrun by the Japanese. They consisted of British and Australian civil servants, anthropologists, telegraph operators, traders: and they were admirably served by bands of local natives. They were able to communicate by wireless with MacArthur's headquarters. In war of unorthodox character

*Willoughby and Chamberlain, op. cit.

of this kind information about Japanese strong-points and the distribution of Japanese manpower was often worth a whole division of troops. The exploits of these men are one of the most exciting chapters of war history; and it is very extraordinary that they have not become part of the folklore of the war.

To MacArthur's military tasks were added the military and diplomatic ones of welding Australia and the United States in a close alliance. The Australians, in spite of all their positive qualities, were at this period surprisingly hard to deal with: they were touchy, quick to take offence where none was intended, hypercritical as a kind of self-defence. In spite of a grotesque side to his character—which was self-assertive and boastful and which went with genuine confidence and did not mask self-distrust—MacArthur actually made himself liked, and won the confidence of Australia. He esteemed and got along well with Curtin, the Australian Prime Minister, and the two of them often collaborated in opposing Washington or London. He took an interest in preparing the reorganization of the Australian supplies so that by re-orienting Australian industry his armies in Australia actually received from Australia itself a much larger proportion of its needs than had been supposed possible.

In playing this role, MacArthur was much helped by accidents in his previous career which had detached him from the ordinary life of an American soldier. In his service as military adviser to the Philippine government, he had come to conduct himself with an unusual detachment from the American military machine. This, combined with a natural tendency to a certain Caesarism in politics, had brought it about that in his Pacific command he was often handled by the American government as if he were an independent political power and not a subordinate officer. His relation to the American authorities was very like that of a much-prized condottiere to an Italian city state. The legend of MacArthur as the great American pro-consul was added to by the fact that when the war began he had not been back in America for years, nor was he to return until 1951. Though MacArthur undoubtedly gained from this position, he had as a rule to forgo the ability to influence the military planners by personal knowledge of the officers concerned. A remoteness from understanding American politics complicated his career.

Piercing political insight into fundamentals was combined with a pathetic political incompetence in day-to-day matters.

*

In all this fatal combat in which Americans were locked together with Japanese in a contest from which neither side could free itself, one single fact stood out. The war was waged with the utmost ferocity, but it was under the eyes of relatively idle armies which were spectators of what was going on. Of the vast number of men who were mobilized for the war, the greater part were destined never to come into combat. Japan had an army of fifty-one divisions: until the very end of the war, forty of these divisions were either occupied in China, which for most of this period had a totally inactive front, or were employed in guarding the frontier with Russia. And on the American side the number of troops employed in the actual offensive by MacArthur and later in the reduction of the Pacific islands, was very small indeed in comparison with the vast army which the United States had concentrated for war in the Far East. (Similarly in this Far Eastern war the British troops who had actual combat experience were limited to the four or five divisions in Burma.) The western allies could not make use of a larger force. They had chosen to fight the Japanese on narrow fronts—in New Guinea and in the Pacific islands—and the circumstances of the war were such that there was no room for a great concourse of troops. Thus the war came to resemble the war at Troy. The serried ranks stood and watched the combat fought between the heroes. Their fate was decided in battle in which they had no part.

In this desperate fighting in the Pacific, Admiral Yamamoto, the one imaginative genius at war whom the Japanese, with their great military gifts, contributed to the conflict, was taken out of the picture. His death was plotted in Washington. It was brought about by arranging an ambush by American aeroplanes which fell on him in great strength as he was flying on a tour of inspection to one of the Pacific bases held by Japan. This was in April 1943, soon after the Japanese withdrawal from Guadalcanal. The details of his flight, the precise time of arrival, were all obtained by intercepting cipher messages which could be read. Yamamoto was always punctual to the moment: the surprise depended on the ambushing planes being able to count to the moment upon his presence at the destined place of the encounter with him. Yamamoto went to his death with a punctuality that was a rare virtue among orientals, even among commanding officers. His end was like the death of Hector who was similarly taken at a disadvantage by a force of Achilles' myrmidons:

> Look Hector how the sun begins to set
> How ugly night comes breathing at his heels
> Even with the veil and darkling of the sun
> To close the day up, Hector's life is done.

The American Admiral, having worked this overthrow, could find no more fitting words to announce it than the following telegram to the exterminators: 'Congratulations Major Mitchell and his hunters; sounds as though one of the ducks in their bag was a peacock.' Democracies have curious lapses of taste when they go to war. At the press conference to celebrate the success of the plan, the same Admiral observed: 'I had hoped to lead that scoundrel up Pennsylvania Avenue in chains with the rest of you kicking him where it would do the most good.' It is said that the audience whooped and applauded.

*

By July 1943 the American planners were already satisfied that they had chosen the right road. They lifted their sights, and began to consider what they should do when they drew near to Japan. Could intense air bombardment, which should be possible from Chinese airfields and from their great aircraft carriers, and unremitting submarine warfare, really reduce this proud people, or would the unemployed army of over a million be ready to dispute their way? Would an invasion be necessary; and, if so, would the history of the fanatical defence of small atolls be lived through once again, this time in the island centre of the terrible and warlike race?

MacArthur and Nimitz were the two American personalities who dominated the Pacific. They had taken up the initiative when it had been dashed from the Japanese by the battle of Midway Island. They had begun to attack, and had succeeded in their campaigns ever since. To halt them began to appear as being beyond Japan's capacity: the only doubt was how long they would take to cross over the Pacific, and to make war on Japan at its gateway.

IV

THE DEFEAT OF JAPAN

17

Mid-1943

In the middle of 1943 the war had resolved itself into a defensive struggle by the Japanese to hold the vast territory which they had overrun, for such little loss, in the hectic days early in 1942. With the crippling loss of their navy at Midway Island, their drive outwards had lost its impetus; it had failed in its purpose of gaining for them a rapid peace. But the Japanese were left in possession of a vast territory, economically very rich; and the operations of MacArthur and of Nimitz had only begun to win this back.

They held, and preparations had hardly begun to expel them from, a line behind which were included Burma, Thailand, Malaya, and the Dutch East Indies; and it extended far out across the Pacific. Behind this line they had obtained 80 per cent of the world's rubber, 54 per cent of its tin, 19 per cent of its tungsten, the oil wells of the Dutch East Indies with a huge reserve, and large supplies of manganese and iron ore. The map and economic intelligence suggested that Japan, if it showed the administrative competence to organize these assets, could, with some equanimity, face a prolonged war. It need have no panic, at least for the time being, before the very heavy counter-attack which America, now at last fully mobilizing for war, was mounting against it.

By 1943, however, it began to become plain that Japan, as an adversary of the United States, was outdated by two or three generations. In the organization for war, the contest was between the Americans, a nation of businessmen, amateurs in war but bringing to it all the skill learned in a century and a half of fierce capitalist struggle, in which lack of imagination and foresight exacted disaster and retirement, and the Japanese, who still regarded American business as vulgar, and who sought to combat it by an economy held together on a basis of command. Japan still thought of war in strictly military terms. Its eyes were fixed on territory which had to be held, on the battles which were taking place, and on the tactics to be used. The fact that the war was to be won or lost in the nation's factories and workshops had never clearly established itself in the mind of the Japanese Supreme Command. Japan had, it is true, passed a law even before Pearl Harbor, which gave the government totalitarian powers to regulate the economy; but the economy, under war conditions, exhibited nothing like the transformation which the United States and Britain underwent in similar circumstances.

Even after it had staked everything on the action at Pearl Harbor, Japan failed to give top economic priority to building aircraft, warships and submarines upon which the defence of the empire it had won must eventually depend. The Japanese had the initial advantage that they began the war with aircraft which surprised their antagonists in their performance. But the Japanese unaccountably failed to exploit this superiority. Japanese aircraft production in 1943, though it had tripled since 1941, was very much less than it might have been. In 1943 it was in fact only one fifth of the total American output. And, even for the use of its restricted air force, Japan failed to mobilize anything approaching the manpower which was needed. The skill and audacity of the pilots at Pearl Harbor, and the extreme popularity which the flying service enjoyed, showed that Japan was not wanting in resource to organize its air force adequately. Moreover, until the end of the war, the Japanese aircraft designers went on improving the standard fighters and bombers. But there was a failure of liaison: the army and navy were unwilling to make their wants clear, and to transmit these to the planners of the Japanese war effort. And even more than aircraft, a territory such as the Japanese had to defend, required warships and submarines. Here, also, the Japanese record is hardly comprehensible. In the months when America was turning out a prodigious number of aircraft carriers—twenty-two were under construction in 1943—Japan, which by the action of Pearl Harbor had shown itself to be a pioneer of naval air strength, was content to build only three new carriers. The disparity was greater still in cruisers and destroyers. The Japanese naval staff had apparently reverted to an older view, recoiled from reading the lessons which they had themselves demonstrated, and put their faith in battleship construction. They did not seem to realize, for example, how fatal it was to be outrun in submarine production. They had begun the war with high-quality submarines, but this arm never played the defensive role which might have been expected in a campaign fought among countless islands.

For Japan to realize the advantages of the economic riches of its empire, a vast, flexible merchant navy was necessary. In scarcely any other department of war was Japanese planning so inefficient. It began the war without a realistic or adequate appreciation of the demands which were likely to be made upon its merchant shipping. In 1941, it possessed 5.3 million tons of shipping; about 35 per cent of Japanese trade had been carried in foreign vessels. The greater part of this fleet was at once requisitioned for service use, 1.2 million tons for the army and 1.4 million tons for the navy; and a large part of this was squandered by the wasteful operations in the Solomon Islands. In 1942 the Japanese lost over a million tons of shipping, and by 1943, the shortage had become acute, and the estimates and forecasts of the Japanese Planning Board had been exposed. The losses, by submarine warfare, by mines, and by air attack, were such as to make ridiculous the attempt to weld together the Japanese territories in a single viable empire. Before this challenge, Japan made no adequate response: there were no interesting tactics, no system of convoys, no asdic, no radar. By 1943 they were forced to replace their dwindling merchant fleet with wooden ships, but these boats were terribly slow, and also vulnerable. Worse, they had neglected their shipyards, which were ill equipped and antiquated, and these were clogged, in the middle of 1943, by a fifth of the entire merchant marine undergoing repair.

These weaknesses must in the first place be put down to unimaginative planning by the Japanese Command, and the fact that civilian Ministries were instinctively held in contempt by service Ministries. At joint conferences the requests of civilians for allocations of manpower and materials tended to be overruled, even though the end product might be one of which the services were badly in need. For such reasons as these Japan was never able to utilize its huge economic assets. Japan had risked war for the sake of obtaining raw materials under its flag; but, when this was brought about, it could not transport them. It had the intense mortification of being in possession in the South Seas of one of the richest economic units in the world, but of being unable to enjoy its usufruct. The iron, the coal, the bauxite, nickel, tin, manganese, lead, salt, graphite, potash, all the vital materials for war, were all of them technically Japanese, guarded by Japanese troops, but they lay as useless to Japan as though they were in the hands of the enemy, because they could not be transported. They were a kind of fairy gold. Japan's plight is vividly shown by one figure. In 1940, before the war, it bought and imported three million tons of iron ore from the Philippines and Malaya. By 1942, though its troops had absolute control over the iron mines, it managed to carry just over 100,000 tons of iron ore from these territories to Japan.

The most acute famine was in oil. This had been foreseen, and the need for oil was the basic reason for Japan's going to war. But the oil had remained elusive. The wells of the Dutch East Indies produced an abundant supply, but it could only be transported in tankers, which were an easy target for the aeroplanes of the western allies and for their submarines. The shutting down of one economic activity after another in Japan was the consequence of this very real blockade. First civilian transportation was hit: then production in one industry after another. Already, by 1943, the oil shortages hampered the operations of the navy and grounded many of Japan's aircraft.

The weakness of the Japanese defensive structure was, then, economic. The Japanese waged a war against the most efficient economic organization of history, and waged it with totally inadequate resources. In vain they put their trust in reeking cube and iron shard, when even their ability to manufacture cubes and shards was being limited. But, though the nemesis worked itself out in an economic form, the weakness was not really economic, but was one of intelligence. The Japanese civil service, Japanese planners, the Supreme Command, failed their country. The economic resources had been there, and they could not be used, because the Japanese Empire failed to remain linked together. Given flexibility and foresight, this weakness might have been overcome. A different organization of their supplies, more local initiative, more skilful prevention of submarine warfare, more adequate use of the submarine and the aeroplane in solving the economic problems—any of these might have availed to prevent the end, which already, in mid-1943, was becoming certain to those who possessed the economic intelligence to see where war was leading Japan.

The desperate reality was, however, still unclear to most people. It was to be found only in economic statistics, which were a military secret. One of the undeniable successes of the Japanese military was in concealing the badness of its Intelligence alike from the enemy, from its colleagues in the government of Japan, and from its own people. It was the consequence of the rigid drill in security which had been practised at least since 1930. Let nobody decry the effects of such a very tight anti-espionage system. The consequence was that, in 1943, Japan, though it was already toppling on its feet of clay, was able to deny this knowledge to a large part of the world, including the Intelligence services of the western allies. They saw the advantages which Japan possessed, its still formidable army, only a small part of which had been so far engaged in battle, and its tremendous morale. They were impressed by the fact that no rumours of mutiny ever reached them, and that there were no strikes or signs of civilian unrest in Japan. They were conscious too of the very great disadvantages under which they had to carry on the offensive against Japan. Japan held the inner lines, and could transport a stiffening of the defence forces wherever these were threatened. The Japanese themselves were conscious of the immense handicap of enormous distance: the handicap that weapons, fuel, ammunition, cement and road materials, were being shot out in an unending flow, and vanishing across the Pacific Ocean. It needed a calm judgement in their adversaries to realize that this would avail against them, and that, sooner or later, the inherent deficiencies of the Japanese would force them to the huge convulsion of surrender.

Many of the lands taken over by the Japanese, and included in their fortress area, were the homes of nationalist movements which had come near erupting against their former white imperialist rulers. Japan, in letting loose its campaign against the western powers had expressed its natural sympathies with Asian aspiration. The pricking of the balloon of western prestige, and the surprising ease with which the West was put to rout, had had a profound effect on everybody's mind; though the Japanese sympathy had largely a propagandist incentive, in fact many Japanese were sincerely committed. The campaigns thus had had the effect of intensifying the nationalist resolve. In some cases, Japanese propaganda had led the people of these South-East Asian countries to believe that Japanese conquests would automatically bring them independence. But time was lost by the Japanese in fulfilling the hopes. Had the peoples of South-East Asia merely exchanged white imperialism to pass under the rule of a Japanese Empire?

The territories, which had been occupied by Japan, were at different stages of political development. In most of them, the British or American influence was strong. They had accepted the way of parliamentary democracy as holding out the best prospects of obtaining their independence, and, since both the United States and Britain could apparently not envisage any other course of progress, they had accepted constitutions of a more or less truncated form of Westminster or Washington democracy. That the Asian nationalists had allowed themselves to be directed along these lines is one of the astonishing facts of Asia at this time. It is a sign of the political vitality in Asia of western ideas, which remained very vigorous in spite of the inefficiency which had been revealed by the western systems administratively. Japan, as was natural, was more open-minded about the forms of government which should ultimately prevail; it was inclined to be suspicious of all forms of democracy, as being intrusions by the West into the East, and favoured instead the forms which emerged from Fascism (though these were as much of western origin), but it recognized that, in the storm of war, it was in no position to apply itself to political experiment in South-East Asia. It preferred to leave this for the peace years which it hoped would follow, and for the time being to make do with provisional, make-shift forms of government. The régimes which Japan set up in the areas under its control usually took the form of a committee of the existing political parties, relieved of control by parliaments, which it declared abolished. The governments themselves used most of the institutions with which they were already familiar.

In Burma the new government was set up by a brief decree. In the Philippines, a Philippine Executive Commission, consisting of seven well-known politicians, took over the government. In Malaya, which was more backward politically, the Japanese were content to preserve the forms of government through the sultanates. It is illuminating to see how, in the more developed countries—Burma and the Philippines—the tracks which they had been following before the war still governed their minds and set the tone to their political life.

The fate of Burma in these years is especially worth study. U Ba Maw, a lawyer, a party leader, and former Prime Minister under the British, was designated by the Japanese as national leader in 1942. He later published a book, *Breakthrough in Burma*, from which a picture of Burma under the Japanese stands out. At first there was confusion. Japan raised the Burmese army, which has already been described, to harry the British, but this, which attracted the elements normally associated with banditry, grew out of hand; it was liable, from the first, to turn upon the Japanese. Ba Maw, once he had been appointed by the Japanese, had, it is clear, the mission of restoring order in Burma, in which he worked closely with the Japanese.

There was a period of euphoria, a festival of feeling Asian. Ba Maw describes in his book how

. . . on both sides we believed in an ultimate Axis victory, which would wipe out the western empires in Asia for ever. This lasted for several months, during which the leaders of the various political and communal groups went out to the districts in mixed teams on a 'trust Japan' campaign. The Japanese on their part reciprocated by giving the central government as much independence as their notion of independence would allow, and also by supplying us with most of the essential commodities and services we lacked and needed. This was the Asian relationship between the two sides in the first months of our administration.*

*Ba Maw: *Breakthrough in Burma*, Yale University Press, New Haven and London, 1968.

Ba Maw recognized that tension rose because of the different aims and interests of the Japanese and the Burmese.

The Japanese wanted the Burmese to put victory in the larger world war before their own limited political objectives in Burma, whereas the Burmese wanted to gain those objectives first and at once. Thus a basic contradiction which already existed when our administration was formed now began to harden and divide the two peoples. My view about this matter is that the blame lay with both sides, but more with the Japanese. They were a far more immature people, in that they proved to be so devoid of judgment in their dealings with others, so domineering and blinded by delusions of their own racial grandeur and Asian destiny when it was most clearly in their interests to move with history by getting rid of all such racial nonsense. They could have achieved so much more if they could only have shown a spirit of true Asian fellowship and equality with the other peoples in Asia instead of claiming, in defiance of the clear world trends, to be 'more equal' than the others. This happened not only in Burma but all over South-East Asia.*

In spite of this, Ba Maw's relations with many Japanese continued to be personally good. It is true that he had continual difficulty with the more brutal type of officer, and claims that he was constantly in conflict with them for the protection of the Burmese people. He condemns utterly the soldiers brought in from China, who had been hardened by long experience of occupying that country of hostile people. He gives details of the Japanese mania for slapping people, of their insensitiveness to Burmese custom and convention. But the Japanese at the top make a very different impression. Of General Iida Shojiro, the Commander-in-Chief in Burma, he says:

I found him to be the best type of Japanese soldier, human, fatherly, and very understanding, a militarist on the surface, but not altogether so deeper down; at least he always tried to see things your way too, which was what made him different from the other militarists. It gave him a good deal of inner perception, particularly of the fact that a war can be won or lost in many ways and for many reasons, one of the surest ways to lose it being to rouse the hostility and resistance of a whole people.†

*ibid.
†ibid.

And of General Terauchi Hisaichi, who was the Supreme Commander of all the Japanese forces in South-East Asia, he says:

> As a person I found him to be really remarkable, a handsome, princely figure, out of a long and mellow feudal past, and yet belonging very much to the present in Japan. I had thought that as the chief of the conquering Japanese army he would most incarnate the dizzy reflexes of the conquest, but I was completely wrong. It may have been because I had least expected to find it in him, but the quality which struck me particularly was his essential humanity. Unlike most other militarists, this consummate war-lord was not afraid to show that he was also human, and precisely because of this he understood us better than many around him.*

Even General Tojo, the Japanese Prime Minister who had begun the war, gets a good report from Ba Maw.

National relations, as distinct from personal ones, however, continued to be bad. The Japanese army continued to insist that the Burmese puppet government was ultimately responsible to it. It continued to make demands on the Burmese civil servants which outraged them; and continued to produce a type of myopic and over-confident officer who angered the Burmese by racial arrogance. They were notorious for seizing the crops and carts of the peasantry; for insisting on forced labour, for intervening everywhere.

Relations became so strained that ultimately the government in Tokyo felt that it must make a great effort at their improvement. Early in 1943 General Tojo announced in the Japanese Diet that Burma would be declared to be independent within a year. Japan had grasped that independence was the deep longing in the soul of the peoples of South-East Asia, and that, if this were granted, Japan could continue in fact to direct their policies. There followed some hard bargaining over the exact form of their future relationship, in which the Japanese army endeavoured to stipulate that it should have the legal right to intervene if the Burmese government departed from agreed principles. In the face of Burmese opposition, it accepted instead a treaty of alliance between the two countries, in which they simply pledged their cooperation for the self-determined development of all the

*ibid.

countries of South-East Asia. These negotiations were completed by August 1943, and the declaration of Burma's complete freedom was made in conditions of apparent reconciliation and confidence. Japan had certainly made an effort at overcoming hostility. But Ba Maw concludes on a disillusioned note:

> On the Japanese side, many militarists went back to their old ways again. They could never remember for long that the Burmese were now a free people. I have already mentioned their charge against me that I took our independence too seriously. The cause of the mischief was that they wanted it both ways; they wanted the Burmese to fight the war as people defending their own independence and yet in other matters they were to behave as if they were not independent. The militarists merely changed their argument; previously they had tried to impose their will upon us in the name of military administration, and now it was in the name of military necessity without bothering to convince us that there was really any such necessity at all; and as the pressures increased they refused even to argue about the necessities, but treated them as Japanese imperatives which ruled out all argument. Knowing how critical the situation had become we tried to go along some of the way with them, but they wanted us to go the whole way, which was clearly impossible unless we were convinced of the need for doing so. Thereupon these little war-lords accused me of trying to subvert their war effort; and so we drifted further apart*

At the end of the same year, 1943, Japan made a further effort at demonstrating that it was really in earnest in seeking, by the gift of independence, to gain the friendship of Asia. It convened a conference in Tokyo between Japan and five governments, those of Burma, the Philippines, Thailand, Manchukuo, and of the anti-Chiang segments of China. It also invited the Indian refugee leader, Subhas Chandra Bose. The conference met for two days at the beginning of November. Opportunity was given for the oratory of several eloquent statesmen; their speeches were widely reported; some of them took the chance of ingratiating themselves with the Japanese. Most of those who took part, and the Japanese, felt that the conference had been helpful to them. At its end a joint declaration was issued, which pledged everybody con-

*ibid.

cerned to work for Asian independence—which had become the fixed idea of all the lesser countries of Asia—and to support each other in the cause.

More than this was hardly to be expected of a political conference which had been called to demonstrate happiness and unity, not to discuss differences. The final resolution spoke, it is true, of economic cooperation. Japan had been pressing the idea of the economic interdependence of the region, and of the benefit, for all the countries of the area, of economic connection with Japan. The concept was of a kind of Asian Common Market. The odd thing was that Japan did not make more rapid progress with economic planning. It had set up in 1942 a Greater East Asian Ministry, and designated to it the task of preparing schemes; but no programme was published, and there were no elaborate accompanying sets of statistics. There was considerable conflict in Tokyo about this Ministry. By some civilians, especially those in the Foreign Ministry, it was feared that it would be regarded as provocative in South-East Asia: it would unmask Japan's determination to plan the life of the region, and would be counter to the policy of granting independence. Tojo, the Prime Minister, was adamant in its favour. The decision, however, cost him the resignation of his Foreign Minister in protest at the setting-up of such a Ministry.

The Dutch East Indies had been omitted from the countries invited to take part. It was barred from this celebration of regional independence. The Japanese attitude towards this territory was always peculiar. The nationalist movement there was as strong as, or stronger than, that in Burma; and the national parties had made it plain that they should receive the same coveted gift of independence. Japan, however, was not so understanding in their case. The Supreme Command firmly refused that Japan should commit itself on its post-war status, either because it was so rich economically that it was unwilling that Japan should forgo the possibility of annexing it and retaining it as a prize of war, or because it wished to keep it as something to bargain over with the western allies at the eventual peace settlement. In the meanwhile, the Dutch East Indies were governed by the Japanese military, tempered by local councils. Some of the Japanese Ministers thought that this was a mistake, and would have been very willing to buy amity at the price of eventual independence;

but, at an imperial conference in May 1943, the views of the Supreme Command had prevailed. They had not changed by the time of the East Asia Conference in November.

The real purpose of that conference had apparently been to embarrass the western allies and, by demonstrating that total independence had become the political currency in Japanese Asia, to deter them from pressing on with plans for its reconquest. A rather more subtle aim may have been to cause dissension between Great Britain and the US. Japan was aware of the American criticism of Great Britain in being behindhand in meeting the demands of nationalism, and it counted on causing further disputes between the allies if it stirred up the nationalist claims still further. The difference in outlook towards nationalism between Britain and America was, in this and many other matters, the chink in their armour which Japan tried to exploit.

Yet the general feeling about the conference was cynicism, disbelief, and amusement. Japan had attempted to convince the people of South-East Asia that it was the sincere friend of the independence of their national units. At the same time Japan, by its action, demonstrated that it was establishing a new empire in place of the one which had been overthrown.

*

Similar experiences to those of Ba Maw with the Japanese were repeated again and again by other people in South-East Asia. Everywhere at first their expectations had been favourably aroused; the Japanese came in through general acclamation; their victories gave them glory; they strode over the vanishing West with pleasure. The *mise en scène* was admirably contrived for Japanese achievement. Restraint, moderation, modesty would have paid them huge dividends. But instead of even pretending to live up to their propaganda about the new age of Asian brotherliness, with which they flooded the countries taken over, most Japanese, and especially the army, made no secret of the fact that they considered that they had won an empire, and were determined to enjoy it. Nearly all instruments of the Japanese state were under the firm control of the Supreme Command, and this was determined not to release any prize which Japanese arms had gained. Those people in South-East Asia with a sophisticated understanding of the ways of government could reckon the callous, and more or less disguised, ways in which the Japanese economic and political instruments set about exploiting them; those who relied upon their eyes for information saw the Japanese, with a naïve disregard of consequence, humiliating the people, insulting their customs, not bothering to learn their languages, and enjoying their disarray.

There were certainly many Japanese, even many Japanese generals and high officers, who, with traditional civilization, understood the sensibilities of subject peoples. The Japanese Foreign Ministry, some Japanese politicians, and some businessmen, struggled hard to get official sanction for more generous policies. They were not blind to the writing on the wall in South-East Asia, and understood the strength of national feeling. That Japan was as receptive as it was, and that, at the top level, it was willing to meet Ba Maw and the other nationalists half way, says much for the quiet pertinacity with which they struggled. This (and the worsening position of Japan in the war) brought independence for the Philippines in September 1943 in the same way that it had come in Burma. But it bore the same sense of sham and unreality as long as the Japanese army and the much more dreaded military police were there and took the law into their hands. The milder Japanese were terrorized into acquiescence by the general will of the Japanese army which was to plunder and oppress. In face of the mass descent on to South-East Asia of the military machine, in face of the reality of Japanese extortion, brutality and incompetence, Japanese good intentions were advertised in vain. In a very short time, their empire had exhausted its credit, and the Japanese uniform had made itself detested.

*

In mid-1943 the British reorganized their command system in Asia. They recognized that Delhi was no longer the ideal centre for the headquarters of the military. It was too heavy with history, and had too many historic distractions. Essentially it was the base of the Indian army; and this was not suited for a war such as this had become, involving amphibious operations and Far East diplomacy. The eyes of a General Staff in India were apt to become fixed upon India's north-west frontier, and on the Middle East. Only by constant effort could they be prevailed upon to study the Burma frontier, and to give due weight to new allies and friends, the hard-pressed Chinese and peoples of South-East Asia. It appeared best to wrench the command away from its old associations, and to locate it at some centre where it could achieve a more correct view of the war. New men were to be brought in, and they would operate from a new place. It would be one in which more attention was paid to voices which went unheeded in Delhi. The command was in fact divided: Delhi continued to be responsible for the Indian army in its home organization; the new command was to be responsible for mobilizing and directing all the forces in the attack against Japan in the East. It would include all three services, army, navy and air force.

At the Quebec conference of the allied powers in 1944, it was decided that the new command should be located at Colombo. It was to be under Vice-Admiral Lord Louis Mountbatten. He was a cousin of King George VI, and it was felt that royal status would give him additional prestige in dealing with Britain's allies, and discharging the political duties which it was clear the post would involve. It was to be international; Mountbatten was to be equally responsible to the British Prime Minister and to the American President. Undoubtedly the arrangement was well conceived; it gave a new tone to the British war effort in the Indian Ocean: it created a new race of military planners who were free from traditional concerns.

A further ingenious tie-up of the command was made by appointing General Stilwell as the deputy of the Supreme Commander. He was the American general who was simultaneously acting as a ranking general of the Chinese army. His aims and objects had diverged greatly from those of the British, of whose military achievements he thought meanly. By this provision, he, and the Chinese, secured a share in the command; at the same time it proved easier to control him.

Mountbatten proved a heavy-weight figure, an ample complement to General MacArthur and to Admiral Nimitz as a member of the triumvirate by which the rest of the war was directed. He was a scientifically minded commander, and many first-rate scientists from England appeared on his staff at Colombo: a happening which in Delhi would have been thought eccentric. He had a gift for the use of public relations, and used this, among other ends, for establishing a rapport with the troops, many of whom had been in a dangerous depression when Mountbatten was appointed. He had in fact something of the personal glamour of the film star, which the public, as the war progressed, increasingly demanded of troop commanders.

With these developments, there faded out one of the most impressive commanders of the war, Lord Wavell. It is true that he continued for a time as Commander-in-Chief in India, and that in the summer of 1943 he was made Viceroy of India; as such he enjoyed political power. But as a maker of war strategy his role was finished. He had played an original, if an inadequately appreciated, part. As Commander in the Middle East in the early part of the war he had borne the brunt of the early attacks by the Italians. He had been starved of resources, and, by bluff and intellectual ability, he had won successes against immense odds. At the beginning of the Japanese war, he had been appointed to the Supreme Command of the troops in Malaya and in the Dutch East Indies, in addition to India, in the hope that, with his quite inadequate force, he might work the same miracle that he had done in the Middle East. The task was a hopeless one; Wavell, also, was by this time a tired man, and had lost a part of his cunning. By temperament an intellectual who combined reflection, and a strange kind of mysticism, with a life of action, a natural scholar whose career had been among soldiers, he failed to achieve recognition among the politicians who mattered because of an inability—or rather an unwillingness—to communicate his personality to his colleagues.

*

The creation of the Colombo Command put new energy into the conduct of British propaganda. It began to be classed as one of the major instruments of war.

Propaganda work had begun before Pearl Harbor. It had been centred in Singapore, in an office called the Bureau of the British Ministry of Information, and had operated through the information sections of different British missions in the Far East, such as the British consulate in Shanghai. The early network, which thus came into existence, was disrupted when the Japanese captured most of these places, including Singapore. They were especially severe on prisoners who had any connection with this organization. This was not because they realized the latent power of propaganda, but because they assumed that a Bureau of Information must be concerned with espionage, of which they were particularly afraid. The officer who was Director General of the Bureau, Robert Scott, formerly in the consular service in China, had a very grim experience during the years of captivity. The Japanese had a curious respect for legality, and were unwilling to execute their victims unless they had made a confession. Time and again, in an effort to extort this confession, they imposed savage tortures on him. He refused to confess, and therefore survived: but when he came out of prison he weighed only five stone.

With Singapore lost, an organization had to be built afresh. It was centred on Delhi; and soon a staff with a highly international flavour was put together—Chinese, Indonesians, Dutch, Frenchmen, Greeks, Hungarians—all the cosmopolitan elements which had escaped from Shanghai and Hong Kong and had taken refuge in India. Some of them were journalists or writers, some were businessmen, a few had been politicians. Their collective knowledge of the Far East was variegated and extensive. The predominant personality was the gifted and imaginative Director of Broadcasting, John Galvin. He was an Irish Australian who, in a crowded life, had seemed to have prepared himself for the role he now had to play. He had a vision of Asia as a force to be reckoned with in the world of the future, when the Japanese should have been thrown back to their own shores. He could appeal to intelligent nationalist sentiment in the occupied territories because of the genuinely democratic quality of his own outlook: upon the organization of propaganda he brought to bear original talents, and extraordinary energy and resourcefulness.

By all the regular methods of propaganda, by broadcasts from a radio station set up by Galvin in New Delhi, by pamphlets and books, by the organization of a news reporting service which was accurate about defeat and could be rusted in accounts of victory, little by little the British version of the war was radiated out. The propagandists in New Delhi exposed the falseness of the Japanese claim for a Greater East Asia Co-Prosperity Sphere. They stripped Japan of the claim to be anything but an old-fashioned imperialist. They gave to the Asian world the lively sense that western power still existed, was preparing for a riposte, and had good hope of a future in which men could live at liberty and in peace. They transformed the image of India from being a country in collapse to being a power house in which returning armies were girding on invincible force.

Of the powerful effect of this invisible arm of the British army there can be little doubt. Ba Maw speaks in his memoirs of the disquieting effect in Burma of British propaganda and the British agent on the minds of a rather mercurial population. The sense that the British were gone was undermined by the awareness that British eyes were still upon them, and that the slightest and most intimate details of the Burmese districts were being discussed in London and Delhi.

*

The propaganda had more effect on the peoples who were subordinate, and rather unruly, allies of Japan than on Japan itself. Showers of propaganda burst unavailingly on the granite of Japanese civilian morale, and the Japanese army was never known to have lost a battle, to have flagged in any way, or to have been at all diverted from its purposes by any of the wiles of psychological warfare.

It was proof against American propaganda no less than against British. A most effective instrument at the United States' disposal was the broadcasting station at San Francisco. Propaganda was backed up by the useful research done in numerous centres. On the whole, however, American arms gained little support from the labour of American propagandists against the monolithic Japanese.

On the other side, only perfunctory use of propaganda was made by the Japanese. Indeed, both Japanese and Chinese seemed to ignore the possibilities of propaganda until the very end of the war. No Japanese figure rose to play anything like the same part as Dr Goebbels, Minister of Enlightenment in Nazi Germany. Japanese propaganda was directed chiefly towards the people of the countries that it had occupied, or planned to attack. The media which it used were the same as those employed by its adversary, predominantly the wireless and the printed word. But there is little to be said of this side of Japan's war effort. On the whole it was parched for lack of imagination.

Thus all the eastern world resounded, both with explosives and with the monotonous exchange of propaganda. *Inter arma silent leges:* but the media of mass communications were busier than ever. Every nation talked with every other; to argue with it, to inform or mislead about the direction of hostilities. America spoke to Japan. Japan spoke to South-East Asia. Britain spoke through numerous languages on the Delhi wireless. In this general post there was one notable exception. Britain did not speak to India. The British political warfare executives operated from Indian soil, and used Indian facilities, but in return for this the British government had given an undertaking that radio propaganda would be directed outwardly, and that it would not use these instruments for arguing with Indian public opinion.

The Indian government had its own propaganda organization. This, though partly operated by British staff, conceived its task rather differently from the outward-directed political warfare. Its task was limited to explaining to the people of India the motives of the government of India in fighting the war, and to demonstrating the progress it was making. It was not to debate with Indians the rights and wrongs of their differences with the British. From this use of the radio, the British barred themselves. They accepted the limitation formally; and investigation shows that on the whole they stuck by this agreement. The British never, for example, put over to Indian opinion its own case on Indian constitutional developments, as it stated this in broadcasts to America. The motive was that the British feared to aggravate India the more by supplying its own commentary on events. As was usual, it put its confidence in bland silence; which of course in the end was the more provoking.

*

The allies announced, at the Cairo Conference of the U S, Britain and China, in November 1943, the severe peace terms which they proposed to exact from Japan. They were not put forward as opening the way to peace, as a bait to negotiation: the allies intended them as declaring their programme of action, and as an encouragement to China, and persuasion of it to remain in the war. Japan's overseas empire was to be forfeit; it must surrender unconditionally. At first, this declaration did not have the deflationary effect on Japanese morale which had been hoped for. Japan, which privately had already begun to envisage the possibility of defeat, was, however, optimistic that it could avoid the worst consequences. It knew the very great defensive strength of its position, due to geography. It was confident that the United States and Britain would not risk the vast losses in manpower which they would have to incur in the last stages of the war when it came to a struggle to land in Japan itself. The United States and Britain would, it was sure, snatch at the possibility of a reasonable negotiation, in which much of what Japan judged to be indispensable could be preserved.

Therefore Japan interpreted the menacing words from Cairo as being a good deal less than their face value. They were reassured also by the absence of a Russian signature to them. Russia, though it was allied to the U S and Britain, was active only in the German war, and had not committed itself to the eastern conflict. The conference at Cairo had been designed to take place without the U S S R being represented, since Russia was unwilling to compromise its neutrality in the Pacific. Japan saw this and was deeply relieved. If Russia was firmly attached to neutrality in 1943, what might be its position in a year or two, when its experience with its western allies had further frayed its nerves? Besides, was it in the real interests of any of the great powers to destroy Japan as an organized force, and open the way to another power to occupy the vacuum? Did the United States or Britain desire to make a ruin there in which Communism would sprout? Japan still had sufficient reason for not regarding the Cairo Declaration as the accurate forecast of history.

Moreover Japan was to nurse, until the very end, false comfort from its long immunity from occupation. Japan, alone of Asian countries, had never known the tramp of invading armies. It had come to believe that it was especially protected by the gods from the hand of war. For a warlike people, the Japanese had been singularly little affected by threats from abroad. Only twice, in the thirteenth century, had Japan itself been in danger from invasion by foreign soldiers. In the time of Kubla Khan, in 1274 and again in 1281, great Mongol armadas set sail to conquer the small island empire, and annex it as a tributary. They were seemingly irresistible; Japan seemed done for; it quaked with terror, while it began to defend every inch of the way against those troops who had managed to land. But on each occasion great storms scattered and wrecked the mighty fleets, and the invaders stood no chance. This history became a part of the national memory. The 'kamikaze' or 'divine wind' which had saved Japan in the thirteenth century was expected, until the very end, to blow again, or the divine protection would manifest itself in some other guise.

The wind was not to blow. Russia entered the war, America put its trust in an army of occupation to avert Communism. The eventual peace was very nearly on the identical terms of Cairo. But no American or British life was lost storming the beaches of Honshu.

18

Subhas Chandra Bose

THE Japanese, after overrunning Burma, had been content for two years to stand on the defensive. They had repelled the attack organized by General Wavell from India in the autumn of 1942, against Arakan. The operation, which was encouraged from London in the hopes that it would repair British prestige, was premature and was made with inadequate force and troops insufficiently trained; the Japanese were never embarrassed by it—except that it restricted a move which they had been intending to make at the same time into north India—and, by outmanoeuvring and outflanking the British, they compelled the British to retreat.

The country between India and Burma was peculiarly difficult; communications almost did not exist; the disease-infestation required that armies, if they were to operate with any degree of efficiency, should be remarkably well organized with medical services, which they were not until 1944. These facts, as much as any other, kept the British and Japanese apart, though great pressure was brought on British troops by Churchill to go on the offensive. In fact, the Japanese had acted on the principle that geography had contrived to give Burma the perfect scientific frontier, and calculated that they would do enough if they posted troops to guard the few practicable approaches from India.

In 1943 took place the adventure of General Wingate in Burma. This man, who had formed his ideas in Palestine and Abyssinia, and who took T. E. Lawrence and the Arab revolt in the First World War as his model, was confident that Burma

could make an ideal field for guerrilla war. If it was hard for
armies to make contact, he suggested that guerrillas should
do their work for them; and that, once these had made a
long-range penetration behind the Japanese lines, they could,
by superior mobility and surprise, produce as much havoc as
would be caused by a successful army invasion.

Wingate convinced the Indian army with great difficulty,
and made an expedition with just over three thousand men.
The higher Japanese officers regarded him without anxiety,
and said that he must starve in the jungle; the more junior
officers were shocked by the boldness of his strategy, and by
their inability to hunt him down. The advance of Wingate
upon T. E. Lawrence was in the use of wireless and of
aircraft. Wingate lost a thousand men, one third of his force,
and had put a Burmese railway temporarily out of action.
Whether his guerrilla successes came near justifying his theory
was an open question; a much larger operation, employing
aircraft, was planned for the next year, but it met with
disaster at the outset, Wingate being killed on taking off.
He is a hard man to assess. England, for prestige reasons,
urgently needed a success, and it possessed at this time a
propaganda machine, which could create heroes overnight.
Wingate's personality and achievement were written up and
blazed across the world. It may be that Wingate demonstrated,
not the success of his own guerrilla strategy, but the success
of British propaganda. He supplied to the waiting and idle
troops of the British army, in the tedious interval of training
and before they were offensively engaged, the spectacle of
exciting warfare and of individual performance. Wingate believed himself to be a man of destiny and that the situation
was also one of destiny.

A far more orthodox, and forceful, attack was intended
by the British in the spring of 1944. The Fourth Army
Corps was preparing it, using the small town of Imphal in
north-east India as its base. The Japanese, who had two divisions in the region, had intelligence that it was coming,
and resolved to strike first.

The campaign inside the borders of India which resulted
was interesting partly because, in it, Japan again put to the
test its claim that it was fighting, not simply for itself, but for
the freedom of the Asian peoples. It is true that the organized forces of allegedly 'free India', which it had among

its troops, played only a minor part; the campaign was so interesting, so stubborn, so terrible, and the 'free Indians' played such a small role in it, that the history of it, and its narration by the Japanese, might well overlook their presence. Yet, symbolically, the event is important, and was certainly seen to be so by the people of India and South-East Asia. Japan had announced that it had opted out of the circle of imperial predatory powers, and could rightly claim to be the patron of free Asia. It had not, until this time, done anything very striking to show that it was living up to this claim. In Japan, all attention was given to the gallantry of the Japanese forces; and the average man scarcely thought of their army as fighting Asian battles, or that their Asian allies could be of much worth to them. The opportunity had come to show that this was a mistaken view.

Chance presented itself in the shape of the Indian leader Subhas Chandra Bose. He played at this stage an extraordinarily decisive part. By accident, and by seizing an exceptional opportunity, he was able to cut a figure which made him outstanding among the comparatively small number of men who influenced the course of the war by their individual qualities. He chanced to be available to the Japanese to lead a movement to free India, and, in retrospect, it appears that this was the last chance of saving itself with which Japan was presented.

*

Bose was a Bengali, the son of a comparatively high civil servant who became a judge. Bengal had a special place in the history of Indian nationalism. It stood by itself culturally, and bred a type which was peculiar in being the exponent of a classical strain of regional loyalty. Bengali patriotism was deeply devotional: it was less associated than in other parts of India with day-by-day economic interests: the Bengali really believed the singularly powerful oratory which surged over the province especially after 1905. The passionate quality of Bengali nationalism, monomaniac, hot, somnambulist, is rather like that of the Sinn Fein patriot who is heard, off-stage, as a repeated theme in Sean O'Casey's play, *Red Roses for You*, repeating his hypnotic oratory. This nationalism expressed itself, to a degree quite unknown in other parts of India, in a fascination with violence and in a cult of terrorism. The typical Bengali nationalist was quite carried away, renounced his home and the ties of ordinary business, and plunged into secret conspiratorial activity in a way which horrified the rest of India as being extravagant and an affront to domestic obligation.

Bengal differed so much in temperament from the other parts of India that political cooperation with it was not easy. Bose became a leader of Bengali nationalism, and was so powerful a personality that his shadow fell over the rest of India. He was in the recognizable succession to the Bengal leaders of his youth who used to be carried away by the poetical implications of 'mother India', Hinduism, and Indian uniqueness. Always, Bose saw himself, and conducted himself, as a man of destiny. He had a great appeal to youth, frustrated, very poor but very proud, liking rhetorical leadership, always responding enthusiastically to the idea of a solution through some act of violence. He sought to turn Indian nationalism into the kind of movement which grew in Bengal.

As a young man, Bose, who was born in 1897, had been sent by his family to England, where he studied so diligently at Cambridge that he passed the entrance examination into the Indian Civil Service. This still enjoyed so much prestige in India that a lifetime spent in it, or a resignation from it, produced equal *réclame*. Bose chose the latter course. By resigning even before he had been posted to any particular duty, he gained a flying start in the Bengal Congress Party. Two decades of serious attachment to Congress, and a spell of office as Mayor of Calcutta, brought him, after a term of imprisonment which he spent in Mandalay Fort in Burma, to the presidency of the All-India Congress in 1938. Though the inner springs of his being may have been poetical, he developed, during his time as Mayor, a business-like aptitude, which won recognition from British officers.

This proved to be a parting of the ways with his non-Bengali Congress colleagues. In his struggle with them, and partly because of his temperament, he moved sharply to the Left, though for him there was no special attraction in socialism, and he was not moved by the conflict between this and free enterprise. The Left meant simply extremism, more determined personalities—a more congenial emotional atmosphere. He advocated ever more extreme Congress policies: and in particular he opposed Gandhi's stubbornly held non-violence. In this contest, Gandhi faced the blind emotional forces of Bengali nationalism, which repudiated Gandhi's homespun philosophy of the spinning wheel and of the virtues of simple peasant life. A religious preoccupation such as Gandhi's—a religion which dwelt on the virtues of the Sermon on the Mount which Gandhi had taken over in his version of Hinduism—was alien to him. Bose's passion was summed up in his favourite slogan: 'Give me blood and I promise you freedom.'

The year of his final breach with Gandhi was also the year of the outbreak of the war in Europe. Bose was not inclined to sit still among such events. For the attitude of Gandhi and Vallabhai Patel, the men he was opposing, it is possible to feel much admiration. They were realists. They were as intransigently opposed to the British as he was himself. But they accepted that military action was not the way to strike at them. They were organizing a vast, poor, ignorant, apathetic nation in the only way it could be mobilized. A military adventure *was* the kind of thing the British would expect and would know how to deal with. They were helpless against this unspeakable groundswell. Subhas Bose was simply too impatient for this Himalayan wisdom.

Bose thought otherwise. The world was being changed by armies, and he was impatient to have an Indian army. His agitation was impatient of bounds. He was arrested, rather oddly for a seditious speech in connection with the agitation for the removal of a memorial to the victims of the Black Hole of Calcutta, which was thought to be hurtful to national sentiment. In prison he meditated upon the progress of the war, on the might of Germany, on the great opportunities for Indian freedom which he felt that Gandhi, with a senile attachment to non-violence (as it appeared to Bose) was at this time allowing to pass by. He was distracted when he thought of what he might be able to effect if he was at liberty. He procured his temporary release by beginning a hunger strike, and assured that he would not thereafter be restored to jail by absconding from his home in Calcutta early on a January morning of 1941, disguised as an elderly Moslem mullah.

By a daring journey he made his way across India, through Afghanistan and through the Soviet Union, into Germany. There he found his spiritual home, and probably would have done better if he had stayed there instead of answering the call of Japan. He had always been attracted by Germany. His temperament was Wagnerian: the Nazi grandees proved attractive personally. The colourful side of Nazism appealed to him profoundly. The heroics, the constant legends, the dangerous and insidious concepts, the affected contempt for weakness and pity, the invocation of history, all seemed congenial to him. Bengali culture is strongly patriarchal, and the Nazi concept of the place of women in the warrior's life appealed to one who, till he went to Germany and married a German, had apparently been indifferent to women. In the Siegfried cult and the heroic life, he saw a model which he found admirable. He was deficient in the sense of humour that was the best preservative against Nazi fantasy; and his Hindu education had given him a natural tendency towards a narrow concentration on whatever happened to appeal to him for intellectual reasons. Even the Nazi brutality he found brisk, salubrious, and invigorating.

In politics he found the Nazi form of state entirely congenial. The rule by the Nazi party, and the authoritarian role of the party by a small caucus of leaders, seemed to him to provide India with a model form of government. Discipline, before all else, was what India seemed to need for overcoming its problems of the division into separate castes and communities, and for dealing with its great economic problem of poverty. The democratic type of government which it might imitate from Great Britain had the fatal weakness of permitting so much liberty that the state might fall in pieces. New vistas opened for an Indian government which would be equipped with a Gestapo, concentration camps and an S S. On the precise details of the policy he would pursue if the war should bring him to power, he was vague. It was enough that he should proclaim the bracing virtues of authoritarianism.

Bose therefore found the situation promising. He was satisfied with his personal reception. The Germans invited him to take charge of organizing the rebellious Indians in their hands into a body which might be useful for war purposes. He was given access to the Indian prisoners captured by the

Germans in North Africa. He broadcast to India over the German radio; and he took part in the controversy over the Cripps mission to India. Volunteers began to come forward to form an Indian Legion, and about two thousand men were enlisted for training. There was much ceremonial feasting and mutual compliment.

Spiritually this was probably the happiest part of Bose's somewhat neurotic life. But after some months Bose had to recognize that his German friends had not acknowledged him as the head of an Indian government in exile. Perhaps this was due, as was explained to him, to the fact that they could as yet, while Russia remained undefeated, have brought no effective aid to an Indian rebel government; perhaps it was because Hitler could not bring himself to recognize that Indians would be equal citizens in the post-war world which he was planning. Hitler, if Germany won the war, intended to dispose of India by a diplomacy in which Indians would not play a part.

Whatever was the reason, the Germans put no obstacles in Bose's way when an invitation reached him from the Indians in South-East Asia to transfer himself to this new sphere, and to take charge of the free India movement which was being organized by the Japanese. His imagination, the dramatic part he might play, the appeal of the idea of pan-Asianism, his calculation of how India, or at least Bengal, would respond to new situations, all impelled him to accept.

*

Bose sailed from Kiel in a German U-boat in February 1943. He left behind some lieutenants to continue the work of organizing the available Indians, though he had failed to come to an agreement with the Nazis on precisely how they were to be used. The U-boat sailed to Madagascar, and there, off shore, it made a rendezvous with a Japanese submarine which carried him for the last half of his journey. He reached Tokyo on 13 June, after a voyage of thirteen weeks. That he was permitted to be so slow suggests that the Japanese, at least at this time, did not found great hopes on the plan for which he had been imported.

Indeed they had been making half-hearted bids at raising the Indians in revolt against the British ever since the first days of the war; and they had suffered a series of disappointments. At first the project had been entrusted to a man named Major Fujiwara Iwaichi, of the Army General Staff, who appears to have been of some amiability, with an understanding of what would appeal to Indians. He was fortunate in lighting, in the first days of the war, on a sick prisoner, Captain Mohan Singh. This was a man of character; he was a cousin of the Maharaja of Patiala, a great prince of the Punjab; he was a capable professional soldier, and had become, apparently without the knowledge of the Indian army, a convinced nationalist. With the backing of Fujiwara, and with the financial aid of some of the leaders of the 800,000 resident Indians in Malaya, he undertook to raise from the Indian prisoners of war a force which might prove useful to the Japanese.

Of the total of 115,000 men who surrendered during the whole of the Malayan campaign, Indians made up a very large number. Though at first a rather blind confidence was put in their loyalty by the Indian government, this had a rather unenviable, if amiable, record, of being deceived. In the Indian Mutiny of 1857, the inquiries held afterwards had shown that an almost insane trust had been placed in troops which had given every sign that they were preparing for rebellion.

Certainly the experience of some of the troops, in the months immediately before the surrender of Singapore, had not been such as to ensure their fidelity. Malaya was in many ways the weakest link in the British imperial chain. Among other disservices, it brought about the demoralization of the Indian army. The culture and atmosphere of Malaya has been described very exactly in the stories of Somerset Maugham, and this society did not seem to most Indians as one worth dying for. Near Singapore there was a very luxurious country club with a much sought-after swimming pool. In the six months before the war, it became known in Singapore that the wives of the planters and of local white businessmen had objected to the swimming pool being used by Indian officers. British officers from the same regiments were eagerly invited, solicitously treated, and competed for assiduously. The Indians were dismayed when this action of the club was officially condoned: at least no protest against it was made from the government or from the military command. This insult, casually offered by the Tanglin Club, did more than many other light-hearted steps to undermine the British Empire in Asia. A dispassionate observer, surveying what was done, must have decided that the English, and especially their wives, were mad. It is not politic to insult a man mortally who is about to defend you.

The Japanese attempts at subverting the loyalty of the prisoners had as their background this resentment at the arrogance of the white society of Malaya. In spite of this preparation of the soil, the first attempts of Fujiwara and of Mohan Singh to set up the Indian National Army, which was inaugurated at Singapore on 12 February 1942, had only limited success. True, they had much to offer the Indian captives—immediate freedom, good wages, the resumption of their military careers, an apparently bright political prospect, exemption from the dreadful forced labour squads, for which Japanese prison camps soon became notorious. Yet the response was poor and Mohan Singh proved anything but an obedient tool. He laid down conditions that the Japanese were unwilling to accept; he stated plainly that if the Japanese aimed at replacing the British in India, they would, after a short time, have to face the aroused opposition of Indian nationalism. In December 1942 Mohan Singh resigned from his position and was arrested by the Japanese, and the first stage of the Japanese experiment at collaboration with Indian nationalism was over.

The Japanese had been handicapped in their efforts because of a deep-seated contempt which they had for prisoners of war, and, still more, for prisoners who were willing to be untrue to their oath of service. Nothing struck them as so contemptible as disloyalty, and they were unable to hide this. Simple-mindedly they judged their prisoners by the same exacting standards which they would have applied to their own people. This made them maladroit in the project of raising an army out of defaulters and deserters.

The decision was, however, taken to persevere in this venture. It was resolved to see whether better results could be obtained from enlisting a politician of standing to head the movement, instead of working exclusively through military men. Subhas Bose, whose mission in Germany had been favourably reported on by the Japanese military attaché there, seemed to be well qualified for this role.

Bose, on returning to Asia, threw himself energetically into organizing the Indian movement, and, in a short time, gave it a life of its own, irrespective of the intentions of its Japanese sponsors. Bose was a different type from the sycophants and commercial adventurers who were usually available to support the Japanese enterprises. The qualities of action he had once displayed as Mayor of Calcutta were now directed to the preparation of a government in exile, which should be ready to replace the existing government of India. On 23 October 1943 the provisional government of Free India (Azad Hind) was set up in Singapore, with Bose at its head. He bled the Indian businessmen white for funds for his enterprise, being given by the Japanese the power to levy taxes on them, and having acquired in the service of Congress the right combination of contempt for millionaires and of business-like respect for money. Bose worked under the great handicap that adequate human material for forming a provisional administration was absent. In spite of this, the sketchy organization of Azad Hind was set up.

Though Bose, between June and October, had transformed the position of the Indians in South-East Asia, and had built them into one of the forces which had to be taken account of, yet he had not succeeded in getting Japan to the point of recognizing a full-fledged government-in-exile. The most that he gained was an invitation to take part as an observer, along with the puppet governments of the Japanese system, in the Greater East Asia Conference in November 1943, although his status was certainly inflated by the oratory of those present; Japan also declared its readiness to hand over the Andaman and Nicobar Islands in the Indian Ocean, to Bose's administration. But as his organization grew in effective power, the relation with local Japanese officials deteriorated. All the vexations which Ba Maw had had to endure, also faced Subhas Bose. The Japanese army was aware of the nuisance which an opinionated exiled government could make, and, deeply suspicious, was anxious to thwart it. However, the Japanese commanders agreed to test out what effect the Indians could bring upon a battle; and Bose glowed at the opportunity.

*

In the meanwhile the Japanese had made their plans for an offensive from Burma which was to be directed against India. Their position was gradually growing dangerous. Large forces were being prepared against them—potentially fourteen divisions from China in the north, three or possibly six divisions from India in the west. In the spring the Japanese in Burma were reinforced, and the decision was made. Basically, the Japanese attack on India was intended to forestall an ultimate offensive against themselves by striking at once and dispersing the gathering British force. The conception was sound, if somewhat optimistic. The Japanese threw into disorder the aggressive plans on the British side.

First the Japanese hoped to overrun the British in Arakan, and then to advance into India, taking in the Assamese towns of Imphal and Kohima. From there they would move into Bengal, though probably they intended no larger action which would have taken them beyond that province. They affected, however, to fall in with Bose's plans for the general invasion of India, as they made stirring material for propaganda. In March 1944 they began their attack and crossed the Indian frontier. The Japanese army employed three divisions.

Bose was determined that they should be accompanied by regiments of the Indian National Army. His provisional government had been transferred to Burma in January 1944. He is described by Ba Maw at the time as a 'bold, khaki-clad figure, carrying with him everywhere the aura of his vast, fabulous country'. In what followed, Bose's sense of reality, his strong point compared with the Indian leaders on the British side of the dividing line, deserted him. He proclaimed the slogan 'Chalo Dehli'. 'On to Delhi.' Its Red Fort, the ancient citadel built by Shah Jahan, hypnotized him, and its occupation became an obsession. In his elation, he foresaw himself sweeping on, made master of the country by a popular upsurge; able, with the strength which this would bring him, to dictate terms to the surrendering British, and to ensure that the Japanese did not misuse their victory, or ride roughshod over the country. He calculated that a Japanese invasion of India would create a very divided feeling among Indians, and might even, the reputation of Japan being what it was, bring a mass of them to the side of the British; but the appearance on Indian soil of an Indian army of liberation would have the most rousing effect all over the country. The world would hear for the first time of the Indian National Army, and thousands of Indians would surge to it. It is strange to find a politician so practical as Bose nursing such illusions. The conversations at this time between Bose and his captains in the Indian National Army, the records of which have survived, are the proofs of his misconception.

The Japanese took a cooler view of his prospects. They wanted to divide the I N A (Indian National Army) up into units of 250 men, who would act as liaison troops, guides and spies, and who would each be attached to a Japanese force. In the end a compromise was arrived at. The I N A had three organized divisions in the expedition, each of two thousand men. The remainder moved as auxiliaries. It became known that the Japanese army had reserved for itself the right of gaining the first victory on Indian soil, and looked forward to offering Imphal as a birthday present to the Emperor, which would be the more welcome because the war was going badly on other fronts.

*

The army against which it moved, the Fourteenth Army, was, like the armies in the Middle East, a joint Anglo-Indian one. Battalions were either British, Indian or Gurkha, but the battalions were mixed up, and the brigade, and still more the division, were heterogeneous. Throughout the war, there was general good feeling and cooperation between the British and Indians. Whatever the grievances, they did not show themselves on the battlefield. This army, by the reorganization of command which took place in 1943, had passed under the supreme direction of Lord Louis Mountbatten, Commander-in-Chief in South-East Asia, with the ultimate command post at Colombo.

The army, which was about to receive its first campaigning experience, represented, at least in part, a new kind of India in arms. Its old pre-war armies had been drawn from a relatively few districts and, among Hindus, from a few chosen castes. Now, under wartime necessity, the army had very much widened its intake of recruits: and with surprising results. For example, Madrasis, who had formed an important part of the armies of Lord Wellesley at the Battle of Assaye, had not been recruited for many years. Now they were offered employment, and the Madrasis celebrated their readmission by supplying the most decorated air force pilots that came from any region of India.

The army undoubtedly gained from opening its ranks; and in so doing the government met a long-standing grievance of the people. The economic benefits of supplying troops were very considerable, and these accounted in part for the prosperity of such regions as the Punjab. It had seemed unjust to favour some parts of the country and to withhold benefits from the others. The lot was cast by a theory, largely arbitrary and false, that some of the people were naturally martial, others not; in fact the distinction dated from the Indian Mutiny, and went on the principle chiefly of rewarding the classes which had not joined the Mutiny, and of discriminating against those which had. At last the army shook itself free from baleful memories, and recruited itself on a more national basis.

This new army began to reflect the new interests of India. Whereas the old army had been entirely non-political, the new entries inevitably brought in with them something of their political interests. The attempt to bar out contacts with political leaders had to be given up: the brightest of the recruits, especially for the officer corps, were the most political: the pride in being above politics had to give way. These new recruits thought it unnatural and absurd to volunteer their lives for use in a war in which they had no say. The mess rooms became forums where every aspect of the world and of government action was under constant scrutiny. This was reflected in the concern of the government in seeing that the reading rooms of the army were well stocked with propaganda. The older generation of professional army officers, and of Indian N C Os looked on disapprovingly, but they could do nothing to stem this constant debate. Increasingly the government was compelled to open the barrack-room gates, so the army became less cloistered. In these months of the war, the old life of India was talked away in the heroic and mock bravura of undergraduate politics conducted by an army of civilians in uniform.

In the campaign which was about to begin, many of the regular Indian officers, whose admission to the army had been the great event in its history during the 1930s, were to be for the first time in action. Soldiers who afterwards became well-known, such as Ayub Khan, later to become President of Pakistan, were tested in this fighting.

About the British soldiers in this army, the main fact was that they began the campaign by being war-weary. They had many of them been on duty for a long time, in an unhealthy climate. They were unsettled by the separation from their families. They were bored by inactivity. They complained that they were the 'forgotten army': an army which had lain in preparation too long and had not the bracing experience of coming into action. It did not take to the atmosphere of the country it was to fight in, to the jungles and the eerie silences, to the leeches and snakes: its medical services were inadequate, and, before the introduction of mepacrin, it was always decimated by malaria.

*

The Japanese advance became bogged down in the siege of Imphal. For over eight weeks, beginning on 8 March 1944, a terrible contest, perhaps the most primitive of the war with the exception of the struggle for the Pacific atolls, took place for the possession of the city: there was resolute hand-to-hand fighting.

At the beginning of the siege, the Japanese, at the start of their offensive, looked very likely to succeed. But the expedition was doomed when the Japanese found it impossible, because of the nature of the country and the blockage of supply routes from the air, to reinforce it with men and materials to overcome the defence. For days the Japanese were convinced that a final effort by them would deliver the city into their hands: but always they were disappointed. They beat off British and Indian sorties, but their own attacks were repulsed. There was great carnage. The fighting was so intense because the Japanese had to be killed at their posts, in the bunkers and wherever they had found cover. A similar struggle took place a little to the north of Imphal for Kohima, where a gigantic battle was waged over the possession of a tennis-court in the garden of the Commissioner's house.

A tactical innovation which deprived the Japanese of one

of their habitual means of securing advantage was made during the campaign. In their drive through Malaya and Burma two years before, they had, using their superior mobility, habitually surrounded British forces; and, when this took place, the British habitually withdrew. This time the British did not retreat; and, though surrounded, relied on being supplied by air. An elaborate organization of the R A F flew in large amounts of food and ammunition. Without this airlift Imphal would have fallen. This change in tactics, which was due to the improved strength of the R A F in the area, changed the situation. The Japanese plans went awry when the troops, whom they thought they had trapped, stayed to fight it out instead of retiring in disorder. They misjudged profoundly the quality of the troops they opposed. They had formed so low an opinion of the British in the Malayan fighting that this betrayed them; the extent to which British troops under British command were underrated turned out to be one of their principal assets.

Another important, significant, hopeful change was that, for the first time in the war the Japanese began to surrender. Not in large numbers: the majority were still faithful to the idea that defeated Japanese are killed or commit suicide. But that some at least, when wounded, depressed, cut off, and cold, acted as other soldiers similarly placed were accustomed to do, was a cheering fact.

The action took place in the country of the Nagas. Some spectacular achievements brought the Naga tribesmen into the light of world publicity. Much more has happened since to these attractive people. Their activities in Intelligence, and as porters, played an unexpected part. A monument erected on the battlefield recalls how two Nagas, disguised as mess servants, stole the Japanese plans of their future lines of advance, passed these to the British, and enabled them to be frustrated.

One Japanese newspaper reporter wrote: 'These fierce battles are comparable with Verdun in the last war.' Finally, logistics were decisive. There was an utter failure of communications, and the Japanese air force was too weak to emulate the British in air transport. The Japanese could bring in neither rice, nor medical supplies, nor essential equipment. The Japanese, who always travelled light, had relied on capturing stores and living on stocks of rice which they might seize; but in this they had failed. The Japanese troop commander issued the following order: 'A decisive battle is the only battle known to a Japanese soldier, or fitting to the Japanese spirit, but now other methods may have to be adopted.' By this he meant a strategic withdrawal. On 4 July the Japanese lifted the siege, and, on their way back, their retreat became a disaster.

They began the campaign with an army of 85,000 men; in it they lost 53,000. British and Indian casualties amounted to 16,700. The result of the campaign was a terrible, wasteful, ignominious defeat. It was one of the worst disasters that the Japanese army suffered in the whole war; comparable in disgrace, if not in magnitude, to that of the Japanese navy at the Battle of Midway Island. Primarily, when all due allowance had been made for the performance of the Fourteenth Army, it had been due to ineffective staff work by an army which was not familiar with campaigning in the tropics. It must be remembered that the war in Malaya had been before this the only large-scale operation of this kind which the Japanese army had fought, and, on balance, its training was still for temperate climates. The higher officers would not cooperate with one another. Perhaps because of this, the Japanese G H Q demanded a rigid obedience to orders and thus checked initiative from the officers in the field, which could often have turned defeat into victory. Another cause of the rout was the numerical weakness of the Japanese air force.

But that the Japanese soldiers had fought like tigers cannot be denied. A quotation may be given from the book on the campaign by Colonel Barker entitled *The March on Delhi*:

> Recruits in the Japanese army were subjected to an intense three-month course of indoctrination which changed them into fanatics, ready to die for their Emperor, their country and the honour of their regiments. This slogan 'Our highest hope is to die for the Emperor' was chanted until it became a positive obsession. The indoctrination of their families was not forgotten either; soon after the new recruit was called up, his relatives received a letter from his commanding officer asking them to be careful not to block his road to an honourable death. The effectiveness of the propaganda may be judged from the fact that there were cases of wives killing their children and committing suicide so that their husbands

would not be reluctant to die. Many officers and men even had their funeral rites performed before leaving for the front to show their intention of dying for their country . . .*

Yet, impressive as their military behaviour was, it was undoubtedly an aberration. There was madness in it, as well as remarkable self-discipline. For, as the war dragged on to its close, and as the Japanese position grew steadily worse, so did the Japanese military behaviour become more ferocious. Its extreme cult of death was a new thing of this century, at least in the form which it took at the time. Early in this century, the Russo-Japanese war had not been particularly savage. And the new sternness was only to be found in the Japanese overseas. As long as they were in the homeland, they did not seem to be possessed, as were the troops in Burma, in the Philippines, and in China. It was as if the Japanese army, once it had had battle experience, succeeded in passing its *furor Japonicus* to all the reinforcements which came to it from Japan. The madness came out in some of the battle orders which were captured:

> You men have got to be fully in the picture as to what the present position is. Regarding death as something lighter than a feather you men must tackle the task of capturing Imphal. You must accept that the division will be almost annihilated. I have confidence in your courage but should any delinquency occur, I shall take the necessary action. In order to keep the honour of his unit bright, a commander may have to use his sword as a weapon of punishment, shameful though it is to have to shed one's own soldiers' blood on the battlefield.†

Some of the men who were the victims of this military discipline, some of the officers who enforced it, are now living quietly in Japan, and they must look back on their wartime experience with surprise and almost with disbelief.

The news of the defeat on 4 July arrived in Tokyo at the same time as the news of the loss of Paris by Germany. It was hard to say which of them faced the blacker prospects, Germany or Japan. The disaster increased the bad relations between the army and the navy: this came, said the navy, of the army 'taking walks' in Asia, and entering on unnecessary

*Colonel A.J. Barker: *The March on Delhi*, Faber, 1963.
†ibid.

adventures instead of concentrating on the problems of the defence of the homeland.

The adventures were nearly at an end. The army would be needed in the Japanese islands. This campaign was nearly the finish of the Japanese in Burma. For a time they were saved from effective pursuit by the monsoon, which put an end to all war. But when the monsoon ended, the Fourteenth Army moved forward; the offensive had already been joined by a bitterly fought advance of Americans and American-trained Chinese troops (who had fallen back on India in 1942) led by General Stilwell; a thrust from Arakan for which the prelude was the taking of Akyab from the sea; and by four Chinese divisions reluctantly introduced by Chiang Kai-shek from Yunnan. This time the offensive progressed. The allies had clear air supremacy, and this was decisive, particularly because it enabled them to keep their armies fully supplied. The Japanese had stirred up opposition from all corners of the world; they must however have felt somewhat surprised at finding among their pursuers divisions of West African and East African troops. They had been raised by the British, and the war in Burma in tropical conditions offered them appropriate employment. That the African people had no quarrel with Japan, that Japan had no significance to them except as the exporter of textiles which were prized by them, did not seem to cause any comment.

As the British slowly reoccupied Burma, they felt the imperial itch reviving. An imperial army in advance bred different sentiments from an imperial army in retreat. 'By English bones the English flag is stayed.' This old line of poetry took on a new meaning.

By April 1945 Rangoon had fallen. It fell actually to the advance from Akyab, which beat by a few hours the advance from the north. The Japanese soldiers continued to fight savagely, but they were the victims of the bad strategy of their generals. Soon all Burma was clear. The end was made more certain because most of the Burmese army, which had been raised and trained by the Japanese, revolted and changed sides at a critical moment.

In the course of this campaign, there had taken place a sharp revision of the complacency of the Japanese about the demerits of the British soldier. Soon after the start of the war, the Japanese had met with such success, and the morale

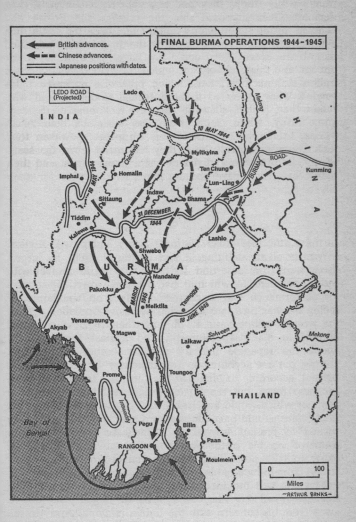

FINAL BURMA OPERATIONS 1944–1945

British advances.
Chinese advances.
Japanese positions with dates.

LEDO ROAD
(Projected)

INDIA

Ledo

10 MAY 1944

Chindwin

Myitkyina

Ten Chung

BURMA ROAD

Kunming

Imphal

Homalin

Lun-Ling

Indaw

Bhamo

Sittaung

Tiddim

31 DECEMBER
1944

Kalewa

Shwebo

Lashio

B   U   R   M   A

Pakokku

Mandalay

MARCH 1945

Meiktila

Taunggyi

18 JUNE 1945

Akyab

Yenangyaung

Magwe

Salween

Laikaw

Mekong

Prome

Toungoo

THAILAND

Irrawaddy

Bay of
Bengal

Pegu

Bilin

RANGOON

Paan

Moulmein

Mekong

0   100
Miles

~ARTHUR BANKS~

of the white troops they had encountered had been so low
that they had supposed that the prestige the British had
enjoyed during the previous century had been the result of a
confidence trick. Caution towards the British was succeeded
by extreme scorn. They could not have held them in lower
esteem, and this probably accounted for their over-confidence
in the Kohima operations, which otherwise appeared light-
headed. They preferred to have British troops to deal with
rather than Indian, since, in the new reckoning of the Japanese army, white troops were less tenacious than Asian
troops. In the vicissitudes of this campaign, however, they
learnt, very expensively, that they had made a wrong assessment. The British troops put on their laurels again, and their
recent campaign gave the Japanese new respect for their
adversary.

*

In the battle, the Indian National Army had proved useless.
In nearly all the fighting, it had disgraced itself. Its largest
losses were from desertion. Its heart was not in combat with
the government to which it had formerly owed allegiance.
Its performance had a depressing effect on the hopes of
seeing the war turn into an Asian defensive operation against
the western counter-attack. Subhas Chandra Bose sustained
himself in his disappointment, and against the contempt
which the Japanese military did not bother to hide, by
putting out an account of near-treachery by the Japanese.
Imphal, according to him, had been helpless before the Indo-
Japanese force, but the Japanese had held back the Indian
advance which would have taken it. They were unwilling that
the Indians should have the great prize of the campaign; they
wished to present Imphal as a Japanese conquest to the
Emperor on his birthday. An Indian governor had been
ready to take possession, but the Indian troops were forestalled from inducting him.

The tale was too inaccurate to be effective. Subhas Bose
lost nearly all his magical appeal. In despair, he turned
away from his concern with the Indian National Army to the
political regimentation of the million Indians living in South-
East Asia. But his fortunes sank with those of the Japanese.
When these were finally overwhelmed, and had finally sur-

rendered, he prevailed on a local officer to let him try to escape by air to Russia. It was a move consonant with his daring and his obstinate opportunism. He foresaw that relations between the West and Russia would be bad, and hoped that Moscow would see the opportunity of letting him set up in Russia his provisional government of India. But the aeroplane in which he was flying crashed on the way to Formosa, on 18 August 1945, and Bose ended his melodramatic life. In spite of his failure, he had, by his daring, so much caught the imagination of the Indians who had been in touch with him, that they refused to believe that he had really been killed. The rumour spread that he had gone underground and had become a Sadhu (there is some evidence that some of the defeated rebels did this in 1858 after the failure of the Indian Mutiny), and that he would emerge again to lead a triumphant rising against the British. The legend was firmly believed in by his brother, Sarat Chandra Bose, a leading, and apparently hard-headed, Congressman of Bengal.

Bose's idea of corrupting the Indian army, and of leading it back in triumph against the British in Delhi, though it turned out to be a fiasco, could have been a formidable threat to Britain. Its concept was sound: it was fortunate for Britain that the morale of the I N A was such as to make the plan unworkable. For months the news of the I N A caused very deep anxiety among the army staff and the informed civilians, in Delhi, and their failure in action was received with intense relief. The enterprise had been kept reasonably secret from the public in India. It was not entirely unknown, for the information about it was contained in the monitoring report which had a fairly wide circulation; moreover, Bose's radio was listened to fairly extensively. But the public was surprised when it learned later from the press how wide the conspiracy had been.

Of 70,000 Indians who had been captives, over half resisted all the lures to serve either Japan direct or else rebel India. They had nothing very much to induce them to remain loyal beyond their oath of service and their regimental pride. These ties held; and their strength was an important factor in determining the history of the war in Asia. For this the main credit goes to the regimental commanders of the previous two or three generations who, by and large, were trusted by their men to stand up for their interests, for fair treatment, and for an honourable status. These men built up the ties which between 1942 and 1945 bore the great strain.

This left the problem of what to do with the soldiers who had been less loyal. Most of these who had enlisted in the I N A had passed into British hands, and for the second time had become prisoners of war. Technically they were all of them guilty of an internationally agreed crime of the darkest nature. For desertion, treason, rebellion, and levying war against the king, a harsh penalty was likely to be exacted. Actually, no drumhead court-martials were held on any of the prisoners upon capture. They were kept in captivity, and what to do about them became a political case which was hotly debated.

It was not decided until the war ended. The Congress leaders, on coming out of their own wartime captivity, saw in it an ideal means of attacking the government. The I N A were presented as the true heroes of the Indian nation, and, if harshly dealt with, would become revered martyrs. The British were impressed by this danger. They were inclined to act in the spirit of Winston Churchill, who advising clemency on another occasion, had said: 'The grass grows quickly over the battlefield. Over the scaffold, never.' They decided to release the undistinguished mass of the prisoners. But they hesitated at the ring leaders, and those who, in the course of the campaign, had been guilty of war crimes, or had tortured their former comrades because these had stood firm against the allurements of the Japanese. They had to keep it in mind that those who felt most bitterly against the Indian National Army were the officers and men of the Indian army who had remained loyal. For the sake of the morale of this Army, it was scarcely possible to release without some punishment at least the more spectacular of the prisoners. Therefore, after much indecision, and much discussion which became involved with the renewed negotiations between the government and Congress, the decision was made to limit prosecution to a few cases, ultimately restricted to three.

The trials were held in the Red Fort of Delhi in 1946. A more peculiarly inept setting could not have been chosen. The Red Fort had become, in Indian national mythology, the shrine of Indian national hopes. It had been built as a citadel

and palace by the Moghul Emperors, and symbolized the
time before the British conquest, when all that Britain meant
had been individual merchants coming to beg for patronage
from the great ones of India. The trials gave so much
publicity to the Congress lawyers, who were able to defend
the prisoners, and to Jawaharhal Nehru who, having once
been a barrister, could appear before the courts, that the government was glad to call them off quickly. It was content
with the simple dismissal from further service of the great
majority of officers and men. Such dismissal was punishment in itself, since service in the army brought with it
economic privilege; and, by confiscating this advantage from
the disaffected, it was thought that the loyal part of the
Indian army would be at ease.

*

Burma had been freed as the result of a sustained thrust of
the British and the Americans against the Japanese army,
which had worn itself out by the offensive at Imphal and
Kohima. From recovered Burma, the victors prepared to
move afresh. Singapore and Malaya, were the next targets:
and Japan had there, and elsewhere in South-East Asia, a
very large army, as yet unscathed, its morale untouched by
allied propaganda, with vast supplies of arms and ammunition. The prospect which this opened up, and the length of
time which would be taken in ejecting Japan from one
well-defended post to another, caused a great upsurge of
criticism of British strategy. Had the drive on Burma, even
though it was ultimately successful, really been justified?
Were there not better ways of using British power than in
following the withdrawal of Japan? Could Britain, using its
recovered naval supremacy, not strike at some vital ports,
less protected?

There is a notable passage in Tolstoy's *War and Peace*
describing men's behaviour on the battlefield. When he is
stricken on the field of Austerlitz, Prince Andrei sees two
opposing men, French and Russian, both seizing hold of a
ramrod, and struggling for its possession. Each would have
done better to release his hold of it, and to free himself to
use his musket. But they were too much hypnotized by the
struggle to let go. So they continued to tussle. In the

circumstances of the war in Asia, it was asked whether the British and Japanese really did any good for themselves, or brought the war nearer to an end, by remaining locked in conflict.

In fact, the decisive fighting was going on in the Pacific. Britain was denied a role in this: it could supply no adequate force, and the American commanders were under pressure to distance themselves from allies who put their cause in such an imperialist colour. Keeping the British at arm's length was held to improve the American image with the national parties of south Asia. The future of that part of the world was held to lie with them.

19

---◆---

China 1942–4

BEFORE describing the end of Japan, and the breakthrough of the American ships from the Pacific, it is necessary to review the fate of China up to this point. After all, China had been the main cause of the war in the Far East. This conflict, which had spread so widely, had begun as the result of the refusal by Chiang Kai-shek to come to terms with Japan. China had not ceased to count. But, after the intervention of the United States, it had taken a relatively minor part in the military affairs of the nations.

Before the conflict was enlarged, Chiang had calculated that, if he held out, sooner or later Japan would come into collision with other powers. He had resolved, and it was more or less public knowledge, that, when this time came, China, which for four years had borne the fury of the Japanese offensive, would retire from the actual fighting, and would leave it to the fresher forces which should become engaged to complete the wearing down of Japan, of which China felt that it had done enough. Without fighting further, Chiang Kai-shek counted on being able to join in the eventual share-out of territory, and in the other benefits, when the world was rearranged at the general peace. In this, events had gone more or less as Chiang expected. Chiang, the simple and, in the eyes of the sophisticated statesmen of the West, rather primitive soldier, seemed at the time to have his judgement vindicated; his diplomacy confirmed.

China, poor in resources for making war, now held the best cards. The United States had chosen to take up the

293

challenge of Japan. But it had handicapped itself by the decision to concentrate on fighting Germany first, Japan afterwards. In the interval before it could concentrate its whole attention on Japan, allies in the East were likely to be of greater moment to the United States than the United States was to them. It became a major preoccupation with it to keep China in the war, at the cost of offering it all possible inducement to stay. China could have all that it asked, in exchange for its willingness that the total commitment of American force in the Far East should be delayed. In the long run, the United States believed that the use of Chinese territory was indispensable for making it geographically possible for the allies to defeat Japan; it had no confidence that Russia, which also had a land army able to get to grips with Japan, would ever, in the way that events were shaping themselves, break its neutrality with Japan. For the United States, China represented the corridor along which their armies might eventually proceed, and get at Japan on level terms. In the meanwhile, China was to be the subject of a holding operation: to be kept in the war at all costs.

The impediment lay chiefly in geography. With the fall of Burma, the precarious link with Chungking along the Burma road was interrupted. China was cut off. Between it and the Americans there was the enormous barrier of the Himalayas. To keep China in the war, the Americans, with ingenuity, tried by every means to circumvent the obstacle. They organized an airlift to China over the mountain ranges from India; they sent American officers to re-train the Chinese army; they put continual pressure upon India to demonstrate that China might eventually find aid there. In immediate aid, China was given a large Anglo-American loan: America subscribed $500 million and Britain £50 million: this relieved its immediate financial problems.

This aid the allies intended for China as a whole. It was directed to whoever in China would fight Japan. Chiang Kai-shek's aim was to engross it all for himself. It was to ensure that his hold over the country was continuously and decisively strengthened; it was to deny aid to those who might threaten it. In his thinking at that time dollars counted for more than morale in the upkeep of government. He saw danger principally in one fact—that the communists, the party of revolution, might obtain the economic backing which would transform the situation, and put them on equal terms with the government. In a China, in which the ferment of revolution was working ever more actively, in which Communism had already mastered the circumstances of the war, it was essential that the communists should be denied their share of foreign aid, even at the cost of their military efficiency as allies against Japan. Technically, the Kuomintang and the communists were still allies; they were pledged together to fight Japan; the American aid, on a reading of the military situation, should have been divided between them. That it should not became the governing aim of Chiang's policy.

At first, the prospects appeared bright for Chiang. His more distant ambitions, of being the supreme force in Asia at the end of the war, buoyed him up when his government, as the result of the intensification of the blockade, suffered blow upon blow. Chiang was sanguine: this perhaps explains why he took phlegmatically even the worst of news. Both his enemies, Japan and Chinese Communism, were being trampled into ruin by the United States. His long-term prospects were heady. His standing in Washington mattered more to him than military realities in the Far East. In this he was served zealously, alike by plausible Chinese and by foreigners over whom China had cast its spell.

Chiang, in order apparently to gratify his sense of importance, struck out in directions which caused surprise, and ways which were unwelcome to his allies. He had insisted on visiting India, in February 1942, and seeing Indian affairs for himself. He could urge that India had suddenly become vitally important for China, both as a base, and as transit territory for American supplies. The bad relations between the government of India and Indian nationalists were a menace to China, because they could result in a situation which interrupted communication. Chiang insisted on studying matters for himself, and tried, by personal diplomacy with the Viceroy and Indian leaders, to bridge the gap between them.

The British were annoyed. They found Chiang extremely ill-informed, and privately judged that, in the guise of a mediator, he was prospecting the ground for Chinese intervention in case the military necessity in Europe should compel a British withdrawal from India. They objected to the need for providing Chiang and his wife with banquets at the moment when, too late in the judgement of many observers, they had become conscious of their desperate state. Especially, though, they demurred at the increased prestige which his interest brought to the Indian Congress in its duel with the Viceroy.

Chiang Kai-shek could not blame the Indian administration for a failure to back him. This somewhat lethargic government went out of its way to provide, with energy and great speed, the institutions which were needed to bind the two governments together in their war effort. On the Indian side, a China Relations Department was brought into being, to whose good offices a thousand things were owing: the Department did everything, from supply to strengthening military cooperation. It was efficient, it was prompt, it cut through delays. It was so much out of character for the government of India that it quite astonished the Chinese.

*

In spite of these inducements to be up and doing, China remained more or less militarily inactive. The performance of Chinese troops, in the rare action in which they were now engaged, was unmemorable. Nor was this surprising. Their armies were shockingly organized; relations between officers and men were deplorable; the officers were increasingly arrogant and corrupt; they embezzled the wages of the soldiers; they were often brutal and ignorant; the soldiers either were separated for many years from their families, or, if they had news of them, were rightly disturbed at the news of worsened conditions in the countryside. The rank and file had nothing to fight for.

Chiang Kai-shek chose, in March 1943, to publish under his name a highly controversial book. It was written in Chinese. The book was called *China's Destiny*. It contained the familiar story of the unjust dealings with China by the Great Powers, the unequal treaties, the shearing away from China of her dependencies. Thus it revealed that China still nursed her grievances when it would have been better policy to have concealed them. The powers which had done China its past wrongs had now shown a willingness to repair the damage, and the exposure of China's wound could only damage their cooperation. The effect of its publication was to cause mistrust, rouse suspicion, and generate bad blood. Madame Chiang Kai-shek shrewdly advised against an English translation: this did not appear therefore until 1947.

Chiang, in his relations with his allies, followed the tactics of 'threatening to fall'. He advertised that his position was calamitous. The weaker he was, the more anxious the Americans were for him, and the greater the efforts which they were willing to make on his behalf. Naturally he led them on; and he was helped by the chance that President Roosevelt revealed, from the United States' entry into the war until his death in 1945, an extraordinary partiality for China. The accidents of personality played here a fateful part. Roosevelt, active in Washington, had an even greater influence on events by the climate of opinion which he germinated, than by the measures he took as head of the American government. He dwelt much on the shape which the world must take as a result of the war; and he became convinced that, round a firm Sino-American axis, the Asian countries were destined to revolve. American aid would supply strength to China; China would revert to its traditional art of radiating its great civilizing influence out across its borders.

Roosevelt saw rightly that the crisis in the Far East was ultimately due to the collapse of the political power of China. The United States would restore it. This time there would be no imperialists to undermine it again; President Roosevelt was satisfied that the eastern role of Britain and other colonial powers was coming to an end. Asia would be safe again, except from its own dissension, and what power would thrive better in this atmosphere than China. He gained comfort from the signs that China's appetite for its historic greatness was beginning to recover. He became convinced that he was serving alike the interests of the United States, and also all the world, by throwing his mantle over China.

Roosevelt had an extraordinary power of communicating his vision to the public. In this case, however, he preached mostly to the converted. The United States' attitude towards China in the later stages of the war was rather unbalanced. If one nation can be said to adopt another, the United States adopted China. The United States has been liable to periodical phases of extreme partiality to certain foreign countries; in its fervent feeling towards China at this time, it outdid itself. The United States was hallucinated; like Titania by Bottom the Weaver. The reality was that the U S became enthusiastic for the tyranny of the Kuomintang, which was passing increasingly into the most reactionary hands; the Americans saw it, not as it was, but as a democratic party full of vigour and promise. In place of a military rabble, the United States saw in the Chinese army an inspiring force, which was a mixture of a romanticized version of the American armies of the Revolution and the Civil War. Where there was evident, and apparently irreparable economic ruin, it saw lively economic promise. Its intellectual and artistic life, which, to the trained eye, was in the ruins of a great cultural past, appeared to the U S A to be full of a fresh, imaginative view of the world. China appeared as nearly a new Utopia. The United States of course produced its realists, who protested against its romantic illusions, but they could scarcely make themselves heard against the newspapers and radio, which all of them followed the fashion.

Roosevelt's policies, the American hallucination, the realities of geography and of logistics in the East, produced, between them, a mood of accommodation of China which bewildered the rest of the world. China was pitied, but the United States postponed coming to its aid with immediate and effective military succour. It was encouraged by the United States to pass its time in discussing its growing ambition. American patronage ensured that China's claims were not regarded as simply ludicrous. Men like Winston Churchill took a sceptical view, but it was hardly worth their while to oppose the U S over this. In war, naked strength is in the last resort the thing which counts; but prestige may be manufactured by the few statesmen who matter, and may, over the short run, pass for strength. China was in this condition, and advanced by several degrees in the world's esteem.

All the while that this was happening, the Chinese press, which was of course under strong government influence, had, as was natural in the relations between states, been biting the hand which fed it. The newspapers were full of articles which attacked the United States very bitterly. They made use of the stale propaganda methods of the Nazis early in the war in Europe. They claimed that the United States would fight until the last Chinaman; they envisaged that China, having made great sacrifices for democracy, would be a certain loser at the peace, and would itself be sacrificed. They painted a picture of the riotous life lived by Americans in luxurious camps in the midst of the poverty of China. This mood, when it became known in the United States, took a little of the glow out of the American feeling for China. But the work of the China lobby had been very far-reaching, and the suspicion that the Chinese were ungrateful was lightly borne by American philanthropy.

Although there was much criticism of Chiang Kai-shek by some Americans with a clearer vision, too much can be made of occasional Sino-American friction. In particular, the incompetence and bad morale of the Chinese were probably overrated by some American experts. There was no real likelihood of China making a separate peace. Chiang Kai-shek had steered China's policy since the earliest years of the conflict, but, by the latest years, China had probably steered itself. The muddle, constant criticism, and apathy misled the United States. China, though it detested war, was averse from surrender. It would have opposed Chiang if he had wished to make a dishonourable peace with nearly as much compulsive force as it had done when it suspected him in 1937. China's mood was frightening. It had not the least enthusiasm for the war; it was profoundly weary of it; but it was determined to continue to resist. If ever a war had in fact been a 'people's war', this was one, even though there were large and respectable elements of the population who were cooperating with the Japanese. The government was forbidden by the nation to make peace: by a nation which, by all reasonable arguments, yearned for peace. The war seemed likely to continue indefinitely.

*

It was the Americans who had to serve in China who were naturally less affected by the extreme American enthusiasm for all things Chinese. Their position was extremely difficult; they suffered much less from the delusions which were making American policy, but they were expected to act as if they did so. The attitude of the much-tried American General, Joseph Stilwell, deserves study. His mishaps are part of the misunderstandings of the time.

He was a naturally bilious man: he was nicknamed 'Vinegar Joe': he was suspicious of everyone, especially of Americans who were fawning on Chinese, of all British, with whom he had to be in alliance but whom he suspected of outwitting the United States, and of the Chinese, above all of Chiang Kai-shek, whom he saw playing a gigantic confidence trick on the United States. The irony was that he, who had few illusions, was inclined to be grimly friendly towards China, and, in a professional manner, to defend its interests.

After Pearl Harbor, when American aid began to pour out on China, it was clearly desirable to appoint someone to be responsible on the spot for its distribution. A commander was needed for the American personnel who were militarily active in or near China. A military expert was also necessary to work out joint military plans with the Chinese. Stilwell, as a person of unquestionable experience, and available immediately, was appointed. He had served for many years in a quasi-diplomatic status in the American Embassy. At Roosevelt's instance, in his instinct to mix up American affairs with those of its allies, Stilwell was given by Chiang Kai-shek the Chinese rank of his Chief-of-Staff.

When, as described earlier, the British formed their South-East Asia command in 1943, Stilwell was appointed as the deputy of Mountbatten. From a comparatively minor position, he had accumulated appointments, all of which gave him authority. Few men in the war were in a position of such power.

The multitude of functions was a mistake. With such divergent pressures upon him, no man could have made a success of being a loyal servant of the United States and China. For a joint post to be workable, there must be coincidence of interests between the countries to which a man is jointly responsible. Stilwell, in serving Roosevelt and Chiang, had an impossible task. Much as Roosevelt respected the role that China was destined to play, the interests of the United States and China were different. Stilwell had decided that he would be through and through American: he would serve the United States and would correct Roosevelt's rather eccentric judgement.

The difficulty was increased because Stilwell's own judgement was defective. He did not see that, for the issue of the war, it really was unnecessary for Chiang to fight much more. Roosevelt himself had probably glimpsed this truth. But Roosevelt erred because he supposed that it was necessary for the United States to make strenuous efforts to keep China in the war. China would have remained belligerent in any circumstances, and its real interests, which Chiang saw very clearly, were all against making a separate peace. Having won credit with the western allies, China would have been suicidal to fling it away by becoming a renegade towards the end of the war, in which the difficult part had been the beginning. Nor would it have gained any advantage by doing so. The United States and Britain were satisfied as long as China remained formally at war, and turned a blind eye to the reality of much of China's wartime record.

Stilwell, however, did not perceive this. He had a mania to drive China back into war: both its bureaucrats living in comfort in Chungking, and its wretched conscripts herded to war by force. Chinese guile, Chinese pretence that it was doing much more than it was, he exposed with relish. Stilwell obtained Chinese agreement that thirty Chinese divisions should be allotted for cooperation with the British from India for the operations in Burma and to reconquer South-East Asia. To facilitate these operations, the road connecting Assam in India with Burma was constructed. It was one of the major engineering enterprises of the war. Stilwell, and his like-minded American staff, made no secret of the fact that they greatly desired that American and Chinese forces should get into many of these regions in advance of the British. They considered the British Empire obsolete and effete, and had no desire to see it re-established. They counted on a peace settlement which would create an Asia of self-determining nation-states, always the American ideal, as 1919 had shown in Europe. For this, they considered it of first-class importance that they should end the war in military possession of disputed territory. But the thirty Chinese divisions proved to be a paper force. Only a fraction was ever available. For Stilwell's aim, there was to be no Chinese manpower.

Stilwell, in his vigour for the war, could get little response from the Kuomintang officials, and from Chiang Kai-shek personally. He became increasingly obsessed with the fact that Chiang was employing 200,000 of his best troops for cordoning off the area that was occupied by the Red Army; and that this army, alone of China's military forces, had proved that it was anxious to fight, and had shown the value of its guerrilla strategy against the Japanese. But it was prevented by the Kuomintang from playing its part in the war. Chiang, in his fear that substantial economic aid would reach the communists, and would make them dangerous to him, blockaded them shamelessly.

Stilwell denounced him to the Americans as a bad ally: Chiang complained that he could have no confidence in such a Chief-of-Staff. To do him justice, he could say that Stilwell had not grasped the fact that the civil war in China was continuing. The merger of the armies, which was to have taken place by the pact which Chiang made with the communists at the time of the Sian kidnapping, had never been carried out. The communists had laid down their own strategy in their war with Japan, and, as by their guerrilla methods of war they penned Japan more and more to the towns, they continually occupied a larger and larger area of the country. All the while the communists were consolidating their hold. Was Chiang to assist them by removing his forces which kept them under surveillance?

The problem was difficult; Chiang was notable for his obstinacy, which had established him where he was; Stilwell was notorious for pertinacity and for courting disfavour. With Stilwell's agreement, a whitewashing of the communists took place in America. The news about them was surprising, and cheered an America which was hungry for hopeful news. It was said that they were not real communists at all; they were Jeffersonian democrats, simple rural reformers, who desired only to fight for their country, and they were held back by Chiang Kai-shek, the real nature of whose government had by this time become plain. They were a brand-new and unexpected ally, waiting to be used against the Japanese if the United States would sanction it. Chiang Kai-shek, treating this as a threat of American repudiation of him, fulminated, and put the blame on Stilwell. He supposed him responsible for the agitation in the press.

By the autumn of 1944 the breach between Chiang and

Stilwell had become wider, beyond reconciliation. Chiang officially demanded that Roosevelt should dismiss Stilwell. Roosevelt, though his confidence in Chiang had been half-changed by Stilwell—but not his confidence in China—consented.

With the fall of Stilwell there vanished a plan which had been dear both to him and to Roosevelt. This was for the re-training and modernization by American officers of the entire Chinese army. The United States was characteristically ready to take responsiblity for this gigantic task; but it required Chinese consent to the extent of being willing to make a reality of the appointment of Stilwell as Chief-of-Staff. Chiang would not trust such authority to any foreigner.

Admittedly it would have been difficult; there would have been storms, and, whilst Stilwell's attitude to the communists was at best ambiguous in the view of Chiang Kai-shek, it was clear that there were many fundamental principles on which the two men were divided in any reform. Stilwell would have certainly wanted to incorporate part of the Red Army, and much of its system of command and administration. Neither of them would compromise. But Chiang, in winning his point that there should be no foreign command in his army, sacrificed the possibility of ending the war with a re-born, modernized force.

*

The war was very depressing when seen in these years from Chungking. Air-raids, which had been plentiful, had died down, and had become rare. But with this there had come hunger and a dreadful boredom, with nothing to distract people from being conscious of their extreme discomfort. The city was overcrowded: it was full of refugees. The lives of most people had become a nightmare because of inflation; it was still under a semblance of control; it was to reach fantastic proportions, as in Germany during the period at the end of the First World War, only when the war was over; but already it cast very deep shadows, and was the main impediment in life.

The extent of the inflation was a novelty in human history. In Chungking, prices rose by two hundred and fifty times in the two years 1942–4. The price index of goods, quoted at

100 in 1937, was 125,000 by 1945. How to cope, how to find money, became the overriding concern of everyone, including all the army officers, and the events of the war sank a long way behind. Another stunning blow had been dealt at human society, and strong suspicions grew up as to whether life could ever be normal again, even if peace was restored. It was the classical effect of an uncontrolled inflation. 'If you wish to make a revolution,' said Lenin, 'first debauch the currency.'

In spite of this, many people were growing very rich, out of wartime enterprises and profiteering, but they hid themselves, and no bright plumage lit up the drab scene. Only the gossip and scandal circulated wildly. The inflation had the usual effects in disintegrating the society. The corruption became impudent. One day, when a general of the Indian army was paying a visit to the city, the cousin of the Chinese finance minister called on him by night, and outlined a plan of partnership by which the two could make a fortune. All that was necessary was the use of the general's means of transport, and of his prestige to keep official interference at arm's length.

To keep their armies in the field, the Chinese had to make more and more use of conscription. It was an ordinary sight to see in the countryside, even close to Chungking, squads of soldiers being deported to fighting areas; the soldiers were all chained together. Across the length of the huge country, there was constant, small-scale, sporadic action, which, though of little military consequence, did much material damage. The Japanese occupying the cities were harried, and in many parts of the country could not venture, except in great force, into the countryside; they raided and massacred sporadically. Insecurity was constant; the war had apparently ceased to have a reason and the possibility of an end.

In parts of the country, however, the war seemed to have run its course, to be exhausted, and to have fought itself out. It was succeeded by the armed forces on both sides following the age-old instincts for trade. The armies became trading organizations. Trading is a passion with the Chinese; with the Japanese it is familiar. As soon as the armies stood still, the Chinese put out their feelers, and the Japanese, who were not paid very highly and welcomed some supplement to their wages, responded. The metamorphosis of the barbaric

Japanese conquerors into the scheming Japanese traders was curious to watch. The attempts by high Japanese officers to restrict the trade were in vain. The Japanese generals, even at the highest level of direction of the Japanese armies, were too deeply engaged. China, by the action not of its government or of its soldiers but by the private enterprise of its merchants, had woven a web of commerce, which within a month or so of conquest snared the Japanese and bound them in all sorts of ways to courses of action which aimed to the satisfaction of private wants rather than the advancement of Japan's public enterprise of subjugation. And so it was to continue until the end of the war. The spectacle is of exuberant trade springing up and flourishing wherever the two belligerents came in contact. Patrolling warships operated most. The Japanese navy was particularly notorious for doing traffic with the Chinese. This was very well attested by watchers in Hong Kong in the months before the island was invaded.

Stilwell's fall in 1944 coincided with the last great military effort in China by the Japanese. During 1943 and the first part of 1944, the Americans had built up a new war machine on Chinese soil with which they had at last succeeded in reaching the heart of the Japanese war effort, and which held out hopes of being deadly. This they did by expanding greatly the activities of General Claire Lee Chennault. This man had begun by recruiting a private air force, mercenaries, drawn from the staff of American airlines and college youths. They were known as Chennault's Flying Tigers. In the summer of 1941, while the United States was still neutral, this force, put at the service of the Kuomintang, proved itself indispensable for the air defence of Chungking. Later, when the United States entered the war, it was incorporated in the American army, and Chennault also returned to it. In the course of time he established airfields in Eastern China, and from there began the first systematic bombardments that the Japanese had had to endure. They were found so effective that the greater part of the material sent painfully to China by the airlift was used for constructing the airfields.

This finally prevailed on the Japanese to renew their military effort against China. They had halted large-scale military campaigning at the end of 1938, and, during the years since, it had seemed that they were best served by letting time work for them. They hoped that discomfort, and the upset from the perpetual strain of relations with the communists, would in the end induce Chiang to submit his stubborn neck to peace negotiations. They could place their trust in Chinese racial dislike of its western allies. During this period there were steady defections from the Kuomintang side to the Japanese and to the Wang Ching-wei government, which satisfied Japan. By 1942, the communists estimated, and published with smugness, that twenty-seven Kuomintang generals had gone over. .

In 1944 Japan decided that it was necessary to renew the offensive. This was also in part prompted by the need to have land contact with its forces in South-East Asia, since its shipping had been so drastically reduced. It began a campaign with the purpose of capturing and dismantling the Chinese airfields. The revived Japanese onslaught burst like a thunderclap on China. Divisions were moved from Manchuria, where they had passed the war in idleness, watching Russia. The Japanese army found in a renewal of the Chinese war the opportunity to work out its feeling of frustration. The new divisions roared through the seaboard of China, and farther inland, destroying one airfield after another, not meeting any Chinese army able to stand up to them in pitched battles. Where there was a struggle, as in Hunan, the Chinese, when they were eventually broken, were set on by an enraged population, which blamed them for having disturbed the unofficial armistice. To such a squalid end had the aims of the Chinese army to defend the country been reduced.

The loss of General Chennault's airfields drew the world's attention once more to China's weakness. It settled a controversy which had been going on among strategists. One side had taken the view that Chennault had proved that land operations were unnecessary: it was enough to build airfields in distant places, lightly protected by guerrilla operations, and leave the air force to carry on the war. The other side argued that, without an army, airfields were entirely vulnerable. The latter view proved correct; it was found that the Chinese armies were inadequate to safeguard them.

But the usefulness and importance of China to the western allies had changed sharply.

The beginning of 1943 had seen the last great western incentive offered to the Chinese. In that year, the West had made the gesture of terminating their right to maintain

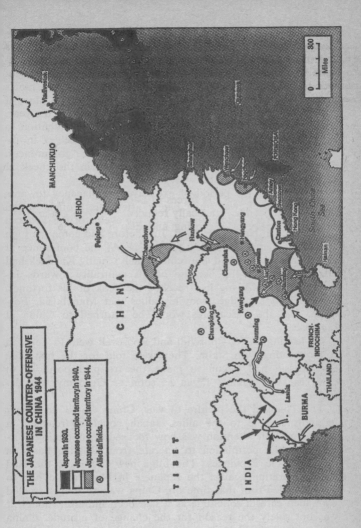

Treaty Ports in China. The largest tool of imperialism was renounced. The negotiations, which they had pursued desultorily since the 1920s, were accelerated, and agreement was reached. If the war had ultimately grown out of China's endeavour to extirpate these foreign footholds in China, it had, by this decision of the allies, been won. Later in the year, Roosevelt had secured an allied statement of the intention to associate China as an equal power with themselves in remoulding the pattern of the world at the peace conferences. Other countries may have had their tongue in the cheek at this, but Roosevelt had his way.

Nevertheless the period of excessive complacency towards Chiang Kai-shek was immediately after this brought to an end, or was very much qualified, by the events of the Teheran Conference in November 1943. Just before had come the high point of Chiang Kai-shek's apotheosis. At the conference at Cairo of Roosevelt and Churchill, which Chiang Kai-shek had attended—but Stalin, because of his neutrality towards Japan, did not—Chiang had reached the peak of his fortunes. He received a pledge from his allies that Manchuria, Formosa, and the Pescadores would be returned to China at the peace.

On leaving Cairo, Churchill and Roosevelt went to Teheran for a meeting with Stalin. They were told for the first time that Russia had begun to make the troop dispositions to enter the war against Japan as soon as Germany was defeated.

This changed the picture of war. China would no longer be indispensable to the allies. Japan could be reached in other ways; all attention was now focused on obtaining Russia's eventual permission to operate from Russian bases in the Maritime Provinces. The huge new factor of the Red Army operating against the Japanese in Manchukuo had to be digested. From that time on, China was no longer treated with such careful solicitude as it had been hitherto, though it was not solely the reason for the change of attitude. China still enjoyed the delusive grandeur which had been built up in President Roosevelt's time, and communicated by him to the public, but this was a wasting asset.

China, as an object of strategic concern, became of secondary importance. Chiang Kai-shek, his suspicions and ambitions, no longer held the centre of the picture. The war, which had originated in the crisis of China, was to come to an end with the fate of China apparently of small concern to the Great Powers, which now pressed on towards the final kill.

*

In the course of the war, a profound change had, however, come over the prestige of the Kuomintang and of the communists. They had both of them engaged in warfare, which they had fought by different means using different arms. They had been in competition with each other. The upshot, though it was not yet definite, was that, in the judgement of the various important groups of Chinese society, the communists had shown themselves more durable than the Kuomintang. True, the Kuomintang was, technically, to be one of the victor powers. But the Kuomintang had lost face irrevocably.

It was not so much that the communists had shining victories to their credit. They had latterly fought very little. But their government survived the war with an infinitely better morale than the Kuomintang.

Soon after the war, the two governments would come into open conflict. Support would vanish away from the Kuomintang. It would transfer itself to the communists.

The Kuomintang had plenty of opportunity to see how unpopular its régime was becoming, and plenty of opportunity to take up some more popular course. But it kept obstinately on its disastrous career. As it became clearer that China, thanks to its allies, was to be on the winning side in the war, there grew up naturally a discussion about the form that post-war politics was to take. Similarly the Kuomintang could have met the public half way, and announced the approaching end of its party dictatorship. But its reply, as the demand for this grew, was to increase the size of the secret police. Its activities became intolerable. The Kuomintang gave every indication that it would continue unreformed.

20

Twilight

THE attention now turns to the American offensive, far across the Pacific, and it turns away from all the other theatres of the Far-Eastern war. Fighting still continued in these, but it became obvious that it was irrelevant. The turmoil in the Pacific dwarfed all other, and this became increasingly so until the end.

In the middle of June 1944, the Americans invaded Saipan in the Mariana Islands. This island, 1,350 miles from Tokyo, was the most vital point in the outer defences of Japan. It had been strongly fortified, so strongly that even the naval experts believed it to be impregnable. Its strategic importance was appreciated; from Saipan, the Americans would be able to bomb Tokyo; they could also disrupt the communications of the remaining forward posts in the Pacific with Japan. Its loss would breach what was called in Japanese 'the absolute zone of national defences'.

The Americans had assembled huge forces. They had an escort fleet, for the troop transports for the invasion, of seven battleships, twelve escort carriers, eleven cruisers, and ninety-one destroyers. It took only half an hour for the assault forces to get ashore at Saipan, but it still remained to be captured. At once the Japanese assembled their still very formidable fleet, and sought a decisive battle. They had foreseen the American moves and were not taken by surprise; they had ample strength in Guam and in the islands of the Philippines. The battle which resulted was the fourth large-scale naval combat of the war. The sense of occasion was in the message of the Japanese admiral to the fleet before the action began: 'The fate of the empire rests on this one battle.'

The result was entirely disastrous to Japan. The successive strikes by Japanese aeroplanes were beaten off, and in the whole battle Japan lost nearly four hundred aircraft. The destruction of these, and the repelling of the Japanese attacks, were more spectacular than the loss of ships, though the operation cost the Japanese two battleships and an aircraft-carrier; two other carriers were disabled. This was far beyond the capacity of the Japanese shipyards, at this stage of the war, to make good. The American damage was very slight.

As was usual, the Japanese navy silenced the news of the defeat. Even high officials of the Foreign Office remained without knowledge of what had been happening. They were especially confused because, after the defeat, they had been invited by naval officers to banquets to celebrate a great Japanese triumph.

The fall of Saipan could not, however, be hidden. The news began to circulate in the middle of July 1944. To most people it came as an entire shock, and for the first time the average Japanese, without any such information as had been weighing on the experts, began to surmise that Japan was in fact losing the war. Saipan had fallen with such ease, the Americans were ahead of their timetable. An evident *frisson* went through the nation, well disciplined though it continued to be.

A result was the resignation of General Tojo, the Prime Minister. He went, after a complicated intrigue of the politicians. This was the first sign of political malaise which had come from Japan during the war; and it was received with relief by those watching among its enemies. The procedures by which government changes were brought about in Japan were as a rule quite different from the official processes laid down in the Japanese constitution. In this instance, a group of high civilian and army officers, especially those who had formerly held official positions, began to agitate that General Tojo's cabinet should resign. Saipan had caused them to open their eyes, and to press their arguments as a matter of life or death. Their dissensions were heard at high level, and they arranged that they should be transmitted to the throne.

As a result, a great agitation was set afoot among a large circle of those holding the various offices of importance. Tojo, who, a week earlier had apparently been completely safe, suddenly found the ground trembling under his feet. He sought to appease his critics by yielding to one of their demands, and proposed that he should no longer combine the posts of Prime Minister, War Minister, and Chief of the Army Staff. The arrangements were made for General Umezu Yoshijiro to become Minister of War. But by this time, the opinion of the inner circle had moved on, and it could be satisfied with nothing less than the resignation of Tojo as Prime Minister. He demurred, and argued in vain. On the day of the announcement of the loss of Saipan, on 18 July 1944, his resignation was in the hands of the Emperor.

The choice of a successor fell to an informal group of seven elder statesmen. Their task was to find somebody able to carry on the war, but who would, in view of the bad prospects for its outcome, also seek earnestly to bring about peace. The Japanese had not abandoned all hope of fighting the war, at least to a drawn peace; they were intent on maintaining a warlike front; they were on their guard against exposing their irresolution and their anxiety; they desired the serious exploration of the possibilities of peace; but they felt that this must be completely concealed, or otherwise the quest would be hopeless.

Their deliberations about Tojo's replacement appear to have been unsubtle. All they could do was to agree on the nomination of General Koiso Kuniaki, an army officer who had a bad reputation from the days of terrorism in the thirties when the army was promoting a series of crises with the civilian Ministers in order to advance its claims of controlling the government. The Emperor, however, appointed him because he had been recommended.

It was a choice which was apparently made under the compulsion of avoiding events such as those which had happened a year earlier in Italy. The elder statesmen judged it necessary to avoid nominating a man who might play in Japan the same part as General Badoglio. The extent to which Badoglio had captured the mind of Japan is curious. It showed perhaps how much the Japanese desired a Badoglio, and for how long they found it imperative not to disclose this.

Toshikazu Kase, a senior Foreign Ministry official, has described these confused and rather dark transactions. He himself belonged to the 'pro-British, pro-American' circles. His book, *Eclipse of the Rising Sun*, is useful in showing how many of these men had continued throughout the war to hold high position in the Foreign Office, in certain Ministries, at the imperial court. They had been inactive from prudence: from the fall of Saipan, however, they began to work for peace. They had still to be very cautious, for they would have been rendered helpless if it had become known how specific, and actively specific, were their intentions. By their sympathies becoming known they would at best have made themselves ineffective: at the worst they would have been assassinated. And there were of course many who, when the war was over, claimed to have been pro-ally, but those memory may have exaggerated its degree.

At the end of 1944, Toshikazu Kase wrote in his diary the following:

> Defeat now stares us stark in the face. There is only one question left: how can we avert the chaos attendant upon a disastrous defeat? The preservation of my fatherland, that is a paramount task assigned to me by fate. The hostile attack is developing so surprisingly swiftly that it may be that diplomacy cannot intervene before it is too late. I must redouble my efforts to expedite the restoration of peace. For that purpose I shall secure friends in the army who will collaborate with me secretly, and enlighten public opinion through wider exchanges of view with politicians, publicists, and press representatives. The chances are that the reorientation of our policy is yet feasible. If so the nation will escape annihilation. Even so, it will probably be accompanied by civil disturbances. Much blood will flow—and who knows that mine, too, will not be spilt? . . . This, in short, is my New Year's Day prayer.*

This sums up very well the feeling of the small class of clear-sighted, non-fanatical men. But a difficult task lay ahead for them. Toshikazu Kase and his friends had to convert a sufficient number of patriotic Japanese to enable them to shift the vital balance against the fanatical, the deluded, and the ignorant. They had to do this with the certain knowledge

---

*Toshikazu Kase: *Eclipse of the Rising Sun*, Jonathan Cape, 1951.

that charges of treason might well be brought against them, and would be paid for either with execution or else by the familiar old Japanese resort of private violence.

*

The American drive from the Pacific continued. After Saipan, the strongly fortified positions of Tinian and Guam were captured in August 1944. These were also considerable victories, made possible only by mobilization of resources, and their concentration upon tiny islands, which were possibly unique in military history. A feature of all these operations was the disparity of the losses. The Americans should in theory, being attackers, have suffered at least three to one more heavily than the Japanese. But, in all three operations, the American dead numbered just over 5,000, while the Japanese lost 42,000. On Guam, for the first time, there had been a dent in Japanese morale: over 12,000 prisoners were taken. Usually these island defences ended in a great *banzai* charge of the remaining garrison, who plunged to death, rather like the death charge of the chivalry among the Rajputs of medieval India, who vowed themselves thus to self-destruction. The generals on both Saipan and Guam committed ceremonial *hara-kiri*.

In October, General MacArthur, in the south-west Pacific, made his expected attack on the Philippines. He was still under the disadvantage of the somewhat complicated command arrangements which shared between him and Admiral Nimitz the control of operations in his area. He could count upon a powerful fleet detached from the central Pacific. Japan chose to regard his attack as a crisis of the war. Its generals recognized that, if the Philippines were occupied by the Americans, the supply lines of the Japanese Empire would be fatally obstructed. Therefore Japan stated that, on its ability to defend the Philippines, the issue of the war would depend.

Such repeated pronouncements were foolish, and, in making them, the Japanese generals should have had in mind their grave embarrassment if their defence proved ineffective. They would be in the position of carrying on the war even while admitting that the war was a lost cause. That they permitted themselves to talk so rashly was the best proof that the morale of the Japanese General Staff was beginning to fail even though the Japanese soldiers fought as tenaciously as before.

The Japanese lived up to the words of their military leaders. They gathered their navy, which was still very powerful in surface ships—only in the loss of the aircraft carriers had it been gravely weakened—and sought, by putting all their effort into a single decisive blow, to turn their great danger into a decisive victory. And circumstances played into their hands. It had been calculated that local airfields would be operational for the landings, but the rainy season broke, and they were flooded. The Japanese had a period of air superiority, flying in from Samar. For a few days it was touch and go whether the American advance would be disastrously defeated.

MacArthur's invasion force, which landed on 20 October 1944 on the shores of the Gulf of Leyte which is a central island of the Philippines, had the protection of very powerful warships. The Japanese sought to lure this naval force away by sending a decoy fleet, and then, with a much larger fleet, aimed to sink the American transports, and to destroy MacArthur's army, which was to be taken at a disadvantage while they were still engaged in disembarkation. The Japanese placed their confidence in the battle upon the greater fire power of the Japanese navy; the days of attacking by waves of aircraft from carriers was over, since the Japanese naval air force had been virtually eliminated. The navy was back to reliance upon its battleship fleet, and among this it included the battleship, *Yamato,* which had been built free of the former limitations on the size of battleships. It was the most formidable ship in the world, mounting eighteen-inch guns.

If they had succeeded in their plan, the Japanese would have achieved a second Pearl Harbor, this time destroying the American army in Asia as formerly they had annihilated the American Asian fleet. Even so, the United States, with its economic might only just beginning to operate at its full strength, could, in all reasonable probability, have regarded a defeat as a temporary setback, and the inevitable conclusion of the war would have been merely postponed by a year or so. But, though this possibility must have been clear to the Japanese admirals, an interruption of the continuous

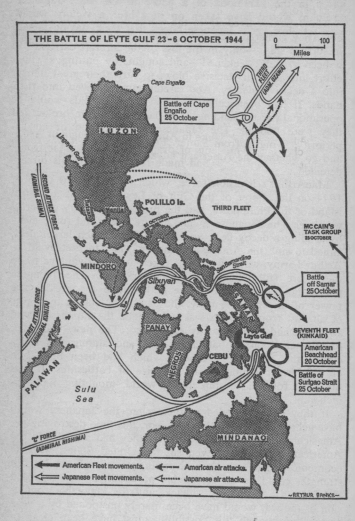

THE BATTLE OF LEYTE GULF 23–6 OCTOBER 1944

0   100
Miles

Cape Engaño

LUZON

Battle off Cape
Engaño
25 October

Lingayen Gulf

SECOND ATTACK FORCE
(ADMIRAL SHIMA)

POLILLO Is.

THIRD FLEET

THIRD FLEET
(ADM. OZAWA)

MC CAIN'S
TASK GROUP
25 OCTOBER

Manila

MINDORO

FIRST ATTACK FORCE
(ADMIRAL KURITA)

Sibuyan
Sea

San Bernardino
Strait

Battle
of Samar
25 October

SAMAR

PANAY

SEVENTH FLEET
(KINKAID)

Leyte Gulf

American
Beachhead
20 October

CEBU

PALAWAN

NEGROS

Sulu
Sea

Battle of
Surigao Strait
25 October

"C" FORCE
(ADMIRAL NISHIMA)

MINDANAO

⟵ American Fleet movements.   ⟵--- American air attacks.
⟵ Japanese Fleet movements.   ⟵···· Japanese air attacks.

~ARTHUR BANKS~

American advance would have been dear to them. They rejoiced in the likelihood of a pause in the war: Japanese optimism would have taken on new life: a victory would have set alive again Japanese hopes that their staying power might outlast America's. Nobody can foresee all the unexpected circumstances which might happen in war. Given time, Japan could begin to hope that the germs of a negotiated peace might sprout.

MacArthur's moves had therefore created a situation more fraught with consequence than even he, with his flair for reading the Japanese mind, at first realized. His landing had created a profound stir, alike in America and throughout Asia. He had chosen the elements of drama. He was not far from the point from which he had made his take-off in his direct contact with the Japanese in 1942, and, as he had promised to do, he had returned. But at once the Japanese navy pounced, and dreamed of plucking from this nettle, danger, the flower, which might be the checking of the American guillotine as it was about to fall, the dismantling of the instrument, and the creation of the necessity to rebuild it if the war were to continue. Its ships, some from Borneo, some from Formosa and Japan itself, converged upon the Gulf of Leyte.

The officer in command of the Japanese fleet was Admiral Toyoda Soemu. There is no doubt of the merit of his overall plan, which he directed at long range from Tokyo. The ships from Japan he formed into a decoy force, with which he aimed at dividing the Americans from their protective force of battleships and aircraft carriers, which were commanded by Admiral W. F. Halsey. This force included what remained of Japan's once formidable fleet of aircraft-carriers; it was less strong than it seemed for, as was discovered afterwards, the Japanese carriers sailed empty of planes. Japan had used up its planes and pilots, many of the last batch of these at the futile battle of Guam, and oil was running desperately short. Nevertheless, the manoeuvre was successful. Admiral Halsey went in pursuit, and left MacArthur dangerously exposed.

With two forces of battleships which were held in readiness in Borneo, Toyoda planned to attack the American transport fleet as soon as it was deprived of much of its protective escort. The first of these forces was exceptionally powerful; it contained five battleships, all of them larger and faster than any which they were still liable to meet. Toyoda gambled on these making unimpeded contact with the enemy, free from the diversion of air attack—which was reasonably certain, as the American transport fleet was beyond the range of land-based aeroplanes—and, by superior fire power, sinking it.

Against reasonable expectation, however, both the Japanese fleets failed in their objects. The lesser of the two was ambushed by what had been left behind of the American navy, which was rather larger than was foreseen by Japanese Intelligence, and was completely annihilated except for one destroyer. The Japanese had the mortification of seeing their ships sunk by ships which were technically inferior to their own. Ironically, in this action, the Americans employed battleships which were obsolete, had already been once sunk by the Japanese—at Pearl Harbor—and which had been dredged up from the mud of the sea bed. The larger Japanese fleet, though it was engaged and disorganized earlier on, got through the American defences, and for a time, if it had but known this, had the American transports at its mercy, but because of muddle, of being let down by other ships, and because of a deep misunderstanding of what was being done by the American ships, the Japanese Admiral did not bombard but sailed away inexplicably. His losses had been heavy; his actual gains were very slight; his potential gains, those which he had unaccountably let slip through his fingers, made this, their final battle of the war, very poignant to the Japanese navy.

Among the warships employed, the Japanese decoy force from the north alone avoided heavy losses. It retired in good order. Similarly Admiral Halsey's powerful battleships, which had been the main concern of the Japanese, were never in serious action throughout. They steamed 300 miles to the north, and when, as was afterwards discovered, they were within forty miles of the decoy force, they steamed 300 miles south. Upon their arrival, they found the battle of Leyte was over. Admiral Halsey was much criticized for having made so powerful a fleet ineffective in the action, but, given the system of communication prevailing among warships, he could hardly have done other than he did.

For the Japanese defeat, the same forces seemed to operate as before in the melancholy history of this navy. Bad Intelligence work, bad coordination between commanders, incompetent naval fliers, and inability of the Japanese commanders to retrieve disaster and to provide a new plan: these, which had dogged the navy since the battle of Midway, continued to do so until the death of the navy at Leyte.

The principle defect was in the quality of the command. The Japanese admirals and captains had been too old for their work. They were too fearful of risking their ships; they were certainly brave, and reasonably competent, but they creaked in manoeuvring a modern fleet, which was beyond their capacity. No common doctrine of strategy or tactics united them, and they were handicapped by the failure of Japanese engineers to provide for the navy some of the devices which had become common among other belligerents. Above all, it had turned out that, where the Japanese had been forced to make an innovation in the arts of naval warfare—in combining naval and air power—this advantage had not been sustained. Yamamoto, whose ideas had first prevailed, had not succeeded in training up a younger section of the navy with ideas similar to his own, and Yamamoto's death at Bougainville on 18 April 1943 ended the innovation. The pilots, who should have become principal commanders, and who had had battle experience, had all of them met their premature death in the Pacific Ocean, and the direction of new recruits was left to men who had never been converts to Yamamoto's ideas, and had seen his successes with a certain amount of envy and scepticism. Especially, the tactics of Yamamoto required an expert and highly trained personnel; he had begun the war with an inadequate supply; it had continued lacking; nobody had come to prominence as a gifted air trainer. The dash, the precision, and the brilliance of his fliers at Pearl Harbor was seen to have been a performance out of character of the Japanese navy.

*

In January 1945 General MacArthur, thus surviving his most perilous passage in the history of the war, overcame the

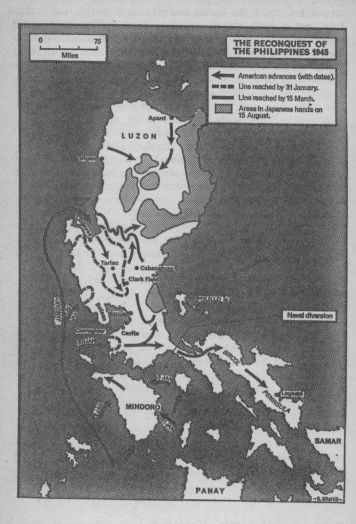

THE RECONQUEST OF
THE PHILIPPINES 1945

0 — 75
Miles

⟵ American advances (with dates).
━ ━ ━ Line reached by 31 January.
━━━ Line reached by 15 March.
▨ Areas in Japanese hands on
15 August.

Aparri

LUZON

Tarlac
Cabanatuan
Clark Field

POLILLO Is.

Naval diversion

Corregidor
Cavite

BICOL

PENINSULA
Legaspi

MINDORO

SAMAR

PANAY

—R. BANKS—

Japanese resistance on Luzon. From there he moved to Mindanao, the main island, and carried through land operations, which followed the same pattern and had the same results as the events in New Guinea. It turned out that the Japanese army, in spite of its emphasizing that the fighting would be decisive, had been unable to assemble a land force strong enough to make the resistance as tenacious as that of the Pacific Islands.

This ended the war for MacArthur. He did no more fighting, though after the war's end, another great historic role fell to him as Supreme Commander for the Allied Powers, with chief responsibility for the occupation of Japan. For the present, MacArthur wore the laurels of having been the most spectacular commander of the allied side, in both the Pacific and the European theatres of war. His victories, usually gained with forces which were in the minority, were due to remarkable imagination; and they were made possible by an extreme cult of efficiency by his staff. For the time, MacArthur busied himself with the preparation for the projected allied offensive against Japan itself, which was to have begun with a landing on Kyushu island; not expected, however, before 1 December. For this projected operation, the command arrangements were changed. MacArthur was given command of all the army throughout the Pacific (with important exceptions); but the American navy was still strong enough to oppose a unified command of all the sea forces.

For the first assault, 5 million men would have been employed. It is notable that they would for the most part have been American; though American allies begged a place in the operation, room was found for only a token force of three divisions from the Commonwealth. The war was coming to an end in a very different way from the war in Europe. The invasion of Normandy and the campaigns in France and Germany had been genuinely joint enterprises: there was not even the pretence of such in Japan. In the war in the Pacific in the later stages America had become very conscious that the United States was first, the allies nowhere. In the conquest of Japan the fact was to be rubbed in. The United States welcomed this sign that European imperialism had little part to play in the new Asia.

*

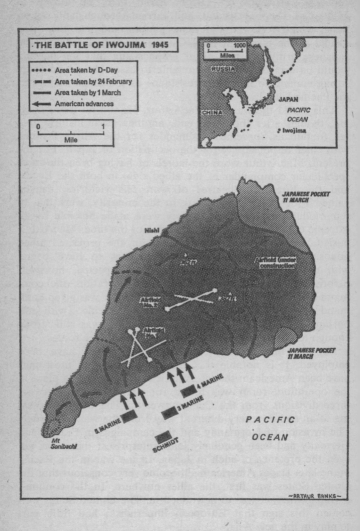

THE BATTLE OF IWOJIMA 1945

•••••• Area taken by D-Day
━ ━ ━ Area taken by 24 February
━━━━ Area taken by 1 March
◄━━━ American advances

0   1
Mile

0   1000
Miles

RUSSIA

CHINA

JAPAN

PACIFIC
OCEAN

? Iwojima

JAPANESE POCKET
11 MARCH

Nishi

Airfield (under
construction)

Airfield
No.2

Airfield
No.1

JAPANESE POCKET
11 MARCH

4 MARINE

3 MARINE

5 MARINE

SCHMIDT

PACIFIC
OCEAN

Mt
Sonibachi

~ARTHUR BANKS~

The way to final assault had been opened by the success of the United States' other campaign which advanced from the central Pacific to the entrances of Tokyo Bay. The fall of Saipan had been an important stage in this advance; it marked a change in Japanese defensive tactics. Hitherto the Japanese had sought to repel American invaders by making mass charges on them as they landed. But at Iwojima, the next island to be attacked after Saipan, the Japanese fought in prepared positions, inflicting great damage on the Americans before they were overwhelmed in March 1945. The island had to be wrenched from them, trench by trench. The Japanese losses were 20,000: the American marines lost 26,000 killed, and the U S navy nearly 900 killed or missing and about 2,000 wounded.

From Iwojima, Nimitz had first intended to make his main target Formosa. He changed his plan, and launched his attack on Okinawa, a heavily fortified island, forty miles long, in the Ryukyu Islands, 500 miles from Japan proper. On 1 April 1945 the Americans landed, and at first met with almost no opposition. But they were in an enormous ambush: they realized suddenly that the northern part of the island was alive with troops, all of them skilfully hidden. A feature of the resistance was their use of light artillery, among the most effective of the war. While the Americans were meeting deadly resistance from the north, their plans were disordered by the Japanese use of Kamikaze planes. These were manned by volunteer squads of suicide pilots, who flew their planes to crash on the decks of ships and there explode. The Kamikaze, who were first used by the Japanese in the battle of Leyte, had by now been incorporated in the general plan for the defence of Japan. The Kamikaze were genuinely volunteers; the Americans were unwilling to believe that such a corps could be formed on a free-will basis, but their efforts to find that they had been conscripted were in vain. By the ferocity of their action, by the unreason of their suicidal intentions, they struck the Americans with peculiar horror. The Kamikaze fought with a peculiar exaltation, they appeared insanely exhilarated, and they went to their death as though to a fascinating ceremony. It was the eschatology of war. In the battle for Iwojima they did very great damage. On one day they sank twenty-four ships. But they could not alter the fact that the number of aeroplanes, as also the number of pilots, was shrinking fast, and would presently be used up.

The battle for Okinawa changed rapidly into nightmare. It progressed like a surrealist film. On the sixth day, on 6 April, the Japanese dispatched from the Inland Sea their huge battleship, the *Yamato*. It was a huge Kamikaze. Its mission was to wreak as much havoc as possible: it carried only enough oil for a one-way trip, and was meant for destruction. In fact it was engaged by American aircraft, and was sunk before it could do much damage. But the madness of the sacrifice in such a way of the world's largest battleship convinced Japan's antagonists that the Japanese staff was near the end of its judgement.

The battle lasted until 21 June. It ended in scenes of horror. The Japanese commander and his deputy both committed ceremonial *hara-kiri*. Over a hundred thousand Japanese were dead. A very small number survived as prisoners.

The Americans were satisfied that a weighty section of the Japanese command, both in the navy and the army, now saw no chance of success in war, and no opportunity of gaining even a temporary respite, and would be glad to make peace. The war might have ended then. But how were these high officers to terminate it? They were afraid of being assassinated if they made any move: the mass of the army and navy was still able to fight, and there was still a minority of the more senior officers who were willing to fight on to the end. No mutinies or outbreaks of any kind took place among the forces.

The difficulty for the United States was that it lacked the means of making contact with the politically reasonable sections in Japanese life. The attempt to signal to the East that the United States would respond favourably to any bid for surrender was made again and again, usually by cryptic speech on the American broadcasting stations; but they met with no reply from any who could speak responsibly in Japan. Still the war went on, and no peace was yet possible, though the majority of all classes of Japan desired it greatly. The civil servants, the industrialists and bankers, the trade union leaders, the considerable classes of the intelligentsia— all despaired of war, and regarded with frenzy the piece by piece destruction worked on them by the American aeroplanes. But the intransigent section of the military, who had gained control of the direction of Japan ten years before, could not be set aside. A dramatic and novel development in the art of war was necessary for this.

*

A picture of the Japanese Empire in twilight, and approaching dissolution, is given by the puppet Prime Minister, Ba Maw. Ba Maw, as has been seen, had had his quarrels with the Japanese, and, though he had made his position tolerable, he had hardly cause to love them. The more remarkable is his sober account of the way in which they faced defeat and international disgrace. He was invited to Japan in November 1944, just as the systematic bombing of Japan's home islands was beginning, in an endeavour to organize Asian support for the tottering Japanese imperial structure. Ba Maw owed his eminence to the Japanese, and knew that he must fall with them. This is the general impression which he describes:

> Tokyo and its people had changed since I had seen them a year ago, visibly subdued and disillusioned by events, but most of them as determined and defiant as ever. They were now a people in the grip of the biggest crisis in all their history and grimly waiting for the worst. But they were facing the situation wonderfully and revealing their latent racial qualities, their almost inexhaustible capacity to take whatever should come, to endure and survive and wait and even hope. They were more or less the same outwardly, but in the course of a long quiet talk they could not help but betray their true thoughts and fears. Unlike before, they now spoke mainly of the Kamikazes, thus showing that they were placing most of their hopes on something which was really an act of desperation. The people were living with a new terror, the threat of American mass air bombing; they knew that they had no real way to protect their millions of paper and bamboo houses; not even, as it turned out, the Imperial Palace.*

The topic of chief concern was the air bombardment, and the damage which that was able to do, especially on the morale of the population. This is what Ba Maw says of this:

*Ba Maw: *Breakthrough in Burma,* op. cit.

One of the worst incendiary bombings of Tokyo occurred when I was there near the end of November 1944. The result was quite literally a holocaust, a mass burning of one of the densest areas of the city. I saw the ghastly devastation the next morning. But there was no panic or self-pity or even audible complaint among the huge mass of victims. In fact some of them were able to express their happiness that the Imperial Palace had escaped. It was a heart-breaking sight but it also lifted one's heart immensely to see so much human endurance and strength of character displayed in so dark an hour.*

Ba Maw was taken round the headquarters of the Japanese army. The Kamikaze were exhibited to him as a kind of Japanese secret weapon. He met Koiso, the Japanese Prime Minister, and General Sugiyama, the Minister for Defence, who was soon to play a decisive part. He took every opportunity of discussing with the Japanese commanders their defence tactics, and represented that a scorched earth policy would be intolerable to the Burmese as was also the plan of using the Burmese forces to fight the rear-guard action against the British. Ba Maw had the satisfaction of saving the Shwe Dagon Pagoda from being incorporated in the Japanese defence perimeter. At least he gives himself the credit of having achieved it by the negotiations of his visit.

*ibid.

21

The End

THE war had entered its final stage. Japan still battled on, but its position was hopeless. The United States, still arming, poured out its fleet and aircraft across the Pacific, and was preparing the great offensive against the sacred Japanese homeland. The expectation was that the American war machine, which had swallowed up so many Pacific islands, would in the long run devour Japan proper. The economic might of the United States must finally prevail. The war machine moved on, and the only uncertainty was the length of time it would take to complete the process. Japan, as Germany before it, was given no time to summon up its resources and to organize them for the optimum defence of its own country.

Japan, in its final phase, was like Macbeth cooped up in Dunsinane, without any rational hope of a happy issue from his adversities, mechanically wound up to continue to shout defiances at the armies investing him.

> Some say he's mad; others that lesser hate him
> Do call it valiant fury: but, for certain,
> He cannot buckle his distemper'd cause
> Within the belt of rule.
> ANGUS: Now does he feel
> His secret murders sticking on his hands; . . .
> Those he commands move only in command,
> Nothing in love; now does he feel his title
> Hang loose about him, like a giant's robe
> Upon a dwarfish thief.

One hope alone sustained Japan. The Soviet Union had not denounced the Non-Aggression Treaty which Matsuoka, Japan's Foreign Minister, had been able to negotiate with it in 1941. In spite of the bad blood between them five years earlier, this treaty, to the surprise of onlookers, had kept the peace between the apparently predestined enemies, though war had raged universally elsewhere. Japan could reckon that peace in Europe would bring to a head the issues between Russia and the United States. Was it too much to expect that Russia, threatened and thwarted by the United States, might see that its true interest lay in accepting the partnership of Japan? Japan could claim that it had already shown, by refraining from striking at Russia when Hitler was at the doors of Moscow in 1941, that no insuperable cause of conflict lay between it and the Soviet Union. It could represent that, in spite of the severe destruction which it had suffered, it still possessed an army which was one of the key pieces on the board internationally. The Japanese army still had fighting spirit, still had ammunition, and could hope to take an immense toll from a threatened invasion. It boasted that to overrun Japan, when all its natural advantages of defence were taken into review, the United States would need a force of 10 million men, a force which it could not hope to transport. If the United States came to be at loggerheads with Russia, it was unlikely that it would willingly force through the attack on Japan to its conclusion, which would be frightful carnage.

In 1945, as the Japanese position grew evidently more desperate, Russia began to unmask its intentions. In April, at the time of the attack on Okinawa, the Soviet government announced that it would not renew the non-aggression pact which was due to expire one year hence. When the Japanese made proposals about the possibilities of a new agreement, the Russian Ambassador was ominously evasive. Russia gave every sign that it was preparing for war with Japan. Thus its final hope was nearly extinguished. 'Despair thy charm' seemed to cry out the omens for Japan.

It seems probable that the Japanese Intelligence had not heard of Stalin's information to Churchill and Roosevelt at the Teheran Conference. Russia was preparing for war with Japan as soon as Germany was defeated. Confirmation of this should have come easily to Japanese spies; but there is no record of Japan having been well served by espionage. There were no figures in its employment comparable to Richard Sorge, the Russian agent, who, in the critical phase before Pearl Harbor, had spied on Japan for the U S S R; he had been able to reassure Russia that Japan had decided not to hasten to the aid of Germany, and refused to attack Russia as Germany wished. Japan was of course under the handicap that, if it employed men of its own nation as agents, they were more conspicuous than others. Japanese could hardly wear the appearance of blank anonymity which is essential to espionage. The same is broadly true of western spies in an eastern country. They may succeed, by exceptional audacity, in exceptional circumstances, as Sorge was able to do. But in a war between East and West, espionage is likely to play less part than in a war in which the contestants share a similar racial background.

Espionage, therefore, paid the Americans only very mean dividends. It is remarkable how little was the knowledge which reached them in this way from Tokyo. Japanese counter-espionage was very capable, but the United States had succeeded in developing the eyes and ears which pried on Japanese moves, though this was done at a distance by code-breaking, and not by means of spies. Its advantage in this has already been noted, for example at the time of the negotiations before Pearl Harbor, and in naval battles; it had continued to read the Japanese codes throughout the war, and never betrayed to the Japanese that it was in fact doing so. It required great restraint by the Americans to take no step by which it should become obvious to the Japanese that they possessed the secret. It is, in fact, recorded in Japan that a few men doubted from time to time the degree of security of Japanese communications, but they were not attended to.

*

Meanwhile the American air-raids on Japan went on relentlessly. Until June 1944 American planes, except for those in Lieutenant-Colonel Doolittle's adventure in 1942, had not been over Japan. Thereafter the Japanese homeland was subjected to a bombardment which was utterly destructive. The officer in charge of American bombardment was General

Curtis H. Le May. He was a skilled technician, with experience of the air war against Germany. He had at first concentrated on organizing bombing expeditions from Chengtu, in Szechuan, but later decided that this base was unsuitable since he could not organize from there the massive squadrons by means of which America hoped to bring the war to an end. In February 1945 he shifted his base to the Marianas.

On 10 March he sent in waves of bombers which flew abnormally low: this was a protection against anti-aircraft guns, which were abundant in Tokyo. The Japanese, even as late as this, did not have their guns adjusted to radar; they were operated manually, and they were made largely ineffective by Le May's strategy. Flying so low the aeroplanes did not even have to carry guns. On this one raid the Americans distributed 2,000 tons of bombs. In this savage assault they used a device of air attack which had been perfected over Germany. The explosions which they employed raised intense heat on a large sale. As a result they caused violent storms of air currents, which were utterly beyond control, and proved one of the most lethal factors in this kind of attack. This one raid is estimated to have caused 125,000 casualties. It was estimated that 40 per cent of the city was destroyed in under three hours. Over a million people were made homeless.

These grim tactics, operated with the thoroughness of General Le May, were new, and marked a change in air warfare. Le May followed this first raid with others through May and June, at the end of which the Americans could see, by air reconnaissance, that they had destroyed half Tokyo and many provincial cities, many of them essential for the war effort. The destruction of civilian life was greater than it had been in Hamburg or Berlin. Much more damage could be done on Japanese cities by fire bombs, because of the light structure of most buildings; the same weight of explosives led to much more widespread destruction. A contemporary Home Ministry report described as follows the behaviour of the populace: 'The consequences of the air raids had caused the people to evacuate the area. In certain areas they neglected to keep the water tanks filled. The people lack a fighting spirit towards the incendiary bombing.' After May the Minister of Home Affairs admitted that civil-defence measures in Tokyo were futile.

The economic consequences were devastating. At first the destruction, as was the case in Germany, had less effect on industrial production than might have been supposed, but, as it became more wholesale, and surpassed the war damage in Europe, so its effects became harder to circumvent. The Japanese government took more sweeping powers to direct the economy of the country; but where was the economy left to direct? The food supplies began to fall dangerously, and could not be distributed because of the destruction of the railways and the breakdown of commercial organization. The description of the life of the Japanese worker at this stage of the war, underfed, harried to inhuman extremes by the government, lacking the elementary comforts of a safe home, must touch even the reader who knows something of the terrors endured by the German population. A great flight began from the towns to the countryside.

For the first time the civilian part of the nation began to turn against the military. In parts of the country it became positively dangerous to wear uniform. Such aberration shook deeply the Army General Staff.

Japanese experts at the time said that the Japanese standard of nutrition in the towns in the last year was below that of Germans in the fateful winter of hunger after the end of the first European war. Even the army, which was the last to be affected, was put on short supplies. The soldiers were found to be bartering military equipment for the scanty food supplies which filtered through to private hands. In spite of all this, both civilian and military morale remained astonishingly high. There were no rice riots in the Japanese towns, such as were already causing great concern in Germany in the First World War as early as 1916. It may be that the Japanese were less shocked by this adversity than were European populations, because they had been inured to it. Twenty years before, the people of Tokyo had experienced similar devastation in their capital city; that time from the horrors of the Tokyo earthquake.

*

In April 1945 the Prime Minister, Koiso, fell from office. He had engaged in negotiations with Chinese emissaries, by which he had intended to split the Chinese and the western allies. They were of course secret, but they leaked out, and when they failed he was dismissed. Baron Suzuki Kantaro, an aged admiral, succeeded. It was remarked that he was sworn in on the day after the loss of Japan's prize battleship, the *Yamato:* Japan had turned to the navy for its Prime Minister just at the time that it had lost its fleet. He had a good record, having been a target of the army conspiracy of 1936, in which he was badly wounded. He was a hero of the Russo-Japanese war. He had a likeable, rather enigmatic, personality. He was almost universally popular, which is a rare thing in Japan. From experience, he believed that the scope for personal intervention in public affairs was limited, and he was apt to preside benignly over them, and to feel philosophically that nobody could have altered what had it past come to pass. In fact, there was, in Suzuki, a touch of Tolstoy's Kutuzov: the much respected figure, clothed with glory from the past, who is wise enough to collaborate with events, rather than to attempt to withstand them—or even to understand them.

But he was eighty years old: too venerable to be effective, even by roundabout means. He had not the decisiveness, the single-mindedness which were essential qualities in a Prime Minister in such a crisis. The choice of Suzuki, however, was a sign that the peace party was gradually prevailing. He was not a born leader, he did not incarnate the Japanese desire to go down fighting. Intellectually he needed no conviction that Japan had lost the war; he was himself more than ready for peace. But he moved too slowly to be able to save Japan. The peace party was looking for a totem, was ready to be rallied, and to assert itself, but this was beyond Suzuki.

In the next month, May, Japan lost its ally, Germany. The Supreme War Council met and approved the decision to carry on the war notwithstanding. It declared, however, that Japan was released from the provisions of the Tripartite Pact. Japan had now to face the switch of the allied forces engaged in the European war, and their addition to the force already employed against Japan in the East; it had also to meet the possible use against it of the Russian army, now disengaged.

*

An outside chance for Japan lay in the complications set up by the death of Roosevelt on 12 April, and his succession by Vice-President Truman. But to have used these to advantage, to have extricated itself from the net which was closing on it, would have required a very flexible diplomacy. Flexibility was never a strong point with the Japanese and the number of neutral centres where Japan could operate, and from which it could obtain its intelligence, had, to the advantage of the United States, become very small.

At the Yalta Conference, in February 1945, Roosevelt had offered Russia a larger bait to enter the war against Japan. He unilaterally raised the stakes. Confident of Churchill's support, he promised Russia the southern part of Sakhalin and the Kurile Islands. He added the recognition of unspecified Soviet interests in the commercial port of Dairen and the reissue of the Russian lease of Port Arthur as a naval base; and he proposed that there should be Russian participation in the control of the Chinese Eastern Railway and the South Manchurian Railway. Roosevelt, by negotiating on these lines, had cancelled out the effect of the Russo-Japanese war of 1904–5, and had taken upon himself to re-make history. Furthermore, Roosevelt, with Churchill's unspoken assent, had behaved in a very cavalier fashion in disposing of huge Chinese assets and settling vast issues in disregard of wholly legitimate Chinese claims.

In spite of this agreement with the Russians, which had been so dearly purchased, the Americans, and to a large extent the British, continued to be profoundly distressed by the memory of the savage Japanese defence of the Coral Islands. The ferocity of their resistance in the homeland was expected to be as formidable. Nothing like the same internal collapse was foreseen as followed the death of Hitler in Germany. The war might continue for as much as a year, and with what was foreseen as the mounting strain of tension with Russia, in spite of the glitter of the terms of Yalta, the upshot was not clear.

In the meanwhile it became known that the Japanese General Staff was pressing on with plans for a fanatical defence of the Japanese islands. Rightly it was supposed that the principal American blow would be directed at Honshu. To deal with this it could assemble two and a half million troops in the home islands. Tales arrived to the effect that a vast underground headquarters was being dug out at Tokyo. The Japanese army was said to be gambling on the blind determination which would halt the Americans on landing. Clearly the Americans had still much effort before them.

*

But very shortly after, a great change came over the situation. It was brought about by the completion of the atom bomb. Partly this was the result of German-Jewish genius, which, barred from Germany by racial madness, had been mobilized in the invention of this device of war, which had been meant in the first place for the overthrow of the Nazi system. Part of the early work was done in England: and, when it was concentrated in the United States, British scientists participated. The war against Germany had come to an end in May 1945, with the bomb still a project, and not realized in fact: but by June it was clear that it was about to become operational. The news that it was to be so, and would be available for use against Japan, had already been grasped by the very small circle in which, at this stage of the war, had been concentrated the making of American policy. Its immense, hardly credible, destructive power could quench the continuing flame of Japanese fanaticism. With its finality there could be no discussion.

By this trick of fate, the need to cajole and coax Russia, the need for Russian complicity and Russian power, were all removed.

By the summer of 1945 it was stated that American policy would be revised: Russian aid was now no longer so necessary for bringing to an end the war with Japan. The United States had initially perceived that through the possible intervention of Russia it could go ahead without perpetually needing to keep China contented, and now it saw that it would be able to discard Russia in its turn.

In fact America was by this time as zealous to deter Russia from entering the war as before it had been to bring Russia in. Truman had succeeded Roosevelt; his period was from the start different from the period of Roosevelt. Other considerations apart, Truman was less inclined to exert himself to maintain good relations with Russia. He was less of a historian. He was less inclined, especially at this point of his career, to look into the future, and to adjust his actions accordingly. Instinctively, Truman was thinking in terms of the containment of Russia, and was anxious that, in the Far East, Russia should make as little headway as possible. If Russia once went to war and invaded Manchuria, there would be little chance of keeping it out of Port Arthur and Dairen (which it had already been promised at Yalta). Even though Truman, who was new to these issues of foreign policy, did not himself stress all these points, he was more available than Roosevelt had been to advisers who suggested a frankly anti-Russian policy. None of the advisers knew, but Truman did, that the atom bomb would be available for putting Japan out of the war. For the time being he was satisfied that Russian demands would not be extravagant. If the effects of the bomb were to be as he was advised, a power without the bomb could not argue aggressively with the power which possessed it.

The condition of Japan continued to deteriorate. It was uncertain that the bomb would ever be required. General Le May was claiming that his air bombardment had totally paralysed life in sixty major cities. He claimed that Japan was being driven back to the stone age. The Joint Chiefs-of-Staff reported at the beginning of July: 'Japan will become a nation without cities, with her transportation disrupted, and will have tremendous difficulty in holding her people together for continued resistance.' By March 1945 Japan had lost 88 per cent of the merchant fleet with which it had begun the war, and it had become almost impossible to import any goods, even the most essential. The service departments of the government cried out for the punishment of those engaged in the economic administration; but this could do no good. American Intelligence was, however, rather less optimistic. It gave due allowance to the putting out of action of much of Japanese heavy industry through the blockade and through air bombardment. But it reported that the Japanese output of combat aeroplanes was still between 1,200 and 1,500 a month (as compared with a peak production of 2,300 reached late in 1944). The greatest shortage was of fuel oil, which was bringing orthodox air operations to a standstill. On the other hand Japan had little to worry about in its stock of ammunition. The Intelligence Committee still thought that the highly trained Japanese army, the greater part of which had as yet never been in action, was a formidable fighting force. It reckoned that it would probably take another twelve months to subdue it. It made its report, it must be noticed, without knowledge of the bomb.

At the Potsdam Conference in July, when the three masters of the world met face to face, Truman, with careful premeditation and calculated misdirection, told Stalin, apparently in passing, that the allies had in their hands a more powerful bomb than any previously used. No word was said about the bomb being nuclear, or about the transformation of the war by its invention. Churchill, who knew the true facts, and who watched Stalin carefully, agreed that he had not suspected the truth behind Truman's apparently routine information. He took it as an announcement that the United States had been able to charge its bomb with a heavier load of dynamite. There is drama in the spectacle of these two men, the pillars of the western world, systematically observing the demeanour of a man whom they both regarded as their potential enemy, while in public they played on him something which resembled a confidence trick. The drama is heightened because Stalin had in his pocket, in the communist offensive which he knew he could release in Europe, something like an atom bomb in politics.

A race, in which one of the partners, Stalin, was in darkness about the true facts and about their urgency, then took place between the Americans, who were about to explode the bomb, and the Russians, who were in the last stages of the preparation to attack in Manchuria. Russia had become aware of the change of attitude by the United States, of the desire that it should not participate, though it may have been partly puzzled about the reason. The United States rushed the preparations. At one time the bomb was to have been used on 1 August. Last-minute delays in completing its manufacture put this back a few days. Further delay came because the weather made it almost impossible to raid Japan accurately.

During the Potsdam Conference it was learnt that Japan had requested Swedish mediation in working out surrender terms. It was plain that peace could not be far off. The

United States, however, showed surprisingly little zeal in developing this initiative.

The United States made at this time the decision to exclude Russians as members of an occupation force in Japan. The plans for occupying Japan were made surprisingly late. Their details were all improvised. For example, the decision to divide the occupation of Korea and to fix the boundary between the American zone and the Russian zone at the thirty-eighth parallel, was made between an American captain and a Russian major. Thus, casually, there came into being a frontier problem which subsequently divided the world. The Americans and the British were informed by Molotov about the repeated, almost frenzied, attempts by Japan to enlist the support of Russia as a mediator. They were being rebuffed by Russia. It was clear that Russia was not going to back Japan as a move in the war that had already begun between it and its allies.

At Potsdam, on 26 July 1945, the allies had issued a final and solemn summons to Japan to surrender. Its terms were broadcast over the wireless. They were that those Japanese who had been responsible for the policies which had led to war were to be forever eliminated; that Japan must renounce all its overseas empire; that war criminals must be punished; that Japan should be occupied. As had become the habit of the United States with beaten adversaries, Japan was required to surrender unconditionally. These demands, though exceedingly radical, were not entirely rejected by Japan, so desperate had its position become.

An answer was understood to have been given in a press conference on 30 July by the Japanese Prime Minister, Suzuki, at which he spoke in Japanese. It was, as might have been expected from an old man, doubtful, temporizing and ambiguous. Apparently he had meant to say that he withheld comment. The allies interpreted the Japanese word he used as meaning that Japan not only would not comment, but would treat the summons with contempt. This was taken by the handful of Americans who knew what was intended as the signal for dropping the bomb. Actually it has been since suggested that a word was mistranslated, and meant much less than was supposed, signifying merely that Japan's first reaction to the summons was not being published. The subsequent controversy about what really happened has been inconclusive. If the confusion in fact occurred, it is typical of the Japanese language, one of the most involved and muddled languages of the world, that it should have betrayed Japan towards its disaster.

The bomb was dropped on Hiroshima, the chosen target, on 6 August 1945. The attack was made from Tinian, not far from Guam, which had been taken in the previous year. The plane, a B 29 bomber, had been blessed for its mission by a Roman Catholic priest. The havoc made was as great as was forecast. It was clear that the war could not be pursued when America could drop bombs of this kind. Within three days a second bomb, of a different and even more deadly type, was dropped on the civilian port of Nagasaki. It did slightly less damage, because Nagasaki had better air-raid precautions and because the bomb did not set off what is technically known as a fire storm; but its blast was greater than that at Hiroshima. This time, to signalize the joint responsibility of the United States and Britain, the death plane was accompanied by a plane carrying British observers, Dr W. Penny, the physicist, and the Wing Commander L. Cheshire, who, by one of the ironies of these events, was later to win celebrity in Britain as the leader of one of the most inspired missions of the day, that of bringing comfort and the opportunity of decent existence to the incurably disabled. With the bomb at Nagasaki, there was released a manifesto to the top Japanese physicist, addressed to him by his American colleagues and explaining some of the details of the bomb. It urged him to enlighten the Japanese government.

Ironically, Nagasaki was one of the parts of Japan which had the connections of longest duration with the West. It was founded in the sixteenth century by a feudal lord who was a Christian, and who wanted the trade between Japan and the Christian world to be based on it. For a time the port was actually ceded to the Jesuit missionaries, who organized its administration. It was subsequently the centre of persecution of Japanese Christians when the Japanese government became alarmed by their number.

The dropping of the atom bomb was so dramatic, the awed shock it provoked throughout the world was so final, and the sense that it was, in President Truman's phrase, 'the greatest thing in history', seemed so incontestable that there was a general instinct to think that it had brought to an end one phase of human affairs. From then onwards everything would be dwarfed by events. But the appalling news of the disaster produced by atomic radiation, the vaporizing and burning of human beings, the whole vast panorama of unutterable suffering, somehow failed to register with most people who lived through those days. Even the horrible details, published some months afterwards and set out with all the technical skill of American publicity, were too terrible for belief. The mind set up impediments to taking in such information. There was born at that time an uneasiness which has affected a whole age.

*

The Americans had thus won the race. They had set themselves against Russia; but it was virtually a dead heat because on the next day, before Japan had had time to surrender, the Russians crossed the frontier of Manchuria. By a two-pronged offensive, one prong from outer Mongolia, the other from the Soviet maritime provinces in Siberia, Russia overran the country as neatly as Germany had picked off countries earlier in the war. Though the fate of Hiroshima has stuck in the world's memory and though it has been regarded as the final cause of Japan's capitulation, it seems, in point of fact, that it was the Russian invasion that tilted the Japanese over to put an end to the war.

The effects of the atom bomb and the grim finality of its consequences were not immediately clear. Among most people outside Hiroshima itself, even among those in Tokyo, there was doubt about what had really happened. A great bomb had fallen; terrible destruction had been wrought; but Japan had become thoroughly used to such calamities. Actually the loss of life in the atomic phase, though it was rendered peculiarly horrible by atomic radiation, was less than that in the great B 29 raids, to which Japan had been subjected since March 1945. But all Japan knew the significance of the dreaded invasion of Manchuria, the advent of the Russian hordes, the coming into reality of that threat which had, as long as man could remember, been the governing fact in Japan's foreign policy. Japan could not face war with another Great Power. It was this which made it 'despair its charm', and accept the facts.

*

The history of the way Japan surrendered is dramatic, and even today, has probably been only partly told. At least, new accounts are constantly appearing in Japan with new details, which, true or false, require the narrative of events to be considered afresh.

A new personality in Japan played a large part at the conclusion. This was the most august person in the land. Hitherto he had been content to be a spectator of the great events, but now he entered the arena. This was the Japanese Emperor.

He was a virtuous prince. The irony is that such dark proceedings had been allowed to happen under his aegis. In the whole range of personalities who held positions of distinction in the war, whether of actual power or of decorativeness, he, and the English monarch, George VI, were the only ones without serious blemish. Like George VI he had a stammer; like him, he held in reality very little political power. It must have been discouraging for this young man, entering on his life's career, that he succeeded his father, who had been an idiot during almost the whole of his reign. Yet that fact had not compromised the monarchy, and this speaks highly of the reserves of credit which the institution enjoyed. In one respect the Emperor was ahead of George VI. He had strong intellectual interests, though these were concentrated on a single subject, marine biology. The corollary of the secure eminence of the Japanese Emperor was that ordinarily public opinion severely restricted the range of his activities; he was expected to do almost nothing because his role was almost deified. And Hirohito could not be said to have contributed anything remarkable to the political debates of his time. From the day he ascended his throne in 1926, to the day when he nearly lost it at the time of Japan's defeat, he did what was expected of him. He was reliable; he was thoroughly constitutional: he gave no trouble to the politicians by threatening to use the stored-up prestige of the Japanese monarchy to embarrass them. The inner circle of Japanese with knowledge of what went on behind the façade of public life knew that the course of Japan's affairs—the autonomy of the military, and a foreign policy which brought it into collision with the United States and Britain—was profoundly antipathetic to him. But beyond asking the occasional awkward question at imperial conferences, he gave no sign of his continual vexation.

However, at the crisis of Japan, he acted with much common sense. He borrowed from the Confucian philosophy of China the maxim by which he governed his actions. The Confucian wisdom was not to stand up like an oak tree before a raging tempest: in a storm, the oak tree is uprooted and perishes. The willow tree has the better chance of survival; it bends before the wind, but, when the hurricane is over, its root is unsnapped, and it stands up once again by its own resilience. Thus, before the storm of the Japanese military, which was to blow away many persons in its time, the Emperor bowed, and was inconspicuous. Now the storm was nearly blown out, and the opportunity came for the reassertion of the powers of the monarchy, which were real and legitimate even if they had been so long unused. He was guided, in the crucial days when he felt that his personal intervention was timely, that in fact the spirit of the Japanese constitution called for it, by a suave and subtle sense of correct timing. He was capable of choosing the right men to collaborate with—or he was very lucky in these being available, and in offering their services. His conduct at the time suggests that this marine biologist had developed a political instinct during the years of inoffensive constitutional practice.

Throughout July the conviction of defeat had been gripping one person after another and one institution after another. In the past year the fortunes of the civilian elements of government in their control of the military had begun to revive. In the complex balance of forces which made up Japanese politics, the centre of authority began to pass a little away from the soldiers and towards the civilians. A significant date had been the fall of the Tojo government (July 1944), which happened after the fall of Saipan. It was overthrown under pressure from the Jushin, the former Prime Ministers, who had formed a more or less informal

council. This body was unknown to the written constitution;
it had in consequence no rights, such as access to government papers; it came, however, to exercise great power. It
had an influence like that of the Genro, or elder statesmen,
though the power of the Genro had been openly recognized.
The re-entry to Japanese politics of such an influence was
important. It was the more so at this period because the
Jushin had tended, with some exceptions, to work for peace.
Most of them thought that the war was irrevocably lost,
that the leaders knew this well, but that, floundering and
indecisive, they saw no means of terminating it.

But the services, both the army and navy, were obdurate
for continuing war: and the senior officers, even if compelled by reason to admit the hopelessness of their case,
could point out that they were powerless to assent to peace.
They would have been assassinated. The spirit of the nation
had passed into the custody of the patriotic societies which
would have employed the sanction of murder against anyone who dared to speak of surrender. Both the Jushin, and
the more reasonable service officers, had to mask their
intention, to carry on their intrigue behind walls of extreme
secrecy, and had to say one thing while in fact strenuously
doing another. As a result, Japan's resolution to fight on
appeared undented. It had become as good as impossible
for it to capitulate. Japan, having made a cult of the principle that no Japanese ever surrendered to the enemy, now
found it impossible to accept the findings of common sense.

Behind the scenes, however, and with every secrecy, Japan had been sounding the possibilities of an honourable
peace; and peace, with honour that would satisfy Japan
meant, in effect, a peace on the simple condition that Japan
was allowed to keep its Emperor. In every other respect
Japan was ready, except for the irreconcilables in the army,
to surrender unconditionally; with the Emperor's position
guaranteed, the Japanese would sigh with relief and cease
their hopeless resistance. There is undeniable pathos about
these last days of Japanese agony. Japan was willing to
trade the entire substance of capitulation for this one concession to a principle which, to its western conquerors, appeared perverted and of no worth. To the West, attachment
to an Emperor was sentimental; a defeated Japan must
eventually have a chief executive, and the title he would

use of himself was no matter. But to the Japanese it was beyond price. Even so, some of the Jushin were frankly disposed to sacrifice the Emperor, if peace could be gained by this.

President Truman had to take account of the fact that feeling against the monarchy was strong in the United States. Those in favour of tolerating it were accused of being appeasers. Truman himself, backed by Henry L. Stimson, the Secretary for War, was in favour of accepting the Japanese terms on this point. They were influenced by the argument that the American occupying force would find it much simpler to do its work if it had the Japanese Emperor on its side. His prestige was so immense that he would, as it were, legitimize the occupation in Japan's eyes. Also, an American commander, able to speak through him, would be able to gain control of the surrendering Japanese armies; which, otherwise, would have presented a problem. Truman did not directly meet the Japanese condition. But he drafted the American reply in terms that, while avoiding all mention of the Emperor problem, conveyed the general sense that the Emperor would be kept.

These exchanges came between two vital meetings in Tokyo, the first on 13 August, between the Japanese Emperor and the Supreme Command, the committee of which directed the war; the second on the next day, a conference of the Emperor with the Japanese Cabinet. The meetings were held in a dug-out in the imperial palace. In spite of the belligerent circumstances, a certain formality was observed. All those taking part wore full dress uniform, or morning dress; the long table at which they sat was covered with a precious gold brocade. But the Emperor himself, appearing unshaven, increased the general sense of gloom. At the first meeting, no decision was reached: the case for further resistance, the case for immediate capitulation, were fully argued. But the Prime Minister Admiral Suzuki succeeded in getting agreement that the Emperor should be asked to decide personally what should be done. To follow such a procedure was revolutionary in Japan: the convention was that he should never be embarrassed by having to give instructions to his Ministers. At the second meeting, after those present had again expressed their views, and the American attitude towards the Emperor had been weighed up, the decision was taken by the Emperor. 'The unendurable must be endured', was the imperial pronouncement which terminated the war.

With the last military hope gone, with the Red Army pouring into Manchuria, and with further air attacks expected, which nobody had the remotest idea of how to resist, the Japanese Emperor, in form using the procedure with which he had committed Japan to the calamity of Pearl Harbor, but in fact having taken on himself the personal responsibility for what was now done, gave instructions that hostilities were to cease and, on 14 August Japan replied, accepting the Potsdam declaration.

Until the last moment, it continued to be uncertain if even the intervention of the Emperor would succeed. The military, which had made the war, would not lightly abdicate. It was one thing for the Emperor to forbid further war; it was another for him, great though the Imperial prestige was, to be obeyed. Moreover the United States, in refusing all bargaining, had not satisfied the army that it stood to gain nothing by forcing American troops to fight their way ashore in Japan. Action was precipitated because a fairly accurate account of the peace negotiations had leaked to the army. On the night after the decision to end the war was taken, a melodrama took place in Tokyo which was equal to any of the sensational passages in the history of conspiracy. It recalls Hitler's night of the long knives, in which there culminated the feud between him and the S A leaders; St Bartholomew's Eve in Paris four centuries earlier; the fight, again at Paris, on the night of Robespierre's fall, between the moderate politicians and those who wanted the terror to continue. A group of young, well-connected, passionately unappeasable officers tried to halt the negotiations, make a coup, and seize the sacred person of the Emperor.

To succeed, they needed the support of three or four generals, who were in key positions in Tokyo. Their plot began in the office of the general commanding the First Guards division, which was garrisoning the imperial palace. For hours they pleaded with him: then, their tempers breaking, and pressed for time, they abruptly murdered him. In these bloody proceedings, there is an odd atmosphere of a family quarrel which had passed out of control and become terribly serious. Many of the officers were related to the generals with whom they were pleading. One of them was the son-in-law of General Tojo, the former Prime Minister. Another was the brother-in-law of General Anami, the War Minister.

The officers went to the part of the palace where the Emperor was. Comedy then took over. On the evening before, the Emperor was known to have recorded a wireless address, which would be broadcast to the people of Japan on the next morning, 15 August, and in which he had declared the Japanese decision to surrender. When it was once played on the air, the act would be irrevocable; it was therefore vital to the officers to seize the record and destroy it. It was known to be present in the palace until it was needed for broadcasting, and the soldiers in the plot spent some hours searching for it in vain. Some of those taking part, with the curious detached Japanese aestheticism, remarked on the great beauty of the night, the uncanny and eerie moonlight which provided a backcloth of deep peace for these disordered events. The Emperor, the occasion of this wild conspiracy, was sleeping peacefully, a few yards away, and when it came to the point nobody would commit the impiety of waking him. In a cellar, directly underneath, the Lord Keeper of the Privy Seal, Marquis Kido, who was deeply committed to the peace negotiations, was quaking for his life, for, if the officers had discovered him, they would certainly have slaughtered him. Some radio officials, who had played a part in manufacturing the record, were rounded up and kept prisoner for a while. Their lives were also in danger.

The conspiracy ended because, with the passage of time, the officers began to ask themselves whether they were not going too far. *Sake* flowed; but this did not avail to stifle doubt. The failure to find the gramophone record put a lesion on the unfolding of the plot. Resolution drained away, and the band dispersed. Fake orders, which they had issued to the Guards division to rise and seize the palace, were intercepted. They did not dispose of a sufficient body of rank and file troops.

As a result of this sacrilege of army officers in seizing the imperial palace, the War Minister committed *hara-kiri*. He had been on the verge of this supreme act as a gesture of atonement for the behaviour of the Japanese army in losing the war; the night's doings probably overcame his natural hesitancy, and made death the way out of a situation which had become unbearable to him. In the ministerial debates of the previous days he was one of those whose opinion was most consulted, and had been the most vacillating. He had readily agreed that the military situation was hopeless; but he had been withheld from advising surrender as the only rational course by doubts over what the Americans intended to do about the Emperor. Now he was for capitulation, now he veered towards those who suggested that Japan should try again to save itself by force. His attitude, even towards those who attempted the military coup, was ambiguous. He was not taken by surprise; for days he had known that something was afoot. He had said to those around him that a coup would be impious and impossible; but, at the same time, he had shown marked favour to the more irresponsible officers. He summed up in himself the weakness that was general in the higher ranks of Japanese officer, considered from the point of view of their reliability to the state. He took it as axiomatic that a general need not in all cases obey instructions which reached him, but should be free to connive at gangsterism when the situation required. It was clear that his heart yearned for a coup: and his head only partially restrained him from siding with the young officers. Very distressingly, and rather characteristically, he bungled his suicide, and lived in great agony until the following day.

In the anti-climax which followed these exciting events, the rumours of which began to get about, Hirohito's speech was played over to the Japanese people. It was still touch and go how the speech would be received. In fact, the speech was not generally or at least clearly understood, and that for a very curious reason. The Japanese Emperor spoke the language of the court, very flowery, with a strange lilt, which it was hard for modern Japanese to grasp, at least auditorily. This, combined with sentiments so unexpected— to the uninformed—coming from such a source, produced at first a general bewilderment.

Meetings of colonels and majors were taking place the whole time in all parts of Japan. The plan for a final national effort by air force pilots who had sworn themselves to act as suicide squads was nearly put into effect. The proposal was to bomb the United States warship, the *Missouri*, which was steaming into Tokyo Bay, to accept the Japanese surrender. This was narrowly averted. Hirohito's speech contained a notable sentence, probably inserted on the Emperor's own responsibility, which may have irritated American and British listeners, but which represented the Emperor's own, perhaps naïve, views. He said:

> We declared war on America and Britain out of our sincere desire to ensure Japan's self-preservation and the stabilization of South-East Asia, it being far from our thought either to infringe upon the sovereignty of other nations or to embark upon territorial aggrandizement.

He continued with a statement of the incontrovertible fact of Japan's utter helplessness, and the lunacy of continuing the war. He was aware of the danger of seeming to break faith with those who had been killed, but the plight of those still alive required peace absolutely.

The Japanese people wept tears of disbelief and shame, but also of relief, when the imperial message at last sank home. The long nightmare of hypnosis under which they had been held by the military at last was shaken off. With the disciplined self-control of their race, which usually succeeded in clamping down upon their very volcanic emotion—which always so surprised the onlookers—they switched their behaviour overnight, and became the welcoming hosts to the advancing wave of American occupiers. By one of the psychological swings, irrational and extraordinary, which are evident among people under severe strain, the Japanese passed abruptly from regarding the Americans as barbarians, who were contemptible and to be treated with unappeasable hostility, to accepting them as a people who had incontestably proved their superiority by victory, and who had earned their consequent respect. Peace had come partly because of the effort, at the risk of their lives, of the peace party, and, when they had succeeded, it was plain that it had the support of the majority of the people. But this mass had, to the very end, remained completely unorganized. Peace was brought about with the Japanese public still as spectators of the event. They contributed nothing to it.

*

Everywhere the Japanese Empire surrendered, or crashed. In Burma it was already a memory, and the Japanese were gone. In Indonesia they had delayed too long to proclaim independence under Japanese auspices. This move, which was calculated to earn them plaudits in defeat, had been sabotaged by the Japanese army, which had no confidence in the return which could be gained by apparently serving the Asian cause. On 17 August 1945, the impatient leaders of the Indonesian National Party declared independence for themselves, thus forestalling the return of the Dutch. They persudaded Sukarno, the apparently fiery but in reality circumspect principal leader of the revolution, to read out the document which, in Indonesia ever since, has been famous. Sukarno's courage had failed him at the last moment, but his confederates held him to his task, and induced him, at pistol point, to go through with his broadcast statement. Thus a national leader was compelled to go through a historic act for which he must have been very grateful ever afterwards. Soon British troops would arrive to supervise the Japanese surrender, and soon their relation with the Indonesian nationalists would deteriorate. Within a matter of days an action would take place between the Indonesians and the Japanese, who were fighting under the command of British officers. To such a topsy-turvy condition had affairs been brought in that country.

In Manchukuo the Russians streamed in; the administrative structure erected by the Japanese vanished in a flash. Their puppet Manchu Emperor, Pu-yi, has recorded the final scene which took place at his capital at Changchun:

> My brother, sisters, brothers-in-law and nephews were already at the railway station, and, of my entire family, only I and two of my wives were left in the palace. Yoshioka addressed me and the servants who were still with me in a peremptory tone:
> 'Whether we walk or go in automobiles, the sacred objects to be carried by Toranosuke Hashimoto will go in front. If

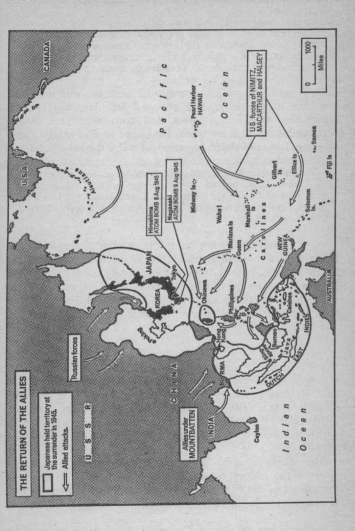

THE RETURN OF THE ALLIES

- Japanese held territory at the surrender in 1945.
- Allied attacks.

Russian forces

Allies under MOUNTBATTEN

US forces of NIMITZ, MACARTHUR and HALSEY

0 1000 Miles

CANADA

U.S.A

Pacific Ocean

Pearl Harbor HAWAII

Aleutians

Gilbert Is

Ellice Is

Samoa

Fiji Is

Hiroshima ATOM BOMB 8 Aug 1945

Nagasaki ATOM BOMB 9 Aug 1945

Midway Is.

Wake I

Marshall Is

Solomon Is.

JAPAN

Tokyo

KOREA

Peking

Okinawa

Marianas Is

Guam

Carolines

NEW GUINEA

AUSTRALIA

Philippines

Hong Kong

Celebes

Borneo

BURMA

Siam

DUTCH EAST INDIES

Java

U S S R

CHINA

INDIA

Ceylon

Indian Ocean

anyone passes the sacred vessels they must make a ninety-degree bow.'

I stood respectfully and watched Hashimoto, the President of the Bureau of Worship, carry the bundle containing the sacred Shinto objects to the first car. I got into the second and, as we left the palace, I looked around and saw flames rising above the National Foundation Shrine.*

Pu-yi set off to make his way to Japan. He was informed that the American government had left Hirohito on his throne. He sank to his knees, and kow-towed to him, expressing his relief at the news. He hoped to find safety under his wing. But at Mukden he was arrested by the Russians.

The airfield reverberated to the sound of aircraft engines as Soviet planes landed. Soviet troops holding sub-machine guns poured out of the planes and immediately disarmed all the Japanese soldiers on the airfield, which was soon covered with Soviet troops.†

Pu-yi remained for five years the captive of the Russians. He was then handed over to the Chinese communists for 'brainwashing'. It took time, but eventually the Chinese were satisfied that he was in a desirable state of mind. From 1959, until his death in 1967, he was in Peking, employed as a gardener in the former imperial gardens of the city, and was a striking national monument.

*

Power was everywhere passing away from those who had held it; and a new world was being created. It was the same in those parts of Asia which were, at least formally, on the victors' side. In India the negotiations were beginning which resulted in its complete emancipation within two years.

The war was at an end, and no attempt will be made to trace the history of the countries further, or to examine the effects of the rewards and penalties which they incurred. It is arbitrary to mark a step anywhere in history, and the

---

*Pu-yi: *From Emperor to Citizen: the Autobiography of Aisin-Gioro Pu-yi*, Foreign Language Press, Peking, 1965.
  †ibid.

new age in Asia which began in 1945 is really the pendant of Asia at war, and is inseparably connected with that. It would take decades to work out the consequences of the great struggle. But the history of the world must be arbitrarily chopped into lengths. For the purpose of this book the dropping of the bomb is the terminus.

By dropping the atom bomb the Americans had done much more than put an end to the war with Japan. They had put an end to a chapter of human history, and had transformed the nature of war. In the future neither governments nor people would enter on a war as lightheartedly as the Japanese had done. The interest of the historian lies in the question of what induced Americans to take the responsibility of dropping it.

Why did the Americans, who had it in their power to terminate the war by simply notifying Japan of the terrible effectiveness of the new weapon which had come into their hands, go to the lengths of actually dropping it? Why did they not content themselves with one bomb, but in a matter of hours, and without waiting to see the consequences of Hiroshima, drop the second bomb on Nagasaki?

The answer to these questions is, and is likely to remain, the greatest single matter of controversy of the war. The documents do not clarify the reasons. Churchill, for instance, is hardly enlightening. In his memoirs, he says, quite simply:

> The historic fact remained, and must be judged in the after time, that the decision whether or not to use the atomic bomb to compel the surrender of Japan was never even an issue. There was unanimous, automatic, unquestioning agreement around our [Council] table.

The United States was nearly as well aware as Japan of the desperation of the Japanese. Virtually they had conceded defeat at the end of July, and had put out peace feelers, first asking the Russians to act as mediators, and, on finding them unobliging, had approached the Swedish government. Anyone with experience of diplomacy could perceive that the upshot, after a few days' natural hesitation, must be the surrender so much desired. In the days of decision during the Potsdam Conference anything like a sustained Japanese defence, from strong defensive positions, had clearly become impossible. By ending the war in a ghastly and fearful massacre, the Americans cast over their triumph a dark shadow, and one which may, as is the way in great historical transactions, return to plague the doers in the future.

After the bomb had been exploded, Russian policy became, for the time being, very conciliatory. It was in this period that Truman announced his recent decision that the occupation of Japan should fall exclusively to the Americans. The details of the occupation of Germany had been discussed inexhaustibly, and continued to be a major issue among the allies: by contrast, the occupation of Japan seemed to have been arranged at very short notice, and by the United States alone. Great Britain made no demur at the American decision. Russia limited its protests to a proposal that the surrender on the battleship, the *Missouri,* should have its counterpart on Hokkaido with a ceremony of the surrender of the Kwantung army to Russia. This was rejected. Probably the existence of the bomb frustrated Russian plans for insisting on a joint occupation of Japan, and the consequences of this were incalculable. It avoided endless intrigue, and conflict of puppet parties: probably it saved Japan from a great deal of hardship: it made the return to normal life in Japan much quicker: by taking out Japan as a major question of dispute, it probably made the relations of Russia and the United States by that much easier to handle. It may even have kept them from war. It was perhaps the only good thing which came out of the dropping of the bomb.

The fateful decision to drop the bomb was made within a matter of days. Most of the men who were responsible for Japan's policy had not known a fortnight before that the atom bomb was in existence. Even General MacArthur, who, more than any other man, was responsible for the overthrow of Japan, was given the information only a very brief time before the bomb was due. He had said that he deplored it, but he had no time to make his protest effective. Admiral William D. Leahy, the Chief-of-Staff of the President, was consulted in advance and said, bluntly, that he thought that the use of the bomb was brutal, and served no rational end. It is possible that President Truman, whose subsequent decisions about the bomb were on the whole sober and responsible as, for example, during the later Korean war, may have acted in these days very much in the dark; and it is at least charitable to suppose that he did so. Churchill remarked that, as soon as the news of successful tests arrived, the President seemed to be determined to use it. Churchill judged it useless to press for discussion. All these statesmen suddenly found the bomb at their disposal, and they had no reasonable opportunity to think out the implications of atomic warfare, nor, it seemed, was the phenomenon of fall-out clear in their minds. The real essential difference between an atom bomb and a larger conventional weapon had not been grasped. Most Americans supposed, like Stalin, that it was simply a bigger and more lethal weapon. The discovery of atomic power required that men of exceptional vision and judgement should have been in power, who could see the consequences of the action they took then upon the politics of the next half century or longer. Those men were hardly likely to have been thrown up by the circumstances of directing the war.

Epilogue

I T may have been useful to recapitulate the facts of this conflict. There can seldom have been fought a war which engaged so much of the attention of so many powers, the details of which have so rapidly been allowed to become vague. Within a generation the dramatic events of Japan's surrender, the particulars of the relations between Japan and China, the great struggle at Imphal, the island-hopping across the Pacific by the United States, the great naval battles, have all begun to be touched by the waters of Lethe. Even Pearl Harbor, which has naturally entered into the folk-lore of the U S A, today appears far-off, and what happened there is vaguely understood.

The eastern war was inevitably overshadowed by Hitler's war in Europe. It was interdependent with it, and its events criss-crossed with those of the western conflict. But, in retrospect, they have assumed a subordinate part. The events of the European war stand out clearly; they are remembered sharply; the events of the war in the East are, by contrast, hazy in the public memory, and are heaped together in a certain confusion. Ask any young man born at or after the dropping of the bomb at Hiroshima, be he of Asian or European origin, to outline the events which led up to the fearsome drama, and you will be surprised to find what lacunae lie in his narrative.

And yet the events which had to be settled by arms, and by the atom bomb, were as great as the issues in Europe, the suffering was as widespread, the events spread over as many continents, involved more civilizations, and left as

357

large a dent in the history of world culture. For this reason, it has seemed to be worthwhile seeking to protest a little at the progress of the waters sweeping away the recollection of those years—even if the waters are fundamentally healthful, doing the saving work of washing away the memories of brutality and the hatred of nations for one another, and other things which are best forgotten. The famous feats of endurance of the peoples, the daring projects of the national leaders, may, with justice, be offered up as alms to oblivion; yet no people can afford to neglect the history which has made them what they are.

The war, for all the damage it had done, was not, by the standards of past wars, a particularly long one. Three wars, which were needed to settle the opposition of deep conflicting forces, and which turned upside down the affairs of all the participants, took much longer. One was the Thirty Years War between Protestant and Catholic Europe. Another, the Peloponnesian War, which checked finally the Athenian attempt at imperialism, lasted nineteen years. The war which rose out of the French Revolution ran a course which ended at the Battle of Waterloo, and covered twenty-three years. The present war, from the time that the fighting set in in earnest on the Chinese mainland in 1937, and excluding the opening skirmishes between China and Japan, was over in eight years.

The comparatively shorter duration of the great modern wars reflects the deadly nature of modern armaments. The causes nevertheless have been weighty and complex. The issue of the strife in Asia settled a number of conflicts which, but for the war, might have dragged on for years, causing constant unrest, and keeping the region in continual uncertainty. It had been decided which of various trends were to continue, and which, among those which had seemed strong and flourishing a few years before, were either to stop abruptly or else to fade away.

The decision was sharpest for Japan. The attempt to maintain Japan's unnatural pre-eminence in the Far East, and to spread it over the lands to the south, had failed. Japan's empire was dissolved. Japan's efforts had been astonishing. A relatively small country, whose principal assets were the ardent will of its citizens and their regimentation, had had the temerity to challenge the three corners of the world to come against it in arms; and had withstood their reply for more than three years.

The Japanese of that generation had passed through a strange phase of their national history. In the past there had been little to single them out for peculiar reprobation. They were always very vigorous, usually artistic, always somewhat muddled intellectually, which was apparently due to the imprecision of their language. They were also perhaps outstanding for an exaggerated conformism, though they also had the tradition of lifting the tyranny of society over the older members of the community, and giving them a licence to do and say what they pleased. And always, as with any generalization about an entire people, one is conscious at once of many eccentric members of the community, for whom the general rule did not apply.

The main fact in the twentieth century is the acute military phase that the Japanese lived through. It was an aberration. It was not really traditional. It may be that Japanese society has a Samurai streak, and a prolonged feudal period had left it too ready to respond to the call of arms. Many of its ways of thought were military in origin. But, if one looks back on Japanese history, the Japanese do not appear to have been an unduly military people. At one period they were predominantly artists, and would not allow matters of soldierly concern to interfere with the artistic life. In the great Heian period, which is perhaps the outstanding example in history of a leisured class giving up all its time to artistic living, there was once a complaint that the imperial bodyguard could not be properly sustained. The soldiers could not ride horses: they constantly fell off them. The detailed history of the society of this time is full of anecdotes of the extreme lengths to which Japanese aestheticism would go. The men of the Heian period are strange ancestors of the Japanese who took Singapore.

The Japanese who were born in the most recent generations were conditioned by the institutions of their society to offer themselves in the bid to establish a Japanese imperialism. These institutions, most of them borrowed from the West though given a peculiar slant in their development, are the monument of the Meiji Restoration. Gradually they induced in the mass of the people the willingness to support a more and more aggressive national policy. The institutions took on a life of their own. In the end, they carried the Japanese people into a great war, and brought down half a continent.

The prime evil of Japan was certainly the ascendancy of the military. This led, in time of war, to the Supreme Command conducting the war as a state secret from the civilian parts of the Japanese administration. Whatever else may be said of such a system, it proved to be most incompetent militarily. Thus Japanese militarism held within it the seeds of its own defeat. It was unable to organize Japanese society so that in modern warfare it could compete with the powers which were organized to be more flexible.

The same militarism, as far as it was able to prevail in making Japanese foreign policy, was responsible for the basic error which brought about Japan's downfall. This was to found Japan's policy on fear of the outside world, and to meet this by seeking to spread a counter-fear of Japan. Because Japan was in a difficult position internationally, because it was vulnerable, because its economic position required that it should have unimpeded access to imports and a constantly growing market overseas for its exports, and because it feared that these might be interrupted by force by an unfriendly power, it counted that prudence required it to be ever on its guard, to arm and show its teeth in a way that would fend off dangerous intentions in its rivals. There were Japanese voices which protested at such a policy, and pointed, rightly, to the inevitable end; but they were not attended to. The result was a long period of tension, culminating in a war in which Japan lost everything, a war which could not possibly have safeguarded the things which Japan had armed itself to save.

The contradictions of Japan's foreign policy are stated compendiously by the Foreign Ministry official, Toshikazu Kase, who played such a useful part as intermediary of the court circles in bringing the war to an end. 'For a poor country like Japan,' he said,

> the construction of costly warships meant a crushing burden upon the national treasury. And yet we built a good number of them. We also maintained a vast Army and an ever expanding Air Force. In the end we became like the mammoth whose tusks, growing ever bigger, finally unbalanced its bodily structure. As everything went to support the huge

tusks, very little was left to sustain the rest of the body. The mammoth finally became extinct.

Why did the mammoth arm itself with weapons such as ultimately to bring about its own destruction? Because it was apprehensive. In its desire to defend itself against external enemies the poor creature forgot the very fact that its tusks were its own mortal enemy! Why did Japan arm herself to the teeth? Because she was apprehensive? Why was she apprehensive? Because she had enemies. Why were there enemies? Because her aggressive policy excited suspicion in others. Rather than abandon that objectionable policy she augmented her armaments. But armaments are a relative affair. There is no end to an armament race.*

The men who served ruthless, imperialist Japan were not by nature particularly ruthless or imperialist. They bore no signs of predestination, and there was nothing about them which marked them as enemies of the human race. The Japanese generals, though superficially they might seem to conform to a rather brutal and disgusting pattern, were often men of singular eccentricity. In other circumstances, they might have appeared as rather engaging. Many of them had a vivid and vigorous interior life, and the most varied traits of personality. Some of them practised Japanese archery and fencing each day, not for athletic reasons but for the self-control which these disciplines induced, and for greater proficiency in the art of meditation. They were an interesting contrast to the British army, much more emotional, much more given to adjusting their philosophy and their actions. The contrast between them and the commanders of the Anglo-Saxon forces was often richly comical. Rigid behaviour patterns in their native environment made them what they were and, uprooted from this environment, their behaviour was unpredictable. It could of course, be terrible; occasionally, however, it was the reverse.

The behaviour of the Japanese soldiers, and their cult of non-surrender, may have seemed to those fighting them to mark them out as an especially desperate, unreformable species of military man. Here too, is only an example of the lengths to which institutions may go in marking their victims. Biologically similar young men, transported to another society and brought up under other institutions, turned out

*Toshikazu Kase: *Eclipse of the Rising Sun,* op. cit.

to be enthusiastic liberals or democrats, and found most reprehensible the Japanese cult of military national aggrandizement and the pursuit of death.

The Japanese, in the last war, were shocked at finding a most rigid refusal to respond to the call of their country and race on the part of the Nisei, the children of the Japanese emigrants to America, who had most of them continued to marry with Japanese. In this they were much disappointed: they had counted on being able to convert this class, and if they had succeeded, would have disposed a valuable ally for their war-making. The Nisei had some reason to attend to their call, for the United States was less than generous in its treatment of them, and did not hide its suspicion. The deportation or preventive confinement of the large masses of Americans of Japanese origin, who had given no reason for doubting their loyalty, was one of the blots on wartime American government. But the Nisei, almost without exception, refused the appeal of their blood relations, and were almost fanatical in their devotion to the new institutions among which they had been brought up.

The Nisei show that there is no such thing as a militarist through and through, made such by his physical make-up, and a stranger to civilization because of the military activities of his ancestors.

Most significant of all, the Japanese, since their surrender, have undergone a thorough change of heart. In no country in the world is militarism so thoroughly reprobated. All Japan's energies are now concentrated on remaining a friendly civilian state. Possibly the very completeness of the emotional swing is suspicious. What is today so violently renounced may tomorrow be once more violently espoused. But all the signs are that the world has, as the result of the war, gained a new Japan.

At the end of the war an international tribunal was set up by the allies in order to put on trial a large number of those who had allegedly been responsible for war crimes. The Japanese had wished to reserve a trial of war prisoners to themselves as a condition of Japanese surrender, but they had been overruled. At the major War Crimes Tribunal in Tokyo, twenty-five Japanese leaders were sentenced, seven of them to death, others to life imprisonment: among these were General Tojo, the Prime Minister; General Koiso, his successor; the wily court chamberlain, Marquis Kido, who played so large a part in bringing about Japan's surrender; Shigenori Togo, the Foreign Minister who had showed a most un-Japanese independence of judgement; and Koki Hirota, another former Prime Minister. The conveners even proposed trying Prince Konoye, but he evaded arrest by poisoning himself. These doubtful proceedings went like a swath through all those who had been in any way prominent in Japanese politics of the period. The biographical footnotes of a book on Japanese history at this time make heavy reading because of the end of most of the characters. The major good that came out of these proceedings at Tokyo was that they are the most complete, exhaustive account of Japanese politics in the militarist period.

Other war crimes trials were held in Hong Kong, Singapore, Borneo and elsewhere in the recent Japanese Empire. Detainees were arraigned for cruelty towards local populations and prisoners of war, and over 900 were executed. The thought of these melancholy figures, and the deeds which in many cases preceded this toll of life, leads to the reflection that had the war had a different result, the subsequent years might have been the age of Japanese imperialism. Asia has been spared that. The war, with all its horrors, had achieved this positive good. A reluctant admiration for Japan's military feats must not block out the consciousness of the sinister shadow which for a time hung over the eastern world.

Search the record how one will, it is almost impossible to find anything good to say of the Japanese Empire. Its liquidation was an unqualified benefit to the world. In the years before the conflict, Japan had had its opportunity to develop its empire in miniature—in Korea, in Formosa, and in the parts of China which it came to dominate—and in this exhibition of the Japanese spirit it failed to show any virtues. An empire, which by its definition is a political structure housing peoples of different cultures and languages, is different from the nation-state, which is the most approved political form in the twentieth century. Nations object to being included in an empire. Empires are out-of-date. But some empires are more tolerable than others. They may have qualities which actively catch the imagination of their people. In the case of a very few, their peoples will actually be willing to die in their defence, though instances of this have become increasingly rare. The classic case, in comparison with which other empires may be judged, was Rome of antiquity. That empire seems to have offered a wider life, richer opportunities, a larger destiny, than could be looked for within the confines of small states.

The Japanese Empire, if it is judged from its beginnings, was not at all likely to develop into one of these rarer structures. In its origin it was essentially primitive and of petty conception. It was put together by conquest, and its prime aim was to plunder the subjected peoples for the benefit of the Japanese. The empire offered hardly anything to its citizens which led them to take pride in membership of it beyond a pride in being Asian. This should not be neglected. The Japanese made considerable play with pan-Asianism. The contemporary writing is all about the joy of being Asian. It was the outstanding fact of the time. But it was not long before the contrast between Japanese idealism and Japanese practice took away this enthusiasm.

The Japanese system was founded on no great code of law. In its organization it embodied no exhilarating concepts such as have led men elsewhere into giving their loyalty, even if divided—concepts such as liberty, equality and fraternity; the career open to talents; the greatest good of the greatest number or restraint of the evil of exploitation. The Japanese Empire signified no large cult of reason, no vision, no distinctive habits of thought or behaviour, no corpus of books which set the tone of people's thought, no pattern of individual behaviour which might have given people a liberating vision. It was the starting-place of no system of philosophy which was likely to appeal to men of all races and different cultures: in other words, it lacked the universalist appeal. The most to which it invited its citizens was to the enjoyment of Japanese culture, and there the difficulty was that, though this culture is not inferior, it is one which most Asians find uncongenial and it is at best provincial and not a universal civilization. In particular, the Japanese language was unsuited as a medium of communication for holding the political machinery together. Nobody talked Japanese as a form of intellectual pleasure, as the subjects of the French Empire often spoke French: nobody preened himself upon its use: the language was thought to be muzzy and imprecise.

Japanese culture is especially strong on the inculcation of the correct attitudes for aesthetic appreciation: but aesthetics has never been strong enough to hold an empire together. Besides, this quality of mind was already considered out-of-date in Japan itself.

Calling on the people of its empire to share Japanese culture was summoning them to a Barmecide feast. Responding to the call, the Chinese felt themselves sitting with more primitive people than themselves. They found that Japanese culture was a tiresome and constricting limitation on their minds.

A peculiarly evil feature of the system was that it had within itself no ability to evolve, to change, to end itself, and to merge with other forces in Asia. It would endure only as long as Japanese military power lasted: it was sustained by that and by that alone: it invited head-on collision with all the emerging forces of Asia, and if it had not been destroyed in war, it would sooner or later have led to bloody wars of liberation.

When the war was over, when Japan had given up the pretence at founding a new political order, and gave free play to its natural talents, the Japanese surprised the world, and themselves, by solving their problems by simple hard work, and without any use of force or creation of grandiose political structures. They recovered economically in the minimum of time; they rapidly became a beacon-light in Asia, they proved that an Asian people could save itself by its own exertions. And all this without even the dream of empire. Energy, skill in planning, imagination in enterprise, ability in the application of techniques to the economic processes proved enough to get Japan over all its obstacles; and Japan has discovered the political advantages in having a foreign policy which is audacious by reason of its modesty.

*

The war also precipitated everywhere the downfall of western power in Asia. The western powers withdrew from China. Treaty Ports were at an end: also the rights of extra-territoriality. Within two years Britain withdrew from India. This was a change which plainly doomed the French Empire in Indo-China, and the Dutch in Indonesia. Within ten years, they had each of them passed away. They did not go voluntarily, as did the British Empire in India; they attempted to stay, and they were willing to go to war against the national parties which rose up to extrude them. But they were too weak to prevail. Moreover they were too much concerned with their problems in Europe to be able to give the war their whole-hearted attention.

The Japanese Empire having been destroyed and the western empires put down, a power vacuum existed which only the nationalist organizations could fill. These were left to organize most of Asia in the pattern they desired. The West, including the United States, tried to influence them in one way or another, using their economic power to make their will effective, and in the case of the U S, their armaments when the situation did not respond to economic manipulation. By indirect means they hoped to prevail as effectively as in the days when they sat with political power in Delhi and in the eastern capitals. This was the phase of neo-colonialism, and the emancipated countries of Asia have been on their guard against it and have sought to render themselves really free.

*

China, released from the incubus of an imperial Japan, has been free to develop as the inward forces in the country directed. Within four years of the ending of the war China became communist. The excessive corruption, the paralysis of will and venal incompetence of the later years of the Kuomintang were increased by its unnatural isolation from the rest of the country. Once this was removed its downfall was inevitable.

The prolonged agony which had been suffered by the Chinese people as the twentieth century wore on, opened the way to a violent remedy. The chief leaders of the Kuomintang escaped the vengeance of the opposing party by retiring, with vast fortunes, to the island of Formosa whence they kept up, under an American umbrella, a somewhat ludicrous show of still exercising an influence in world affairs. In the first flood of revenge, many of the landlords, who had lived for so long in the sun of prosperity in China, were violently put down, with sufferings as cruel as any

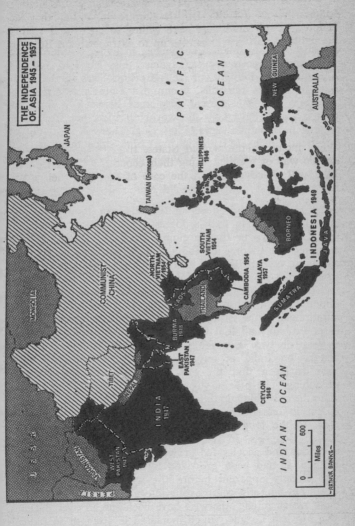

which they had, by past insensibility and negligence, occasioned among the poor. Later, 're-education' was the term used to describe the method by which the bourgeoisie were broken in. The mass of the people were liberated into a new life of undreamed-of sufficiency in living standards and educational opportunity: as against this, freedom for the individual—of thought or self-direction—was largely absent. In foreign relations, communist China's extreme isolationism, and the mutual suspicions between it and the United States, have kept the world on edge, but from time to time have shown signs of relaxing. There is no doubt of the greatly recovered prestige of China since the war, and its natural re-emergence as a major power in Asia.

*

What had been the effects in India? Great though the upheaval had been in India's domestic life, the war simply affected the pace of the development of its history, and accelerated the divorce of India and Britain: it did not give events an essentially new turn. Its chief effect was to bring to a head the emancipation of the country, and to accelerate the industrialization. Though these two occurrences were undoubtedly a consequence of the war, one of them, the withdrawal of the British had been bound to happen in any case. Probably all that the war did was to advance this by a year or two. Everybody who looked with the eye of history on India at any time from 1930 onwards must have foreseen that the end of the British Raj was approaching. The precise steps by which it would come about were the only thing doubtful.

Yet in one fateful respect the war gave an unexpected twist to the long process of the freedom struggle by the Indian Congress. In the circumstances of wartime politics, a sudden and accelerated growth took place in the Moslem League. It had been provoked by the Congress success; it was already apparent before the war; but the war acted like a hot-house in compressing into a few years the development which might otherwise have been spread over decades. The Moslem League, which increased in strength so radically, was emboldened to press for the creation of the Moslem state of Pakistan.

CHINESE COMMUNISM 1934–1950

USSR

MONGOLIA

Under Soviet Control

1945–1948

Vladivostok

PEKING

NORTH KOREA
Occupied by USSR 1945–1948
Cease-fire line 1953

Yenan

SOUTH KOREA
Occupied by US 1945–1948

Seoul

Nanking

Okinawa
US military
Government since 1951
Japanto is
US Administered since 1945

FRENCH

Hong Kong British since 1842

Portuguese since 1557

TAIWAN (FORMOSA)
Main Nationalist stronghold under Chiang Kai-shek

HAINAN

THAILAND

SOUTH

INDO

Cease fire line 1954

CHINA

CHINA

Saigon

SEA

0   300
Miles

★ Communists active in these areas 1934.
← Mao Tse-tung's 'Long March' 1934–1936.
◄-- Soviet attacks against Japanese-occupied China 1945.
← Retreat of Chinese Nationalist forces 1949.
▨ Chinese Nationalist-held areas following expulsion from mainland 1949.

THE GROWTH OF CHINESE COMMUNISM
Areas held by communists 1936–1949.
Communist acquisitions April 1947.
Communist acquisitions July 1948.
Communist acquisitions December 1949.
Communist acquisitions 1950 onwards.

Today this state has come into being. It is an exceptional creation which reminds us of the continuing force of religion in politics. Religion was the driving force in making for the existence of this state. As such, the creation of Pakistan seems to be a digression from the ideas of the Enlightenment, and a return to the Middle Ages. Its establishment was accompanied by forebodings and very great reluctance on the part of the British government. If independence had come in 1937, instead of 1947, it would undoubtedly have been given to a united India. The intensity of the divisions did not appear until later: they only manifested themselves in their full significance during the war years. But an undivided India would not have held together. The Hindu–Moslem cleavage would have declared itself under the strain of self-governments. Sooner or later, unified government would have been made impossible: communal tension, and eventually communal civil war, would have brought it to a standstill. The same process would have taken place which later placed obstacles in the path of Nigeria, which, when it became independent, had appeared so gigantic and stable.*

It is easy to forget how at the end of the war the decision to partition the sub-continent was on a knife edge. Without the war, the British would hardly have considered the creation of Pakistan as a necessary act. The state of Pakistan is therefore one of the monuments to the war with Japan. It is an unlikely one: nobody today sees any special connection between its history and that of Japan: yet the two are linked causally.

*

For the U S the war was an incident in its rise to be one of the two greatest powers in the world. It received its baptism

---

*This was written in 1968. Since then serious divisions have arisen between East and West Pakistan which have made an end of their conjunction in a single state. One of the fundamental factors which have produced this break has been the immense obstacle of geography, which a look at the map on page 367 makes clear. In addition, the populations of the two wings differed in race, language and character, and had little to combine them, except religion.

of fire. For many years before 1941, America had distorted
the natural play of international affairs by utterly refusing to
act the part of a Great Power. Its people, in general and
except at certain conjunctures, appeared to be without the
political instincts of the citizens of a major state. Because
of their unique behaviour, and of the influence of this upon
the official conduct of the American government, the United
States, at a time when fate and its economic power called
upon it to exert tremendous influence, limited its voice in
world affairs to be hardly of more account than that of a
third-class European state. Doubtless the reasons for this lay
far back in American history, and touch on George Washington, the fear of 'entangling Alliances' and the belief that
foreign governments were very wily and would inevitably
bamboozle an American government which was rash enough
to negotiate with them. But the United States had been in
the First World War; its reaction from this experience and
withdrawal into isolation, had been a setback to normal
growth. When Pearl Harbor happened, the United States, in
a world at war, still had an army of about the same size
as Sweden's; it still made the gestures, to which it had accustomed itself before its entry in 1917 into the First World
War, of being 'too proud to fight'. It is true that American
ideas and American business influence were very prevalent,
as also was the uncontrollable propulsive power of American culture. But the American state did not set itself to
propagate them.

In the course of the war, the United States developed
amazingly. It grew with the alarming speed of Alice when
she swallowed the potion in the bottle marked 'Drink me'.
It began the war with organs and Ministries for taking part
in foreign affairs which seem like toys. But, with the creative
wind of improvisation which swept through the U S, the
institutions developed rapidly. Simultaneously its public opinion, and the institutions by which this was made effective,
grew in self-confidence. By the end of the war, the United
States was moving in international affairs with professionalism and boldness.

American democracy was to show that while it was surprisingly persevering as long as the war lasted, it was, once
peace was restored, capable of a rapid, revolutionary change
of mood. The fires died as swiftly as they had blazed fierce-

ly. Within seven years America had come to feel towards
Japan as towards its protégé: and had transferred to Japan
some of the abnormally cordial feeling which it had held
towards China, until China became communist.

Finally, this was probably the last war which Great Britain took part in as a world power, certainly an Asian
power. For the last time Britain manoeuvred as a government with interest and concern in every part of the world
especially in Asia. It ended its Asian history with panache
It was nevertheless an end. Within two years of the dropping
of the bomb on Hiroshima, Britain ended its responsibility
for India. By this one act it terminated its empire every
where in Asia; for a British Empire in Asia which excluded
India was not really a possibility.

Great Britain, at that time, was more than a small country, with a restricted part to play, as seemed to befit one
of a cluster of west European islands. By the accident of
history, by the energy of its peoples it had, for the previous
two centuries, been shot out of its natural sphere. It had
risen to a height of power and prestige which obviously it
could not retain but to which people in Britain had become
accustomed. The leaders of institutional life had risen to their
opportunity, and for some decades this had been reflected
in politics. These seemed to have an influence totally out of
the proportion which would naturally be expected of such a
numerically small people. Living in Britain at this time had
a magnifying effect, so that what was done seemed to be
done with a deep sense of responsibility. The proceedings of
the parliament at Westminster were gazed at by so many
people that those who took part in it had the uneasy sense of
acting on a great stage of the world, and being the cynosure
of the world's eyes. This sense was often embarrassing. It
often invested relatively trivial affairs with a false glamour.
It would have been healthier if they had been dealt with
without these overtones. Even so, thought in Britain was
still apt to be large; small conceptions were still at a discount.
It was this quality which perhaps most separates the Britain
of those days from what it has become.

Within ten years of Indian independence, Britain had
liquidated practically all that was left of its Asian empire.
Ceylon, Malaya, Burma—let them go all. It was not a matter
of no longer discouraging their instinct to break away from

the empire which had once been thought of as a supra-national organization, a house where all the rising national-isms of the empire might, of their own free will, find asylum. They were positively conducted to the door. They were given a golden handshake—financially a rather mean one—and were sped into independence with expressions of goodwill.

Britain, which had enjoyed in Asia the great romantic period of its history, turned back, as a result of the war, and after an interval for readjustment, to the more sober task of discovering the contrast between being a world pow-er and being a small country off the north-east corner coast of Europe. It became preoccupied with the total revolution which should adapt Britain for its new role; with anxious debate as to whether it should think once more to become a European power as it had been under is Angevin monarchs, or whether it could exist as a small island alone.

It is irony that, at the end, Britain finds itself in very similar circumstances to those which worried Japan at the start of this history. Transpose the islands off the north coast of Asia to the islands off the northwest of Europe, and the parallel is strangely apt. Its history, as Dean Acheson rightly diagnosed—only to be the object of bitter vitupera-tion by people in Britain—was that it had lost an empire and not found a new part to play. The British may count them-selves fortunate that the public opinion of the world has moved on, and it is unlikely that Britain will be tempted to try and solve its problems in a similar way to Japan.

*

And the human side? What of the war for the Little Peter-kins of Asia?

The conflict had a recognizable pattern, though there were so many confusing cross-currents. One purpose of this book has been to trace it out. It settled the influences which were to be dominant in the lives of people for the next generation or so—until new pressures meet new obstacles, and all is again in the melting pot, the issue having again to be settled by conflict. For this last great cataclysm, the price paid in human life and suffering was truly prodigious. The numbers of those killed in the war on all fronts have been analysed in the earlier Epilogue. Of two of the great Asian families of people engaged, the Chinese casualties, difficult to estimate, have been given by Chiang Kai-shek in his book, *A Summing-Up at Seventy*, as over 3 million. 'These figures,' he says, 'do not include the heavy losses in life and property sustained by the people in general.'* Japanese losses in battle and air-attack have been estimated at around 2 million. Of the people elsewhere in Asia, by far the largest proportion had no wish to take part in the quarrel. They neither understood, nor cared for, nor were consulted about, the objects of conflict. From first to last they viewed the war as a fact of destructive nature, which everyone in his senses sought to evade, but which was fated to make enormous waves. Those who voluntarily went to war, or felt passionately about the issues to the extent of being genuinely willing to die for them, were very few. Submitting to the economic inducements because of poverty and destitution was the nearest that most combatants came to acting by a reasonable decision. The only Asian people of whom this was not really true were the fatally indoctrinated Japanese.

It is, however, economic pressure alone which interests nine tenths of the population of Asia. It is idle to think that people living in conditions of Asian poverty, and with so much mass illiteracy, can be capable of acting in any other way. Any system of government which offers them the prospects of seeing a barely tolerable life, barely tolerable though it be, for six months ahead, will be more than welcome. Frills of government, freedom, choice, are suspect to them. Those combatants who came from a society in which the compulsion of hunger was less present were swept together by conscription, and had even less say in their destiny.

The war was probably the last major conflict which will be fought in Asia in which all the Asian antagonists except Japan were predominantly agrarian. This gave the war its peculiar, and rather antiquarian flavour. Time will ensure that, before another great contest can happen, large segments of society will have become heavily industrialized, and with industrialization, will have come the special type of social organization which renders society so different in behaviour from that which was traditional.

*Chiang Kai-shek: *A Summing-Up at Seventy*, Harrap, 1957.

Even the very few of the educated classes—the Chinese university professors, the Japanese, the Indian leisured upper classes—who had the inclination and the ability to trace out the pattern of events behind the confusion, to understand the whys and wherefors, derived little consolation when they were compelled to live among a collapsing economy and the dangers of loot and arson from the fact that to them was vouchsafed the understanding of what the war was all about.

It is clear that, to the many millions who fought and suffered unvocally, to the ignorant armies clashing by night, unselfconsciously, those who survived owe an inexpiable debt. It seems, at some points in history, that only through a convulsion involving millions is understanding painfully acquired. 'The cut worm forgives the plough', said the poet Blake. By invoking this kind of charity, there can perhaps be forgiveness for the ungovernable fury of the instruments by which history is made.

Chronological Skeleton

1937

July	7	Japanese attack Chinese at Marco Polo Bridge
Dec	14	Fall of Nanking to the Japanese

1938

July	11	Japanese-Soviet battle of Chang-kufeng
Oct		Chiang Kai-shek's Government withdraws to Chungking
Oct	21	Fall of Canton to the Japanese
Oct	25	Fall of Hankow to the Japanese
Nov	5	Prince Konoye declares 'New Order' in Asia

1939

Sept	1	Germans invade Poland
May–Sept		Battle of Nomonhan between Japan and USSR

Sept	3	Great Britain and France declare war
Sept	17	USSR invades Poland
Oct		USSR exacts mutual assistance treaties from Estonia, Latvia and Lithuania
Nov	30	USSR invades Finland
Dec	17	*Graf Spee* scuttled

1940

Mar	12	Finland capitulates
Mar	30	Setting up of Wang Ching-wei's puppet government at Nanking
Apr	9	Germans invade Denmark and Norway
May		British occupy Iceland
May	10	Germans invade Low Countries and France. Churchill Prime Minister
May	15	Dutch lay down arms
May	20	Germans reach English Channel
May	28	Belgium capitulates
May 27–June 4		Dunkirk

June 10 Italy declares war	June 10 Italy declares war	June 10 Italy declares war
June 14 Germans enter Paris		
June 22 France signs armistice		
July 3 British action against French fleet at Mers-el-Kebir		July–Oct Closing of the Burma Road
July 10–Sept 15 Battle of Britain		
	Aug 4 Italians invade British and French Somaliland	
Sept 3 Anglo-U S bases destroyers deal	Sept 14 Italians invade Egypt	Sept 27 Tripartite Pact between Japan, Germany and Italy
	Oct Hitler confers with Mussolini (4), Franco (23), Pétain (24)	
	Oct 28 Italians invade Greece	
Nov 5 Roosevelt re-elected President	Nov 11 British attack Italian fleet at Taranto	Nov Hungary, Rumania and Slovakia brought into Tripartite Pact
	Dec British Offensive in North Africa captures Tobruk (Jan 22) and Benghazi (Feb 7)	Dec American embargo on sales of scrap iron and war material to Japan

1941

Mar 11 Lend-Lease Act signed

Mar 1 Bulgaria joins Tripartite Pact

Mar 27 Simovic coup: Yugoslavia refuses to join Tripartite Pact

Mar 28 Battle of Cape Matapan

Mar 31 First German offensive in North Africa; takes Benghazi and invests Tobruk

Apr U S occupies Greenland

Apr 6 Germans invade Yugoslavia and Greece

Apr 13 Non-aggression pact signed between Japan and Russia

May 2 British invade Iraq

May 20–June 2 Germans take Crete

May 27 *Bismarck* sunk

June 8 British defeat Vichy French in Syria and Lebanon

June 22 Germans invade U S S R

July U S joins occupation of Iceland

July 2 Japan decides on extensive moves into Indo-China

July 12	Anglo-Soviet Treaty of Mutual Assistance		
July 28 & 29			U S, British and Dutch East Indies impose embargoes on the sale of oil and steel to Japan
Aug 14	Roosevelt-Churchill conference, Placentia Bay; Atlantic Charter		
Aug 17	Fall of Kiev		
Aug 25	Anglo-Russian occupation of Iran		
Sept	U S 'shoot at sight' order		
Sept 8	Leningrad invested		
Oct 17			General Tojo replaces Konoye as Prime Minister of Japan
Oct 30	Sebastopol invested. German thrust for Moscow		
Dec 1	Russian counter-attack		
Dec 7			Japan sends a declaration of war to the U S
Dec 7			Japan attacks Pearl Harbor, the Philippines, Hong Kong and Malaya
Dec 8			U S and Great Britain declare war on Japan

Dec 9 China officially declares war on Japan and Germany

Dec 10 Japanese sink the *Prince of Wales* and the *Repulse*

Dec 10 Japan captures Guam

Dec 11 Japan attacks Burma

Dec 23 Fall of Wake Island

Dec 11 Germany and Italy declare war on U S

Dec 24 British re-capture Benghazi

1942

Jan 11 Japan attacks the Dutch East Indies

Jan 28 Germans re-capture Benghazi

Feb 8 Fall of Rangoon

Feb 15 Fall of Singapore

Feb 19 Japanese bomb Port Darwin in Australia

Feb 27– Battle of the Java Sea
29

Mar 2 Fall of Batavia

Mar 11 Cripps mission to India

Mar Bomber Command raids Baltic towns

Apr German 'Baedeker' raids

Apr 4– Japanese raid into
9 the Indian Ocean, bombing Ceylon

May 30 '1,000-bomber' raid on Cologne		
June Destruction of PQ 17		
	July 3 Fall of Sebastopol	Apr 9 US surrender of Bataan
July Regular raids on Ruhr and Hamburg begin		Apr 18 US air raid on Tokyo
		May 1 Surrender of Mandalay
		May 6 Surrender of Corregidor
		May 6–8 Battle of the Coral Sea
		June 4 Battle of Midway Island
		June 4 Japanese attack on the Aleutian Islands
Aug 12–15 Stalin-Churchill meeting in Moscow	Aug 12–15 Stalin-Churchill meeting in Moscow	Aug 7 US landings on the Solomon Islands
Aug 17 First US raid on Germany		Aug 9 Civil Disobedience campaign announced in India
Aug 19 Dieppe raid		
Aug 31 Battle of Alam el Halfa: German-Italian advance stayed		

	Sept 13	Battles for Stalingrad begin
	Sept 21	Opening of the Arakan offensive under Wavell
	Sept 21	Opening of U S offensive in New Guinea
Oct 23	Battle of Alamein	
Nov 8	Allied landings in Morocco and Algeria	
Nov 11	Germans occupy southern France and Tunisia	
Nov	Record months for sinking by U-boats	
Nov	Regular raids on Berlin begin	

1943

		Jan 11 Treaty relinquishing extraterritorial rights between the US, Britain and China
	Jan	German retreat from Caucasus
Jan 14–24	Casablanca conference	
	Feb 2	German surrender at Stalingrad. Russians recover Kursk (8) and Rostov (14)
		Feb 8 Wingate's expedition into Burma
		Mar 2 Battle of the Bismarck Sea
Mar 29	Battle of the Mareth	
		Apr 18 Death of Admiral Yamamoto, at Bougainville

May 11   U S begin to liberate Aleutian Islands

Apr 19- / May 16   Rising and extinction of Warsaw Ghetto

May 12   German-Italian surrender in Tunisia

May 17   Attack on Ruhr dams

May 26   Discovery of Katyn massacre and severance of Russo-Polish relations

June 29   U S landings in New Guinea

July 5- / 6   Battles in the Kursk salient and Russian recovery of Orel and Belgorod

July 10   Invasion of Sicily

July 25   Dismissal of Mussolini

Aug 17   Quebec Conference: setting up of South-East Asia Command, under Mountbatten

Aug 17   U S daylight raids on Regensburg and Schweinfurt

Aug 23   Russians recover Kharkov

Sept 3   Invasion of Calabria and signing of Italian surrender

Sept   Russians recover Novorossisk and Smolensk (25)

Sept 9   Landings at Salerno

Sept 12   Rescue of Mussolini

Oct 13 Italy declares war on Germany	Oct Russians recover Zaporozhe (14) and Dnepropetrovsk (25)	Nov 5–6 Greater East Asia Conference held in Tokyo
	Nov 6 Russians recover Kiev	Nov U S landings in the Gilbert Islands
		Nov 22–26 Cairo Conference: unconditional surrender demanded of Japan
Nov 28– Dec 1 Teheran Conference		Nov 28– Dec 1 Teheran Conference
		Dec Opening of the assault on the Marshall Islands
1944		
Jan 12 Landings at Anzio	Jan 27 Leningrad relieved	Feb–Mar Beginning of Japanese offensive on borders of India, siege of Imphal and Kohima
Feb 15 Bombing of Monte Cassino	Apr 2 Russians enter Rumania	Apr 17 Renewed Japanese offensive in China
		Apr–July U S advances through Dutch New Guinea

Western Front	Italy	Eastern Front	Pacific / Far East
June 6 Invasion of Normandy	May 17 Germans evacuate Monte Cassino	May Russians recover Sebastopol and Crimea	June 15 Americans invade Saipan
June 12 First V 1s hit London	June 4 Americans enter Rome	June 23–July 3 Russians recover Belorussia	June 15 First B-29 raid on Japan
July 20 Attempt on Hitler's life		July 23 Russians take Lublin and establish Polish Committee of National Liberation	July 4 Japanese defeated at Imphal
	Aug Kesselring mans the Gothic Line	Aug 1–Oct 2 Warsaw rising against the Germans	July 9 Fall of Saipan
Aug 15 Allied landings in southern France			July 18 Resignation of General Tojo
Aug 17 Final victories in Normandy. Paris rises			Aug U S recovery of Tinian and Guam

Aug 24 Leclercq enters Paris		
Sept 3 Brussels liberated		Sept Allied counter-offensive in Burma, under Mountbatten
	Sept 5 USSR declares war on Bulgaria	
Sept 8 First V 2s hit London		
	Sept 12 Rumania signs armistice	
	Sept 19 Finland signs armistice	
Sept 17–30 Arnhem operations fail		
	Oct 20 Partisans and Russians enter Belgrade	Oct 20 US landings in the Philippines
		Oct 25 Battle of Leyte Gulf
		Nov Beginning of systematic US bombing of Japan
Dec 16 German offensive in the Ardennes		
1945		
Jan 12 General Russian offensive begins		Jan 9 US landings on Luzon
Jan 17 Russians enter Warsaw		
Feb 4–12 Yalta Conference		
Feb 13 Surrender of Budapest		
Feb 13–14 Dresden raids		

Mar	7	Americans cross the Rhine at Remagen
Apr	12	Death of Roosevelt
Apr	13	Russians enter Vienna
Apr	16	Last Russian offensive begins
Apr	28	Death of Mussolini
Apr	30	Death of Hitler
May	2	Berlin in Russian hands. Germans in Italy capitulate
May	5	Prague rises
May	7	Germans surrender at Rheims
May	9	Russians enter Prague
July	17	Potsdam Conference

Apr	1	U S landings on Okinawa
Apr	4	Japanese Prime Minister Koiso resigns and is replaced by Suzuki
Apr		Russia refuses to renew her non-aggression pact with Japan
May	3	Japanese surrender Rangoon
July	26	Allies at Potsdam call on Japan to surrender
Aug	6	Hiroshima
Aug	8	Russia declares war on Japan
Aug	9	Nagasaki
Aug	14	Japan capitulates
Sept	2	Japanese surrender signed

Books: the Eastern Hemisphere

This section compiled by D. E. T. Luard

It is one of the joys of Guy Wint's superbly spare style of writing that his texts are never cluttered with innumerable footnotes giving references to doubtfully relevant learned sources for every statement made. His own reading in this field was, none the less, very wide and it may be that, if he had not tragically died before this book was completed, he would have added a short booklist at the end, or possibly even separate lists for each chapter. In any case, for the sake of those readers who may be inspired by the book to explore in greater detail some of the subjects it has opened up, these notes on further reading may prove useful.

PART 1

On the background of the differing responses of China and Japan to the incursions of the West, described in the first chapters of this book, a good deal has been written. So far as China is concerned, the longest and most complete account, still very readable, is contained in H. B. Morse's *The International Relations of the Chinese Empire* (London, 1910–18), which is in three volumes and covers Chinese relations with the outside world until the fall of the empire in 1911. A more succinct account of the same period, including more analysis of events within China itself, is given in E. R. Hughes's *The Invasion of China by the Western World* (London, 1937). A superb, first-hand picture of the reaction of Chinese officials and others to the problems created by the West, and their image of the western world, is given in *China's Response to the West* edited by J. K. Fairbank, and S. Y. Teng (Cambridge, 1954). A somewhat similar book, covering a longer period, also containing original texts, is that edited by R. Pelissier, *Awakening of China, 1783–1949* (New York, 1967).

Japan's response to a similar stimulus is described in a number of books on modern Japan. Richard Storry's admirable *A History of Modern Japan* (London, 1960) contains a highly readable account of the dynamic reaction of Japan to its first contacts with the West in the middle of the last century. A longer perspective is given in I. Nish's *The Story of Japan* (London, 1968), an elegant and scholarly account of Japan's history; and in M. Hürlimann and F. King's *Japan* (London, 1970).

On the international political developments in the Far East from the middle of the nineteenth century to the 1930's, the best account is still Geoffrey Hudson's brilliantly written *The Far East in World Politics* (London, 1945). Other books, covering roughly the same period, less readable but giving rather more detail is N. Peffer's *The Far East: A Modern History* (Ann Arbor, 1958) and *Far Eastern International Relations* (Boston, 1931) by H. B. Morse and F. H. McNair.

China's history in the years before the Sino-Japanese War began is only rather patchily covered in works in English. There have been a spate of excellent books about the growth of the Chinese Communist Party and its early struggles, of which B. Schwarz's *Chinese Communism and the Rise of Mao* (Harvard, 1952) and Conrad Brandt's *Stalin's Failure in China, 1924–27* (Oxford, 1958) are among the best. A vivid, if highly partisan (that is, Trotskyist), view of this period is given in A. Isaac's *The Tragedy of the Chinese Revolution* of which the first edition appeared in 1938, full of revolutionary fire, and a second, somewhat watered-down version in 1951 (Stanford, Calif.). Another work of considerable historic interest is that of M. N. Roy, who was the Comintern representative in China at this time, *Revolution in China* (Calcutta, 1951). The best accounts of life in the communist-controlled areas of China at the time, are given in Edgar Snow's *Red Star Over China* (London, 1937) and Simone de Beauvoir's *The Long March* (London, 1958).

There are, so far as I know, no other books in English describing the general situation in China at the period covered by Guy Wint's chapter 4. A good general work is O. E. Chubb's *Twentieth Century China* (New York, 1966) which gives some account of China under the Nationalist Government, including both debits and credits. A fascinating picture of Japanese rule in Manchuria is given in the book by Pu-Hi, the last Chinese Emperor, later placed on the throne of Manchuria by Japan, quoted several times by Guy Wint: *From Emperor to Citizen* (Peking, 1965). Life in Peking in this period is described in G. N. Kates's *The Years that were Fat: Peking 1933–40* (New York, 1952). Finally, a readable, somewhat journalistic general picture of Far Eastern politics in the late 1930s is given in John Gunther's *Inside Asia* (New York, 1939).

On the Manchurian 'incident', and the West's response to it, two books giving very different view-points are W. W. Willoughby's *The Sino-Japanese Controversy and the League of Nations* (Baltimore, 1935), which exposes convincingly the weakness and ambiguity of the western reaction to Japan's encroachment and the total ineffectualness of the measures taken by the League. A far more lenient view of western actions, and especially British action, is taken in R. Basset's *Democracy and Foreign Policy* (London, 1952), which is something like an apologia for the passivity of western governments in the face of the Japanese attack. An account of U S policy during this period is contained in Dorothy Borg's two books *American Policy and the Chinese Revolution, 1925–28* (New York, 1947) and *The U S and the Far Eastern Crisis of 1933–38* (Cambridge, 1964). J. W. Christopher's *Conflict in the Far East, American Diplomacy of China 1928–33* (Liden, 1950) fills the gap between these two books. U S policy at a somewhat later stage is covered in T. A. Brisson's *American Policy in the Far East, 1931–40* (New York, 1941) and in C. A. Beard's classic *President Roosevelt and the Coming of the War, 1941: a Study of Appearances and Realities* (Yale, 1945).

On Japan's policy at this time, and especially the growth of Japanese militarism, there are a number of books: Y. C. Maxon's *Control of Japan's Foreign Policy, a Study of Civil-Military Rivalry, 1930–45*, gives a brilliant account of the factional fights within the Japanese government, and especially the struggle between the Ministry of Foreign Affairs and the military for the control of Japanese foreign policy during this period, showing very clearly the responsibility of the armed forces for expanding and intensifying Japan's ambitions in the outside world, and often, as in Manchuria and North China, pursuing virtually a foreign policy of their own. R. Butow's *Tojo and the Coming of the War* (Princeton, 1961) looks at the same period, examining especially the sinister role of Marshal Tojo in these events. Other books on Japanese militarism are R. Storry's *The Double Patriots* (London, 1957), H. Lory's *Japan's Military Masters* (New York, 1943) and J. M. Maki's *Japanese Militarism: its Cause and Cure* (New York, 1945).

PART 2

On Japanese actions in China after 1931 T. A. Brisson's *Japan in China* (New York, 1938) is valuable. D. J. Lu's *From the Marco Polo Bridge to Pearl Harbor* (Washington, 1961) describes Japanese policy and actions during the period between the outbreak of full-scale war in China in 1937 to the attack on Pearl Harbor in 1941; and some of the same ground is covered in more journalistic style in H. S. Quigley's *Far*

Eastern War 1937–41 (Boston, 1942). A. N. Young's *China and the Helping Hand* (Harvard, 1963) gives a detailed account of U S policy in assisting China during this period. An account of the Burma Road and the diplomatic and military discussions which surrounded it, is given in *Behind the Burma Road* by W. R. Peers and D. Brelis.

There are a number of books which describe the diplomatic maneuverings preceding the Japanese attack on Pearl Harbor. Among the best of these are P. W. Schroeder's *The Axis Alliance and Japanese-American Relations* (New York, 1958) and F. W. Ikle's *German-Japanese Relations, 1936–40* (New York, 1956). For those who are prepared to delve into more voluminous official records there are *The US Department of State Papers Relating to the Foreign Relations of the US: Japan 1931–41* (Washington, 1943); *The Archives of the Japanese Ministry of Foreign Affairs, 1868–1945*, which were published in Washington in 1954; and the relevant volume of the British Official Documents. (The British Official Documents are in any case now open until 1941).

On Pearl Harbor, its approach and its aftermath there are a number of books. Of special interest is a work by Joseph C. Grew, U S Ambassador in Japan at the time of Pearl Harbor and later Under Secretary of State, *Ten Years in Japan* (New York, 1944) and that of Sir Robert Craigie, British Ambassador at the same time, *Behind the Japanese March* (London, 1946). A straight-forward account of the diplomatic history preceding Pearl Harbor is given in H. Feis's book *The Road to Pearl Harbor* the first of a series of books by this author on diplomatic history in the period from the late 1930s to the late 1940s.

PART 3

A basic source book for the war itself is of course Churchill's *History of the Second World War*. All the volumes contain some material regarding to the Far East, but perhaps the most relevant are volume III *The Grand Alliance* and volume VI, *Triumph and Tragedy*. Even larger in scale is *The Official British History of the Second World War* of which the five volumes on *The War against Japan* (London, 1957–69) are by S. W. Kirby. There is also J. Ehrman's *Grand Strategy, October 1944–August 1945* (London, 1956) which is volume VI of the British official history and deals with the discussion and diplomatic dealings concerning the war strategy to be adopted in the Far East. Other military histories are the volume produced by C. Romanus and R. Sunderland, for the U S Department of the Army, which gives a detailed account of U S Army activities in China, Burma and India (the titles of the volumes are *Stilwell's Mission to China, Stilwell's Command Problems* and *Time runs out in CBI*); and the corresponding volumes on the Army and Air Forces in World War II by W. L. Craven and J. L. Cate (Chicago, 1958). On the British side of the war an interesting account is contained in Field Marshal Slim's *Defeat into Victory* (New York, 1961). Finally the official British diplomatic history of the period is contained in L. Woodward's *British Foreign Policy in the Second World War* (London, 1962).

For those who want something rather more condensed, a good general military history is given in B. Collier's *The War in the Far East, 1941–45* (London, 1969). There are a considerable number of books on individual campaigns and battles. Among the best and most famous is Spencer Chapman's *The Jungle is Neutral* (London, 1949) about the campaign in Malaya. The battle for Singapore is described in an English version *Singapore: The Battle that Changed the World* (London, 1965) and in a Japanese version by the Chief of Operations and Planning Staff of the Japanese 25th Army who designed the Japanese operation, M. Tsuji's *Singapore, the Japanese Version* (London, 1968). The American campaign in Guadalcanal is vividly depicted in a book by Sam Griffith, a Brigadier in the U S Marine Corps, *The Battle for Guadalcanal* (New York, 1963).

Of the struggle in other parts of S. E. Asia, A. W. H. Harterdorp's *Japanese Occupation of the Philippines* (Manila, 1967) based on personal experiences in a Japanese prisoners-of-war camp and many personal interviews, describes Japanese conduct in that country. *Japanese Military Administration in Indonesia* (Yale, 1965) gives an account from Japanese documents of the way that country was administered. On the battles in Burma and China the *Stilwell Papers* (New York, 1948), which were published by his widow after his death, presents General Stilwell's own justification of his activities in the Far East sector. M. Collis's *Last and First in Burma, 1941–48* (London, 1956) is more concerned with political and social developments in that country during and after the war. On the attitude of many educated Burmese to the Japanese conquest, Ba Maw's *Breakthrough in Burma*, quoted a number of times by Guy Wint in this book, is especially enlightening; as is the book written by U Nu *Burma under the Japanese* (New York, 1954). A. Gilchrist's *Bangkok, Top Secret* (London, 1970) provides an exciting account by a British Army officer of S.O.E. activities in Japanese-occupied Siam. The struggle for India, and the real threat that developed to that country for a time, is described in A. J. Barker's *The March on Delhi* (London, 1963). Two first-class books presenting the Indian picture, are B. R. Nanda's *Mahatma Gandhi* (London, 1958) quoted by Guy Wint, and Penderel Morn's *Gandhi and Modern India* (London, 1968), both of which include accounts of the attitude of Gandhi and other Indian leaders to the war.

The naval war in the Pacific is described in two excellent books by S. E. Morison, the great American historian, *Two-Ocean War* and *The Rising Sun in the Pacific* (Boston, 1948). There are also two interesting books by Japanese writers on the naval war: M. Ito's *The End of the Imperial Japanese Navy* (London, 1962) and M. Fuchida and M. Okumiya's *Midway: The Battle that Doomed Japan*. Two other interesting books presenting the war through their eyes, are: T. Kase's *Eclipse of the Rising Sun* (London, 1951) filling a diary of the reactions of a Japanese to his war-time experiences and increasing disillusion with his government, and J. D. Potter's *Admiral of the Pacific* (London, 1965), a biography of Admiral Yamamoto.

The diplomatic history of the war period, including relations between Japan and Germany and between Japan and the Soviet Union (in the curious situation when Germany and Japan were allies, though one was linked in deadly combat with the Soviet Union, while the other remained in diplomatic relations with her) has been the subject of several works. One of the best is E. L. Presseisen's *Germany and Japan, A Study in Totalitarian Diplomacy* (The Hague, 1958). The same theme is studied over a much shorter period (1941–2), in J. M. Meskill's *Hitler and Japan: The Hollow Alliance* (New York, 1966). H. von Dirksen's *Moscow, Tokyo, London* (Oklahoma, 1952) includes an account of some of the diplomatic complexities of this period. Also of some interest is *Stalin's Correspondence with Churchill, Attlee, Roosevelt and Truman* published in Moscow in 1957.

Accounts of Japan's Empire in the Far East and the way she governed it are contained in F. C. Jones's *Japan's New Order in East Asia, 1937–45* (London, 1954). And a good general account of developments in the Far East throughout the whole of this period is contained in a book by the same author, together with H. Burton and B. R. Pearn, produced by Chatham House, *The Far East, 1942–46* (London, 1955).

PART 4

On the diplomatic to-ings and fro-ings in the year or two before the defeat of Japan there is now an enormous volume of material. There are first a large assembly of the memoirs and papers of those who were involved. These include *The Memoirs of Cordell Hull* (New York, 1948); D. W. Leahy's *I Was There, A Personal Story of the Chief of Staff to Presidents Roosevelt and Truman* (New York, 1950); James Forrestal's *The Forrestal Diaries* (New York, 1951); Roosevelt's *Victory and the Threshold of Peace; The Collected Papers of FDR, 1944–45* (New York, 1950); R. E. Sherwood's *Roosevelt and Hopkins* (New York, 1948); McArthur's *Reminiscences* (New

York, 1964) and Truman's *Memoirs*—volume I (which includes his account of the decision to use the atomic bomb).

On the British side, besides the books of Churchill and Slim already mentioned, there is the second volume of Eden's autobiography *Memoirs* (London, 1960–65).

Among Chinese books Chiang Kai-shek's *China's Destiny* (London, 1947) is in a sense the official bible of KMT policy towards the end of the war (it was written in 1942–3) and his *Summing up at 70* is a more personal review of his life and political aims. There are also two interesting memoirs by Japanese statesmen of this period, both (inevitably) among the doves within the Japanese government, describing their effort to secure peace: *The Case of Japan* (New York, 1956) by Shigenori Togo, who was the Japanese Foreign Minister towards the end of the war; and *Japan and Her Destiny: My Struggle for Peace* (New York, 1958) by M. Shigemitsu.

On the closing period of the war, and especially on the thinking behind the decision to use the atomic bomb, two differing views are put forward in H. Feis's *Japan Subdued, The Atomic Bomb and the End of the War in the Pacific* (Princeton, 1961), which stresses that the bomb was used for a strictly military purpose and with the minimum loss of life which it was thought was necessary to bring about a Japanese surrender; and G. Alperovitz's *American Diplomacy: Hiroshima and Potsdam* (London, 1966) which seeks to show that an important motive in the use of the bomb was to improve U S bargaining power in dealing with the Russians in Europe and elsewhere. *Behind Japan's Surrender* by L. Brooks (New York, 1968) looks at the same events from the Japanese side, describing the deliberations in the Japanese capital after the bomb had been dropped and its effect in bringing about the decision to surrender.

Acknowledgements

The author and publishers wish to thank the following for permission to reproduce photographs:
The Associated Press Ltd: 8, 14; Black Star: 7, 27; BCP: 3, 4, 10; Camera Press: 1, 6, 19, 21, 22, 23, 24, 28, 29, 31; Central Press Photos Ltd: 5, 13; Imperial War Museum: 11, 15, 16, 17, 26; Keystone Press Agency Ltd: 32, 33; Navy Department, National Archives, U.S.A.: 20; Novosti Press: 2, 9, 12, 25; Paul Popper Ltd: 18; Ullstein GmbH, Berlin: 10.

About the Authors

Peter Calvocoressi, who writes on the war in the
Western Hemisphere from the social conflicts of
the 1930s and Hitler's rise to power to the Nuremberg Trials, is a graduate of Eton and Oxford,
and served at the Nuremberg War Trials. A member of the Royal Institute of International Affairs
and the author of its Annual Surveys, he has
taught at the University of Sussex, has written a
weekly syndicated column for the British press for
seventeen years, and is currently Editorial Director of Penguin Books. Among his books are
*Nuremberg: The Facts, The Law, and the Con-
sequences,* and *Suez: Ten Years After.*

Guy Wint deals with Asia, from the century-old
struggle between China and Japan to the ultimate
defeat of Japan. He was educated at Oxford and
Berlin University, and served on a 1932 technical
mission to China, and in India, Singapore, America, and China during World War II. The author
of *Spotlight on Asia,* and *Asia: A Handbook,*
among others, he was at St. Antony College, Oxford, and wrote for the *Observer* until his death
in January 1969.

The never-before-told story of the most deadly chess game in history—with spies as the chessmasters and nations as the pawns

THE WAR IN THE SHADOWS

Charles Whiting

World War II

While nations clashed openly, a select group of men and women deliberated moves and counter-moves behind the scenes. These were the spies—whose activities have up until now been only partially chronicled and who have been romanticized to a credulous public.

Now, Charles Whiting has ripped the veil of illusion from the tortured face of spying and reveals the true story and how the players—whether British, American, Czech, French, Dutch, Russian or German—lost.

To order by mail, send $1.50 per book plus 25¢ per order for handling to Ballantine Cash Sales, P.O. Box 505, Westminster, Maryland 21157. Please allow three weeks for delivery.

OUTSTANDING
BALLANTINE
WAR BOOKS

Gehlen,
  Charles Whiting $1.25

Nazi Olympics,
  Richard D. Mandell $1.50

The War in the Air,
  Gavin Lyall $1.65

The Day the Red Baron Died,
  Dale Titler $1.50

The Hunt for Martin Bormann,
  Charles Whiting $1.25

Fork-Tailed Devil: The P-38,
  Martin Caidin $1.65

The Blond Knight of Germany,
  Trevor Constable and Raymond Toliver $1.65

War Fish,
  George Grider and Lydel Sims $1.50

Reach for the Sky,
  Paul Brickhill $1.25

PLOESTI,
  James Dugan and Carroll Stewart $1.95

To order by mail, send price of book(s) plus
25¢ per order for handling to Ballantine Cash
Sales, P.O. Box 505, Westminster, Maryland
21157. Please allow three weeks for delivery.

CLASSIC
BALLANTINE
WAR BOOKS

SUICIDE SUBMARINE!, Yutaka Yokota with Joseph D. Harrington

BRAZEN CHARIOTS: An Account of Tank Warfare in the Western Desert, November-December 1941, Robert Crisp

THE THOUSAND-MILE WAR: World War II in Alaska and the Aleutians, Brian Garfield

ZERO!, Masatake Okumiya & Jiro Horikoshi with Martin Caidin

THE BRIDGE AT REMAGEN, Ken Hechler

THE MIDGET RAIDERS: The Wartime Story of Human Torpedoes and Midget Submarines, C. E. T. Warren & James Benson

CURRAHEE!, Donald R. Burgett

THE FIRST AND THE LAST: The Rise and Fall of the German Fighter Forces, 1938–1945, Adolf Galland; translated by Mervyn Savill

STUKA PILOT, Hans Ulrich Rudel, translated by Lynton Hudson

U-BOATS AT WAR, Harald Busch, translated by L. P. R. Wilson

THUNDERBOLT!, Robert S. Johnson with Martin Caidin

DECISION AT ST.-VITH, Charles Whiting

WING LEADER, Group Captain J. E. Johnson

THE DESTRUCTION OF DRESDEN, David Irving

U-BOAT 977, Heinz Schaeffer

To order by mail, send price per book plus 25¢ per order for handling to Ballantine Cash Sales, P.O. Box 505, Westminster, Maryland 21157. Please allow three weeks for delivery.